Public Governance in Denmark

Public Governance in Denmark: Meeting the Global Mega-Challenges of the 21st Century?

EDITED BY

ANDREAS HAGEDORN KROGH

Royal Danish Defence College, Denmark

ANNIKA AGGER

Roskilde University, Denmark

And

PETER TRIANTAFILLOU

Roskilde University, Denmark

United Kingdom – North America – Japan – India – Malaysia – China

Emerald Publishing Limited
Howard House, Wagon Lane, Bingley BD16 1WA, UK

First edition 2022

British Library Cataloguing in Publication Data
A catalogue record for this book is available from the British Library

ISBN: 978-1-80043-713-5 (Print)
ISBN: 978-1-80043-712-8 (Online)
ISBN: 978-1-80043-714-2 (Epub)

ISOQAR certified
Management System,
awarded to Emerald
for adherence to
Environmental
standard
ISO 14001:2004.

ISOQAR
REGISTERED
Certificate Number 1985
ISO 14001

INVESTOR IN PEOPLE

Table of Contents

Foreword

Denmark and its neighbouring Nordic nations have attracted a global gaze for the better part of a century, far greater than their relatively small size would seemingly merit. The reason for such significant attention is rooted in the recognised successes of the Nordic societies. 'Nordic countries are a model of cooperation and they consistently punch above their weight in meeting the challenges of our time', remarked United States President Barack Obama at the Nordic Leaders' Summit in Washington DC in 2016.[1]

The Nordic nations are positioned to receive an explosion of heightened global attention. The world needs leadership to tackle the international mega-challenges of the early twenty-first century as examined within this important volume: economic and social equality; democracy and participation; public sector effectiveness and efficiency; climate change and the environment; and demographic changes and immigration.

These mega-challenges are also expressed through the Sustainable Development Goals (SDGs) for which Denmark and its Nordic neighbours are measured as comparable global leaders, regularly topping the annual SDG Index. I stress the word *comparable* because as the young Swedish activist Greta Thunberg reminds us, Nordic societies do not live up to the utopian characterisations they are sometimes prone to receive. Overconsumption is a significant problem. Each Nordic country consumes resources at a level greater than the earth can support, exceeding planetary boundaries and contributing to climate change and loss of biodiversity; racism exists across Nordic societies with concerning levels of extreme nationalists having gained power; and inequalities are growing. Nevertheless, for all their flaws, Nordic nations are comparable global leaders from whom many important lessons can be learned.

Denmark deserves focused attention to better understand its comparable successes, its continued challenges and what lessons those of us elsewhere in the world can draw. Andreas Hagedorn Krogh, Annika Agger and Peter Triantafillou have pulled together a superbly edited volume, attracting the contributions of leading scholars that brings important messages both for academics

---

[1]Remarks by President Obama, President Niinistö of Finland, and Prime Minister Solberg of Norway at the Nordic Leaders' Summit Arrival Ceremony'. The White House Office of the Press Secretary, 13 May 2016. Retrieved from https://obamawhitehouse.archives.gov/the-press-office/2016/05/13/remarks-president-obama-president-niinist%C3%B6-finland-and-prime-minister.

and policymakers alike. Each chapter has a lessons learned section that serves as a space for reflection and most constructive context when considering potential paths forward.

The editors and authors throughout this volume go to quite some length in pointing out what could be learned while also taking care to share the particular historical conditions in Denmark. These contextual features are so important to consider in efforts to transfer policy to other countries with very different political systems, such as the United States and France. Transferring policy lessons is always a challenging task, and as every nation is uniquely unique, the lessons provided in this volume can help to better ensure more likely success in such learning efforts.

Denmark is often characterized as a welfare state, but I share the feeling with others that it is better characterized as a 'well-being state' or as an 'enabling state'.[2] Denmark is constantly in development in order to meet new societal challenges – or 'punching above its weight' as President Obama put it. These changes mean that any easy characterisation of Denmark's public governance system is difficult and calls for continued research and debate, something for which this volume makes a significant contribution.

The volume concludes with an indispensably important message: Even if Denmark is in no way a utopia, and it still faces all kinds of societal challenges, 'The chapters in this edited volume go to show how the collaborative governance model in Denmark is relatively stable and largely based on socio-political cooperation, equality, trust, pragmatism and an inclusive compromise culture. Despite shifting minority governments and emerging political parties on both wings, the political middle, which embraces gradual reforms of the welfare state, is wide and strong. A generally content and happy citizenry along with both formal and informal institutions of cooperation and pragmatic compromise dampen the radicalism of new governments and ensure a steady reform path' (see Chapter 14).

21 June 2021

Dr Robert Strand
Berkeley, California, USA

---

[2]Gilbert, Neil, and Barbara Gilbert. The enabling state: Modern welfare capitalism in America. Oxford University Press, 1989.

Chapter 1

Why Look North? Scrutinising the Danish Way of Governing Societal Challenges

Peter Triantafillou, Andreas Hagedorn Krogh and Annika Agger

Abstract

In the twenty-first century, societies around the world are facing a wide range of daunting global mega-challenges: poverty, unemployment, income inequality, unequal distribution of political power, ageing populations, uncontrolled migration, segregated urbanisation, increasing greenhouse gas emissions and a massive decrease in biodiversity. In recent years, politicians, journalists and academic observers have singled out the Nordic countries, Denmark in particular, as model societies of trusting and happy people that have handled many of these challenges with remarkable effectiveness. And yet others warn against 'becoming Denmark,' painting a picture of a dysfunctional, socialist nightmare with high taxes, low job motivation and a general lack of private initiative. In this introductory chapter, the editors cut through the noise of the international debate and set the scene for the nuanced analyses presented here of contemporary public governance in Demark and its capacity to tackle some of the most pressing problems of our time. Specifically, the chapter discusses various conceptualisations of the Danish welfare state, delineates some of its most important historical and structural traits and outlines the main empirical features of contemporary Danish public governance. Finally, it outlines the structure of the book and briefly introduces each of its subsequent chapters.

Keywords: Nordic welfare states; Denmark; mega-challenges; public governance; public policy; public administration

Societies around the world are currently facing daunting problems (United Nations, 2015). The contemporary global mega-challenges include poverty, persistent unemployment and income inequality as well as unequal distribution of political power and participation among groups. Many mature liberal democracies are struggling with ageing populations, uncontrolled migration and

Public Governance in Denmark, 1–18
doi:10.1108/978-1-80043-712-820221001

segregated urbanisation. At the same time, rising greenhouse gas (GHG) emissions and a massive decrease in biodiversity are changing and often eroding the livelihoods of large parts of human populations. These diverse developments have complex causes and rest on contingent forces that vary from society to society. Some have long-standing and deeply embedded structural causes, such as highly mobile forms of capital, which erodes tax bases, fossil-based industrialisation and uncontrolled population growth. Moreover, contingent events such as the 2007/2008 financial crisis and the 2020 COVID-19 pandemic accelerate and exacerbate many of the social and environmental problems of our time.

The global political, economic, social and environmental challenges of the day are testing the capacities of states and their public administrations to provide adequate services, mobilise civil society, pursue innovation and adopt digital solutions. A wide range of politicians, journalists and academic observers have singled out the Nordic countries, Denmark in particular, as model societies with trusting, happy people who have handled many of these challenges with remarkable efficiency. Pitching socially, economically and environmentally sustainable policy proposals, they refer to the Nordic welfare state model and praise its impressive governance capacity (Friedman, 2020). Others, however, warn against 'becoming Denmark,' painting a picture of a dysfunctional, socialist nightmare and calling attention to the high taxes, low job motivation, long completion times for university degrees, and a general lack of private initiative (Regan, 2018).

Much of this debate over the (lacking) merits of Denmark revolves around its welfare state model and its ability to address societal problems. Somewhat surprisingly, the kind of political system and state–society relations underpinning the welfare state have attracted much less attention, at least outside the circles of dedicated scholarship. If politicians, journalists and laypersons disagree over the nature and merits of the Danish welfare state, we could perhaps expect a certain scholarly consensus. Yet even scholars disagree on the contemporary status of the Danish welfare state and its continued ability to deal with the new economic, social and environmental challenges.

To address several urgent societal problems of the twenty-first century, this book aims at providing a nuanced account of the how public governance is exercised in Denmark. It aims both to provide up-to-date academic analyses of Danish public governance and to encourage an informed and balanced debate about formulating and adopting political reforms with reference to 'the Danish model.' Accordingly, the book's target group is both scholars within the fields of public administration, governance and politics, and policy professionals who are engaged in analysing, designing and evaluating public policies and governance strategies. In contrast, it seeks neither to provide an exhaustive account of Danish politics (Christiansen, Elklit, & Nedergaard, 2020) nor to explore everyday Danish life (Jenkins, 2011).

In the reminder of this chapter, we provide some key assertions and images about the Danish welfare state in the international public media and policy organisations, after which we examine its key empirical features. We then give an account of some of the most prominent conceptualisations of the Danish welfare state and delineate some historical and structural traits of public administration and governance in Denmark.

Political Discourses and International Public Debates Regarding the Danish Welfare State

In both scholarly and public debates, we have witnessed growing interest in the Nordic welfare state as societal model. International observers and politicians have highlighted Denmark as an inspiring standard-bearer that is relatively successful in tackling pressing challenges and enabling citizens to live fulfilling lives. In the USA, for instance, former Democratic presidential candidate Pete Buttigieg stated that the 'number one place to live out the American dream right now is Denmark' (Silva, 2020). Similarly, Senator Bernie Sanders (Sanders, 2013) has argued that:

> In Denmark, there is a very different understanding of what "freedom" means. In that country, they have gone a long way to ending the enormous anxieties that comes with economic insecurity. Instead of promoting a system which allows a few to have enormous wealth, they have developed a system which guarantees a strong minimal standard of living to all – including the children, the elderly and the disabled.

Others find President Joe Biden to be a true Scandinavian (Friedman, 2020). For example, Biden's economic stimulus package of April 2021 draws inspiration from the Danish welfare system, such as two years of tuition-free community college and better access to childcare as strategic tools for reducing income inequality and improving social mobility.

Pragmatic critics of such leftist praise contend that it relies on an outdated and idealised notion of Danish society (Friedman, 2020). Other US commentators and politicians dispute the positive image of Denmark and the other Nordic countries more intensely. Prior to the US midterm elections in the autumn of 2018, Fox News issued a feature claiming that all Danes work for the government and that the student allowance results in youth not caring to find a job (Regan, 2018). Two months later, a report by former President Donald Trump's Council of Economic Advisers argued that the standard of living in the Nordic countries is 15% lower than in the United States and that the US GDP would fall by 9% if they adopted a fully federally funded health system akin to that of the Nordic countries (The Council of Economic Advisers, 2018). Several observers, including Danish Minister of Climate, Energy and Utilities Dan Jørgensen (2018), have dismissed these apparent facts and arguments as false.

In the European Union (EU), we generally find a positive image of the economic robustness of the Danish welfare state. For quite some time, the EU Commission has considered the Danish welfare state to be an economically successful model. The European Employment Strategy of the late 1990s stressed its potential for developing into a competitive knowledge economy, and systematic benchmarking analyses in the early 2000s ranked Denmark high on the list of best-performing labour markets (Triantafillou, 2008). The low unemployment rates were largely attributed to the Danish flexicurity model; that is, a labour market model combining low barriers to hiring and firing workers (flexibility) with relatively high levels of unemployment benefits (security), which the EU Council recommended to all of the EU member states (Council of the European Union, 2007; see also Madsen, 2002; Mailand, 2010). Subsequently, several delegations of French parliamentarians and high-ranking ministerial civil servants visited Denmark to understand how the flexicurity model could be adapted in France (Barbier, Colomb, & Madsen, 2009). Today, French President Emmanuel Macron demonstrates a strong interest in the Danish labour market model, which served as an inspiration for his 2017 attempt to reform French labour market policies (NN, 2017).

Contrary to the largely positive conception of the Danish governance model in the EU, the Organisation for Economic Co-operation and Development (OECD) has long warned Danish politicians that the generous Danish social welfare and labour market policies inhibit labour supply by driving wages and taxes up, thereby eroding economic competitiveness (Kaspersen & Svaneborg, 2004). More recent OECD assessments have been more benevolent, however, recognising the persistently high levels of wealth and life satisfaction (OECD, 2020b). A recent study ranks Denmark as the country with the highest social mobility in the OECD: while it takes five generations for low-income families in the USA to enter the middle class, it only takes two generation in Denmark to achieve the same (OECD, 2018, p. 27). Still, the OECD remains somewhat lukewarm about Denmark and its progressive taxation system featuring high marginal income taxation, which the OECD considers an obstacle to growth and investment (OECD, 2014, p. 2; 2019a, p. 10).

As such, the desirability of the Danish welfare state model is disputed. However, the general tendency among policymakers and international institutions is to view the ability of Denmark to manage key societal challenges in a positive light. But what are the foundations of the Danish welfare state? How has it developed? How has it transformed? And how well does it perform today?

What Is the Danish Welfare State?

For decades, measured in GDP per capita, Denmark has enjoyed status as among the richest countries in the world (see Fig. 1 below). Among the Nordic countries, only Norway is wealthier according to this metric, which is largely due to its abundant oil and gas resources. It is noteworthy that Denmark has a higher GDP per capita than the world's most affluent liberal democracies, such as Germany, France, the United Kingdom and Japan. Outside the Nordic countries, only the United States, Switzerland, Luxembourg, Ireland, Singapore and the small Gulf states enjoy a higher GDP per capita. Apart from the United States, many of these countries owe their wealth, at least in part, to their status as tax havens or to vast gas and oil reserves.

Danish citizens enjoy access to a wide range of either wholly or partially tax-funded public services, including childcare, education at all levels, student grants, healthcare, eldercare, unemployment benefits, social security and old-age pensions. Even in the Nordic context, the Danish government expenditures are high

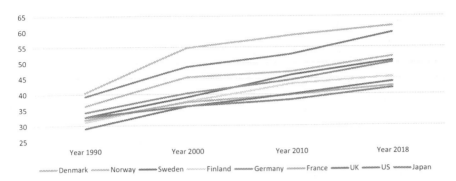

Fig. 1.   GDP per Capita (1000 US Dollars, 2015 Constant Prices, PPP). *Source:* Own production based on data from OECD (2020c).

and consistently make up more than half of total GDP (see Fig. 2 below). Outside the Nordic countries, only France, with its demanding public pensions system, has comparable government expenditures. Obviously, the Danish tax rates must be relatively high to enable the government to sustain such high levels of public welfare spending. Conversely, Danes do not have to pay high insurance premiums to enjoy access to healthcare, pensions, etc. Moreover, it is worth noting that these aggregate figures cover huge inter-country variations regarding the purpose of this spending; for example, the various levels of Danish government spend three times more on social services – relative to GDP – than is the case in the United States, which allocates relatively more resources to defence and justice (OECD, 2020a).

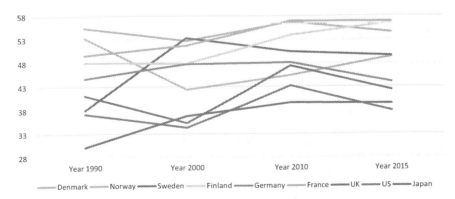

Fig. 2.   Government Spending in Percentage of GDP. *Source:* Own production based on data from International Monetary Fund (2020).

The Danish welfare state has developed and changed significantly over the past 100 years. While a number of late nineteenth century social reforms set Denmark on track to become a welfare state, it did not develop its universal features until the early 1930s, when a Social Democrat–Liberal coalition introduced the 'Public Assistance Act,' the 'National Insurance Act,' the 'Employment Exchange and Unemployment Insurance Act' and the 'Accident Insurance Act' (Greve, 2014). Together, this legislation amounted to the first systematic attempt at securing universal coverage of welfare services financed by general taxation. After World War II (WWII), the welfare state expanded into new areas, notably the 'old-age pension' without a means test, and state-financed healthcare services, which had been covered by collective insurance until the early 1970s. Unsurprisingly, overall state spending on social services grew rapidly – from around 10% of GDP after World War II to some 18% in the late 1960s.

In an attempt at containing the vast economic problems following the two consecutive oil crises in the 1970s, the trend since the 1980s has been welfare state reform rather than expansion. Successive governments have introduced numerous reforms aimed at curbing public expenditures and a more competitive labour market. In later years, a broad coalition of parties in the Folketing has cut unemployment insurance and social assistance schemes to get as many persons working as quickly as possible. In 2013, then-Minister of Finance Bjarne Corydon, a Social Democrat, publicly embraced the notion of 'the competition state' as a 'modern welfare state,' encapsulating the idea that government should play a major role in stimulating markets and strengthening the competitive advantages of the state in a globalised economy (Campbell, Hall, & Pedersen, 2006). While critics warn that reforms in the 2000s and 2010s have led to a gradual hollowing out of the Danish welfare state and dismantling of its successful flexicurity model, proponents of the more market-oriented reforms credit them for the strong Danish economy.

One might think that the large state role in welfare service funding would imply the immobilisation of civil society. But the contrary seems true. Firstly, private organisations provide many publicly subsidised services, such as kindergartens, schools, out-of-hospital medical care and many infrastructural amenities, such as energy and water supply. Secondly, Denmark has an active and highly organised civil society. Exceptionally high and increasing levels of voter turnout – for both general and local elections – and high levels of participation in voluntary associations illustrate the point.

As Table 1 shows, Denmark consistently displays some of the highest voter turnout rates in the world. Only countries with mandatory voting, namely Australia, Belgium and Luxembourg, enjoy higher voter turnout.

The rate of participation among Danish citizens in voluntary (unpaid) work is higher than in most other influential OECD countries. Considering how civic engagement is often seen as the lynchpin of Anglophone liberalism, Table 2 below interestingly illustrates that volunteerism in all the three Scandinavian countries (DK, SW and NO) is higher than in the United Kingdom This is surprising, since the large public sector in the Nordic countries is often accused of crowding out voluntarism and other civil society activities.

Table 1. Voter Turnout (Percentage of Total Eligible Voters) – Perhaps a Column Diagram?

Country	1990s (Average)	2010s (Average)
Denmark	84	87
Norway	77	78
Sweden	85	86
Finland	67	67
Germany	80	74
France	68	49
United Kingdom	75	67
United States	62	55
Japan	61	56

Source: Own production based on data from OECD (2019b).

Denmark is also characterised by many non-profit organisations operating within the infrastructure, retail food and housing sectors. Non-profit companies have played a very influential role in utilities (electricity, gas, water and waste management) and retail food since the late nineteenth century, which saw the emergence of the cooperative movement and development of infrastructure services by local governments. The cooperative movement evolved mainly around independent farmers wanting to retain larger profits from their produce by arranging for their own storage and sales facilities and around labour unions seeking to provide affordable housing for their members. The advent of the EU Internal Market in the mid-1980s forced Danish gas and electricity producers to sell their transmission systems to the state, which now operates them in accordance with EU competition law. The point remains, however, that local government-owned, non-profit companies play a crucial role in Danish utilities

Table 2. Percentage of Population Older than 15 Years Engaged in Formal or Informal Voluntary Work 2015.

Country	Percentage
Denmark	38.7
Norway	48.0
Sweden	35.5
Germany	28.6
France	23.0
United Kingdom	23.3

Source: Own production based on data from Eurostat (2021).

As we have seen, major reforms have developed, shaped and altered the Danish welfare state significantly in recent decades. Today, the strong state/strong civil society mix appears to be a recipe for success. But is the contemporary Danish welfare state and its related mode of governance really that different from those found in other developed countries? And if so, how exactly does it stand out? How have scholars conceptualised the Danish welfare state vis-à-vis other welfare states? And do the established conceptions and distinctions still hold true?

Conceptual Understandings of the Danish Welfare State

Since World War II, scholars have developed a host of different – and at times conflicting – welfare state typologies (Abrahamson, 1999). Yet there can be little doubt that Danish sociologist Gøsta Esping-Andersen's *The Three Worlds of Welfare Capitalism* (Esping-Andersen, 1990) made the tripolar welfare regime typology highly influential. It distinguishes between *liberal regimes*, characterised by modest, means-tested assistance for low-income recipients (e.g. the United Kingdom, United States); *conservative regimes* encouraging family-based assistance and social insurance systems, typically excluding persons without employment (e.g. France, Germany) and *social democratic regimes* providing universal access to public services such as education, healthcare, childcare, eldercare and unemployment benefits (e.g. the Nordics). While the typology is meant to be value-neutral, Esping-Andersen and many following him preferred and commended the social democratic regimes, with their universalistic ambition of promoting equal and high standards for all (Erikson, Hansen, Ringen, & Uusitalo, 1987). Esping-Andersen argued that the universal welfare model is politically strong because it is based on a class compromise between the working class and the new middle class, serving the interests of both. This class compromise was facilitated by various models of corporatism; that is, institutionalised patterns of dialogue and negotiations between the state, organised employers and labour unions. Similar patterns of class dialogue can be found in Austria and Germany, but are wholly foreign to France, the United Kingdom and United States, where trade union membership is much lower. Still, in 2000, Esping-Andersen recommended Denmark and the other Nordic welfare states as a regulatory template for the other EU member states (Esping-Andersen, 2000), conveniently ignoring the many political battles it took in Denmark and the other Nordics to develop the class dialogue necessary to build their respective welfare states.

The notion of universalism is central to the conceptual understanding of the welfare state. It implies that every citizen is entitled to a wide range of tax-financed social services. However, access to most of these services is criteria-based. For instance, social assistance is only granted if the citizen has no other way of ensuring their livelihood, access to specialised health care is dependent on referral from a GP, etc. Moreover, many services in Denmark are partly or wholly user-financed. For instance, Denmark has a substantial number of private schools that are partially financed by user fees, which also plays an important role in many medical services, such as dentistry, physiotherapy and psychotherapy.

Scholars often treat the Nordic welfare states as representative of a single, more or less uniform welfare model. And doing so is justified by the fact that the countries have similar political histories, languages and customs, although this applies more to the three Scandinavian countries, Denmark, Norway and Sweden, than to the other Nordic countries, such as Finland and Iceland (Alestalo & Kuhle, 1987). The Scandinavian welfare states began developing in the late nineteenth century with inspiration from Germany, the United Kingdom, Belgium and even each other. Yet they did so in rather different directions and at different tempi (Kuhnle, 1978). Many of these differences related to different patterns of corporatism. However, the post-WWII ascendancy of social democratic rule in the Scandinavian countries and the expanding political cooperation between the Nordic countries reduced most of these differences (Alestalo & Kuhle, 1987).

Despite these trends of convergence, there are a few notable differences. For example, while the Nordic countries offer much more generous parental leave schemes than do other OECD countries, the Swedish model is ensuring more gender equality than do the other Nordics, including Denmark. Sweden offers the longest paid parental leave, 16 months, three months of which are earmarked for fathers and mothers, respectively (Cederström, 2019), whereas Danish mothers and fathers can share 32 weeks in addition to six weeks earmarked for mothers and two weeks for fathers. Consequently, Swedish fathers take around one-third of the total parental leave, whereas the corresponding figure in Denmark is a mere 10%. Such differences have begged the question whether it makes sense to treat the Scandinavian states as expressions of the same welfare model (Rauch, 2007).

If scholars have not always agreed on the conceptualisation of a common Scandinavian welfare model, there is strong consensus that the Scandinavian countries have all moved (further) away from the universal model since the 1990s. In the case of the Danish welfare state, numerous studies have suggested that it is gradually being transformed into a 'multi-tiered welfare state,' where individual choice and the financing of welfare services is playing a fundamental role for the overall functioning of the welfare state (Kvist & Greve, 2011). Policy examples include the introduction of a mandatory labour market pensions scheme, requiring workers and employers alike to contribute to pensions payment, as well as the aforementioned reformation of unemployment insurance schemes, which has gradually eroded compensation levels in Denmark and the other Nordic countries (Kuivalainen & Nelson, 2012). Other studies of recent Danish welfare reforms show how a mix of budget cuts and work-first approaches reduces the magnitude of redistribution, undermines the Danish flexicurity model and increases economic inequality (Greve, 2016; Trenz & Grasso, 2018). With slight variations, the Nordic countries have all turned to work-first approaches supplemented with individualised activation schemes since the 1990s (Kildal, 2001).

Denmark stands out from the other Nordics in at least three important policy areas: pensions, immigration and the environment. While the Nordic countries all started out with universal, flat-rate pensions, the Danish pension reforms have moved in a more liberal direction. Today, Norway and Sweden rely on a predominantly public earnings-related social insurance system, whereas Denmark has introduced a dual system in which a private pension system supplements the universal public system (Andersen & Larsen, 2002; OECD, 2017). In terms of immigration, the Danish welfare state has introduced strong restrictions on immigration and a number of measures that, in principle or in practice, apply differently to Danish citizens and to immigrants from outside the EU (Andersen, 2007). The differential access to welfare services has moved Denmark away from the universal model and the other Nordic countries, Sweden in particular, where leading political parties have rejected any dialogue with Sverigedemokraterne, a nationalist party. Finally, Denmark is experiencing different environmental problems than its neighbours. Like the other Scandinavian countries, Denmark was an early mover in adopting relatively stringent anti-pollution and environmental protection laws in the 1970s. In contrast to Norway and Sweden, however, Danish land territory is dominated by agricultural production and suffers from huge problems with nutrient pollution of its inner waterways. Having decided against the use of nuclear power, Denmark depends largely on fossil fuels for its energy supply. Accordingly, Denmark consistently produces very high per capita CO_2 emissions.

In sum, the Danish welfare state model has seen some fundamental changes since the 1980s that have moved it away from a near universal welfare state model in which the state played a crucial role in providing health, education and other social services via high levels of taxation. However, Denmark – and the other Scandinavian countries – still stands out as a distinct and in many ways relatively successful mode of governing economic and social problems. The following section will zoom in on the public administration and political dynamics underpinning the Danish mode of governance.

Danish Public Administration and Politics

Public administration and governance researchers see the Danish welfare state as a neo-Weberian state in which strategic management, increased user choice, citizen participation and digitalisation have generally increased the efficiency of its public administration (Greve & Ejersbo, 2016; Johnston, 2013). In general, the Weberian-style bureaucracies in the Nordic welfare states ensure low levels of corruption and high trust in government (Jensen, 2018; Transparency International, 2019). One of the upsides to these high levels of trust is seen in the close adherence to government health recommendations during the COVID-19 pandemic, even though many of the initial guidelines deviated from those of the WHO and other health experts.

While the Nordic countries are all unitary states, they have delegated substantial parts of the design and implementation of public services to sub-national government levels. In Denmark, more than two-thirds of total public spending is thus administered by elected politicians at the regional (counties) and local (municipalities) levels (Nielsen & Rasmussen, 2012). The Nordics also enjoy effective national audit institutions (although Sweden has recently experienced some problems, see Radio Sweden, 2016), and all have a long tradition of ombudsmen catering to citizens' rights vis-à-vis government authorities. Moreover, they have all seen an influx of New Public Management (NPM) reforms since the 1980s, with Finland and Sweden as the front runners and Denmark and Norway as more hesitant, gradual reformers (Knutsson, Matisson, & Näsi, 2016). Generally sceptical of centralised leadership and governance based on market models, however, the Scandinavian countries have been slow and selective when introducing NPM reforms compared to more liberal welfare states, such as the United Kingdom (Pollitt & Bouckaert, 2011). In recent years, post-NPM reforms and collaborative practices have increased the vertical and horizontal integration across governmental levels and public–private divides, further dampening the fragmenting and competition-enhancing effects of NPM (Christensen & Lægreid, 2011).

Notwithstanding these similarities, the public administration and political systems do display certain noteworthy differences. With the exception of Sweden, the government ministers in the Nordic countries are singularly responsible for the affairs under their jurisdiction, which deeply involves them in a wide range of decisions. In Sweden, the central agencies are accountable to the cabinet as a collegium, not to their parent ministry or minister (Greve, Lægreid, & Rykkja, 2016, p. 14). Apart from this collective responsibility for ministerial affairs, Swedish central administration differs by ascribing significantly more autonomy to expert civil servants vis-à-vis government ministers. For example, the Swedish health authorities almost completely monopolised the COVID-19 response in the spring of 2020, whereas the governments took charge of the public health strategy in the other Nordic countries. Another difference relates to the government openness to public scrutiny. As mentioned above, these countries all have strong public audit and ombudsmen institutions. Still, Denmark stands out by virtue of its restrictive public disclosure regulations, which confine access to internal ministerial documents and documents exchanged between government ministers and MPs (Jørgensen, 2014). In fact, a majority in parliament further tightened the two most important laws in this area in 2013, which has reduced public access to internal government documents (Jørgensen, 2014, p. 34). More recently, a series of scandals has smeared the Danish Ministry of Defence, including the military intelligence services (NN, 2020), putting the high level of trust in government to the test.

Like the other Nordic countries, Denmark is characterised by frequent minority government rule (Strøm, 1986). With a proportional election system and 2% electoral barrier for parties to gain parliamentary representation, the Folketing has housed between 5 and 10 parties for almost a century. The prevalence of minority governments has forced the adoption of consensus-style politics, where the four old parties (the Conservatives, Social Democrats, Liberals and Social Liberal) have played a crucial role. While consensus politics has often (but not always) blocked radical reforms, it has ensured a sense of stability and enabled minority governments to muster comprehensive support for long-term reforms, such as the pensions reform of the late 1980s (Green-Pedersen, 2001).

High levels of trust in government and a political culture of consensus- and coalition-building may explain why Denmark has not experienced a wave of populism as radical or divisive as seen in the United States, the United Kingdom and other liberal democracies. Building on lengthy traditions of citizen involvement in policymaking and governance, the Danish democracy has developed robustness through user responsiveness and interactive forms of political leadership. Populist attacks on political, social and cultural elites have had neither a strong voice nor a large audience. Still, moderate expressions of elite criticism have gained some political ground. For instance, the political attacks on experts portrayed as 'arbiters of taste' launched by the right-of-centre government in the early 2000s resulted in the disbanding of several expert committees that tended to be critical of right-wing policies. Another anti-elite sentiment has been expressed as an urban–rural divide, with Copenhagen as the epitome of highbrow elitism (at least in the eyes of the Danish People's Party). This paved the way for a political decision made by another right-of-centre government, this time in 2015, to move several state institutions from the capital to other parts of Denmark, as well as the 2018 decision to cut the budget of the national broadcasting service, the Danish Broadcasting Corporation, by 20% and to allocate some of this funding to rural broadcasters. Finally, the current Social Democratic government continues to carefully avoid accusations of elitism by accepting these decisions and taking a more EU-sceptical stance than previous governments.

In conclusion, the existing social and political science literature suggests that the Danish welfare state and its system of governance are generally well equipped for handling many of the pressing societal problems of the twenty-first century, including poverty, income inequality, unemployment, unequal distribution of political power, ageing populations, mass migration, segregated urbanisation and rising CO_2 emissions. At the same time, however, it points to an array of major challenges to the contemporary mode of governance in Denmark that call for further analysis. The proceeding chapters of this edited volume take up this task.

Outline of the Book: Sections and Chapters

The book is organised in four sections dealing with the five mega-challenges of the early twenty-first century: economic and social equality; democracy and participation; public sector effectiveness and efficiency; climate change and the environment and demographic changes and immigration.

Section I Economic and Social Equality

In Chapter 2, Bent Greve and Daniel Beland investigate the conditions of the Danish welfare state model by examining the progressive tax system and extensive redistribution via state-funded health services, education and generous social benefits. The chapter highlights recent interventions that Denmark has adopted to balance concerns for economic competitiveness against concerns for social equality.

Most OECD countries are striving for effective labour markets with high employment rates; they also provide passive and active support for unemployed individuals, yet of very different scope. In Chapter 3, Magnus Paulsen Hansen and Janine Leschke explore the Danish 'flexicurity model,' a labour market model combining flexibility, security and activation with a strong role played by the social partners.

Securing affordable housing, avoiding segregation and offering good, well-functioning housing are current concerns for many policymakers. In Chapter 4, Elizabeth Toft Kristjansen and Jesper Ole Jensen offer perspectives on how the Danish social housing sector seeks to provide affordable housing and strengthen the democratic participation of the sectors' residents. The chapter highlights how the initiatives balance between the formal resident democracy and an increasingly project-based approach to participation.

Section II Democracy and Participation

Denmark represents an apparent paradox in the international literature, with its high number of parties in the Folketing, prevalence of minority governments and their ability to remain in power and pass important public policy reforms. In Chapter 5, Flemming Juul Christiansen, Peter Heyn Nielsen and Bonnie Field provide an institutional explanation for this anomaly.

Democratic disenchantment and declining trust in elected politicians are widespread phenomena in many well-established representative democracies. In Chapter 6, Eva Sørensen and Jodi Sanford demonstrate how long traditions for involving citizens in policymaking and governance have served as the basis for developing 'hybrid democracy,' combining representative and direct democracy leading to an interactive form of political leadership.

Section III Public Sector Effectiveness and Efficiency

The level of trust between citizens and public authorities as well as between public leaders and employees is quite high in Denmark compared to other countries. In Chapter 7, Jacob Torfing and Tina Øllgaard Bentzen demonstrate how a long-lasting political-administrative culture based on trust and a pragmatic, non-ideological combination of different governance paradigms have generated a positive feedback loop between trust and public governance.

Denmark is often ranked as one of the most digitalised countries in the world. This exacerbates the dilemma between the quest for efficiency and respect for privacy. Based on a detailed analysis of strategies and policies of central and local governments in designing digital services, Peter Aagaard and John Storm Petersen account for the handling of this dilemma.

Section IV Climate Change and Biodiversity

Climate change, global warming and extreme weather conditions have made sustainable development and CO_2 emissions reduction two of the most important points on the contemporary policy agenda. In Chapter 9, Karsten Bruun Hansen and Peter Enevoldsen demonstrate how Denmark, despite initial political and industrial resistance, through balanced top-down and bottom-up governance approaches became a world leader in energy efficiency and wind turbine production and sustainable energy integration in existing energy infrastructure.

Agricultural production is impinging crucially on both biodiversity and global warming. In Chapter 10, Sevasti Chatzopoulou and Kostas Karantininis examine the resilience and adaptability of Danish agriculture to these challenges. The chapter shows how the Danish agri-food system and politics respond to biodiversity and climate change challenges through organisational and policy changes together with the active participation of cooperative movements and the integration of a bottom-up agri-food system.

Section V Demographic Changes and Immigration

The Danish old-age pension system is internationally renowned as one of the most economically sustainable and just pension systems in the world. In Chapter 11, Jon Kvist and Fritz von Nordheim show how major new income inequalities in old age are likely to emerge in the light of rising pensionable age, not just from differences in savings, but from a growing gap between effective exit ages and the statutory pension age. It discusses the need for balancing fiscal needs with fairness and social sustainability when reforming pension systems.

The mainly tax-financed Danish healthcare system has proven relatively successful in securing easy access for all Danish citizens regardless of income. In Chapter 12, Erik Bækkeskov and Peter Triantafillou analyse how the Danish healthcare system has performed in securing equal access and healthcare outcomes. It accounts for the growing costs of health services and examines the key attempts at seeking to contain these costs. It pinpoints some of the economic and political trade-offs implied by the Danish attempts to ensure affordable health, contain growing expenditures and to react in adequate ways to pandemics like COVID-19.

For more than a century, Denmark has been characterised as a cultural homogenous welfare state with high levels of interpersonal trust, solidarity and trust in political institutions. This has been challenged by an increasing influx of immigrants from non-Western societies. In Chapter 13, Carina Bischoff and Anders Ejrnæs analyse how the Danish welfare state has performed in terms of integrating immigrants into Danish society (economically, socially and politically) and the extent to which increasing immigration has influenced societal cohesion.

In the concluding chapter, the editors summarise the key insights from the preceding chapters and relate them to the conceptual welfare state models and the theoretical approaches explored in Chapter 14. We discuss the merits and shortcomings of how Danish public governance strategies and reforms have tried to tackle the societal challenges identified in this volume. Finally, we consider some of the key dilemmas facing policymakers and public managers in other liberal democracies trying to find inspiration in the Danish public governance model, and we contemplate possible avenues for future research.

References

Abrahamson, P. (1999). The welfare modelling business. *Social Policy and Administration, 33*(4), 394–415.

Alestalo, M., & Kuhle, S. (1987). The Scandinavian route: Economic, social and political developments in Denmark, Finland, Norway and Sweden. In R. Erikson, E. J. Hansen, S. Ringen, & H. Uusitalo (Eds.), *The Scandinavian model. Welfare states and welfare research* (pp. 3–38). New York, NY: M.E. Sharpe.

Andersen, J. G. (2007). Restricting access to social protection for immigrants in the Danish welfare state. *Benefits, 15*(3), 257–269.

Andersen, J. G., & Larsen, C. A. (2002). *Pension politics and policy in Denmark and Sweden: Path dependencies, policy style, and policy outcome.* Aalborg: Department of Economics, Politics and Public Administration, Aalborg University.

Barbier, J.-C., Colomb, F., & Madsen, P. K. (2009). Flexicurity–An open method of coordination at the national level? *CES Working Papers,* 46. Retrieved from https://halshs.archives-ouvertes.fr/halshs-00407394/document

Campbell, J. L., Hall, J. A., & Pedersen, O. K. (Eds.). (2006). *National identity and the varieties of capitalism: The Danish experience.* Montreal, QC: McGill Queen University Press.

Cederström, C. (2019). *State of Nordic fathers.* Copenhagen: Nordic Council of Ministers.

Christensen, T., & Lægreid, P. (2011). Post-NPM reforms: Whole of government approaches as a new trend. In S. Groeneveld & S. Van De Walle (Eds.), *New steering concepts in public management* (pp. 11–24). Bingley: Emerald.

Christiansen, P. M., Elklit, J., & Nedergaard, P. (Eds.). (2020). *Oxford handbook of Danish politics.* Oxford: Oxford University Press.

Council of the European Union. (2007). *Towards common principles of flexicurity-council conclusions.* 16201/07. Brussels.

Erikson, R., Hansen, E. J., Ringen, S., & Uusitalo, H. (1987). *The Scandinavian model. Welfare states and welfare research.* New York, NY: M.E. Sharpe.

Esping-Andersen, G. (1990). *The three worlds of welfare capitalism.* Cambridge: Polity.

Esping-Andersen, G. (2000). *A welfare state for the 21st century? Ageing societies, knowledge-based economies, and the sustainability of European welfare states.* Report to the Portuguese presidency of the European Union, prepared for the Lisbon Summit. Retrieved from http://lege.net/nnn.se/seminar/pdf/report.pdf

Eurostat. (2021). Participation in formal or informal voluntary activities or active citizenship by sex, age and educational attainment level. Retrieved from https://appsso.eurostat.ec.europa.eu/nui/show.do?dataset=ilc_scp19&lang=en

Friedman, T. L. (2020, March 10). Joe Biden, not Bernie Sanders, is the true Scandinavian. *The New York Times.*

Green-Pedersen, C. (2001). Minority governments and party politics: The political and institutional background to the 'Danish Miracle'. *Journal of Public Policy, 21*(1), 53–70.

Greve, B. (Ed.). (2014). *Historical dictionary of the welfare state* (pp. 60–67). Plymouth: Rowman & Littlefield.

Greve, B. (2016). Denmark: Still a Nordic welfare state after the changes of recent years? In K. Schubert, P. de Villota, & J. Kuhlmann (Eds.), *Challenges to European welfare systems* (pp. 159–176). Münster: Springer.

Greve, C., & Ejersbo, N. (2016). Denmark: Towards the Neo-Weberian state in the digital era. In G. Hammerschmid & S. van de Walle (Eds.), *Public administration reforms in Europe* (pp. 119–128). Cheltenham: Edward Elgar.

Greve, C., Lægreid, P., & Rykkja, L. H. (2016). Introduction: The Nordic model in transition. In C. Greve, P. Lægreid, & L. Rykkja (Eds.), *Nordic administrative reforms. Lessons for public policy* (pp. 1–22). Basingstoke: Palgrave Macmillan.

International Monetary Fund. (2020). IMF data mapper. Retrieved from https://www. imf.org/external/datamapper/exp@FPP/USA/JPN/GBR/SWE/ZAF/IND/CHL/FRA/GRC/NLD/ESP/RUS

Jenkins, R. (2011). *Being Danish. Paradoxes of identity in everyday life.* Copenhagen: Museum Tusculanum.

Jensen, M. F. (2018). The building of the Scandinavian states: Establishing Weberian bureaucracy and curbing corruption from the mid-seventeenth to mid-nineteenth century. In H. Byrkjeflot & F. Engelstad (Eds.), *Bureaucracy and society in transition: Comparative perspectives* (pp. 179–203). Bingley: Emerald.

Johnston, M. (2013). The great Danes: Successes and subtleties in corruption control in Denmark. In J. S. T. Quah (Ed.), *Different paths to curbing corruption* (pp. 23–56). Bingley: Emerald.

Jørgensen, O. (2014). *Access to information in the Nordic countries. A comparison of the laws of Sweden, Finland, Denmark, Norway and Iceland and international rules.* Gøteborg: NORDICOM.

Jørgensen, D. (2018). Something is rotten at Fox News. *Facebook*, 18 August. Retrieved from https://www.facebook.com/danjorgensen/videos/something-is-rotten-at-fox-news/1458262054275440/

Kaspersen, L. B., & Svaneborg, M. (2004). The OECD as a scientific authority? The OECD's influence on Danish welfare policies. In K. Armingeon & M. Beyeler (Eds.), *The OECD and European welfare states* (pp. 32–43). Cheltenham: Edward Elgar.

Kildal, N. (2001). *Workfare tendencies in Scandinavian welfare policies.* Geneva: ILO.

Knutsson, H., Matisson, O., & Näsi, S. (2016). New public management in a Scandinavian context. In I. Lapsley & H. Knutsson (Eds.), *Modernizing the public sector: Scandinavian perspectives.* London: Routledge.

Kuhnle, S. (1978). The beginnings of the Nordic welfare states: Similarities and differences. *Acta Sociologica, 21,* 9–35.

Kuivalainen, S., & Nelson, K. (2012). Eroding minimum income protection in the nordic countries? Reassessing the Nordic model of social assistance. In J. Kvist, J. Fritzell, B. Hvinden, & O. Kangas (Eds.), *Changing social equality: The Nordic welfare model in the 21st century* (pp. 69–87). Bristol: Policy Press.

Kvist, J., & Greve, B. (2011). Has the Nordic welfare model been transformed? *Social Policy and Administration, 45*(2), 146–160.

Madsen, P. K. (2002). The danish model of "flexicurity" – A paradise with some snakes. In *Interactions between labour market and social protection.* Brussels: European Foundation for the Improvement of Living and Working Conditions.

Mailand, M. (2010). The common European flexicurity principles: How a fragile consensus was reached. *European Journal of Industrial Relations, 16*(3), 241–257.

Nielsen, P. B., & Rasmussen, M. H. (2012). Public expenditure management in Denmark. *Monetary Review*. Copenhagen. Retrieved from https://www.national banken.dk/en/publications/Documents/2012/07/MON2Q_P1_2012_PublicExpendi tureManagementinDenmark.pdf

NN. (2017, November 15). Macron finds elitist tag hard to shake, but he has the upper hand. *The Guardian*. Retrieved from https://www.theguardian.com/world/2017/nov/15/macron-finds-elitist-tag-hard-to-shake-but-he-has-the-upper-hand

NN. (2020, August 24). Danish military intelligence head Lars Findsen suspended. *BBC News*. Retrieved from https://www.bbc.com/news/world-europe-53889612

OECD. (2014). *OECD economic surveys. DENMARK*. Paris. Retrieved from http://www.oecd.org/economy/surveys/Overview_Denmark_2014.pdf

OECD. (2017). *Pensions at a Glance 2017–Norway*. Paris. Retrieved from https://www.oecd.org/els/public-pensions/PAG2017-country-profile-Norway.pdf

OECD. (2018). *A broken social elevator? How to promote social mobility*. Paris. Retrieved from https://www.oecd.org/social/soc/Social-mobility-2018-Overview-MainFindings.pdf

OECD. (2019a). *OECD economic surveys. Denmark, January 2019*. Paris. Retrieved from http://www.oecd.org/eco/surveys/Denmark-2019-OECD-economic-survey-overview.pdf

OECD. (2019b). *Trends shaping education 2019*. Paris. Retrieved from https://read.oecd-ilibrary.org/education/trends-shaping-education-2019/declining-voter-turnout-in-oecd-countries_trends_edu-2019-graph13-cn#page1

OECD. (2020a). *General government spending by destination (indicator)*. Paris: OECD. doi:10.1787/d853db3b-en

OECD. (2020b). Life satisfaction. Retrieved from http://www.oecdbetterlifeindex.org/topics/life-satisfaction/

OECD. (2020c). OECD.Stats. Retrieved from https://stats.oecd.org/Index.aspx?DataSetCode=PDB_LV

Pollitt, C., & Bouckaert, G. (2011). *Public management reform. A comparative analysis* (3rd ed.). Oxford: Oxford University Press.

Radio Sweden. (2016, September 15). Third national auditor resigns over scandal. Retrieved from https://sverigesradio.se/sida/artikel.aspx?programid=2054&artik el=6517548

Rauch, D. (2007). Is there really a Scandinavian social service model? A comparison of childcare and elderlycare in six European countries. *Acta Sociologica, 50*(3), 249–269.

Regan, T. (2018). *Everyone in Denmark is working for the government*. New York, NY: Fox News. Retrieved from https://video.foxbusiness.com/v/5820602221001/#sp=show-clips

Sanders, B. (2013, May 26). What can we learn from Denmark? *Huffington Post*.

Silva, C. Da (2020, February 20). Pete Buttigieg praises Denmark as best place to live the American dream during debate–The country has universal healthcare. *Newsweek*. Retrieved from https://www.newsweek.com/pete-buttigieg-democratic-debate-denmark-american-dream-healthcare-1488215

Strøm, K. (1986). Deferred gratification and minority governments in Scandinavia. *Legislative Studies Quarterly, 11*(4), 583–605.

The Council of Economic Advisers. (2018). *The opportunity costs of socialism.* Washington, DC. Retrieved from https://www.whitehouse.gov/wp-content/uploads/2018/10/The-Opportunity-Costs-of-Socialism.pdf

Transparency International. (2019). Corruption perceptions index 2019. Retrieved from https://www.transparency.org/en/cpi/2019/results/table

Trenz, H.-J., & Grasso, M. (2018). Toward a new conditionality of welfare? Reconsidering solidarity in the Danish welfare state. In C. Lahusen & M. T. Grasso (Eds.), *Solidarity in Europe. Citizens' responses in times of crisis* (pp. 19–42). Basingstoke: Palgrave Macmillan.

Triantafillou, P. (2008). Normalizing active employment policies in the European Union: The Danish case. *European Societies, 10*(5). doi:10.1080/146166907017 44398

United Nations. (2015). *Transforming our world: The 2030 Agenda for sustainable development.* New York, NY: United Nations Department of Economic and Social Affairs.

Section I
Economic and Social Equality

Chapter 2

Redistribution, Inequality and Nordic Welfare States: Challenges in a Global World

Bent Greve and Daniel Béland

Abstract

As elsewhere, inequality has increasingly been on the agenda in recent years in Denmark, which has led to discussion about the redistributive role of welfare states across existing welfare regimes. Perhaps surprisingly, the Danish debate on inequality has revolved more specifically around how the country's tax system influences labour supply, especially the high level of marginal income taxation. The debate on poverty and inequality has become more prominent in Denmark in recent years, with a focus on the living standards of pensioners and children as well as the dynamic relationship between inequality and social policy. Thus, if there is a willingness to reduce inequality, a central challenge is to determine which instruments are available to counter rising inequalities in Denmark. In this context, the interaction between the issue of poverty and political support for specific social policies in Denmark is a challenge. Overall, the analysis suggests that tax reforms focusing on labour market supply have helped increase inequalities, thus indicating a possible trade-off between different aspects of welfare state development. Furthermore, the universality of the Danish model might be questioned in the coming years, which might also imply a debate on the generosity of a number of social security benefits, including those targeting the unemployed.

Keywords: Inequality; social policy; universality; labour supply; progressive taxation; Denmark

Public Governance in Denmark, 21–37
Copyright © 2022 by Emerald Publishing Limited
All rights of reproduction in any form reserved
doi:10.1108/978-1-80043-712-820221002

Introduction

In contrast to liberal welfare states, the universal Danish welfare state, like its other Nordic counterparts, is well known for the combination of relatively high levels of taxation and duties with comprehensive welfare services and economic redistribution across the life course and between the rich and the poor (Greve, 2019a; Kangas & Kvist, 2019). Furthermore, overall, Denmark and the other Nordic countries have low levels of poverty, despite increased global competition, a particularly significant issue in small, open economies. Still, recent years have seen an increase in inequality making the Danish welfare state less distinct than it used to be.

The rising inequality has come onto the political agenda, in Denmark as well as in other countries (Atkinson, 2015; Piketty, 2014; Stiglitz, 2012). This has led to a renewed debate about taxation and the redistributive role of social policies across welfare regimes because the welfare state's traditional equalising role has not been effective in all countries and, in some of them, this role has even declined (Bussolo et al., 2019; Leventi, Sutherland, & Tasseva, 2017). Specifically, in Denmark, the debate has been revolving not only around inequality but also around the influence on labour supply of the tax system, especially the high level of marginal income taxation, which remains a key aspect of tax progressiveness. Like in many other countries, the argument at the centre of the Danish debate on taxation has been the slogan 'it should pay to work,' which could, given the focus on high marginal tax rates, undermine support for progressive income taxation. This as well as the trickle-down argument is discussed below.

Rising inequality is important because it tends to have negative consequences for societies' development. This includes low social trust, high levels of crime, and even bad health outcomes across the entire population (Atkinson, 2015; Dabla-Norris, Kochhar, Suphaphiphat, Ricka, & Tsounta, 2015; Stiglitz, 2012; Wilkinson & Pickett, 2018). It has further been argued to have a negative impact on economic growth (Berg & Ostry, 2011; Cingano, 2014), which implies that the perceived historical trade-off between equality and efficiency (Okun, 1975) might not be there any longer. The question of why, at a time when many call for evidence-based policymaking, these elements no longer permeate policy decisions can be explained by several factors, including different interpretations of data, the consequences of interaction and the possible policies available to cope with different types of inequality, as they also might influence other aspects of social development. As one study concludes: 'High inequality may have several negative side effects: an increase in crime, political dysfunction, macroeconomic instability, worsening public health, and lower social mobility' (Dimick, Rueda, & Stegmueller, 2018, p. 48). This is also confirmed in another study comparing New Zealand and Denmark (Richmond-Rakerd et al., 2020).[1]

Importantly, given that tax and social policy are national prerogatives within the European Union (EU), with a few exceptions, the rising inequality calls for a Danish solution, though this obviously has to take into account concerns over Denmark's international economic competitiveness. Simultaneously, in Denmark, there is an argument that there would be dynamic impacts of lowering taxes, especially the high marginal tax rates, and this should make all richer, due to which the increase in labour supply should imply a higher total production (and thereby higher GDP to share). This has been part of the arguments for social policy change, in this way resembling arguments on trickle-down economics.

The present chapter will assess whether this trend of lowering especially income taxes is one of the core reasons for the recent increase in inequalities in the universal Danish welfare state. Furthermore, changes in generosity of social benefits, a central issue in Nordic welfare states, will also be discussed as another potential factor behind the rise in inequality. In recent years, the debate on poverty has also become more central in Danish politics, especially with a focus on children, the living standard of pensioners, and working-age people located outside the labour market. This debate is linked to ongoing discussions about measures that might help those living with low income. As in other countries, voters and, often, populist parties have rallied behind a demand for greater economic and services for older people (Greve, 2019b).

Four main sections comprise the remaining of this chapter. Section 'Change in Inequality – And Some Reasons Therefore' explores the dynamic relationship between inequality and social policy in Denmark while featuring a comparative discussion of the other Nordic countries and of Germany and the UK, which are examples of continental and liberal welfare regime, respectively. Section 'Development in Poverty – Some Reasons' studies the interaction between the issue of poverty and political support for specific social policies in Denmark. Section 'Discussion' discusses recent social changes and the lessons we can draw from them, including a short comparison to liberal welfare states, such as the US. Finally, Section 'Implications for Practice' sums up the chapter's main claims. Overall, the analysis suggests that tax reforms focusing on labour market supply have helped increase inequality, thus indicating a possible trade-off between different aspects of welfare state development.

Change in Inequality – And Some Reasons Therefore

In this section, the analysis of inequality in Denmark focuses mainly on changes to the tax system and to spending patterns in both social services and social security benefits. Although it is true that the 'welfare systems play a major role in levelling inequalities' (Eurofound, 2019, p. 16), such a focus on the relationship between inequality and the welfare state obscures the fact that, in Denmark as in other countries, the increase in inequality is also tied to changes in age structure, labour market participation, higher earnings-inequality, educational attainment, skill-based technological change, and alteration in cohabitation (increasingly rich with rich and poor with poor, which when using data on household income will show increasing levels of inequality) (Causa, Hermansen, Ruiz, Klein, & Smidova, 2016; Cohen & Ladaique, 2018; Pareliussen, Hermansen, André, & Causa, 2018; Søgaard, 2018). Yet, the following discussion focuses on recent Danish tax reforms and the generosity of social benefits while studying their possible influence on patterns of inequality.

In general terms, inequality is shaped by wage differentiation in the labour market, which is determined by uneven 'access to education, labour market institutions, unions and minimum wage' (Piketty & Cantante, 2018, p. 227). However, wage differentiation is less important in Denmark given the Nordic traditions for tri-partite agreements and a pressed wage structure, albeit educational attainment level plays a role with regarding employment opportunities and income levels. This can thereby have an impact on the level of inequality, including between men and women; even Danish women has seen higher level of educational attainment in the last decades.

Our analysis does not include the possible impact of public in-kind transfers on inequality, which is difficult to measure (Egholt Søgaard et al., 2018). A few observations on in-kind transfers, though, are in place. The services provided by the Nordic welfare states are often either free or cheap, which indirectly helps reduce inequality, even if free higher education especially benefits higher income groups. Inequality of opportunity is not included either, but it is well known that inequality has a strong relation, among other things, to the educational attainment level. Finally, in contrast to reforms affecting cash benefits, much less change has occurred in the area of social services, which should not hide the existence of a debate on the future of universality in this area (Greve, 2020a). Yet, due to the lack of solid data, we are not focusing on such an area. Simultaneously, if these services are not provided by the welfare state then the individual has to buy it on the market. This requirement of user payment could foster inequality in accessing such services. Furthermore, from an economic perspective, economies of scale justify collective action and, more specifically, it is not rational because if people save on their own, for example for long-term care, and then end up not needing it, it does lead to non-optimal levels of (high) savings detrimental to society (Barr, 2010). At the same time, educational services might imply that middle- and high-income earners get more from the welfare states, as children from these families use this service more than people from low-income families.

As argued in the first section of this chapter, increases in inequality are known to have a number of negative impacts on social development. Given this knowledge, it is surprising in the Nordic countries with the historical focus on equality, that economic inequality has increased as indicated in Fig. 1.

Fig. 1 below which shows the evolution of the Gini-coefficient since 2000 in the Nordic countries, in the UK and in Germany before and after social transfers (although pensions is the only social transfer included in data before social transfers).[2] The Gini-coefficient is the most common indicator of economic inequality and using a longer time frame is necessary to assess its evolution. In Denmark, since around the mid-nineties, when the Gini-coefficient stood at 19.9, there has been a slow but gradual increase in the level of inequality (Finansministeriet, 2020).

Fig. 1 shows that income inequality is lower in the Nordic countries and higher in the UK, a liberal country, and Germany, a continental country. This contrast is consistent with the classical understanding of differences across welfare regimes. Fig. 1 also shows that, among Nordic countries, the increase in inequality has been highest in Denmark and Sweden since 2005. While inequality also increased

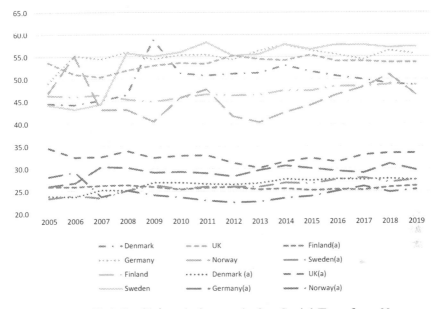

Fig. 1.   Gini-Coefficient before and after Social Transfers. *Note:*
Equivalised disposable income is used. 'A' after country name indicates it is
after social transfers. Time from 2005, as this is the first year with data for all
countries. Given that there is not for all countries data for 2019 the Figure
use 2018 as the latest year. *Source:* Eurostat, ilc_di12 and ilc_di12b, accessed
9 February 2021.

in Germany and Sweden, it declined in Norway, making it the country in Fig. 1
with the lowest level of inequality. The Figure also indicates that welfare states
across different regimes still help reduce income inequality, which is in line with a
study showing across 31 countries that after the financial crisis and changes in the
welfare systems, countries still go through the use of taxes and transfers, which
reduces the Gini-coefficient with 31% (Caminada, Goudswaard, Wang, & Wang,
2019). Overall, because the consensus is that welfare states reduce inequality, the
remaining question is whether or not inequality has been reduced.

In order to paint a more nuanced picture of the evolution of inequality in
Denmark since 2005, Table 1 features three indicators of inequality over time:
Gini-coefficient, 80/20 ratio (income distribution between the top and the bottom
income quintile), and the income share for the top 1%.

Table 1 shows that all indicators point towards higher levels of inequality, e.g.
whether we look at the Gini-coefficient, the income of the top income quintile
compared to those in the lowest quintile (80/20), or the share of the 1% with the
highest income. In fact, in the late 1970s and early 1980s, the income share of the

Table 1. Development in 80/20, Gini and Share of Income for 1% in Denmark since 2005.

	2005	2008	2011	2014	2016	2018	2019
80/20	3.5	3.6	4.0	4.1	4.1	4.1	4.1
Gini	23.9	25.1	26.6	27.7	27.7	27.8	27.5
Share 1%	10.8	10.2	11.2	12.7	12.3	11.2	11.2

Source: Eurostat and World Income Database Data – WID – World Inequality Database, accessed 9 February 2021.

top 1% was around 6%, compared to more than 11% in 2019. This increase in the income share of the top 1% is one of the reasons why inequality in Denmark has been rising, albeit given the relatively modest nature of the increase, this is not the central reason for growing inequality. In addition to changes in the labour market, also growing income from accumulated wealth has favoured this development.[3] This is the case despite the fact described earlier that, since 2009, the top 1% in Denmark have not seen an increase but a decrease of their share of wealth. The share of top-income earners' wealth would even be lower if it included the wealth saved in pension funds, as they are especially important at the lower end of the wealth distribution (Finansministeriet, 2020).[4] This trend is also significant because the changing situation of the top 1% is seen as an indicator of the overall change in patterns of inequality (Atkinson & Søgaard, 2016).

If we look at the reasons why inequality has increased in Denmark, the two main explanations are the changes to the social security system and the (mainly income-based) tax system and how it has developed over time. Overall, redistribution by the welfare state policies has declined in Denmark (Cohen & Ladaique, 2018). When the top 1% gets an increasing share of the income, this also has an impact on the overall level of inequality. The size hereof albeit depend on from whom they get it, e.g. if it is from those already having a high income (such as others of the 20% with the highest income), the changes is not influencing the 80/20 and this is also being a reason for using different measures for the development. At the broadest level, the change in the 1% highest earners' share of income is still a good supplementary indicator for change in overall level of inequality.

The two main factors for the increase in inequality discussed above deal most directly in principle, with two types of argument that have been used to legitimize recent welfare state change in Demark:

(1) It should pay to work
(2) Trickle down will make everyone richer.

Since the 2008 financial crisis, these two arguments have informed the policies of successive governments that have embraced a 'politics of necessity' (*den nødvendige politik*) as a consequence of growing international economic competition and demographic changes (ageing population) are also expected to be there in the years to come. The basic argument here is that, if the incentive to work is too low, people will prefer to rely on social benefits, and indirectly that those not working have a less legitimate demand for welfare. However, this economic argument about work incentives ignores the impact of the level of demand for labour (e.g. the availability of jobs), but also that having a job is not only an economic reality but also socially desirable by the vast majority of the working-age population (Brooks, 2011). Furthermore, we know that being unemployed (Helliwell & Huang, 2014) or at risk of becoming unemployed has a negative impact on well-being and happiness (Chung, 2016; De Neve, Krekel, & Ward, 2018; Greve, 2012). These realities might be mitigated by activation; however, this is the case only if this implies getting a job. Overall active labour market policy is not so effective as sometimes argued (see Chapter 3 in this volume; Card, Kluve, & Weber, 2018; Nordlund & Greve, 2019). Beyond narrow economic factors, the complex social realities mentioned above are seldom included in the analysis of whether people actively search for a job or not (Wulfgramm, 2011).

Despite the many negative consequences of economic inequality, it has consistently been argued – and not only in Denmark – that cutting taxes so that it 'pays to work' would increase labour supply and, in turn, stimulate prosperity. In Denmark, 'making work pay' has been done by changing tax and duty rates, but also by gradually increasing the distance in disposable income between those on the labour market and those outside because benefits of indexation has been lower than the increase in labour market income, a move that has remained largely hidden from public view, as in other countries (Otto & van Oorschot, 2019). This stealthy policy development has taken place through an increase in the earned income tax credit (EITC) (*beskæftigelsesfradrag*) introduced in 2004, which implies that the distance between disposable income received for having a job and for being unemployed increases without reducing the absolute level of the benefit. EITC has increased from 13.600 DKK (app. 1800 EURO) in 2010 to 39.400 DKK (app. 5220 EURO) in 2020, and besides starting in 2014, there has been one extra EITC for single providers at 17.700 (app. 2345 EURO) from 2014 to 22.900 (app. 3030 EURO) in 2020.[5] Moreover, changes in income transfers (such as unemployment and pension) policy have not fully compensated for changes in income and prices, and thereby implied reduction by decay (Saxonberg & Sirovátka, 2009) or as also labelled by drift (Hacker, 2004). Furthermore, there is no clear empirical evidence of how large the difference between benefits and income on the labour market is needed to create work incentives.

This as, it can also be discussed whether there will be a change in supply of labour because of change in the tax rates as often argued do not only depend on the individual persons labour supply elasticity, but will also depend on the income of the entire household. The reason why being that if one person gets a higher income when working, this person or the one cohabiting with might lower their supply as an indicator of preference for leisure.

Apart from issues related to work incentives, there is also the claim that the overall increase in labour stemming from tax cuts would create more saving and due to higher level of production, higher GDP to distribute. This might be the case, although it depends on people's actual income level, in part because people with higher incomes typically have a lower level of elasticity in their supply of labour than people with lower incomes, implying that if taxes are cut, they are likely work less, not more. This may explain why 'no study to date has been able to show convincing evidence in the short or medium run of large real economic activity responses of upper earners to tax rates' (Piketty, Saez, & Stantcheva, 2014, p. 231).

Simultaneously, increasing labour supply should imply more wealth to distribute, which should then benefit all in society. This idea is associated with trickle-down economy, known in the US as Reaganomics (Chomsky, 2007), which is grounded in the assumption that if taxes, especially those on corporations and high-income earners, are cut, levels of economic activity would increase. The additional wealth created is then expected to trickle down to the rest of the population, so that also people with lower income will benefit. Yet, scholars have argued that trickle-down economics has had a negative impact on welfare state development, which calls into question the claim that cutting the taxes of corporations and the wealthy benefits society as a whole (Blyth, 2013; Greener, 2018).

In Denmark, nine tax reforms were adopted between 1987 and 2012, 7 of which took place between 1995 and 2012.[6,7] These reforms were supplemented by several adjustments during these years and later on. These reforms focused primarily on the income tax system. The 'middle-income' tax was abolished from 2010 and the top income tax bracket was raised.[8] Change in rights to certain deductions were enacted and the value of deductions was reduced. Simultaneously, the general personal tax allowance was increased. Overall, this has triggered an increase in fiscal inequality, as higher-income earners benefited disproportionately from these tax reforms. This is the case because, on average, their tax burden decreased more than the one of other income categories, which was especially true between 2000 and 2010 (Greve, 2020b). For instance, after peaking at 21% in 2008, the proportion of the Danish population paying the high-income tax rate fell to only 15% in 2015.[9] An analysis from a Danish think tank (Arbejderbevægelsens Erhvervsråd) also shows that, between 2001 and 2016, tax reform was most beneficial to the top 1% and top 10% of income earners, with close to 8 percentages point increase for the 10% richest and around 1% for those at the bottom of the income distribution.[10] At the same time, in Denmark as in other countries, fiscal welfare is further exacerbating income inequality (Avram, 2018; Barrios, Moscarola, Figari, Gandullia, & Riscado, 2019; Sinfield, 2019). Finally, besides tax reform, Denmark witnessed a movement away from the taxation of labour, capital and property towards more indirect forms of taxation, such as consumption taxes, as the overall tax level remained at the same level, which also exacerbated income inequality given the higher propensity to consume by low-income earners (Causa et al., 2016).

Change in benefits, including above-mentioned lower levels of indexation, has implied that many income transfers today are less generous than in the past, which has also influenced the development in inequality. Furthermore, there is a push to only allow people who have lived in Denmark for at least a number of years to receive certain social benefits, such as family allowance and social assistance. If this is not fulfilled, people will only be eligible for a benefit which is lower than social assistance (kontanthjælp). Thereby, some people, especially migrants, will receive lower benefits than others, a situation that would exacerbate inequality.

Development in Poverty – Some Reasons

Denmark does not have an official poverty line in part because of a lasting controversy over whether one, in fact, can measure it effectively. Measurement complications include the following:

- Dealing with students who often get higher income after they graduate,
- Whether low-income status should be measured over one or more years, and
- What the actual poverty line should be.

Therefore, here we use the poverty line used by EUROSTAT, which is 60% of median income, for a critical account on measuring poverty see Greve, 2020b.

Table 2 shows the development in poverty in selected years and selected age groups.

Table 2 shows that there has been a slight increase in poverty in Denmark, and also that the impact on men and women is the same, although after the 2008 financial crisis, poverty among men was slightly higher. In general, these data are based upon household and, thus, not always strong in explaining gender differences, as well as whether resources are used equally within each household (Daly, 2018). The most remarkable development is the decrease in poverty among those aged 65 and older. This situation is related to the impact of occupational welfare (Greve, 2018), as labour market–based pensions have increased in value since the late 1980s, as related to collective agreements in the private sector reached at the time. As far as the relationship between age and poverty is concerned, there is a

Table 2. Development in the Proportion Living at Risk of Poverty since 2005 for Different Age Groups as Well as Men and Women.

	2005	2008	2011	2014	2017	2018	2019
All	11.8	11.8	12.1	12.1	12.4	12.7	12.5
<18 years	10.4	9.1	10.3	9.2	10.0	11.0	10.3
From 18 to 64 years	11.0	11.3	12.2	13.8	14.3	14.5	14.4
From 25 to 29 years	20.7	22.9	26.8	24.4	28.3	27.2	21.1
>65 years	17.6	18.1	13.9	9.8	8.8	8.9	9.0
Men	11.6	11.7	12.1	12.4	13.0	12.6	12.5
Women	12.1	12.0	12.0	11.8	11.7	12.8	12.5

Source: Eurostat, ilc_li02, accessed 9 February 2021.

higher level of poverty for those aged 25–29, a situation due to the fact that some are still in university, and that recent graduates face higher levels of unemployment (Greve, 2020b).

Changes in poverty patterns can partly be explained by cuts in social benefits and added conditionality to access them. Combined with new changes to the income tax system enacted between 2016 and 2018, this reality has led to a deterioration of the economic situation of the lowest income groups.[11] These transformations took place amidst international knowledge that growing up in poverty can create emotional stress (McGarvey, 2018), and that living in poverty reduces the option to act rationally (Markussen & Røed, 2016). Acting rationally to economic incentives is what has been the core of the economic argument for that 'work should pay,' as lower benefits would increase the incentive to take any available job. Certainly, the increase in poverty due to an increasing number of young people having a lower income because they stay in school longer (Pareliussen & Robling, 2018) is not in itself a problem. Yet, it is a problem for people who stay below the poverty line for longer periods. Here there seems in Denmark – and in many other welfare states – to be a consistent knowledge that this is a more common situation facing unskilled workers than people with higher levels of education. There is regional variation in the availability of jobs that make people living in certain regions more likely to fall into poverty because of higher levels of unemployment. The risk of living in poverty as a consequence of the general decline in the generosity of unemployment benefits is combined with the fact that most benefits fall behind the general increase in Danish living standards. Furthermore, a ceiling on social assistance payments for those not working at least 225 hours per year has also exacerbated inequality. Lastly, implementing an integration benefit (integrationsydelse) later renamed the 'Self-support and repatriation benefit' (selvforsørgelses-og hjemrejseydelse), which offers lower benefits than Social Assistance (Greve, 2020b).

Discussion

There is a continued high support for the welfare state in Denmark and, as in other countries, this is especially the case for healthcare and old-age care (Greve, 2019b; Roosma, Van Oorschot, & Gelissen, 2016). Part of the recent policy discussion has been about the idea that increased labour supply would stimulate economic growth, and that its short-term negative impact on inequality is an economic and political necessity.

Recent years have also seen a growing awareness of the fiscal sustainability challenges facing the welfare state stemming from new technology, globalisation (including global tax evasion) and change in age structure. The current fiscal debate revolves around the ability to find measures that can both finance the welfare state and allow for the preservation of the universality of the Danish welfare state. Supporting human-capital development is one way to do this, but flexibility and flexicurity are also seen as possible ways forward, see also Chapter 3 in this book. Again, several of these issues transcend the Danish welfare state, and they are part of global pressures and issues facing welfare states in general.

In Denmark, there is also a focus on how key actors, such as labour market partners and the business organisations, perceive potential policy alternatives as they relate to inequalities. It has especially been the business sector and a liberal think tank (CEPOS), who has sought to shape the policy agenda by legitimizing cuts to both corporate and personal income taxes (especially the high marginal taxes). These changes are said to improve competitiveness, partly as that it would increase labour market supply. The increase in labour supply should then generate more wealth over time, a situation that would benefit the entire society. This has over a long time been supported by analysis from the Ministry of Finance, using the Danish macro-economic model, arguing not only for changes to the tax and duty system, but also to public spending, which can have a negative impact on labour supply (Finansministeriet, 2018).

Thus, policy changes benefitting the wealthy have been legitimized in the name of national economic interest, even if there is little evidence that trickle-down economics really works, and growing evidence inequality has several problematic consequences both for the individuals affected and for society.

Redistributive policies are still important for both inequality and poverty. Between 2006 and 2017, in this area, we witnessed key differences among the Nordic welfare states, despite the fact they belong to the same welfare regime. For instance, in terms of poverty and inequality alleviation, Finland did better than Denmark, where the policy changes discussed above triggered an increase in the Gini-coefficient of 0.8 point (Palviainen, 2019). Weaker income redistribution in Denmark is also evidenced in other studies, which also point to other drivers of change in Nordic welfare states such as demographic changes (Aaberge et al., 2018) and a more dualised labour market (Dølvik & Oldervoll, 2019).

The fiscal and inequality trends witnessed in Denmark are also apparent in other OECD countries, including those belonging to the liberal welfare regime. To illustrate this, we can turn to the United States, the more 'liberal' welfare regime in rich democracies, within which income inequality has increased since the beginning of the Reagan years (1981–1989). In part because of both economic transformations and changes to the tax system that have often favoured the wealthy in the name of 'trickle-down economics,' the United States has the highest Gini-coefficient in the G7. For instance, in 2017, the United States had a Gini-coefficient of 0.434, compared to 0.326 in France and 0.392 in the United Kingdom (Schaeffer, 2000). Simultaneously, the evidence that the 'rich are getting richer' at the expense of poorer segments of the population is an undeniable reality in the United States:

> Over the past 50 years, the highest-earning 20% of US households have steadily brought in a larger share of the country's total income. In 2018, households in the top fifth of earners (with incomes of $130,001 or more that year) brought in 52% of all US income, more than the lower four-fifths combined.
>
> (Schaeffer, 2000)

It would be easier to mention more economic and social indicators that would further illustrate the well-documented increase in inequality in the United States. Yet, more interesting here is to connect this multifaceted increase in inequality to both policy decisions such as tax cuts that disproportionately advantage higher-income individuals and families and to 'non-decisions' leading to policy drift, which refers to the absence of policy changes necessary to compensate for economic and social trends (Hacker, 2004). For example, a study suggests that, despite the enactment of reforms such as Obamacare, relative policy inaction in key policy areas such as old-age pensions has exacerbated policy drift in the United States (Béland, Rocco, & Waddan, 2016). This suggests that, if one is preoccupied by rising inequalities, they should take into account changes to tax and social policies, but also inaction, which may exacerbate inequality because nothing is done to address ongoing socio-economic trends. As far as inequality is concerned, policy inaction can prove extremely consequential in society, amidst changing socio-economic circumstances that welfare can and should temper or even compensate for (Hacker, 2004).

Implications for Practice

There is a continued debate about the structure of the Danish welfare state, including the consequence of a very complicated system with built-in risk of contradiction between economic efficiency and social equality. Important questions in this debate include whether or not unemployment benefits are sufficiently generous to combat poverty. What type of policies might ensure a decrease in inequality and how can these policies be compatible with the ability to finance the welfare state in the long run amidst accelerated population aging are questions we can address by drawing lessons from other countries and from the comparative social policy literature more generally.

Thus, this section will point towards that types of policy instruments are available if one wants to reduce inequality and the risk of living of poverty. Whether to use them is a political decision.

Overall, as in the past, using the tax and duty system, not only to finance the welfare state, but also as an instrument to reduce inequality, remains an option, so that progressive income taxes and also, as pointed to by Piketty (Piketty, 2014), wealth taxes would foster more equality in society, albeit there does not seem to be political support for raising wealth taxes in Denmark, as the large parties do not support it. Furthermore, there is less to support to redistribution in Denmark than in the other Nordic states (Greve & Azhar Hussain, 2021) Financing is still important, if one wants to ensure that the social benefits are so generous that those outside the labour market do not face the risk of poverty, and that the welfare state continues to reduce labour market inequalities.

Still, if one wants to ensure legitimacy it will also, as in the past, imply that, in order to preserve the legitimacy of the welfare state, the middle class benefits from it (Korpi & Palme, 1998), but also that some fields such as long-term care, pensions, and care for older people have a higher popular support (Greve, 2020a). At the same time, in the wake of the recent COVID-19 crisis, the weakening fiscal ability to finance welfare states is a significant issue, albeit it is less pressing in the Nordic countries, including Denmark, than in other regions of the world, given sound public finances and balance of payments.

Conclusion

Overall, the above analysis has pointed towards the contradictory reality that universality remains a central feature of the service sector, at the same time as the income transfer systems and the income tax system have seen reforms leading to growing inequality.

Thus, because of policies inspired by trickle-down economics and the idea that 'work should pay,' inequality has grown in the Danish welfare state, a situation that makes it less distinct than in the past. This does not imply that the historical factors that triggered the development of an encompassing and highly egalitarian welfare state have vanished altogether. The combination of tax and duty system with redistribution through income transfers remains a reality in spite of some recent increase in inequality as highlighted above. Moreover, the existence of an effective active labour market policy embedded in the flexicurity approach, which is further discussed in Chapter 3, might help people back onto the labour market. Overall, Danes, like the inhabitants of the other Nordic countries, remain the happiest in the world and the welfare state no doubt has a key role in ensuring this (Martela, Greve, Rothstein, & Saari, 2020). Notwithstanding the reforms described in this chapter, we find that it is likely that the welfare state will continue to have this positive effect on happiness and well-being as they still are supportive with regard to reducing the insecurity in case of different social contingencies occurs.

Notes

1. See Section 'Implications for Practice' for the possible impact on legitimacy.
2. The argument for this being that without this it would imply that many older people do not have any income, so this is the classical way of dealing with the issue.
3. See http://kraka.dk/small_great_nation/stigende_topindkomstandel_i_danmark, accessed 12 May 2020.
4. There is no detailed information available on change in the distribution of housing wealth. Wealth is furthermore difficult to measure as a lot of data is not available, including art, cash, and non-registered shares. Moreover, in Denmark the value of housing is imprecise due to lack of uprating. Still, housing has a negative impact on wealth distribution and on income, even though its size is difficult to measure. Furthermore, wealth is very age dependent and given that many young have a negative wealth, this makes it not possible to use the GINI-coefficient as this is skewed by negative values. Therefore, the focus is on income inequality.
5. From www.skm.dk, accessed 7 May 2020.

6. From www.skm.dk: Skattereformer og skatteomlægninger siden 1987, accessed 7 May 2020.
7. https://www.dst.dk/Site/Dst/Udgivelser/nyt/GetAnalyse.aspx?cid=28125, accessed 7 May 2020.
8. The middle-income tax was 6% above a certain income threshold.
9. https://www.skm.dk/skattetal/statistik/indkomstfordeling/bund-mellem-og-top-skatteydere/, accessed 7 May 2020.
10. See https://www.ae.dk/analyser/15-aars-skattereformer-har-tilgodeset-de-rigeste, accessed 12 May 2020.
11. See http://www.oecd.org/els/soc/benefits-and-wages/Analysis-of-policy-reforms-in-the-EU-2016-2018.pdf, accessed 12 May 2020.

References

Aaberge, R., André, C., Boschini, A., Calmfors, L., Gunnarsson, K., Hermansen, M., ... Pareliussen, J. (2018). *Increasing income inequality in the Nordics. Nordic economic policy review 2018* (Vol. *TemaNord 2*). Copenhagen: Nordic Economic Council. doi:10.6027/TN2018-519

Atkinson, T. (2015). What can be done about inequality? *Juncture*. doi:10.1111/j.2050-5876.2015.00834.x

Atkinson, A. B., & Søgaard, J. E. (2016). The long-run history of income inequality in Denmark. *The Scandinavian Journal of Economics, 118*(2), 264–291.

Avram, S. (2018). Who benefits from the 'hidden welfare state'? The distributional effects of personal income tax expenditure in six countries. *Journal of European Social Policy, 28*(3), 271–293. doi:10.1177/0958928717735061

Barr, N. (2010). Long-term care: A suitable case for social insurance. *Social Policy and Administration*. doi:10.1111/j.1467-9515.2010.00718.x

Barrios, S., Moscarola, F. C., Figari, F., Gandullia, L., & Riscado, S. (2019). The fiscal and equity impact of social tax expenditures in the EU. *Journal of European Social Policy, 30*(3), 1–19.

Béland, D., Rocco, P., & Waddan, A. (2016). Reassessing policy drift: Social policy change in the United States. *Social Policy and Administration, 50*(2), 201–218.

Berg, A. G., & Ostry, J. D. (2011). Inequality and unsustainable growth: Two sides of the same coin? IMF staff discussion note. International Monetary Fund.

Blyth, M. (2013). *Austerity: The history of a dangerous idea.* Oxford: Oxford University Press.

Brooks, D. (2011). *The social animal: The hidden sources of love, character, and achievement.* New York, NY: Random House.

Bussolo, M., Krolage, C., Makovec, M., Peichl, A., Stockli, M., Torre, I., & Wittneben, C. (2019). *Vertical and horizontal redistribution: The case of Western and Eastern Europe. 1/19.* EUROMOD Working Paper Series.

Caminada, K., Goudswaard, K., Wang, C., & Wang, J. (2019). Income inequality and fiscal redistribution in 31 countries after the crisis. *Comparative Economic Studies, 61*(1), 119–148. doi:10.1057/s41294-018-0079-z

Card, D., Kluve, J., & Weber, A. (2018). What works? A meta analysis of recent active labor market program evaluations. *Journal of the European Economic Association.* doi:10.1093/jeea/jvx028

Causa, O., Hermansen, M., Ruiz, N., Klein, C., & Smidova, Z. (2016). *Inequality in Denmark through the looking glass, no. 1341.* doi:10.1787/5jln041vm6tg-en

Chomsky, A. (2007). *'They take our jobs!': And 20 other myths about immigration.* Boston, MA: Beacon Press.

Chung, H. (2016). Dualization and subjective employment insecurity: Explaining the subjective employment insecurity divide between permanent and temporary workers across 23 European countries. *Economic and Industrial Democracy, 40*(3), 700–729. doi:10.1177/0143831X16656411

Cingano, F. (2014). *Trends in income inequality and its impact on economic growth, no. 163.* doi:10.1787/5jxrjncwxv6j-en

Cohen, G., & Ladaique, M. (2018). Drivers of growing income inequalities in OECD and European countries. In R. M. Carmo, C. Rio, & M. Medgyesi (Eds.), *Reducing inequalities: A challenge for the European Union?* (pp. 31–43). Cham: Springer International. doi:10.1007/978-3-319-65006-7_3

Dabla-Norris, E., Kochhar, K., Suphaphiphat, N., Ricka, F., & Tsounta, E. (2015). *Causes and consequences of income inequality: A global perspective.* Washington, DC: International Monetary Fund.

Daly, M. (2018). Towards a theorization of the relationship between poverty and family. *Social Policy and Administration, 52*(3), 565–577.

De Neve, J.-E., Krekel, C., & Ward, G. (2018). Work and well-being: A global perspective. In *Global happiness policy report* (pp. 74–128). Retrieved from https://www.happinesscouncil.org/report/2018/global-happiness-policy-report#:~:text=Global%20Happiness%20Policy%20Report%20The%20Global%20Happiness%20Policy,on%20best%20practices%20to%20promote%20happiness%20and%20well-being

Dimick, M., Rueda, D., & Stegmueller, D. (2018). Models of other-regarding preferences, inequality, and redistribution. *Annual Review of Political Science, 21*, 441–460.

Dølvik, J. E., & Oldervoll, J. (2019). Averting crisis through coordination and Keynesian welfare policies. In S. Ólafsson, M. Daly, O. Kangas, & J. Palme (Eds.), *Welfare and the great recession: A comparative study* (pp. 210–227). Oxford: Oxford University Press.

Egholt Søgaard, J., Roine, J., Robling, P. O., Parcliussen, J., Orsetta, C., Lindgren, P., … Aaberge, R. (2018). Nordic economic policy Review 2018: Increasing income inequality in the Nordics (TemaNord 2018: 519). Copenhagen: Nordic Economic Council. doi:10.6027/TN2018-519

Eurofound. (2019). *Age and quality of life: Who are the winners and losers?* Luxembourg: Luxembourg Publications Office of the European Union.

Finansministeriet. (2018). *Regneprincipper og modelanvendelse: Dynamiske effekter af offentligt forbrug og offentlige investeringer.* Copenhagen: Finansministeriet.

Finansministeriet. (2020). *Ulighedsredegorelsen, 2020.* Copenhagen: Finansministeriet.

Greener, I. (2018). *Social policy after the financial crisis: A progressive response.* Cheltenham: Edward Elgar.

Greve, B. (2012). The impact of the financial crisis on happiness in affluent European countries. *Journal of Comparative Social Welfare, 28*(3). doi:10.1080/17486831.2012.736354

Greve, B. (2018). At the heart of the Nordic occupational welfare model: Occupational welfare trajectories in Sweden and Denmark. *Social Policy and Administration, 52*(2), 508–518. doi:10.1111/spol.12380

Greve, B. (Ed.). (2019a). *Routledge handbook of the welfare state* (2nd ed.). Oxon: Routledge.

Greve, B. (2019b). *Welfare, populism and welfare chauvinism*. Bristol: Policy Press.

Greve, B. (2020a). *Austerity, retrenchment and the welfare state. Truth or fiction?* Cheltenham: Edward Elgar.

Greve, B. (2020b). *Velfærdssamfundet: Enkelt, retfærdig og effektivt?* Copenhagen: Hans Reitzels.

Greve, B., & Azhar Hussain, M. (2021). Support for governmental income redistribution in Nordic countries. *European Review*, 1–19. doi:10.1017/s1062798721000089

Hacker, J. S. (2004). Privatizing risk without privatizing the welfare state: The hidden politics of social policy retrenchment in the United States. *American Political Science Review*. doi:10.1017/S0003055404001121

Helliwell, J. F., & Huang, H. (2014). New measures of the costs of unemployment: Evidence from the subjective well-being of 3.3 million Americans. *Economic Inquiry, 52*(4), 1485–1502.

Kangas, O., & Kvist, J. (2019). Nordic welfare states. In B. Greve (Ed.), *Routledge handbook of the welfare state* (2nd edn, pp. 124–136). Oxon: Routledge.

Korpi, W., & Palme, J. (1998). *The paradox of redistribution and strategies of equality: Welfare state institutions, inequality and poverty in the Western countries*. 174. LIS Working Paper Series. Luxembourg.

Leventi, C., Sutherland, H., & Tasseva, I. V. (2017). *Improving poverty reduction in Europe: What works (best) where?* EUROMOD Working Paper Series. doi:10.1177/0958928718792130

Markussen, S., & Røed, K. (2016). Leaving poverty behind? The effects of generous income support paired with activation. *American Economic Journal: Economic Policy, 8*(1), 180–211.

Martela, F., Greve, B., Rothstein, B., & Saari, J. (2020). The Nordic exceptionalism: What explains why the Nordic countries are constantly among the happiest in the world. In J. E. De Neve, J. Helliwell, R. Layard, & J. D. Sachs (Eds.), *World happiness report, 2020*. New York, NY: Sustainable Development Solutions Network. Retrieved from https://worldhappiness.report/ed/2020/#read

McGarvey, D. (2018). *Poverty safari: Understanding the anger of Britain's underclass*. London: Picador.

Nordlund, M., & Greve, B. (2019). Focus on active labour market policies. In B. Greve (Ed.), *The Routledge handbook of the welfare state* (2nd ed., pp. 366–377). Oxon: Routledge.

Okun, A. M. (1975). *Equality and efficiency: The big tradeoff*. Washington, DC: Brookings Institution Press.

Otto, A., & van Oorschot, W. (2019). Welfare reform by stealth? Cash benefit recipiency data and its additional value to the understanding of welfare state change in Europe. *Journal of European Social Policy, 29*(3), 307–324. doi:10.1177/0958928718796299

Palviainen, H. (2019). *Changing Nordic model? A policy analysis*. EUROMOD at the Institute for Social and Economic Research. EM 15/19.

Pareliussen, J. K., Hermansen, M., André, C., & Causa, O. (2018). Income inequality in the Nordics from an OECD perspective. In *Nordic economic policy review* (TemaNord 2018: 519, pp. 17–57). Copenhagen: Nordic Economic Council.

Pareliussen, J., & Robling, P. O. (2018). Demographic change and inequality trends in the Nordic countries. In *Nordic economic policy review* (Vol. *519*, pp. 136–166).

Piketty, T. (2014). *Capital in the twenty-first century*. London: Harvard University Press.

Piketty, T., & Cantante, F. (2018). Wealth, taxation and inequality. In *Reducing inequalities* (pp. 225–239). Berlin: Springer.

Piketty, T., Saez, E., & Stantcheva, S. (2014). Optimal taxation of labor income: A tale of three elasticities. *American Economic Journal: Economic Policy*, *6*(1), 230–271.

Richmond-Rakerd, L. S., D'Souza, S., Andersen, S. H., Hogan, S., Houts, R. M., Poulton, R., ... Moffitt, T. E. (2020). Clustering of health, crime and social-welfare inequality in 4 million citizens from two nations. *Nature Human Behaviour*, *4*(3), 255–264.

Roosma, F., Van Oorschot, W., & Gelissen, J. (2016). A just distribution of burdens? Attitudes toward the social distribution of taxes in 26 welfare states. *International Journal of Public Opinion Research*. doi:10.1093/ijpor/edv020

Saxonberg, S., & Sirovátka, T. (2009). Neo-liberalism by decay? The evolution of the Czech welfare state. *Social Policy and Administration*. doi:10.1111/j.1467-9515. 2009.00655.x

Schaeffer, K. (2000, February 7). *6 facts about economic inequality in the U.S.* Washington, DC: Pew Research Center. Retrieved from https://www.pewresearch. org/fact-tank/2020/02/07/6-facts-about-economic-inequality-in-the-u-s/

Sinfield, A. (2019). Fiscal welfare. In B. Greve (Ed.), *The Routledge handbook of the welfare state* (2nd ed., pp. 23–33). Oxon: Routledge.

Søgaard, J. E. (2018). Top incomes in Scandinavia – recent developments and the role of capital income. *Nordic Economic Policy Review*, *519*(1), 66–94.

Stiglitz, J. E. (2012). *The price of inequality: How today's divided society endangers our future*. New York, NY: W.W. Norton & Company.

Wilkinson, R., & Pickett, K. (2018). *The inner level: How more equal societies reduce stress, restore sanity and improve everyone's well-being*. St. Ives: Allen Lane.

Wulfgramm, M. (2011). Can activating labour market policy offset the detrimental life satisfaction effect of unemployment? *Socio-Economic Review*, *9*(3), 477–501.

Chapter 3

Reforming the Ideal(ised) Model(s) of Danish Labour Market Policies

Magnus Paulsen Hansen and Janine Leschke

Abstract

Globally, Denmark stands out in terms of achieving high employment rates, containing unemployment and providing a labour market model combining flexibility, security and activation with a strong role for the social partners. The Danish labour market institutions and policies are seen as the catalyst for the transformation from industrial economy to a globalised, post-industrial and knowledge-based economy in which socio-economic equality and workforce security go hand in hand with competitiveness and the adaptability of business. In the 2000s, this mutual relationship came to be known as the Danish flexicurity model. Meanwhile, as a policy blueprint, 'flexicurity' has never really influenced Danish politics, and the reforms implemented since the 2000s have deviated from the premises of the model. This paper critically assesses the Danish model and its institutional components. It tracks the emergence of the Danish collective bargaining model as well as the flexicurity model. It scrutinises the challenges and performance of the current Danish labour market institutions and policies in a comparative perspective and discusses the extent to which the Danish experiences *can* and *should* be imitated abroad.

Keywords: Flexicurity; activation; social partners; unemployment benefits; the Danish model; active labour market policies

Introduction

Denmark stands out globally as having contained unemployment and provided a labour market model combining flexibility, security and activation with a strong role for the social partners. Accordingly, scholarly and political debates since the 1990s have pointed out the uniqueness and success of the Danish model for tackling labour market challenges. These challenges include regaining

Public Governance in Denmark, 39–56
doi:10.1108/978-1-80043-712-820221003

competitiveness in the face of increased globalisation and the Europeanisation of the economy and labour; mitigating the risks of long-term unemployment and social exclusion and ensuring high employment despite changing demographics. But does the Danish labour market model still deliver what it promises?

The Danish labour market institutions and policies are seen as the catalyst for the transformation from an industrial economy to a globalised, post-industrial, knowledge-based economy in which socio-economic equality and workforce security go hand in hand with international competitiveness and adaptability of business. In the 2000s, this mutual relationship came to be known as the Danish flexicurity model, which, according to scholars, is deeply rooted in long-standing historical traditions of cooperation between employers and trade unions, where the state plays a limited role; but the model can also be explained with reference to the distinct way of introducing so-called active labour market policies (ALMPs) in the 1990s.

The Danish flexicurity model involves a combination of flexibility for employers, due to lax employment protection legislation, and security for workers, who can rely on relatively generous unemployment insurance, ALMP and life-long learning. It has attracted numerous visits from foreign governments, the EU, OECD and IMF, all seeking inspiration for reforms, and it has become a prominent blueprint among European policymakers (OECD, 2004; Wilthagen, 2007; Zhou, 2007). For instance, both former French President Nicolas Sarkozy and current President Emmanuel Macron have pointed to Danish labour market policies as source of inspiration for French reforms. At the European level, the Danish flexicurity model (along with the Dutch one) came to play an important role in reconfiguring EU benchmarking of member state performance and the advocacy of structural reforms in the late 2000s. In this manner, the Danish model (along with other Scandinavian countries) contributed to legitimising centrist and 'third way' narratives (Green-Pedersen, Kersbergen, & Hemerijck, 2001) of a socially inclusive alternative to both the uncompetitive and dualist model of post-war Europe, with which the Continental and Mediterranean countries were still stuck (Emmeneger, Häusermann, Palier, & Seeleib-Kaiser, 2012), *and* the competitive yet socially flawed neoliberal model making inroads in Anglophone countries (Hansen & Triantafillou, 2011).

There is an irony in the role that the 'Danish model' and 'flexicurity' concepts have played in Danish politics and the public debate. On the one hand, the Danish model has been an important national marker of consensus since the 1990s, contributing to safeguarding the collective bargaining traditions between the social partners, often in spite of EU regulatory initiatives, such as a pan-European minimum wage (Due & Madsen, 2013) or European Court of Justice rulings on Viking, Laval and Rüffert, which questioned the relationship between the free movement of labour and services and collective bargaining rights. On the other hand, despite the international fuss, 'flexicurity' as a policy blueprint has never really influenced Danish politics; in fact, the reforms implemented since the 2000s have deviated from the premises of the model (Bekker & Mailand, 2018).

In the following, we critically assess the Danish model and its institutional components. Section 'Analysis: Emergence of Collective Bargaining and

Flexicurity Models' historically tracks the emergence of the Danish collective bargaining and flexicurity models; section 'Discussion: Comparative Outlook on Current Labour Market Trends' discusses the challenges and performance of the current Danish labour market institutions and policies in a comparative perspective; and section 'Lessons Learned and Implications for Practice' discusses the extent to which the Danish experiences *can* and *should* be imitated abroad.

Analysis: Emergence of Collective Bargaining and Flexicurity Models

The 'Genius for Compromise'

The current Danish labour market model owes its existence to a series of developments occurring in the 1890s, a decade that marked a period of substantial industrialisation together with the rapid unionisation of both professions and unskilled labour, which was concurrent with the organisation of employers (Knudsen, 2011). At the same time, unions were centralising efforts to better organise and regulate strike actions in response to the ability of employers to force through centralised bargaining (Due, Madsen, Jensen, & Petersen, 1994, p. 78). The collective bargaining system, known today as the 'Danish model,' was established in 1899 in the so-called 'September Compromise.'

The September Compromise acknowledged both the right to union organisation and the employers' right to management control, the latter referring to the right to manage and allocate work and to employ the labour they deem suitable (Due et al., 1994, pp. 81–83). It established a legal framework recognising the two central organisations as juridical subjects with responsibility for reaching and upholding future collective agreements (Pedersen, 2014, p. 290). The agreement, the first of its kind to settle fundamental labour market principles and the relations between labour market parties (Høgedahl, 2020, p. 560), thus induced the gradual 'juridification' of relations through institutions, such as the permanent arbitration court and the conciliation board to mediate between parties, constituting the unique collective-based legal system that remains in place today (Høgedahl, 2020, p. 561; Nielsen & Pedersen, 1991, p. 137).

The international attention to and positive recognition of the Danish system already started in the 1950s, when American labour historian and economist Walter Galenson wrote *The Danish System of Labor Relations: A Study in Industrial Peace*, in which he praised the 'Danish genius for compromise' (Galenson, 1952, p. 101 in Due & Madsen, 2013). To Galenson, the Danish system was 'the most detailed and complete system of collective bargaining in existence,' and he concluded that if 'there is any nation that can peacefully adjust the social conflict arising from industrialization, with equal regard to the welfare of the individual citizen, whether worker, farmer, or businessman, it is Denmark' (Galenson, 1952, p. 1). Following the economic slump in the 1970s and 1980s, when few viewed the Danish labour market system as desirable, similar ideas were taken up by Danish labour market scholars in the early 1990s, pointing out the renewed relevance and resilience of the system in the increasingly globalised economy. Jesper Due and

Jørgen Madsen, drawing on inspiration from Galenson, coined the term 'the Danish model' to describe what they saw as the core features of the Danish labour market: (1) a highly organised labour market (on both the employee and employer sides); (2) two-year centralised negotiations with the state as mediator; (3) consensus- and compromise-based relationships between the social partners and (4) regulation through collective agreements between the social partners, not state legislation (Due et al., 1994). In this way, the system grants employers unlimited managerial rights between rounds of centralised negotiations, while workers are guaranteed the right to organise, including to strike and impose blockades against employers without collective agreements. Thus, the system was a catalyst for the increasing organisation of both sides, peaking on the workers' side in 1985 with a trade union density of around 91% (OECD, 1991).

The Danish model has since become a common term in Danish politics, as when marking joint opposition against an EU minimum wage (which would allegedly violate the autonomy of the social partners to set wages) (Lovén Seldén, 2020).

To other scholars, the 1899 September Compromise and the 'civilisation of class confrontation' was seen as the starting point of the establishment of a 'negotiated economy' capable of adapting to world markets through a 'multi-centred and pluralist political structure' allowing for the 'co-ordination of decisions made by autonomous organizations' (Nielsen & Pedersen, 1991, p. 149). Along the same line of thought, scholars have been pointing to the tripartite organisation of several innovative institutions around the labour market, such as parental leave funds and pension funds that grant rights that are not tied to the workplace or sector and the extensive system of labour market education that supports the continuous upskilling of the workforce without a higher education, which in modern lingua would be termed 'life-long learning' (Mailand, 2020).[1]

The Unemployment Problem

In contrast to many other unemployment insurance systems, employers only play a marginal role in the Danish system, which was established in 1907. The system was partially funded by the state and members but run by the unions through member-funded unemployment funds, organised (originally) according to occupational dividing lines. The union control over the unemployment funds meant that access to insurance *de facto* required union membership, which thereby served as an important vehicle for unionisation (Høgedahl, 2020).

Unlike the rest of the Nordic countries, extending the unemployment insurance scheme was the main strategy for the Social Democrats regarding the labour market, leaving the existing poor-relief system largely intact until the 1960s (Korpi & Esping-Andersen, 1987). As the last country in Western Europe, recipients of poor relief were granted the right to vote in 1961, and the former moral logic of deserving/underserving poor was gradually replaced by a social rights perspective, peaking in 1974 with the introduction of a close-to-unconditional benefit combined with a needs-oriented approach to social work (Petersen, 2014, pp. 125–127).

Meanwhile, the unemployment insurance system basically stopped being a contribution-based and union-controlled scheme in 1967, as most expenses became state financed through general taxation (Christensen, 2012, p. 493). The generalisation of the scheme to all sectors increased coverage from 35% to 65% (Christensen, 2013, p. 528). The significant rise in unemployment rates in the aftermath of the energy crises (from around 1% in 1973 to around 12% in 1993) exposed many recipients to the risk of losing their right to compensation. In response, rights were extended through various pragmatic solutions, such as the 'job offers scheme' (*jobtilbudsordningen*), aimed at allowing recipients to re-qualify for unemployment benefits through nine months of subsidised (but regularly paid) work. In practice, this meant a nearly unconditional and nearly universal income with high compensation rates.

This radical extension of social rights in the field of unemployment and other fields (pensions in particular) led to yet another depiction of what constitutes the Danish approach to the labour market. In the most cited work by a Danish social scientist, *The Three Worlds of Welfare Capitalism*, sociologist Gøsta Esping-Andersen coined his 'three welfare regimes' typology: the (Anglo-Saxon) liberal model, the (Continental) conservative model and the (Scandinavian/Nordic) social democratic model. While this regime typology has since become commonplace, the specific normative standard of evaluation of the original typology is less known (Hansen & Triantafillou, 2011). To this standard, Denmark was not merely a prime example of the social democratic model but also of the ideal welfare state, the *raison d'être* of which was the capacity to 'de-commodify.' Along with Norway and Sweden, Denmark had the highest 'de-commodification score' and exemplified a state where 'citizens can freely, and without potential loss of job, income, or general welfare, opt out of work when they themselves consider it necessary' (Esping-Andersen, 1990, p. 23). As we shall see, this ability to opt in and out of the labour market is later recast in the notion of flexicurity. But just as Esping-Andersen's appraisal of the de-commodified Danish labour market gained international attention, Danish reforms would aim towards the exact opposite: *re*-commodifying the labour force.

The Birth of Activation and the Invention of Flexicurity

In line with broader trends in the EU (e.g. Clasen & Clegg, 2006), Danish labour market reforms saw a gradual but radical reorientation towards activation in the 1990s (Hansen, 2019; Kvist, 2003b; Larsen, 2013). Several reforms were initiated, but the landmark reforms were the 1993 reform of the unemployment insurance system (the active labour market policy act) and the 1998 reform of the system of social assistance (the active social policy act), both designed by centre-left, Social Democrat-led governments. The reforms introduced the concept of 'rights and obligations' (established in individual employment plans) to enrol in activities aimed at labour market re-integration as well as to be at the disposal for the labour market (accept job offers and actively seek employment). For recipients of unemployment benefits (UB), the job offer logic for re-qualifying for compensation was changed to mandatory activation, which put an end to unconditionality.

Both reforms were justified by experts and in public discourse by a diagnosis of 'structural unemployment,' a term coined by US economists and Nobel Prize winners Milton Friedman and Edmund Phelps, encompassing a variety of explanations based on the idea of unemployment as a cyclical phenomenon. Danish economists started pointing out the lack of economic incentives to work, questioning the 'generosity' of benefits and the need for upskilling in a knowledge-based economy together with problems of 'social heritage' and 'social exclusion'; similarly, politicians on the right and left alike began depicting unconditional benefits as 'passive,' thereby emphasising the need to 'activate' the unemployed (Hansen, 2019).

In the same decade, unemployment fell from more than 12% in 1993 to around 5% in 2000. This triggered yet another wave of interest in the 'Danish miracle' (Kvist, 2003a; Torfing, 1999) or 'paradise' (albeit with some snakes in the garden) (Madsen, 2002). According to these explanations, Denmark had chosen a soft 'human capital' strategy as opposed to the punitive 'work first' strategy adopted in most Anglophone countries since the 1980s (Torfing, 1999, p. 17). The Danish case proved, they argued, that it was possible to have 'workfare *with* welfare' (Torfing, 1999, our emphasis). Others went further, suggesting a *complementary* relationship. A 1999 report from the Ministry of Labour described the Danish success as a consequence of a 'golden triangle' consisting of (1) high flexibility (easy to hire and fire together with many job openings; (2) high degree of compensation and long duration of benefits and (3) active labour market policies (upskilling, right and obligation to accept offers) (Arbejdsministeriet, 1999, p. 13). Borrowing the concept from scholars describing the Dutch labour market (Wilthagen, 1998), economist Per Kongshøj Madsen referred to the Danish 'golden triangle of flexicurity,' describing the 'successful combination of adaptability to a changing international environment and a solidaristic welfare system, which protects the citizens from the more brutal consequences of structural change,' hereby exemplifying a 'third way between the flexibility often ascribed to a liberal market economy and the social safety nets of the traditional Scandinavian welfare state' (Wilthagen, 1998, pp. 2, 7).

Madsen was not alone at the time in referring to Denmark as a 'best case' for 'Third Way' politics. According to Third Way inventor Anthony Giddens, the Nordic performance confirmed 'that high tax levels are compatible with economic growth and job creation,' which was due to their 'social investments' (Giddens, 2006, pp. 110–111). In the first decade of the millennium, both the EU and OECD would use the Danish (and sometimes Nordic) case to encourage their member states regarding flexicurity reforms (European Commission, 2007; OECD, 2004). Within the same social investment perspective, other scholars pointed to additional factors underpinning the flexicurity model beyond the 'golden triangle,' such as the extensive but adaptive vocational training system, to explain the high competitiveness and innovative capacity of Danish commerce (Campbell & Pedersen, 2007; Lundvall, 2009), resulting in Danish workers (by the late 1990s) spending more time in training and skill formation programmes than workers in any other EU country (Lorenz & Valeyre, 2004), as well as the high expenditure on childcare, the possibility to transfer pension and insurance rights from one job to another and a decentralised, user-oriented public sector (Kristensen, 2013; Kristensen, Lotz, & Robson, 2011).

It is not without irony that while the then centre-right government was touring Brussels, proudly explaining the secrets of Danish flexicurity to envious colleagues (Bredgaard, Larsen, & Madsen, 2007), their reforms back in Denmark would in fact jeopardise two of the three corners of the triangle. Firstly, in an attempt at 'making work pay' and increasing incentives to work, reforms of the 2000s were rendering social security systems substantially less generous. The maximum duration for receiving unemployment insurance was successively reduced from seven to two years, and benefit levels for both unemployment benefit (UB) recipients and social assistance were reduced, the latter in particular targeting immigrants (Kvist & Harsløf, 2014). Secondly, the training element of activation was significantly downplayed in favour of 'work first' instruments and the intensified control and sanctioning of the unemployed. The reforms were further underpinned by a series of instruments inspired by New Public Management, introducing municipal one-stop 'jobcentres,' which were subject to tight budget-control and performance-measurement systems, effectively sidetracking the unions from direct influence (Larsen, 2013).

Despite the financial crisis and changes in government, the 2010s did not result in radical changes to the labour market regime of the 2000s (Hansen, 2019). As regards the unemployment insurance system, the eligibility criteria have been eased somewhat, and control mechanisms loosened to some degree. The opposite trend has characterised the reform of the social assistance system. As a result of ardent public debate questioning the deservingness of social assistance recipients, reforms were intensifying control and the obligation to work for the benefit (Hansen, 2019; Hedegaard, 2014; see also Chapter 2). Some of the measurable outcomes of reforms since the 1990s are illustrated in Fig. 1. One of the most remarkable changes is the decline in the overall expenditure on so-called 'passive labour market policies' (PLMPs) (see 80 and 90 in Fig. 1) as a result of generally stricter eligibility criteria, shorter benefit periods and the rolling back of early retirement programmes. While expenditure on ALMPs has remained relatively stable, the type of measures used changed substantively in favour of sheltered and supported employment and rehabilitation and to the detriment of training and employment and start-up incentives (see items 10–70 in Fig. 1).

The interpretation of the post-1990 reforms is somewhat contested. Some see the 'work first' reforms of the centre-right government as a radical break with the 'human capital' path from the 1990s (Kvist & Harsløf, 2014), turning 'a beautiful swan into an ugly duckling' (Jørgensen, 2009). Others have argued that the radical break occurred earlier and that the reforms since 2000 simply intensified the path initiated in the 1990s, where the economic thinking and modelling of the labour market was turned upside down in the shift from Keynesian to monetarist thinking (Larsen & Andersen, 2009), and welfare institutions were problematised for 'pacifying,' 'de-responsibilising' and 'disincentivising' citizens (Hansen, 2019). This may also explain why the vast majority of reforms since the 1990s have been supported by the Social Democrats, Liberals and Conservatives alike.

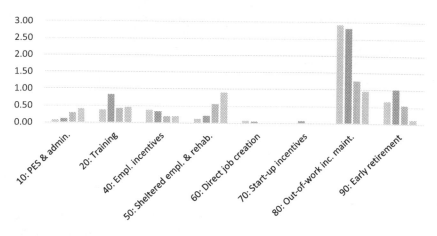

▓ 1986 (unemp. 6.1%)   ▓ 1996 (unemp. 6.9%)   ▓ 2006 (unemp. 3.5%)   ▓ 2017 (unemp. 5.9%)

Fig. 1.   Development in Active and Passive Labour Market Policy Expenditure (% of GDP), Denmark, Detailed Categories, 1986, 1996, 2006, 2017. *Source:* OECD.STAT.

Discussion: Comparative Outlook on Current Labour Market Trends

Active Labour Market Policies: High Spending, Modest Effects

The historical tracking of reforms leads to discussion of the question of how the *current* Danish labour market is faring in a comparative perspective. Despite reforms, from a comparative perspective, Denmark still spends a high share of GDP on both PLMP and ALMP (Fig. 2); it is the top OECD spender, and expenditure is particularly outstanding when taking the comparatively low unemployment rates into account. The active-to-passive benefits ratio is only higher in Sweden in 2017, but the Swedish spending on both PLMP and ALMP was considerably less despite a higher unemployment rate.

In line with earlier studies, a Card, Kluve, and Weber (2010) meta-analysis finds that public sector employment programmes are relatively ineffective; however, specific public programmes (e.g. sheltered employment in Denmark) do not usually have integration into regular employment as their main objective (Bengtsson & Mateu, 2009). Job search assistance and similar programmes have been found to yield generally positive outcomes, particularly in the short run, whereas on-the-job training is not very effective in the short run but has more positive outcomes after two years (Bengtsson & Mateu, 2009). The evaluation measure plays an important role for the overall assessment, with evaluations focussing on the duration of benefits, showing more positive short-term effects than those focussing on employment or earnings (Bengtsson & Mateu, 2009; for an overview on evaluation studies on Denmark, see Kluve, 2010).

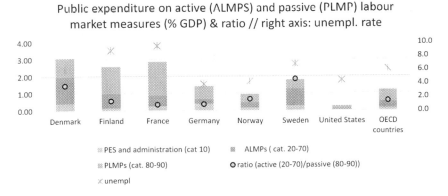

Fig. 2.   Public Expenditure on Active and Passive Labour Market Measures (% of GDP), 2017.[2] *Source:* OECD.STAT (Public expenditure and participant stocks on LMP).

Unemployment Compensation – Still Generous?

However, turning to one of the other corners of the 'golden triangle,' the 'generous compensation,' in Denmark today appears less remarkable. Comparing UB coverage for 2019, Denmark takes a mid-way position, with lower benefit coverage than Germany and Finland – both countries which in contrast to Denmark have means-tested unemployment assistance schemes – but substantively higher UB coverage than Sweden and the United Kingdom (OECD.STAT, not shown). Denmark has seen substantially reduced unemployment insurance coverage rates beginning in the mid-1990s; among the Nordic countries, however, Sweden has seen the most drastic cuts to welfare provision (Fritzell et al., 2014), which becomes apparent in steep decreases in UB coverage.

Replacement rates (i.e. the ratio between unemployment benefits and salary levels) have dropped significantly since the 1990s: from 75% in 1994 to less than 60% in 2018 for an average blue-collar worker. Unions have problematised this tendency, accusing it of threatening the 'cohesiveness of the flexicurity model,' as rising insecurity will lead to labour 'demands of longer terms of notice' when laying people off, thereby 'hampering flexibility' (LO, 2018, p. 4).

Working Conditions – Is the Danish Model Sufficiently Inclusive?

This brings us to the current Danish labour market dynamics (Table 1). On par with the other Nordic countries, with Sweden leading the way, Denmark has very high labour force participation rates (79% overall, 76% for women). As in the other Nordic countries, female employment is largely in the public sector (e.g. nursing, eldercare, childcare and teaching). The generous, tax-funded welfare state relies on high male and female labour market participation, which is

Table 1. Key Labour Market Indicators and Institutions.

	Labour Force Partic. Rate, Total (2019)	Labour Force Partic. Rate, Women (2019)	Employer org. Density (Latest Year av.)	Trade Union Density[a] (2017)	Collective Bargaining (2017 or Latest)	Childcare Coverage 0–2 Years (2017)	Gender Wage Gap[b] (2019 or Latest)
Denmark	79.0	76.0	68	66.1	82.0	55	4.9
Finland	78.4	76.6	76	62.2	89.3	31	18.9
France	71.7	68.2	75	8.9	98.5	56	13.7
Germany	79.2	74.9	58	16.7	56.0	37	15.3
Norway	78.3	75.7	68	49.3	72.5	56	5.0
Sweden	82.9	81.1	83	65.6	90.0	47	7.6
United Kingdom	78.8	74.4	35	23.2	26.0	38	16.0
United States	74.1	68.9	:	10.3	11.6	:	18.5
OECD	72.8	65.1	:	:	32.4	:	12.9

[a]Where available administrative data, otherwise survey data.

[b]The gender wage gap is defined as the difference between median earnings of men and women relative to median earnings of men. Data refer to full-time employees.

Note: Labour force participation rate refers to 15–64 years.

Source: OECD.STAT and OECD Employment Outlook 2017 (employer organisation density); OECD Family database (PF3.2 Enrolment in childcare and pre-school).

supported by comprehensive and generous subsidised childcare for young children (0–2) combined with – as in the other Nordics – high-quality, public childcare. This goes hand in hand with family-friendly employer practices, including flexible arrangements allowing mothers (and fathers) to combine work and care (OECD family database, not shown).[3] However, parental leave, despite generally being relatively generous in terms of (transferable) time and compensation, is organised in a less progressive manner in Denmark compared to the other (Nordic) countries (LO, 2018).

Earnings quality, a measure that takes into account both the level and distribution of earnings, is very high in Denmark and higher than in the other Nordics (OECD.STAT 'job quality database').[4] The findings on high earnings quality for Danish women are also in line with comparatively low gender pay gaps when displayed as the share of median earnings of full-time employees (see Table 1). Important contributing factors for earnings equality in Denmark are a compressed wage distribution due to high collective bargaining coverage (see Table 1).

High collective bargaining coverage, which even saw a slight upward trend over the last decade, is facilitated by high trade union and employer organisation density (see Table 1). Having said this, as most countries, Denmark has seen steadily declining trends in trade union density since the late 1980s, which can partly be explained by the reforms to the unemployment insurance system breaking the ties between funds and unions, hereby allowing for the rise of so-called 'yellow unions' that provide services to members but restrain from collective action (Høgedahl, 2020).

Unlike countries such as Finland and Norway (for some sectors), Denmark does not use extension mechanisms to make collective agreements applicable to employers and employees in the same sector otherwise not bound by the agreement. This has created challenges in terms of low wages and sub-standard working conditions in sectors such as industrial cleaning, agriculture and construction (e.g. Trygstad, Larsen, & Nergaard, 2018). These sectors are characterised by migrant labour and are prone to phenomena such as sub-contracting and/or posting, with strong impacts from the 2004 and 2007 EU enlargement rounds as well as North–North competition further fuelled by the 2008 economic and financial crisis (Trygstad, Larsen, & Nergaard, 2018); nevertheless, like the other Nordic countries, Denmark still has comparatively low in-work poverty rates.

The Nordic countries, with Denmark taking a mid-way position, have generally fared considerably worse than the United Kingdom and United States regarding the employment (and unemployment) of foreign-born individuals (see Chapter 13). This gap is particularly pronounced among women (OECD.STAT, NUP rates by place of birth and sex). Since 2001, Denmark has successively restricted immigration by third-country nationals (see introduction to volume) and is following a work-first approach regarding migrants (Kvist & Harsløf, 2014). In the intra-EU labour mobility setting, Denmark has taken a mid-way position between Norway (top) and Sweden (bottom) in terms of attractiveness for Central and Eastern European (CEE) workers, who have made up the bulk of mobile citizens in the EU since the 2004 and 2007 enlargement rounds (Friberg & Eldring, 2013). Friberg, Arnholtz, Eldring, Hansen, and Thorarins (2014) have shown poor working conditions for Polish workers, the most important group of CEE workers in Nordic countries, in Copenhagen, Oslo and Reykjavik. Felbo-Kolding, Leschke, and Spreckelsen (2019) have emphasised hierarchies in terms of wages between Central Eastern European and Western European migrants in Denmark (Germany and the United Kingdom).

Precarious employment is not a phenomenon widely experienced in the Danish (or Nordic) context. Aggregate job quality, using multi-dimensional indices, has been assessed as very high for Denmark (Green et al., 2013; Leschke & Watt, 2014). Denmark tops the European job quality index, which covers 28 countries, for overall job quality, with Sweden and Finland in places three and four (2015 figures), Norway not included (Piasna, 2017). Denmark – usually together with the other Nordics – is in the leading group in most job quality sub-dimensions, including wages, working hours and work–life balance, skills and career development and collective interest representation. Denmark also does well on forms of employment and job security, whereas Finland and Sweden rank in the middle on this dimension due to higher shares of involuntary non-standard employment. Denmark (and more so Sweden) fares poorer on the working conditions sub-dimension; for Denmark, this is exclusively driven by high work-intensity (Leschke & Watt, 2014; Piasna, 2017). Collective bargaining coverage, trade union density and employee representation in the companies are shown to have a positive impact on overall job quality as well as sub-dimensions such as wages and skills and career development (Piasna, 2017). Some groups are, however, left behind; so-called outsiders consist mainly of migrants and their descendants: young, unskilled, low-wage workers (Larsen, 2011).

Writing in the midst of the COVID-19 pandemic, it is far too early to assess the impact on the Danish labour market. However, a half year after Denmark and most other Western countries 'locked down,' Denmark was among the countries with relatively low spikes in unemployment. Most parts of the economy have remained relatively open, and the state initiated large-scale tripartite agreements in which it agreed to cover the cost of private sector employee salaries as long as companies refrain from laying off personnel; additionally, short-time work or temporary lay-off schemes were extended (see COVID-19 EU-PolicyWatch for details on Denmark and other European countries).[5] Compared to the United States, the Danish model seems to have avoided socio-economic crisis in terms of rising unemployment and poverty.

Lessons Learned and Implications for Practice

So what can policymakers seeking inspiration from the Danish labour market experience(s) hope to learn? In our interpretation, the 'Danish model' is neither stable nor, in fact, *a* model; rather, it is a composite mix of institutions and policies constantly adapting to shifts in the economy, society and ideas that have retrospectively been 'modelised' in a variety of ways. Importantly, one must emphasise the unique historical framing conditions for the evolvement of the institutions described above: a small, open economy with large representation of crafts-based small- and medium-sized companies, a homogenous population, a certain constellation and coalition of classes (workers and smallholders), the folk high-school tradition and the electoral and parliamentary system.

Thus, policymakers face two (equally challenging) conditions when seeking inspiration from the Danish reforms and institutions. The first relates mainly, but not solely, to the Danish collective bargaining model based on a high degree of organised labour and employers (strong social partnership), which may be the element of the policies and institutions described above that has proven most stable over time. It is worth remembering that the origin of the model, the September Compromise, was in fact a set of formal legal rules and institutions that, at least in principle, could be copied. However, the story of the Danish collective bargaining model is also that of particular historical, enabling conditions and the gradual expansion of a particular way of handling conflicts underpinned by informal institutions (e.g. mutual trust between social partners, pragmatic compromise-seeking approach and inclusion of social partners in policymaking) as well as formal institutions. Similar arguments can and have been made regarding the flexicurity model; for instance, that since the Danish flexicurity model relies on a high degree of 'public-spiritness,' it is

> ...hardly sustainable in countries displaying weak public-spiritedness, because the unemployment insurance design raises moral hazard issues that are much more difficult to overcome in countries where individuals are more prone to cheat over government benefits.
>
> (Algan & Cahuc, 2006, p. 2)

The second challenge facing policymakers is that it is not straightforward to copy from model(s) that, as presented above, are in fact unstable. The flexicurity models of the 1990s and 2020s are quite different, to the extent that one may question if the triangle remains 'golden.' While the flexibility corner is more or less unchanged, the ALMP corner can no longer be described as the non-coercive empowering and upskilling approach, and the security corner is certainly less generous than previously. Hence, there is a need to revisit critically the question of what makes the Danish labour market perform as well as it still does. Rather than the 'golden triangle,' the answer possibly lies in the framing institutions and policies that have only changed modestly during the last half century. They comprise a continuing investment in high-quality early-childhood education and comprehensive public eldercare – two sectors that have served to create workplaces mainly for women. Together with family-friendly workplace practices, these institutions allow women comprehensive labour market participation as a fundamental component of the Scandinavian welfare model (Abrahamson, 2010).

As suggested above, the 'golden triangle' of the 1990s was in fact never 'golden' in the sense that it never represented an 'equilibrium.' As discussed above, the reforms in the 1990s introducing ALMPs were not so different from the later reforms; they merely had a different starting point. In other words, even the praised reforms of the 1990s were problematising (and reducing) security while increasing conditionality and activation. These unresolved tensions have yet again become visible in the approach of the current Social Democratic government to labour market reforms. Three examples illustrate this. First, as a response to protests from users and a number of cases of unworthy client treatment (in particular, related to sickness leave and the strengthened criteria for enrolling in early retirement), the government has initiated a benchmarking of jobcentres according to 'dignity goals.' These goals accommodate much of the criticism but also seem to reduce the problems to a *local* problem of bad administration (rather than of the rules they administer). The same ambiguity can be found in two government-appointed commissions. The first, the 'Benefits Commission,' has been tasked with 'rethinking' the social assistance system. While recognising that the current system is 'imbalanced' due to recent reforms, its solutions should nonetheless be 'cost neutral.' The mandate of the second, the so-called 'Second Generation Reforms Commission,' recognises that while the labour market reforms since the 1990s ('first-generation reforms') have 'reduced unemployment, increased labour supply, increased the level of education and strengthened long-term resilience of the Danish economy,' there is a need to pursue a new reform track that has 'a broader focus, underpins the Danish welfare model and contributes to reducing social inequality' (Finansministeriet, 2020). The latter commission was convened in light of the COVID-19 crisis. It thus remains an open question whether the post-crisis developments will also mark a break with the existing reform path.

Notes

1. The elaborate Danish approach to life-long learning, however, also has origins in the extensive apprenticeship programme for folk high-school students dating back to the 1890s (Campbell & Pedersen, 2007).
2. UK no data available. United Kingdom has not provided data on this indicator since 2012; it has traditionally been at the lower end of spenders in the EU context (2011 expenditure figures were as follows: PES: 0.19, ALMPs: 0.22, PLMPs: 0.31 at Unemployment of 8.2%).
3. PF3.1 Public spending on childcare and early education, MF2.4. Family-friendly workplace practices, PF2.1. Parental leave system.
4. Earnings quality is measured by considering both the level and distribution of earnings across the workforce using the general means approach originally proposed by Atkinson (1970) with 'high inequality aversion.' A lower value corresponds to higher inequality aversion, which in turn translates into lower earnings quality for a given distribution.
5. https://www.eurofound.europa.eu/data/covid-19-eu-policywatch

References

Abrahamson, P. (2010). Continuity and consensus: Governing families in Denmark. *Journal of European Social Policy, 20*(5), 399–409.

Algan, Y., & Cahuc, P. (2006). Civic attitudes and the design of labor market institutions: Which countries can implement the Danish flexicurity model? IZA Discussion Papers 1928.

Arbejdsministeriet. (1999). Arbejdsmarkedsreformerne - ét statusbillede. Copenhagen: Arbejdsministeriet.

Atkinson, A. B. (1970). On the measurement of inequality. *Journal of Economic Theory, 2*(3), 244–263.

Bekker, S., & Mailand, M. (2018). The European flexicurity concept and the Dutch and Danish flexicurity models: How have they managed the Great Recession? *Social Policy and Administration, 53*(1), 142–155.

Bengtsson, S., & Cayuelas Mateu, N. (2009). *Beskyttet Beskætigelse – en kortlægning*. Report 09:09. Copehagen: SFI.

Bredgaard, T., Larsen, F., & Madsen, P. K. (2007). Flexicurity – afklaring af et begreb i bevægelse. *Tidsskrift for Arbejdsliv, 9*(4), 8–25.

Campbell, J. L., & Pedersen, O. K. (2007). The varieties of capitalism and hybrid success: Denmark in the global economy. *Comparative Political Studies, 40*(3), 307–332.

Card, D., Kluve, J., & Weber, A. (2010). Active labour market policies – A meta analysis. *The Economic Journal, 120*(November), 452–477. doi:10.1111/j.1468-0297.2010.02387

Christensen, J. (2012). Arbejdsløshedsforsikring og arbejdsanvisning. In J. H. Petersen, K. Petersen, & N. F. Christiansen (Eds.), *Dansk velfærdshistorie: Velfærdsstatens storhedstid* (pp. 487–545). Odense: University Press of Southern Denmark.

Christensen, J. (2013). Arbejdsløshedsforsikring og aktivering. In J. H. Petersen, K. Petersen, & N. F. Christiansen (Eds.), *Dansk velfærdshistorie: Velfærdsstaten i tidehverv*. Odense: University Press of Southern Denmark.

Clasen, J., & Clegg, D. (2006). Beyond activation: Reforming European unemployment protection systems in post-industrial labour markets. *European Societies, 8*(4), 527–553.

Due, J., Madsen, J. S., Jensen, C. S., & Petersen, L. K. (1994). *The survival of the Danish model: A historical sociological analysis of the Danish system of collective bargaining*. Copenhagen: DJØF Publishing.

Due, J. J., & Madsen, J. S. (2013). 20 år med den danske model. *Tidsskrift for Arbejdsliv, 15*(1), 94–103.

Emmenegger, P., Häusermann, S., Palier, B., & Seeleib-Kaiser, M. (2012). *The age of dualization: The changing face of inequality in deindustrializing societies*. Oxford: Oxford University Press.

Esping-Andersen, G. (1990). *The three worlds of welfare capitalism*. Cambridge: Polity.

European Commission. (2007). *Towards common principles of flexicurity: More and better jobs through flexibility and security*. Brussels: CEC.

Felbo-Kolding, J., Leschke, J., & Spreckelsen, T. (2019). A division of labour? Labour market segmentation by region of origin: The case of intra-EU migrants in the UK, Germany and Denmark. *Journal of Ethnic and Migration Studies, 45*(15), 2820–2843. doi:10.1080/1369183X.2018.1518709

Finansministeriet. (2020). Kommissorium: Kommission for 2. generationsreformer, de nye reformveje. Accessed on October 21, 2020.

Friberg, J. H., Arnholtz, J., Eldring, L., Hansen, N. W., & Thorarins, F. (2014). Nordic labour market institutions and new migrant workers: Polish migrants in Oslo, Copenhagen and Reykjavik. *European Journal of Industrial Relations, 20*(1), 37–53.

Friberg, J. H., & Eldring, L. (Eds.). (2013). *Labour migrants from Central and Eastern Europe in the Nordic countries Patterns of migration, working conditions and recruitment practices.* Copenhagen: Nordic Council of Ministers.

Fritzell, J., Bacchus Hertzman, J., Bäckman, O., Borg, I., Ferrarini, T., & Nelson, K. (2014). Sweden: Increasing income inequalities and changing social relations. In B. Nolan, W. Salverda, D. Checchi, I. Marx, A. McKnight, I. G. Tóth, & H. G. van de Werfhorst (Eds.), *Changing inequalities and societal impacts in rich countries – Thirty countries' experiences.* Oxford: Oxford University Press.

Galenson, W. (1952). *The Danish system of labor relations: A study in industrial peace.* Cambridge, MA: Havard University Press.

Giddens, A. (2006), Debating the social model: Thoughts and suggestions. In *The Hampton Court agenda: A social model for Europe* (Vol. 95). London: Policy Network.

Green, F., Mostafa, T., Parent-Thirion, A., Vermeylen, G., Van Houten, G., Biletta, I., & Lyly-Yrjanainen, M. (2013). Is job quality becoming more unequal? *International Labor Relations Review, 66*(5), 753–784.

Green-Pedersen, C., Kersbergen, K. Van, & Hemerijck, A. (2001). Neo-liberalism, the 'third way' or what? Recent social democratic welfare policies in Denmark and The Netherlands. *Journal of European Public Policy, 8*(2), 307–325.

Hansen, M. P. (2019). *The moral economy of activation: Ideas, politics and policies.* Bristol: Policy Press.

Hansen, M. P., & Triantafillou, P. (2011). The Lisbon strategy and the alignment of economic and social concerns. *Journal of European Social Policy, 21*(3), 197.

Hedegaard, T. F. (2014). Stereotypes and welfare attitudes: A panel survey of how 'Poor Carina' and 'Lazy Robert' affected attitudes towards social assistance in Denmark. *Nordic Journal of Social Research, 5,* 139–160.

Høgedahl, L. (2020). The Danish labour market model: Is the bumblebee still flying? In P. M. Christiansen, J. Elklit, & P. Nedergaard (Eds.), *The Oxford handbook of Danish politics* (pp. 559–576). Oxford: Oxford University Press.

Jørgensen, H. (2009). From a beautiful swan to an ugly duckling: The renewal of Danish activation policy since 2003. *European Journal of Social Security, 11*(4), 337–367.

Kluve, J. (2010). The effectiveness of European active labor market programs. *Labour Economics, 17,* 904–918.

Knudsen, K. (2011). *Dansk fagbevægelses historie frem til 1950.* Copenhagen: SFAH.

Korpi, W., & Esping-Andersen, G. (1987). From poor relief to institutional welfare states: The development of Scandinavian social policy. *International Journal of Sociology, XVI*(3–4), 39–74.

Kristensen, P. H. (2013). The distinctiveness of Nordic welfare states in the trans-formation to the projective city and the new spirits of capitalism. In P. du Gay & G. Morgan (Eds.), *New spirits of capitalism?* (pp. 206–230). Oxford: Oxford University Press.

Kristensen, P. H., Lotz, M. M., & Robson, R. (2011).Tailoring Danish flexicurity for changing roles in global games. In P. H. Kristensen & K. Lilja (Eds.), *Nordic capitalisms and globalization: New forms of economic organization and welfare institutions* (pp. 86–140). Oxford: Oxford University Press.

Kvist, J. (2003a). A Danish welfare miracle? Policies and outcomes in the 1990s. *Scandinavian Journal of Public Health, 31*(4), 241–245.

Kvist, J. (2003b). Scandinavian activation strategies in the 1990s: Recasting social citizenship and the Scandinavian welfare model. *Revue française des affaires sociales, 4*, 223–249.

Kvist, J., & Harsløf, I. (2014).Workfare with welfare revisited: Instigating dual tracks for insiders and outsiders. In I. Lødemel & A. Moreira (Eds.), *Activation or workfare? Governance and the neo-liberal convergence* (pp. 48–68). Oxford: Oxford University Press.

Larsen, T. P. (Ed.). (2011). *Insidere og outsidere, den danske models rækkevidde.* Copenhagen: Jurist- og. Økonomforbundets Forlag.

Larsen, F. (2013). Active labor-market reform in Denmark: The role of governance in policy change. In E. Brodkin & G. Marston (Eds.), *Work and the welfare state: Street-level organizations and workfare politics* (pp. 103–123). Georgetown: Georgetown University Press.

Larsen, C. A., & Andersen, J. G. (2009). How economic ideas changed the Danish welfare state: The case of neoliberal ideas and highly organized social democratic interests. *Governance, 22*(2), 239–261.

Leschke, J., & Watt, A. (2014). Challenges in constructing a multi-dimensional European job quality index. *Social Indicators Research, 118*(1), 1–31.

LO. (2018). 30 års dagpengeforringelser: En teknisk gennemgang af kompensationsgraden og lønmodtagernes anvendelse af dagpengesystemet. Retrieved from https://fho.dk/wp-content/uploads/2020/01/baggrundsrapport-om-dagpenge.pdf

Lorenz, E., & Valeyre, A. (2004). Organisational change in Europe: National models or the diffusion of a new 'one best way'? DRUID Summer Conference 2004, Elsinore, Denmark.

Lovén Seldén, K. (2020). Challenges posed by the EU minimum wage initiative to the ETUC and European trade union cooperation. *Transfer: European Review of Labour and Research, 26*(3), 325–343.

Lundvall, B.-Å. (2009). *Innovation, growth, and social cohesion: The Danish model.* Cheltenham: Edward Elgar.

Madsen, P. K. (2002). The Danish model of 'flexicurity': A paradise with some snakes. In *Interactions between labour market and social protection, 2002.* Brussels: European Foundation for the Improvement of Living and Working Conditions.

Mailand, M. (2020). *Corporatism since the Great Recession: Challenges to tripartite relations in Denmark, The Netherlands and Austria.* Cheltenham: Edward Elgar Publishing.

Nielsen, K., & Pedersen, O. K. (1991). The negotiated economy: The structure, the processes, and the instruments. In J. Hausner, B. Jessop, & K. Nielsen (Eds.), *Markets, politics and the negotiated economy: Scandinavian and post-socialist perspectives* (pp. 127–152). Cracow: Cracow Academy of Economics.

OECD. (1991). *Employment outlook.* Paris: OECD.

OECD. (2004). *Employment outlook.* Paris: OECD.

OECD. (2017). *OECD employment outlook, collective bargaining in a changing world of work (Ch. 4)*. Paris: OECD.

OECD Family Database. Retrieved from http://www.oecd.org/els/family/database.htm

OECD.STAT. Retrieved from https://stats.oecd.org/

Pedersen, O. K. (2014). *Markedsstaten*. Copenhagen: Hans Reitzels.

Petersen, J. H. (2014). *Pligt og ret, ret og pligt*. Odense: University Press of Southern Denmark.

Piasna, A. (2017). *'Bad jobs' recovery? European job quality index 2005–2015*. ETUI Working Paper no. 2017.06. European Trade Union Institute, Brussels.

Torfing, J. (1999). Workfare with welfare: Recent reforms of the Danish welfare state. *Journal of European Social Policy*, 9(5), 5–28.

Trygstad, S., Larsen, T. P., & Nergaard, K. (2018). Dealing with austerity and migration in the northern European cleaning sector: Social partner strategies to strengthen wage floors. *European Journal of Industrial Relations*, 24(8).

Wilthagen, T. (1998). *Flexicurity: A new paradigm for labour market reform? Flexicurity research programme paper*. Berlin: Wissenschaftzcentrum.

Wilthagen, T. (2007). *Flexicurity pathways: Turning hurdles into stepping stones*. Brussels: European Commission.

Zhou, J. (2007). *Danish for all? Balancing flexibility with security: The flexicurity model*. IMF Working Paper WP/07/36.

Chapter 4

Innovating Democratic Participation in Social Housing

Elizabeth Toft Kristjansen and Jesper Ole Jensen

Abstract

This chapter examines how democratic innovations can strengthen participation in the social housing sector. In Denmark, social housing offers affordable housing to a large number of Danes. The sector is grounded in traditions for resident involvement and engagement, and the democratic model in the sector is unique to Denmark. The residents have the majority say in all decision-making boards, which enables them to influence both the physical surroundings and social initiatives. Despite the positive merits, the sector faces challenges concerning increased segregation, municipalities allocating an increased share of socially and economically marginalised people to the sector, and less participation in the residential democracy. This chapter studies two cases of initiatives that experiment with democratic innovations to enhance participation in local housing associations. The two cases are innovative initiatives in the social housing sector and illustrate the potential benefits of increased participation. The chapter concludes that project-based initiatives might be on the rise and seem to hold considerable potential for enhancing participation. The challenge, then, is still to secure the coordination and strategic direction of the initiatives while combining them with the formal resident democracy.

Keywords: Democratic innovation; citizen participation; social housing; resident democracy; resident involvement; local democracy

Introduction

A well-functioning housing sector offering affordable dwellings is essential for securing citizens a good, stable life (United Nations, 2016). Internationally, policymakers are working to avoid segregation and to provide affordable housing and liveable neighbourhoods. Resident involvement is a cornerstone in the

Public Governance in Denmark, 57–73
doi:10.1108/978-1-80043-712-820221004

development of the Danish social housing sector (Nielsen & Haagerup, 2017). Although the Danish social housing sector is regarded internationally as an example of high resident influence, the sector has faced several challenges in recent decades (Hansen & Langergaard, 2017), which calls for ways to re-think participation and to increase the sense of ownership and the liveability of these communities. This chapter outlines these challenges and presents two cases involving democratic innovations.

The Danish housing sector represents an interesting case in several ways, especially due to the large proportion of social housing that provides affordable housing. Resident democracy is fundamental to the understanding and identity of Danish social housing. Internationally, it is recognised for its participatory democracy and the level of decision-making allocated to residents (Jensen, 1998). The residents have the majority say in all governing boards and a high degree of collective influence on the physical surroundings and social work in their homes and housing estates.

Today, the social housing sector constitutes around 21% of all Danish dwellings, which makes the sector the second most prevalent in the country.[1] Approximately one million people live in the approximately 500,000 dwellings, and there are around 700 social housing associations of varying sizes. They are all democratically governed by representative assemblies that elect an organisational residents board, and local representative assemblies elect the local housing boards (Jensen, 1997). The sector is non-profit, meaning that the construction of new estates is financed by low-interest state loans. The monthly rent covers the cost of the loans, maintenance, administration and investments in improvements. The purpose of social housing organisations is to make suitable housing available to everyone in need of a reasonable rent and to give the residents influence on their own living conditions (Almenboligloven, 2020).

Despite the many positive merits of the sector in providing affordable housing and granting a high degree of decision-making competence to the residents, the social housing sector is also facing numerous challenges. This includes increasing segregation, municipalities allocating people with social problems to the sector, and less participation in the resident democracy. On other levels in contemporary societies, tendencies of democratic challenges can also be seen (Pitkin, 2004; Stoker, 2006). Citizens are sceptical regarding the legitimacy of political systems, as seen in the growing distance between citizens and their political representatives, declining participation and waning support for political decisions (Geissel & Newton, 2012). These challenges can lead to polarisation and division that exacerbates social and ethnical inequalities. The democratic participation of residents is a cornerstone in the Danish social housing sector. It is important because it secures inputs from the affected residents to the resident boards in each social housing association, which helps to voice concerns and to produce better-anchored solutions and joint ownership of the physical surroundings.

This chapter considers how initiatives produced by democratic innovations may help spur the democratic participation in resident democracy. We review some of the literature on democratic innovation to underline the importance and potential of citizens having influence on their lives and living conditions. We introduce two empirical studies of innovating democratic participation in Danish social housing that also present our overall thesis of how we see a shift towards project-based activities, where the enhancement of legitimacy, influence and ownership help to supplement the participation. The final sections will discuss the experiences and challenges, present learned lessons and points requiring special attention, before concluding and summing up the main points.

Democratic Innovation

There are different approaches to citizen mobilisation. Some researchers point to the need to rethink how democratic models function by introducing democratic innovations and new forms or modes of participation to renew participation and enhance support for democratic solutions (Geissel & Newton, 2012; Smith, 2009). Democratic innovations generally aim to increase democratic legitimacy and to improve policy effectiveness through participation and/or deliberation (Elstub & Escobar, 2019). Smith (2009) defines democratic innovations as: 'institutions that have been specifically designed to increase and deepen citizen participation in the political decision-making process' (p. 1). Citizen participation can assume multiple forms and serves just as many purposes, depending on the aim (Michels, 2011). Some forms or modes of participation occur via the development of new channels and arenas that can supplement the existing ones and, furthermore, strengthen the citizen–politician connection. Part of the literature suggests the introduction of arenas and platforms to gather the relevant actors in collaboration and joint problemsolving or as a combination of democratic participation through representative democracy and direct democracy (Sørensen & Torfing, 2019).

Citizen participation can contribute to a more robust democratic culture in several different ways. It can give citizens a say in decision-making, contribute to the inclusion of individual citizens in the policy process, encourage civic skills and virtues, lead to rational decisions based on public reasoning, and increase the legitimacy of decisions (Michels, 2011). This can also enhance citizen support for political solutions (Elstub & Escobar, 2019) by creating new channels for stakeholder participation and influence. Other initiatives focus on inviting citizens to create and solve solutions and welfare, which can also augment the sense of ownership (Bekkers, Dijkstra, Edwards, & Fenger, 2007).

Drawing on the insights from the literatures above, the Danish examples from the social housing sector can be characterised as attempts at using resident board participation as a vehicle for active local citizenship. More specifically, the participation can contribute to enhancing resident empowerment (and/or their sense thereof) and developing ownership of the local community, as well as learning democratic culture. The resident democracy lives and functions as its own small-scale democracy within the larger national democratic frame. From a micro-level perspective, this chapter contributes by studying local democracy in a social housing context, thereby illustrating some of the potentials and challenges that occur when mobilising residents in the operation of their buildings and local community. Worth mentioning is that the resident democracy is different from other democratic platforms due to the resident composition of the sector, as elaborated in the following section.

The Social Housing Sector

The Danish social housing sector is unique compared to similar housing forms in Europe and other Western countries (Hansen & Langergaard, 2017) due to its history and strong democratic traditions granting residents opportunity to decide matters of concern to their housing community (Jensen, 1998). The resident democracy and collective ownership concepts have been important principles relating back to when the sector was founded in the early 1900s. In Danish, the sector is termed the *almen boligsektor*, which translates to 'general housing'. The term points to the fact that, in theory, the sector is meant to offer housing to the general population. The sector offers diverse types of dwellings for those with different needs. Besides family homes, there are specialised facilities such as youth residences, senior housing and assisted living facilities (Landsbyggefonden, 2019). The social housing sector helps to solve a large societal task in offering dwellings to a section of the population with certain needs, which is why we use the 'social' terminology in this chapter (Nielsen & Haagerup, 2017). The social housing sector is still *general* in the sense that it is possible for everyone to join a social housing waiting list. Funded in legislation, Danish municipalities dispose over every fourth or third dwelling for the placement of refugees and those with social problems or pressing needs in a vacant dwelling. To achieve a socio-economic mix of residents, municipalities can make use of 'flexible letting' (Nielsen & Haagerup, 2017), which allows people with jobs or students to skip the waiting list.

There are multiple opportunities for resident participation, both in the formal resident democracy (Fig. 1) and through local activities. As seen in other member-driven associations and democracies operating at the international, national and local levels, democratic participation is currently challenged (Demokrati-kommissionen, 2020; Pitkin, 2004). Difficulties relating to engaging residents in the formal resident democracy have been discussed for years (Jensen, 1998). Today, 26% of housing estates do not have their own local housing board (Landsbyggefonden, 2019). Although this relates to structural factors (e.g. small estates, many elderly residents), the numbers also reflect the challenge to get residents to engage in democratic work in their own community. The resident boards often lack young people, families with children and ethnic minorities, and they are therefore not necessarily representative of the residents (Bech-Danielsen & Christensen, 2017).

Since the 1960s, the Danish social housing sector has been hit by a 'residual-isation process' (Poggio & Whitehead, 2017), where the middle class has largely left the sector, and the percentages of economically and socially challenged residents have increased. This has amplified the social and cultural segregation between the social housing sector and the rest of the housing market (Nielsen & Haagerup, 2017). The result is a situation where, compared to the rest of the

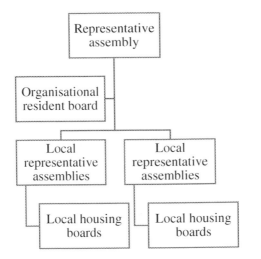

Fig. 1.   The formal resident democracy in social housing associations. Each association has a representative assembly and one organisational resident board. Each estate can then have multiple local representative assemblies and local housing boards.

country, many of the social housing associations have disproportionate numbers of unemployed individuals, ethnic minorities and residents placed by the municipality. Because socio-economic resources correlate negatively with general political participation (Lipset, 1963; Quintelier & Hooghe, 2013), this could limit the expected participation in the social housing sector. Conversely, the social housing sector features historical traditions of collaboration through the resident democracy. However, there is a need to secure involvement, and the social housing sector might be able to reach the socially deprived residents.

The social housing sector and successive governments have been aware of the problems with concentrations of specific citizen groups. Effort has been made to identify the social housing areas with large concentrations of socially disadvantaged residents, and initiatives have been launched in such areas, which have officially been labelled 'ghettos' since 2004. Ghettos are characterised as areas that are 'physically, socially, culturally and economically secluded from the rest of the society' (The Government, 2004 – own translation). Since 2021, based on a number of indicators (residents' income, education, ethnic background and criminal record), the Ministry of Housing updates the list of 'ghettos' annually. The 'ghetto list' requires that housing associations and municipalities launch programmes in the affected areas, mainly in the form of physical and social regeneration master plans (Nielsen, Beckman, Blach, & Andersen, 2016). These plans have been initiated on a large scale over the last decade, the aim being to make physical improvements and socially to activate, integrate and empower the residents while at the same time creating a higher sense of ownership for their area. The social regeneration master plans have included a number of different activities and projects, such as giving young people after-school work (so-called 'pocket-money jobs') and running programmes to establish networks for neighbourhood mothers (*Bydelsmødre*). Thus, a vast number of innovative ways of enhancing resident participation are undergoing project-based participation, where residents can participate in projects and influence the outcome (e.g. by co-designing meeting places and facilities for people in the area). However, such projects have also been criticised for being short-sighted and un-coordinated, with the need for a shared direction to pursue change (CFBU, 2020). This has led to other projects that encourage collaboration with partners outside the housing area, which present a more open approach to the collaboration and organisation of the projects together with strategic support of the local initiatives (CFBU – Center for Boligsocial Udvikling, 2020). However, recent changes to the regulation of the social housing sector have resulted in more top-down steering of these social activities. The social regeneration master plan projects are marked by a professionalisation due to the management of large budgets together with the involvement of consultants, social employees, housing association professionals and other actors. This has made it more difficult for the formal resident democracy to have a say in the decision-making processes, and the resident representation in the project steering groups has gradually waned (Nielsen, Mechlenborg, Hansen, & Jepsen, 2018). This has been reinforced by recent changes to the 'Housing Agreement', resulting in more top-down steering, meaning that the housing associations are not free to decide which projects to run locally (Nielsen et al., 2018).[2] Moreover, the government's plan to counteract social segregation, 'The Act of Parallel Societies' (The Government, 2018), has made it possible for national decisions on demolition if certain criteria regarding the resident composition are not met; decisions which overrule the formal resident democracy.

From this perspective, the formal resident democracy seems to have lost influence to the project-based activities. This is due to the recent political changes mentioned above together with a lack of development of the formal resident democracy, which has been criticised from different sides. For instance:

> To organize shared housing is normally the largest driver for engagement. But in the resident democracy, this element has somehow disappeared and been replaced by a closed organization, where the focus is on influence and not on active participation.
>
> (CFBU, 2020, p. 49)

Numerous attempts have been made at engaging residents in resident democracy through more project-based participation (Niras, KAB, and SAB 2011), as surveys indicate this to be the most efficient way to increase participation among youth. Changes to the formal resident democracy might also increase the participation of younger residents (Boliglaboratoriet, 2014), and better communication between the local board and residents increases the interest among residents to participate in meetings and initiatives (Agger, Tortzen, De Jong, & Skoven, 2013).[3,4] Other development projects targeting participation include the involvement of children in the resident democracy and in activities related to the social master plans (Boligselskabet AKB, Rødovre, & Konradi, 2016). Many projects aim at the basic dimensions of democracy in the housing association, for example, by teaching the younger residents about their democratic rights and how to achieve influence through resident democracy. Although the different models have neither given any clear answers on how to enhance resident democracy nor led to any substantial re-definition of its form and/or content, they might have provided experience with how to proceed with new forms of resident involvement. These projects illustrate a certain level of resident democracy innovation, but questions remain about how to implement the innovations more permanently (and the barriers that are in the way). If participation declines, several challenges can occur that thwart the intentions of the sector, which will fumble with the sector's foundations: decisions will lack legitimacy, and the historical norms and intentions pertaining to resident influence, joint ownership and social responsibility will also decline.

Cases of Democratic Innovation in the Social Housing Sector

The motivation for spurring participation in the social housing sector reflects specific obvious challenges in the sector. For instance, creating after-school jobs increases social integration but also helps to save money on repairs for vandalism; empowering neighbourhood mothers increases their ability to promote the social integration and competences of peers and potentially also saves social costs related to a lack of integration. Many projects under the social regeneration master plans are not only spurred by an ethical ambition to promote democracy and participation but also by pragmatic, cost-saving ambitions. Moreover, the recent policies aimed at reducing the number of 'ghettos' have increased the motivation for the local housing associations to promote more specific goal-oriented initiatives to keep estates off the ghetto list.

We will now dive into two specific cases to discuss the possibilities and barriers to innovations in the Danish social housing sector. The empirical foundation of the cases consists of documents, observations of meetings, interviews with residents and administrators and survey data.

Democratic Innovation through Task Groups

Task Groups represent a new attempt at recruiting more residents and involving them in democratic activities. The task group concept was developed by 3B, a housing association, with inspiration from the Municipality of Gentofte. 3B's argument was that it might be easier to attract residents because the groups are temporary and focused narrowly on specific, concrete challenges. The introduction of the task groups was in reaction to several initiatives and policy solutions launched by resident boards that failed to solve community problems. An example was the implementation of a new policy regarding the sum allocated to each local housing estate to spend on meetings and events for residents. The policy concerned how the money should be disbursed and accounted. The new policy was at odds with everyday practices, and there was an *outcry of indignation from the residents* (Interview manager). The chair of the organisational resident board explains how he *saw a need to supplement the resident democracy to secure a broader scope of perspectives to strengthen decision-making* (Interview 3B chair). The organisational resident board needed more input from and dialogue with the residents to secure the right solutions. The task groups are meant to involve residents in problem-focused discussions with their resident representatives that stimulate democratic participation and the quality of the political solutions.

Institutional design choices regarding such groups must be made concerning theme, participants and mandate (Alexander, 2005). There is no bulletproof recipe, which makes it even more important to consider matters such as the balance between democratic norms (e.g. openness) and productive collaboration (e.g. a good process, useful result) (Kristjansen, 2020). 3B has completed eight task groups in the period 2016–2020. The groups hold three to six meetings over a six-month period and dissolve after reaching a solution. Four task groups have been followed over the course of one year. Each group has a theme chosen by the organisational resident board or as suggested by the administration. The themes all stem from 'wicked problems' (Rittel & Webber, 1973) and can be divided into 'organisational themes' concerning administrative or organisational challenges and 'resident themes' originating from residents.[5] Most groups have had organisational themes.

The 3B task groups have closed access in the sense that participation is by invitation only. The participants are a mix of residents, political representatives and administrative facilitators. Employees or external actors can also be invited to make presentations. When setting up the task group, the organisational resident board and the administration invite residents to participate:

> We make sure that we unfold the complex of problems that the Task Groups revolves around. My role is to think about whom to invite. That is no secret. Sometimes we point out someone we think will be exactly right for this specific task.
>
> (Interview 3B vice-chair)

The strategic selection and invitation of participants can be a tool of control to set the right group of people to solve a task. The residents who have participated in a task group have mostly been active or formerly active in resident democracy (e.g. in local resident boards). There have also been a few participating residents without prior resident democracy experience. The participants have developed a better understanding of each other's points of view across organisational boundaries. Misunderstandings have been cleared up regarding political solutions and administrative measures, which has made it easier for residents to understand certain choices. As one resident explains:

I could give my input and express my concerns while at the same time listening to others' concerns. It has provided a good foundation to think more broadly and to view the world differently. But the starting point was also that output should be something that everyone can use. And I think I actually succeeded really well.

(Interview resident)

The group results have been presented to the organisational resident board, who then decided whether to implement the group's suggestions. All of the task groups have had their results implemented. The participants have indicated a sense of pride in their work and ownership of the results. In 2018, several new residents ran for election for the organisational resident board (Observation Representative Assembly meeting, Copenhagen 2018). It is not possible to draw causational relationships, but residents did mention feeling more comfortable running for the board after, among other things, having participated in a task group. Both the overall task group initiative and some of the results have spread to other housing associations, which are now working with task groups themselves. Such initiatives spreading and being implemented in other organisations is a sign of anchoring and long-term change.

The question is whether the task groups help renew the resident democracy. While it is important to note that it is possible to experiment with innovative forms of democratic participation in the sector, the task groups have also faced challenges and there are important lessons to be drawn. How the group themes are chosen and managed might discourage some residents from participating, and the themes might only interest those who already participate (as opposed to recruiting new residents). To succeed in producing innovative solutions, it is necessary to allow participants to discuss and explore ideas in an easy-going manner, with high levels of trust among themselves, which takes time to develop (Torfing, 2016). The task groups might have been a bit too tightly managed by the administration, which possibly inhibits innovation. The task group format resembles the formal resident democracy to some degree, which might pose another barrier for residents without prior experience with democratic traditions.

Democratic Innovation in SocialHousing+

SocialHousing+ (SH+) is a new social housing concept developed by the Copenhagen Social Housing Association (KAB) in 2007 in response to the lack of affordable housing in the city. Affordability is achieved via a combination of low production costs and high levels of self-management, the latter being highly unusual for the social housing sector. The residents receive the monetary benefit of savings on cleaning and maintenance, which keeps rent down. Even with residents who are unable to participate in maintenance and administration (e.g. senior citizens, persons with disabilities), the argument is that such people can contribute in other ways (e.g. helping with food and refreshments on workdays) or that the other residents accept their absence. The SH+ case represents an example of how to activate residents in the formal resident democracy and in the maintenance of the physical surroundings in the local estate. More than 1,500 SH+ housing units have been built thus far, mainly in the metropolitan region, and rent levels have been kept roughly 20% below new, comparable social housing estates projects. An evaluation based on surveys and interviews among the residents and local boards cast light on the experiences in relation to participation in the various activities (Jensen & Stensgaard, 2016), for instance, *'When you invest time or money in it, then you feel greater ownership'* (Interview resident), and *'I think that the concept of giving a hand is great because [...] I need to know my neighbours, and I think I get to do that... I think it gives a greater sense of responsibility'* (Interview resident).

This indicates that the self-management concept has led to a stronger sense of ownership in the SH+ estates. The surveys revealed that 80% fully or partly agreed that the responsibility for maintenance and administration leads to a greater sense of ownership of the property together with the investments that most people make in the sparsely decorated dwellings. It also indicated a high level of participation in joint workdays and maintenance activities (+80% of the residents), and that a majority (66%) found the maintenance of the shared spaces satisfactory.

The survey revealed that the resident participation in board activities was less pronounced (around 33% of the residents had participated in administrative duties). In the interviews we heard comments such as: *'It has been insanely demanding. Had I known that, I never would have joined the board'* (Interview board member, SH + estate). This probably reflects that the self-management workload is high and more complex in the social housing sector than in private co-ops, where many residents came from. Problems with the recruitment of new members to the boards have been limited, but many board members find the administrative work exhausting.

Another debated issue related to the concept is self-management freeriding, which is perceived as a risk and often a frustration among the participating residents. Before moving in, residents must sign an agreement that they will participate actively in the maintenance of the area. In practice, however, sanctions for freeriding are limited, and few of the residents are willing to police their neighbours.

The results should be seen in relation to the resident composition in SH+, which has a lower rate of single-person households, a higher share of couples with children and residents aged 25–49, and higher numbers of residents with long- or medium-long educations compared to the social housing sector in general. The resident composition in SH+ is therefore more socially resourceful compared to other parts of the social housing sector (Jensen & Stensgaard, 2016). This is hardly incidental, as it is the result of the flexible-letting model, which ensures that primarily those with paid employment and/or the skills to carry out DIY-work receive priority when applying for a dwelling.

While SH+ can be seen as an innovative response to the lack of affordable housing, it is also linked to other agendas, such as the residualisation of the social housing sector and the challenge of shrinking participation in formal and informal housing activities. However, the high level of ownership and participation in SH + should be seen in relation to the relatively narrow and homogenous composition of residents. There is a general sense among those involved in the concept that it would not work in a housing estate with a 'typical social housing resident mix', as there are too few residents who are able, willing or competent to carry out the required work; or they lack the tradition to do so. Conversely, it is also acknowledged that the traditional 'service approach' in the social housing sector does not spur sufficient ownership and participation among the residents. The question then becomes if and how the experiences from the SocialHousing + concept can feed into changing the operation and participation in 'traditional' social housing departments. An important lesson from the SH + concept is that it also requires new roles for the housing administration to support and facilitate a higher level of self-administration; for instance, new types of technical and administrative support, more digital communication, risk-management, as well as information and awareness regarding resident responsibilities.

Discussion

We will summarise and discuss some thematic observations from the two cases of democratic innovation in the social housing sector.

Tailored approach: One of the general conditions is that the structural barriers for participation have increased as a result of the residualisation in the social housing sector, increased globalisation resulting in larger numbers of residents from different cultures, and the increased professionalisation of social projects. Many residents in the challenged housing estates might lack the background to be able to participate in the formal resident democracy, possibly lacking the skills, confidence and/or interest in formal participation, and to develop attachment and ownership to their area. We must therefore work with a tailored approach to participation, both in terms of residents and different participation types. The two cases we have presented represent housing estates with few social challenges (e.g. unemployment, education, attraction, image), and they might be transferrable to similar local estates. However, these approaches are less likely to succeed in estates where the social and physical challenges are greater.

Project-based participation: A general trend is that local participation runs through projects – and apparently less through traditional resident democracy. While this is likely to increase participation, as it (in principle) targets the residents' own interests and needs, it has also increased the steering and professionalisation, which actually reduces the influence from the formal resident democracy. Moreover, in the project-based participation, the residents tend to become social service *receivers* (although roles can be mixed), whereas the residents are service *providers* in the formal democracy. Another danger is that the project-based approach needs anchoring strategies if the projects are to have a more permanent effect: Who will continue the initiatives? Will the participants be able to find the resources to do it themselves? Which networks will support them or be responsible to keep them going? And so on. The project-based participation risks creating a culture wherein participation depends on the local or external financing of activities but where the basic framework is not changed. An alternative to the project-based participation is to alter the conditions for living in the estate, as exemplified by the SocialHousing+ concept. Here, instead of projects, there is an innovative framework that requires active resident participation in exchange for a lower rent. Although this framework is not without challenges, it suggests another possible road to take. An interesting SH+ spin-off is the 'VenligBolig+' (Friendly Neighbours) concept, where young immigrants live together with Danish students in affordable housing. Besides sharing the responsibilities such as maintenance and housekeeping, the concept also helps to support friendships, education and a feeling of community. This indicates an innovative approach to how to possibly integrate ethnic minorities in general and to resident democracy in particular by changing the framework for participation. From a theoretical perspective, the social housing sector experiences reflect the general observations on the crisis of participation and trust and the need to develop new, innovate forms of participation. The project-based participation might help diffuse the democracy and enhance trust, knowing your neighbours etc.

Organisational change: It can be difficult to institutionalise democratic innovations if they are developing in an experimental setting and not synchronised to the everyday practices in the organisation (Nesti, 2018). Overall, the experiences indicate how there are ample opportunities to increase the resident participation in the formal democracy, as the task groups illustrate (e.g. through better dialogue or more bottom-up approaches). Here, the basic challenge seems be the existing organisations (and not necessarily the residents), as the resident boards risk developing over time into closed groups with pre-defined understandings of problems, solutions, communication, norms, traditions etc., which might render it difficult for outsiders to join. The housing association must therefore be aware of this and identify ways of opening up for change, such as task groups. This includes a more elaborate understanding of the value of participation in resident democracy and the necessity to surrender power to residents outside the boards. The SH+ case also illustrates how the housing association needed to alter its organisation to support the self-management approach, which in turn led to new forms of service delivery and to the development of new concepts.

Lessons Learned and Implications for Practice

One of the main lessons from our study is that giving residents influence enhances participation and increases the sense of ownership. It also shows, however, that it is necessary to develop the existing platforms for participation (in our case, formal resident democracy), as well as to develop new arenas for participation. These lessons are generally in line with the theoretical literature that emphasises new modes of civic participation as supplements to traditional representative democracy (Geissel & Newton, 2012; Michels, 2011). Some of the challenges mentioned in the literature also occur in our study; for example, that participation is skewed towards resourceful citizens (Smith, 2009). It is also necessary to be aware of how the new arenas for participation (in our case, mainly project-based participation) interact with the traditional arenas (Sørensen & Torfing, 2019). Our study shows that the physical and social master plans in place in many social housing estates tend to squeeze out the power of the local boards, which poses a clear threat to the traditional democratic model. On the other hand, in the longer run, the local participation transpiring in the many project-based initiatives might generate interest in also taking part in the formal resident democracy. When considering the social housing sector, one could argue that the micro-scale of democratic participation and development of new forms of local-level participation might also enhance participation on a more general scale (i.e., in local boards, local associations or national politics) to better understand the role of the formal democracy on a national scale (i.e., the procedures, implications and opportunities for influencing decisions).

Based on our study, one might see the future role of the formal democracy – which is the cornerstone of the Danish social housing sector – as somewhat uncertain. Our two cases illustrate possibilities to develop increased participation and engagement in the formal resident democracy. Again, the lesson is that gaining influence and benefits from participation is essential. The benefits of democratic innovations could potentially secure influence from relevant and affected citizens, augment the legitimacy of political solutions, strengthen the sense of ownership and boost efficiency.

So why hasn't this been done already? As our cases show, there are several challenges to developing local arenas for participation and democratic innovation. Democratic innovation is no quick fix. The processes consume time and resources, and they require already established relations and trust between the different levels in the organisation. Furthermore, the introduction of democratic innovations takes courage, risk-willingness and alternative plans should the initiatives collapse (which are not characteristics typical of the social housing sector). Based on our study, we suggest that decision-makers consider the following issues to support democratic innovation:

- Change or develop existing structures that inhibit participation.
- Develop structures to support democratic innovations (e.g. an ongoing programme for project-based participation), establish knowledge sharing between residents and housing managers, and collect international experiences and best practices etc.
- Collect evidence of outcomes from different participation innovations: It is important that the successes and failures from different participation models are evaluated and discussed.
- Develop ways to manage possible risks from outsourcing responsibilities to residents. Most project-based activities are 'low-risk', but increasing the level of responsibility in the outsourced tasks might increase the sense of ownership of the sector. This needs to be carried out 'in the shadow of hierarchy' (Scharpf, 1997); thus, an organisational backbone structure must be in place should the local participation fail.

Initiatives like the presented cases do not solve the challenges in the sector alone, but they could potentially strengthen the democratic participation and mobilise resources within the sector. There are many exciting initiatives and projects going on, but there is 'inertia' in the transformations that must be dealt with. If the sector is unable to develop solutions from within, there is a risk of external authorities making decisions that affect the sector.

Conclusion

Our chapter has illustrated different initiatives for democratic innovations taking place in the Danish social housing sector. In a broad sense, we see a need to expand resident democracy, including democratic participation, in the Danish social housing sector. We can conclude that project-based initiatives have increased in the sector and seem to have great potential for enhancing local participation. The risk of the project-based approach is that these initiatives might seem un-coordinated and lack strategic direction. In the Danish context, formal resident democracy has been challenged by the physical and social regeneration master plans stemming from the national aim to fight 'ghettos', where decision-making procedures potentially overrule the local boards. Examples to develop the formal resident democracy are rare, but do exist. Our two examples, the task groups and SH+, represent innovative initiatives in the social housing sector that illustrate the potential benefits of increased participation.

The challenge remains of how to transfer the good experiences from those examples to the sector in general. None of the two presented cases of democratic innovation are in underprivileged neighbourhoods; they are actually in rather strong and well-functioning housing areas. The question then remains as to whether one should develop similar concepts in 'less resourceful' areas – or whether other concepts should be developed in such communities. It seems as though there might still be a need for other measures to involve residents in such challenged areas and to develop and innovate democratic participation there.

Acknowledgements

Thanks to the two reviewers, the editors and colleagues from the research group 'Transformation of Housing and Places' at BUILD, AAU for helpful comments on earlier drafts of this chapter.

Notes

1. The other types of dwellings in the Danish housing stock: owner (59%), private renting (9%), co-operatives (7%) other (4%) (schools, hospitals etc.) (BL – Danmarks Almene Boliger, 2019).
2. Political agreement that defines the way the national fund finances the social regeneration master plans in the housing estates.
3. This includes more young people being on boards, being offered competences and courses to run and facilitate meetings etc., making it count on a CV, larger

influence on decisions, more strategic decisions involving the entire department, greater use of digital platforms for meetings.

4. For instance, more shared activities, resident surveys, ad-hoc groups working on specific projects, making meetings less formal and more inclusive, and more openness to residents' suggestions.

5. Past task group themes include 'Roles, respect and trust', 'Wishes and needs for future services', 'Renovation management', 'Internal moves on waitlists', 'Using shared premises', 'Digitalization and IT', 'Easier to be a local housing board' and 'From strategy to everyday life' (3B, 2017).

References

3B, Boligforeningen. (2017). Opgavegrupper. Retrieved from https://www.3b.dk/bestyrelse/opgavegrupper

Agger, A., Tortzen, A., De Jong, M., & Skoven, J. (2013). Håndbog i Bestyrelsesarbejde: 7 Redskaber Til Bestyrelsesarbejdet i Boligafdelingen. Taastrup.

Alexander, E. R. (2005). Institutional transformation and planning: From institutionalization theory to institutional design. *Planning Theory*. doi:10.1177/1473095205058494

Almenboligloven. (2020). Almenboligloven. Bekendtgørelse af lov om almene boliger m.v. LBK nr 1203 af 03/08/2020. Retrieved from https://www.retsinformation.dk/eli/lta/2020/1203

Bech-Danielsen, C., & Christensen, G. (2017). Boligområder i Bevægelse: Fortællinger Om Fysiske Og Boligsociale Indsatser i Anledning Af Landsbyggefondens 50 Års Jubilæum. Copenhagen.

Bekkers, V., Dijkstra, G., Edwards, A., & Fenger, M. (2007). *Governance and the democratic deficit: Assessing the democratic legitimacy of governance practices.* London: Routledge.

BL – Danmarks Almene Boliger. (2019). Boliger. Retrieved from https://bl.dk/politik-og-analyser/fakta-og-tal/boliger/

Boliglaboratoriet. (2014). De Unge Beboerdemokrater – Hvor Er de Henne? Copenhagen.

Boligselskabet AKB, Rødovre, & Konradi. (2016). Børnedemokrati i Almene Boligområder – Erfaringer Fra AKB Ved Milestedet. Rødovre.

CFBU – Center for Boligsocial Udvikling. (2020). Fælles Om Lokalsamfundet – Inspiration Til at Kickstarte Strategisk Lokalsamfundsudvikling i Udsatte Boligområder. Hvidovre.

Demokratikommissionen. (2020). Er Demokratiet i Krise? Copenhagen. Retrieved from www.demokratikommissionen.dk

Elstub, S., & Escobar, O. (2019). *Handbook of democratic innovation and governance.* Cheltenham: Edward Elgar.

Geissel, B., & Newton, K. (2012). *Evaluating democratic innovations: Curing the democratic malaise?* New York, NY: Routledge.

Hansen, A. V., & Langergaard, L. L. (2017). Democracy and non-profit housing. The tensions of residents' involvement in the Danish non-profit sector. *Housing Studies*, *32*(8), 1085–1104. doi:10.1080/02673037.2017.1301398

Jensen, L. (1997). Stuck in the middle? Danish social housing associations between state, market and civil society. *Scandinavian Housing and Planning Research.* doi: 10.1080/02815739708730429

Jensen, L. (1998). Cultural theory and democratizing functional domains. The case of Danish housing. *Public Administration.* doi:10.1111/1467-9299.00093

Jensen, J. O., & Stensgaard, A. G. (2016). *Evaluering Af AlmenBolig+.* Copenhagen.

Kristjansen, E. T. (2020). Design matters: Tensions between democratic quality and productive collaboration. *The Innovation Journal: The Public Sector Innovation Journal, 25*(3), 1–24.

Landsbyggefonden. (2019). Boligerne i Den Almene Boligsektor 2019. Copenhagen.

Lipset, S. M. (1963). *Political man. The social bases of politics.* Garden City, NY: Doubleday. Retrieved from http://www.garfield.library.upenn.edu/classics1986/A1986C804200001.pdf

Michels, A. (2011). Innovations in democratic governance: How does citizen participation contribute to a better democracy? *International Review of Administrative Sciences.* doi:10.1177/0020852311399851

Nesti, G. (2018). Co-production for innovation: The urban living lab experience. *Policy and Society, 37*(3), 310–325. doi:10.1080/14494035.2017.1374692

Nielsen, R. S., Beckman, A. W., Blach, V., & Andersen, H. T. (2016). DIVERCITIES: Dealing with urban diversity: The case of Copenhagen. Copenhagen.

Nielsen, R. S., & Haagerup, C. D. (2017). The Danish social housing sector: Recent changes and future challenges. *Critical Housing Analysis, 4*(1), 142–149. doi:10.13060/23362839.2017.4.1.333

Nielsen, R. S., Mechlenborg, M., Hansen, A. R., & Jepsen, M. B. (2018). Strategisk Styring Og Udvikling i de Boligsociale Indsatser under 2015–2018-Midlerne. Førmåling Og Foreløbige Resultater. Kongens Lyngby.

Niras, KAB, and SAB. (2011). Evaluering Af Projektet Projektorienteret Beboerde-mokrati. Allerød.

Pitkin, H. F. (2004). Representation and democracy: Uneasy alliance. *Scandinavian Political Studies, 27*(3), 335–342. doi:10.1111/j.1467-9477.2004.00109.x

Poggio, T., & Whitehead, C. (2017). Social housing in Europe: Legacies, new trends and the crisis. *Critical Housing Analysis, 4*(1), 1–10. doi:10.13060/23362839.2017.3.1.319

Quintelier, E., & Hooghe, M. (2013). The impact of socio-economic status on political participation. In K. Demetriou (Ed.), *Democracy in transition: Political participation in the European Union* (pp. 273–289). Berlin: Springer. doi:10.1007/978-3-642-30068-4_14

Rittel, H. W. J., & Webber, M. M. (1973). Dilemmas in a general theory of planning. *Policy Sciences, 4,* 155–169. doi:10.2307/4531523

Scharpf, F. W. (1997). Games real actors play: Actor-centered institutionalism in policy research. In F. W. Scharpf (Ed.), *Games real actors play: Actor-centered institutionalism in policy research* (1st ed.). New York, NY: Routledge.

Smith, G. (2009). *Democratic innovations: Designing institutions for citizen participation.* Cambridge: Cambridge University Press. doi:10.1017/CBO9780511609848

Sørensen, E., & Torfing, J. (2019). Towards robust hybrid democracy in Scandinavian municipalities? *Scandinavian Political Studies, 42*(1), 25–49. doi:10.1111/1467-9477.12134

Stoker, G. (2006) *Why politics matters: Making democracy work.* Basingstoke: Palgrave Macmillan.

The Government. (2004). Regeringens Strategi Mod Ghettoisering. Copenhagen.

The Government. (2018). Ét Danmark Uden Parallelsamfund – Ingen Ghettoer i 2030. Copenhagen.

Torfing, J. (2016). *Collaborative innovation in the public sector.* Copenhagen: Djøf Publishing.

United Nations. (2016). *Urbanization and development: Emerging futures. World cities report 2016.* Nairobi: UN-Habitat: United Nations Human Settlements Programme.

Section II
Democracy and Participation

Chapter 5

Successive Minority Governments – Yet Cooperation and Policy Reform

Flemming Juul Christiansen and Peter Heyn Nielsen

Abstract

Minority governments are more common in Denmark than in any other parliamentary democracy. Internationally, the literature associates minority governments with short-lived, inefficient governments. Yet this is not the case in Denmark. Here, successive governments have served full terms in recent decades and managed to pass large numbers of substantive reforms. This chapter considers how Danish minority governments manage to cope so well and whether polarisation and populism may challenge the solutions to this apparent paradox. The legislative bargaining and agreements *(politiske forlig)* between government and opposition parties are highly institutionalised, giving opposition parties policy influence and procedural privileges almost akin to cabinet parties – but only on the items on which agreement has been reached. The government is therefore able to maintain flexibility. Danish governments have also increased their hierarchical coordination, both in the form of policy through coalition agreements and internally in the form of cabinet committees and a strengthened Prime Minister's Office. The argument here is that these changes make it easier for a government to negotiate as a coherent unit, and the fact that the parties on the respective ideological wings of the Folketing are also included in negotiations and agreements means that polarisation does not seem to affect minority government performance.

Keywords: Minority government; coalition governance; policy reform; executive–legislative relations; polarisation; populism

Introduction

The global populist wave and the polarisation of party systems has led to more ineffective and frequent shifts in governments, often of the minority type, in

Public Governance in Denmark, 77–92
doi:10.1108/978-1-80043-712-820221005

countries such as Spain and Italy. Historically, political scientists have associated minority governments with the instability of the Weimar Republic and the Fourth Republic of France. Even in the two-party United States, increased polarisation has made forming governments more difficult. In this international literature, Denmark represents somewhat of a paradox: On the one hand, Danish politics appear fragmented (many parties in the Folketing) and polarised (increased electoral support for the political outer wings), and Danish governments are almost always minority governments. On the other hand, Danish governments are durable and able to pass important public policy reforms (cf. Green-Pedersen, 2001). A set of informal institutions make this possible. Durable cooperation between government and opposition parties is undergirded by long-term legislative agreements (*forlig*) and various inter-party agreements (Christiansen, 2008). Hence, Denmark has developed viable forms of minority governance (Christiansen & Pedersen, 2014). This minority government viability also extends to internal functionality, with procedures for the centralisation of decision-making in central ministries, such as the Ministry of Finance, and, more recently, in the office of the Prime Minister (PMO) (Nielsen, 2020a). The relatively strong performance of Danish governments regarding agenda control and reform capacity is more in line with recent observations about minority governments, which emphasises the importance of support party agreements (Krauss & Thürk, forthcoming) and agenda control more generally (Thürk, forthcoming).

A key question facing the Danish political system is whether the informal rules for cooperation can withstand the challenges of rising populism or increased support for the political extremes. Thus far, long-term agreements have paved the way for durable, long-term policies enabling reforms and providing predictability and stability about policies when a broad majority of parties can reach agreement. On some occasions, this has been achieved while excluding the political extremes; on others, newer parties on the political wings have been included in legislative agreements, thereby absorbing and in a way disciplining them. This chapter argues that both the survival and vulnerability of this minority-government system is predicated on the ability of minority governments to choose between the 'consensus' politics of broad majorities across policy blocs and forming majorities within such blocs. We argue that this rests on two pillars. First, that moderate opposition parties find it attractive to seek policy influence, despite their intention to replace the government in the next election. Second, parties on the (left and right) wings must remain ready to support minority governments, even if they occasionally seek broad majorities, including parties from the opposite wing. Both pillars could be crumbled by a desire for media attention as a means to winning voters, which would render antagonist strategies attractive for both moderate opposition parties and support parties from the government's own wing. Yet Christiansen and Seeberg (2016) indicate that legislative agreements also take such 'media effects' into account, and Christiansen (forthcoming) shows that while non-centrist parties have grown stronger over time, they have also become more included in legislative work. The chapter also studies how similar developments have affected the internal workings of the government (Nielsen, 2020a).

Analysis

The following analysis begins with a brief presentation of the Danish political system, including its successive minority governments. Next follows possible institutional descriptions of forms of coalition governance both inside and outside the minority governments. Internally, it includes greater emphasis on coalition agreements (Christiansen & Pedersen, 2014) and more hierarchical decision-making (Nielsen, 2020a). This may have strengthened the ability of the top level of government to coordinate policies. Externally, more and more legislation stems from long-term legislative agreements between a minority government and opposition parties. Such external legislative agreements provide the participating parties with policy influence and a number of procedural rights, including veto power, making it attractive for opposition parties to participate rather than merely to criticise the government (Christiansen & Seeberg, 2016). Policy reforms usually result from legislative agreements. Previously, some parties never took part in legislative agreements (Bille, 1989; Christiansen); yet, over time, all parties in the Folketing now take part more or less frequently, meaning that it absorbs new parties into the political system.

The Historical Background of Minority Government and International Comparison

Denmark is a parliamentary democracy, formally headed by a constitutional monarch. Since the last revision of the constitution in 1953, parliament consists of only one chamber: the *Folketing*. Negative parliamentary government was codified by the same constitutional revision, although usually described as customary law since 1901 or at least 1920. This means that a government must call an election or resign if a majority express no confidence in the government in a parliamentary vote. It also means that a government should only be appointed if it can be assumed not to have a majority against it by the time of its appointment.

Denmark is a multi-party system, which is a consequence of an electoral system with proportional representation and a low threshold of only two per cent. Since the 1970s, between seven and 11 parties have been represented in the Folketing at any one time. In combination with negative parliamentary government, this has usually been considered one of the main explanations for why Denmark usually has a minority government (Rasch, 2011). It has been more than 100 years since the last single-party majority in the Folketing. Hence, single-party governments, like the current Social Democratic government, in office since 2019, have all been minority governments. Coalition governments can also be formed without forming a majority, and minority coalition governments have been the most typical form of government since 1982. Governments usually form within one of the two 'blocs', centre-left or centre-right, commonly referred to as 'red' and 'blue', respectively.

In international comparisons of parliamentary democracies, Denmark stands out with its high share of minority governments, minority coalition governments in particular. The other Scandinavian countries, Sweden and Norway, resemble

Denmark with many parties and minority governments (Rasch, 2011). In those countries, the Social Democrats have often formed single-party governments, and centre-right parties have formed coalitions. Single-party minority governments also occur frequently in countries such as Spain, Ireland and Canada, where they have often been close to a majority. In Spain, in particular, multi-level governments are also used to achieve important results (Field, 2014, 2015).

There are currently 10 parties in the Folketing, which renders it difficult to form majority governments, and there has only been one since 1971. Instead, minority governments consisting of one or more parties must find majority support in parliament. According to the international literature, minority governments – minority coalition governments in particular – are typically less durable (Cheibub & Rasch, forthcoming; Lijphart, 1999). Yet Danish minority governments, particularly since the 1990s, have proven quite durable, all remaining in office for at least two-thirds of the electoral term. They have also managed to pass a number of major, long-term public policy reforms on pensions and taxation across policy blocks (Green-Pedersen, 2001). This corresponds with the Potrafke's (2021) finding that minority governments perform as well fiscally as majority governments when they enjoy sustained support. To understand why Danish minority governments perform comparatively well, we must study 'the infrastructure' of coalition building and the internal functioning of government.

Minority Governance: Support Party and Legislative Agreements

In what has become a classic account of minority governments, Strøm (1990) distinguished between those with and without external support party agreements; that is, agreements with parties not in government that nevertheless provide support for the survival of the government, perhaps in return for procedural arrangements or substantive policy concessions. Recent studies have revealed the importance of such arrangements for minority government policy effectiveness (Krauss & Thürk, forthcoming).

Danish minority governments come in both forms. The current single-party, Social Democratic government has an agreement with three parties, belonging to the same centre-left bloc. The agreement contains a set of policies that the government has obliged itself to promote. It remains unclear, though, whether the support parties have all obliged themselves to the same policies. This arrangement is different from that of the three-party, centre-left minority government in office 2011–2015. Here, the Red–Green Alliance formed the parliamentary foundation in the sense that while it neither toppled the government nor prevented it from taking office, the party did not negotiate and thereby directly influenced the content of the government coalition agreement. The Liberal–Conservative governments in office 2001–2011 cooperated closely with the nationalist Danish People's Party, which largely supported the coalition agreement and the economic policies of the government in return for policy concessions on other items of interest in the form of long-term legislative agreements (described below in greater detail) (Christiansen & Pedersen, 2014). Yet the right-of-centre minority government in office 2015–16 and the three-party, centre-right coalition that followed (2016–19) did not manage to establish such tight cooperation (Christiansen, Bjerregaard, & Thomsen, 2019).

Support party arrangements or not, the main source of long-term support for Danish minority governments and their policies stems from legislative settlements (*politiske forlig*). These are negotiated policy compromises between political parties covering single or multiple items (Christiansen & Damgaard, 2008). They usually involve more than merely passing the laws in the Folketing: They bind the political parties over a span of time wherein the parties commit themselves to agree to all changes to that which they have agreed in the first place. Such parties, big or small, thus possess informal veto power, regardless of whether the other parties in the combined settlement hold a majority in the Folketing. The 'circle' of parties in the settlement represented by their legislative spokespersons on the topic usually follow the policies agreed upon closely in more or less regular meetings with the relevant minister and usually receive easier access to information from the minister, which is otherwise usually the privilege of the government. In this sense, settlement parties achieve a 'quasi-governmental' status (cf. Klemmensen, 2005) compared to non-cabinet parties that are not part of a settlement, but only on the items in which they have a settlement, and the group of parties 'governing' may thus vary between policy items. Legislative settlements can be fixed to last for a specified number of years, or they can run consecutively until cancelled. This could result from the parties behind the settlement being replaced after an election by a majority outside of the settlement that are not bound by it and which want to replace it. Alternatively, prior to a general election, settlement parties can also notify the other parties in a settlement that they will no longer be part of it after the election. In that case, the remaining parties may be able to continue the settlement if they fare well enough in the election. Such cancellation notices do occur, although they are rare.

The legislative settlements have no legal or formal foundation in the constitution or in the Order of Parliament, such as the somewhat functionally equivalent legislative institutions found in France labelled 'package deals' analysed in detail by Huber (1996). As such, they form that which Helmke and Levitsky (2004) characterise as an informal institution that substitutes the regular form of majority rule, where the party takes a free vote on the government proposals. They also – negatively – impact the opportunities for voters to affect policies directly by their vote in general elections, since many policies cannot easily be changed.

Legislative settlements come in both *broad* forms, crossing the political blocs, and in *narrow* forms within the blocs. The former survive general elections more easily, since they may more easily uphold a majority and involve future parties in government. Broad settlements provide policy stability.

The political parties generally uphold the legislative settlements of which they have been part. Non-compliance is rare, and not sticking to a negotiated agreement is considered highly problematic in the Folketing, where negotiations are so prevalent (Jensen, 1993). A party breaking an agreement risks exclusion from future agreements. Similarly, MPs place great value on trust and confidentiality in closed-door negotiations. The history of these settlements goes back more than 100 years (Pedersen, 2011). Notably, in 1933, a major settlement between three of the four old, major parties found remedies to handle the worldwide economic crisis. On the very same day that Hitler became German Chancellor on the background of economic and social havoc, the Danish government was able to find broad parliamentary support for comprehensive economic and social policy reforms mitigating the economic crisis. Similar compromises between parties representing workers and farmers were reached in the other Nordic countries. The degree of informal institutionalisation of the legislative settlements is rather unique to Denmark. More generally, much of our knowledge about minority governments comes from the three Scandinavian countries, which possess 'comparatively uncomplicated democratic political systems', with 'small unitary states in which Left–Right ideological issues primarily dominate competition between multiple national or statewide, political parties' (Arter, 2008, p. 56; cf. Field, 2015, p. 1). In more complex institutional and partisan settings, minority governance may at the same time be more complicated while also holding more opportunities. The analyses of Spain by Field (2014, 2015) show how the minority governments there are frequent, show longevity and are effective at passing legislation. Field argues that the minority governments at the state level

> ...can make policy concessions to regional parties in the national parliament where regional parties are policy-seeking *and* offer office concessions *at the regional level* where regional parties are office-seeking, in exchange for achieving its priority goal of governing Spain.
>
> (Field, 2015, p. 3; emphasis in the original)

While the multi-level Spanish state structure is indeed different from the Danish unitary state, the interaction between the state and municipal levels in Denmark is often overlooked in the international context. Much of the public spending is at the local level, and the two parties that dominate government formation – Social Democrats and Venstre/Liberal Party – also dominate local-level decision-making, the vast majority of the 98 mayors coming from one of these two parties. Local Government Denmark (KL), is a private organisation that attends to the interests of the municipalities, and these two parties have alternated in office as chairs. One may argue that the major parties preserve future decisions institutionally at the municipal level. At the same time, its national-level negotiation partners may request greater influence in local decision-making; in that light, this development may come at the cost of local autonomy.

Managing Minority Governments: Top-Down Coordination within Cabinet

A minority government must negotiate with opposition parties to reach agreements and pass policies. As is the case for legislative parties, cabinets can easily negotiate and combine topics across issues if they can coordinate internally – with joint policy goals and effective means of decision-making. Hence, increased coordination within a minority government allows for negotiations with oppositions parties. This could both be across the centre or with the parties within the government bloc, which provides a minority government with manoeuvrability. Since the non-cabinet parties supporting the government are often on the wings of the party system, inclusion in negotiation counters development from populism or polarisation. In times of widespread populism or perhaps an economic crisis, a partisan minister will not necessarily be interested in making unpopular decisions that the Prime Minister wants them to make (Alexiadou & Gunaydin, 2019). On the contrary, line ministers could be expected to use their ministerial position to promote their own personal – and at the same time popular – agenda. This would blur the Cabinet's political profile, possibly spurring division in the electorate (Devillers, Baudewyns, De Winter, & Reuchamps, 2019, p. 249) and intensifying between-minister competition (Nielsen, 2022). Formal and informal coordination mechanisms within Danish cabinets contribute to containing such lost agency.

Danish cabinets are formally organised by the *ressortprinzip*, but the Prime Minister has certain *ex ante* and *ex post* means to reduce agency loss when delegating power to ministers (Strøm, 2000, p. 271). Prior to appointment, potential ministers are screened carefully and, once appointed, monitoring and institutional checks are set in place. These features are elaborated further below.

There are few formal limitations to the Danish Prime Minister's right to appoint and dismiss ministers. This leaves them with considerable flexibility when making ministerial appointments, which makes the system responsive to certain trends in society. The constitution limits neither the number of ministers nor ministries, nor does it regulate how departmental areas are distributed between ministries. It is the Prime Minister's prerogative to determine this. Cabinet members are usually MPs but do not have to be. Junior or deputy ministers are uncommon in the Danish political system. Ministers do not have to undergo a parliamentary hearing or confirmation in an investiture vote. There are practically no non-partisan Cabinet members, whom could be expected to be more prone to moral hazard than partisan ministers (Alexiadou & Gunaydin, 2019).

Danish ministers rarely resign due to political disagreements (Knudsen, 2007, p. 297).[1] A ministerial appointment is generally considered the pinnacle of a career in Danish politics, and most politicians say 'yes' when offered a ministerial post. This has been the case even when certain politicians have publicly disagreed with the political line of the administration prior to their appointment (Nielsen, 2020b, p. 442). These norms give the Prime Minister and other top ministers considerable leverage in controlling the political agenda of line ministers.

The eagerness of Danish politicians to become ministers and not wanting to leave once appointed certainly relates to the central role government plays in the legislative process (Christensen, Jensen, Mortensen, & Pedersen, 2020, p. 223. See also Grøn & Salomonsen, 2020; Jensen, 2011, pp. 220–221). Ordinary MPs make few decisions, as the current Prime Minister once stated (Nielsen, 2016, p. 234). According to the constitution, the Folketing and government hold legislative power jointly, and government can propose bills. Almost all of the more than 200 annually passed laws are proposed by the government. Parliament has very little capacity to formulate legislative proposals, which usually requires extensive legal and technical expertise. These executive–legislative relations reflect tradition but also that the Folketing has refrained from giving itself such capacities, which in turn could be due to the major parties, which alternate in power, preferring not to diminish the capacity of being in government, even (or indeed particularly) as a minority government.

The Prime Minister exercises their right to dismiss or re-shuffle ministers. Ministerial duration has been in decline for some decades (Knudsen, 2020Pedersen & Knudsen, 2005, p. 161), and re-shuffling has been used to discipline ministers (Pedersen & Knudsen, 2005, p. 163). Recent studies have found that portfolio salience affects duration in the sense that the turnover with less important ministerial posts is higher (Hansen, Klemmensen, Hobolt, & Bäck, 2013; Nielsen, 2020c, p. 292). This makes for a hierarchy in the cabinet and a top-down decision-making process.

Once in place, there are several ways for the inner cabinet circles to monitor and control the rest of the cabinet: Certain top ministers write detailed policy programmes, and smaller cabinet committees have gained an increasingly important role in cabinet decision-making. Both provide useful means to contain agency loss.

Since 1993, cabinets have continuously written and published coalition agreements when entering government and renewed them after general elections. Over time, these agreements have become longer and more detailed (Christiansen & Pedersen, 2014, p. 371).[2] They are certainly a means to control line ministers (Jensen, 2011, p. 229), as they are written by top party negotiators, who are typically also central ministers when cabinets are formed. Only top ministers (in practice, central cabinet committee members) decide when to stray from the coalition agreement promises. These coalition agreements are so important that even bureaucrats in the various ministerial departments consider them as guidelines for their daily work (Bo Smith-udvalget, 2015, 127. See also Jensen, 2018, p. 107).

Where the coalition agreements set the joint policies, as indicated, internal cabinet decision-making, involving more ministries or across cabinet parties, takes place within the central coordination committees (Nielsen, 2020b). These are the Coordinating Committee (formed in 1982) and the Economic Committee (formed in 1947, re-organised in 1993), which have come to play a very formal and institutionalised role in cabinet coordination. The Minister of Finance chairs the Economic Committee, whereas the Coordinating Committee is led by the Prime Minister. The committees typically consist of four to six permanent members. With an average number of some 20 ministers in Danish cabinets, committee membership is a clear demarcation of top and bottom in the cabinet hierarchy.

The Economic Committee deals with economic issues, while the Coordinating Committee focusses on the broader political agenda, international affairs and strategy, and serves as the last veto point in the cabinet. Issues not agreed to in the Economic Committee are sent here, but the Coordination Committee generally deals with fewer topics than does the Economic Committee. Both committees exercise tight control over initiatives from non-member ministers, and even small initiatives require approval (Nielsen, 2020b). Consequently, several former ministers mention how membership of one of these committees makes you an *all-around* minister, because they deal with matters concerning all of the ministries. In contrast, the other ministers are *single-issue* politicians, entitled only to deal with matters concerning their own portfolio (Nielsen, 2020b). Each of the committees has a steering group of top-level civil servants preparing the meetings, which are led by permanent secretaries. These can even be veto players in terms of controlling when a non-member can have a case on the committee meeting agenda. The permanent members of the cabinet committees are less likely to be dismissed entirely from the cabinet, suggesting that they are more important to the Prime Minister and party leaders than the other ministers (Nielsen, 2022).

Discussion

The stable Danish minority governments have many benefits: They enable the adoption of long-term political reforms, they keep politicisation and political bigotry at acceptable levels and they minimise populism and political extremism by incorporating and disciplining political parties on both the left and right wings. Yet the relative 'success' of Danish minority governments also comes with a price: Bargaining takes place in closed forums, and the hierarchical decision-making system occasionally decouples public debate, legitimate public interests and even parliament.

Minority Governments and the Opposition Parties

The main expectation in the academic literature is that minority governance is difficult without either stable support or room for manoeuvre. The latter requires a 'responsible' opposition.

Hence, if a minority government is the result of political parties being unable to cooperate and coalesce, the system becomes vulnerable. A situation with 'bipolar' opposition, as described by Sartori (1976), with antagonistic oppositions on the wing attacking the centre, could ultimately undermine this centre, leaving it vulnerable to opposition attack from two sides. If strong parties on the wings did not want to negotiate, the Danish system would become very weak.[3]

It is more ideal for a minority government at times to be able to form a majority in its own bloc, and at other times to form broad majorities across the centre. This is essentially what Danish governments have achieved since the 1990s (cf. Bille, 1989; Green-Pedersen & Thomsen, 2005). The opposition parties that are ready to form government when given the chance often seek policy influence via negotiated agreements and settlements. One may argue that these parties have a 'cartel-like' interest in not making Denmark ungovernable, since they usually alternate in power.

Over time, however, newer parties on the wings also allow themselves to be absorbed or socialised into the legislative agreement system; not following the cooperative logic would most likely mean that these parties remain without policy influence. As such, we can see how wing parties, such as the Socialist People's Party, the Danish People's Party and more recently also the Red–Green Alliance accept these rules of play.

What would challenge these rules? One possibility would be if one party finds it likely that they will be able to win a majority on their own for a significant amount of time; such a party might then rely less on negotiation and cooperation. This is not likely in the highly proportional Danish voting system, however, with a low threshold and 10 parties. It seems more likely for one bloc to remain in power for a long amount of time, removing incentives for 'the responsible opposition' to cooperate.

On a more speculative note, the system of negotiations could become challenged by populism. As seen with the Five Star Movement in Italy, the populist ideology generally holds an aversion to the backroom deals of traditional politics that characterise legislative settlements and that type of consensus. As noted above, however, both the left- and right-wing parties in Denmark that could possibly be inspired by populism have thus far been neatly absorbed by the cooperative agreement systems.

Within-Cabinet Coordination

Strong coordination within Danish cabinets might help to contain agency loss and to maintain political consistency of government. Denmark is among the top-ranking countries in the world in terms of government effectiveness (Grøn & Salomonsen, 2020), and strict, centralised decision-making in Danish cabinets is important for preserving this effectiveness. But the within-cabinet coordination has democratic implications (Marsh, Richards, & Smith, 2019).

Re-shuffling can be used a means to discipline ministers. But short-lived ministers are also considered a sign of an unstable political system (Hansen et al., 2013, p. 228–229). Having less knowledgeable ministers can ultimately lead to inferior political decisions or de facto bureaucratic rule by top civil servants in the ministries. Further, the risk for a Danish minister of being dismissed from cabinet increases when they are recently assessed as being unpopular in opinion polls (Nielsen, 2022). The role of public popularity has often been neglected in international studies of ministerial turnover, which suggests that while the Prime Minister seems responsive to outside pressure, they also care less about ministers' specific knowledge concerning their portfolio or leadership skills, which also are relevant abilities for a minister.

But central, within-cabinet coordination also risks undermining more equal forms of collegiality in cabinet and the departmental authority of line ministers (Nielsen, 2020b). The crucial role of cabinet committees in decision-making processes means by definition that some ministers make decisions impinging on the jurisdiction of other ministers. The ministries of the permanent committee members will also have to advise their ministers on policy matters outside of their own narrow departmental areas, as the committee meetings involve very detailed preparations. But as no constitutional revisions have been made, ministerial departments remain *de jure* autonomous. So line ministers promote and defend the top ministers' policies. By doing so, they create very unclear patterns of responsibility, not least in cases where ministers might not agree completely with the Prime Minister.

The permanent members of the central cabinet committees (and their ministries) deal intensively with matters outside their own departmental area. Aside from the conflict with the principle of departmental autonomy, this necessitates specialised expertise in decision-making neither with the minister nor the bureaucracy.

The centralised control over even small initiatives of line ministers also increases the risk of administrative gridlock. Decision-making processes are slowed down considerably if the PMO must approve even very small details, which has been one of the accusations against the current administration (Christensen, Askim, Gyrd-Hansen, Madsen, & Østergaard, 2021; Nielsen, 2020b), and similar criticism has been raised against former administrations (Nielsen, 2016: *Jyllands-Posten*, 20 March 2018). The delay caused by cabinet committee intervention did not come across in the public debate, however, which instead blamed the formally responsible line minsters for slow policy delivery.

Communication also provides reason for coordination and control across ministries. The appearance of a divided cabinet can harm chances of re-election. Most Danish governments have managed to keep disagreements under wraps, but the three-party coalition government (2016–2019) had many quarrels that made it to the public and even more with its support party, the Danish People's Party.

The exact functioning and how much control is actually vested in the central cabinet committees are questions that have yet to be answered. Future studies should focus on their de facto influence on decision-making, both quantitatively and qualitatively.

Lessons Learned and Implications for Practice

Before making long-term plans or investments, practitioners in both the private and public sectors as well as individual citizens depend on the effective and predictable public decision-making resulting from politics. Increased fragmentation and polarisation are thus highly problematic, as witnessed in many contemporary liberal democracies. The academic literature and lay political opinion often argue that minority governments risk exacerbating unstable political conditions. The Danish case – together with the other Scandinavian countries – shows this to be wrong. Minority governments can indeed be very stable and deliver effective policies via coalition agreements, legislative agreements and centralised cabinet decision-making. If this is how political decision-making takes place – rather than public commissions, hearings, debates and parliamentary votes – what are the implications for practitioners? We argue that it affects the uncertainty under which planning takes place in different ways.

On the one hand, the negotiation of legislative agreements that produce outputs, and ultimately outcomes, depends more on politics in the negotiation room. Committees and commissions that prepare legislation, and where interest groups could be represented, matter less than in the past. Legislative agreements also imply that bills are often introduced post hoc to the agreement. This means that hearings and the involvement of public actors matter less. There is also a risk of too speedy legislation, all of which means that it becomes harder for outside actors to predict the outcome of such processes. The political system remains able to make decisions, but society may come to see the output as 'lightning bolts from Mount Olympus'. On the other hand, both coalition agreements and legislative agreements, particularly those passed by a broad majority of parties and for long terms, do create predictability and stability. The veto power possessed by each political party renders it difficult to change such agreements. For practitioners, this means that at times legislation is stabilised by legislative agreements and at other times not.

This development also has some broader implications. Some of the aforementioned characteristics of Danish cabinets imply that knowledge and expertise that are specific to the area of authority are neglected in decision-making. This is a consequence of short ministerial duration, centralised decision-making in cabinets and the fact that other concerns are taken into consideration when ministers are appointed. Some measures should be taken to counter this trend.

At the informal level, ministers with knowledge related to their portfolio should be valued by politicians and the public alike. Ministers should possibly be allowed longer time in office so as to be able to obtain portfolio-specific knowledge. Line ministers should also stand up to top ministers – or stand down when they do not agree on certain issues. In some cases, ministers should perhaps consider more carefully even saying 'yes' to their ministerial appointment.

At the formal level, some would argue that the role of the Ministry of Finance should be weakened. In recent years, the Danish Ministry of Finance has been accused of having too influential a role in preparing and vetoing proposals concerning policies in other ministerial departments. They claim that the Ministry of Finance does not have the specific knowledge required to intervene in many of the cases that they do in matters beyond strictly economic issues (e.g. in cases of education policy, public sector reform and intelligence service assessments) (Nielsen, 2020b). This would allow the various ministries a more central role when making decisions. Another formal initiative could be to strengthen the capacity of the Folketing to formulate legislative proposals, which might dampen the ministerial aspirations of some MPs. And finally, parliamentary hearings of ministers prior to their appointment could be introduced to ensure 'better' ministers.

There are also questions regarding responsibility and transparency when implementing the Danish way of making centralised decisions. This could be countered by shared legal responsibility of the decisions taken in the central cabinet committees.

Conclusion

Danish minority governments are able to govern in a durable, effective and stable manner. They get legislation through parliament and pass reforms despite increased fragmentation and polarisation. Yet we find that parties on the wings of the political system are included in informal but systematised legislative agreements between the government and opposition parties in parliament. Danish minority governments also issue coalition agreements or government declarations outlining its policies in greater detail than used to be the case, and they have centralised the decision-making process. Danish minority governments also rely on support parties.

Is this decision-making capability and relative stability threatened by increased fragmentation and polarisation? This is less the case than one might expect. On the contrary, parties on the outer wings of the political system, both to the left and right, have become part of the decision-making structure. At the parliamentary level, the polarisation of the party system is therefore reduced, and consensual mechanisms set in. While some of these observations remain particular to the Danish context, we have seen that the idea of systematic and institutionalised exchange as a precondition for effective minority governance is also found in very different political systems (e.g. Spain). This requires more comparison, as do the relations between the national and local levels in the context of legislative bargaining and coalition formation.

All of this has implications for policymakers and top civil servants. The political system is able to make decisions, despite fragmentation, polarisation and minority governments. The decision-making process has become more political, and in that sense, less predictable and less open to influence from interest groups and experts. Yet broad and long-term agreements still secure considerable stability considered valuable for citizens, companies, and other practioners.

Notes

1. An obvious exception for this would be the resignation of the Minister of Transport in October 1981.
2. The most recent cabinet formation (2019) presents something of an exception. The term can be somewhat misleading, as the Lars Løkke Rasmussen II government and Mette Frederiksen I had such programmes when entering office, albeit as single-party cabinets, not coalitions. Since 1929, some coalition governments have on occasion made shorter, written agreements, partly to tie the different parties together (Christiansen & Pedersen, 2014). These were not originally meant for publication, used instead as short internal working papers tying the parties in the coalition together.
3. In their negation of the rules of the system – given by the established parties – such parties would become 'anti-system', as suggested by Bille (1989) in his analysis of the role of now-defunct parties such as the Progress Party and the Left Socialists in the party system. Yet the parties may not be against the democratic constitution (cf. Sartori, 1976).

References

Alexiadou, D., & Gunaydin, H. (2019). Commitment or expertise? Technocratic appointments as political responses to economic crises. *European Journal of Political Research*, *58*(3), 845–865.

Arter, D. (2008). *Scandinavian politics today* (2nd ed.). Manchester: Manchester University Press.

Bille, L. (1989). Denmark: The oscillating party system. *West European Politics*, *12*(4), 42–58.

Bo Smith-udvalget. (2015). *Embedsmanden i det moderne folkestyre*. Copenhagen: Djøf Publishing.

Cheibub, J. A., & Rasch, B. E. (forthcoming). Constitutional parliamentarism in Europe, 1800–2019. *West European Politics*.

Christensen, J. G., Askim, J., Gyrd-Hansen, D., Madsen, H. B., & Østergaard, L. (2021). *Håndteringen af covid-19 i foråret 2020: Rapport afgivet af den af Folketingets Udvalg for Forretningsordenen nedsatte udredningsgruppe vedr. håndteringen af covid-19*. Copenhagen: Folketinget.

Christensen, J. G., Jensen, J. A., Mortensen, P. B., & Pedersen, H. H. (2020). *Når embedsmænd lovgiver*. Copenhagen: Djøf Publishing.

Christiansen, F. J. (2008). *Politiske forlig i Folketinget. Partikonkurrence og samarbejde*. Aarhus: Politica.

Christiansen, F. J. (2021). The polarization of legislative party votes: Comparative illustrations from Denmark and Portugal. *Parliamentary Affairs*, *74*(3), 741–759.

Christiansen, F. J., Bjerregaard, M., & Thomsen, J. P. F. (2019). From marginalization to politcal insider. In B. Biard, L. Bernhard, & H.-G. Betz (Eds.), *Do they make a difference? The policy influence of radical right populist parties in Western Europe* (pp. 79–94). London: Rowman & Littlefield International.

Christiansen, F. J., & Damgaard, E. (2008). Parliamentary opposition under minority parliamentarism: Scandinavia. *The Journal of Legislative Studies*, *14*(1–2), 46–76.

Christiansen, F. J., & Pedersen, H. H. (2014). Regeringsgrundlag i Danmark. Hvordan benytter regeringen dem, og hvordan reagerer oppositionen? *Politica*, *46*(3), 362–385.

Christiansen, F. J., & Seeberg, H. B. (2016). Cooperation between counterparts in parliament from an agenda-setting perspective: Legislative coalitions as a trade of criticism and policy. *West European Politics*, *39*(6), 1160–1180.

Devillers, S., Baudewyns, P., De Winter, L., & Reuchamps, M. (2019). Who do you feel and what future do you want for Belgium? A comparison of candidates and voters' identities and institutional preferences. In A. Vandeleene, L. De Winter, & P. Baudewyns (Eds.), *Candidates, parties and voters in the Belgian partitocracy* (pp. 245–272). New York, NY: Palgrave Macmillan.

Field, B. N. (2014). Minority parliamentary government and multilevel politics: Spain's system of mutual back scratching. *Comparative Politics*, *46*(3), 293–312.

Field, B. N. (2015). *Why minority governments work: Multilevel territorial politics in Spain*. New York, NY: Palgrave Macmillan.

Green-Pedersen, C. (2001). Minority governments and party politics: The political and institutional background to the "Danish miracle". *Journal of Public Policy*, *21*(1), 53–70.

Green-Pedersen, C., & Thomsen, L. H. (2005) Bloc politics vs. Broad cooperation. The functioning of Danish minority parliamentarism. *Journal of Legislative Studies, 11*(2), 153–169.

Grøn, C. H., & Salomonsen, H. (2020). Organizing central government: A pragmatic meritocracy? In P. M. Christiansen, J. Elklit, & P. Nedergaard (Eds.), *The Oxford handbook of Danish politics* (pp. 124–140). Oxford: Oxford University Press.

Hansen, M. E., Klemmensen, R., Hobolt, S. B., & Bäck, H. (2013). Portfolio saliency and ministerial turnover: Dynamics in scandinavian postwar cabinets. *Scandinavian Political Studies, 36*(3), 227–248.

Helmke, G., & Levitsky, S. (2004). Informal institutions and comparative politics: A research agenda. *Perspectives on Politics, 2*(4), 725–740.

Huber, J. D. (1996). *Rationalizing parliament. Legislative institutions and party politics in France.* Cambridge: Cambridge University Press.

Jensen, T. K. (1993). *Politik i praxis. Aspekter af danske folketingsmedlemmers kultur og livsverden.* Frederiksberg: Samfundslitteratur.

Jensen, L. (2011). Steering from the centre in Denmark. In C. Dahlström, B. G. Peters, & J. Pierre (Eds.), *Steering from the centre: Strengthening political Control in Western democracies* (pp. 212–240). Toronto, ON: University of Toronto Press.

Jensen, H. (2018). *Minister – mellem ministerium og Folketing.* Copenhagen: DJØF Publishing.

Klemmensen, R. (2005). Forlig i det danske folketing. *Politica, 37*(4), 440–452.

Knudsen, T. (2007). *Fra folkestyre til markedsdemokrati.* Copenhagen: Akademisk forlag.

Knudsen, T. (2020). *Statsministeren. Bind 1. Kampe om regeringsledelsen 1848–1901.* Frederiksberg: Samfundslitteratur.

Krauss, S., & Thürk, M. (forthcoming). Stability of minority governments and the role of support agreements. *West European Politics.*

Lijphart, A. (1999). *Patterns of democracy. Government forms and performance in thirty-six countries.* New Haven, CT: Yale University Press.

Marsh, D., Richards, D., & Smith, M. J. (2000). Re-assessing the role of departmental cabinet ministers. *Public Administration, 78*(2), 305–326.

Nielsen, P. H. (2016). *Fra kronprinsesse til statsministerkandidat. Historien om Mette Frederiksen og Socialdemokraterne siden 2001.* Odense: Forlaget mellemgaard.

Nielsen, P. H. (2020a). *Historien om dansk regeringsledelse. Udviklingen af det danske statsministerembedes institutionelle ressourcer.* PhD dissertation, Roskilde University, Roskilde.

Nielsen, P. H. (2020b). Ledelse og koordination i danske regeringer fra 1848 til i dag. *Historisk Tidsskrift, 119*(2), 407–445.

Nielsen, P. H. (2020c). Popularity as a measure of portfolio salience? The case of Denmark. *Scandinavian Political Studies, 43*(4), 286–295.

Nielsen, P. H. (2022). Public popularity as a part of the job description? Dismissing unpopular ministers. *West European Politics, 45*(2), 360–380.

Pedersen, H. H. (2011). Etableringen af politiske forlig som parlamentarisk praksis. *Politica, 43*(1), 48–67.

Pedersen, K., & Knudsen, T. (2005). Denmark: Presidentialization in a consensual democracy. In T. Poguntke & P. Webb (Eds.), *The presidentialization of politics: A comparative study of modern democracies* (pp. 159–175). New York, NY: Oxford University Press.

Potrafke, N. (2021). Fiscal performance of minority governments: New empirical evidence for OECD countries. *Party Politics, 27*(3), 501–514.

Rasch, B. E. (2011). Why minority governments? Executive-legislative relations in the Nordic countries. In T. Persson & M. Wiberg (Eds.), *Parliamentary government in the Nordic countries at a crossroads. Coping with challenges from Europeanisation and presidentialisation* (pp. 41–62). Stockholm: Santerus Förlag.

Sartori, G. (1976). *Parties and party systems: A framework for analysis* (Vol. I). Cambridge: Cambridge University Press.

Strøm, K. (1990). *Minority government and majority rule*. Cambridge: Cambridge University Press.

Strøm, K. (2000). Delegation and accountability in parliamentary democracies. *European Journal of Political Research, 37*(3), 261–290.

Thürk, M. (forthcoming). Small in size but powerful in parliament? The legislative performance of minority governments. *Legislative Studies Quarterly*, 1–32.

Chapter 6

Towards Hybrid Democracy and Interactive Political Leadership

Eva Sørensen and Jodi R. Sandfort

Abstract

Although Danish democracy is not currently facing the same decline in the trust in politicians and government as seen in other countries, it faces some of the same destabilising forces as do other 'old' representative democracies. While the various forms of citizen participation introduced in the 1980s and 1990s enhanced politician–citizen tensions, we are currently witnessing a wave of highly innovative, hybrid forms of democracy that both integrate representative and direct forms of democracy and push elected politicians towards an interactive political leadership style. These hybrid forms provide occasion for citizens and politicians to meet and debate pressing political matters. Although we are still in early days and dilemmas remain to be addressed, this development holds considerable potential for democracy in Denmark and elsewhere.

Keywords: Interactive democracy; political leadership; democratic innovation; legitimacy; citizen participation; Denmark

Introduction

Democratic disenchantment and declining trust in government and elected politicians is widespread in many well-established representative democracies, but less so in Denmark (Edelman, 2020). This is not only due to a strong welfare state that helps to reduce inequalities and to provide social security for all Danes but also a strong constitutional protection of citizens' political rights, a strong and vibrant self-governing civil society and a robust market economy (Knudsen & Rothstein, 1994; Laursen & Andersen, 2018). In a highly decentralised political system, Danish local politicians have considerable decision-making power, and the distance between politicians and citizens is relatively low. This decentralised political structure supports a responsive style of political leadership. As described in

Public Governance in Denmark, 93–107
Copyright © 2022 by Emerald Publishing Limited
All rights of reproduction in any form reserved
doi:10.1108/978-1-80043-712-820221006

Chapter 5, a proportional electoral system with a low threshold for gaining seats in local, regional and national representative assemblies also channels the different views and interests in the population into the formal political decision-making process (Christiansen & Pedersen, 2014; Elklit, 2005). The aggregated result of these factors is high levels of voter turnout and political efficacy, as well as the integration of populist political parties and leaders in democratic policy-making (Christiansen & Togeby, 2006; Heinze, 2018; IDEA, 2004; Karp & Banducci, 2008; Mair, 2013).

Despite these fundamental strengths differentiating it from many other countries, Denmark faces some of the same destabilising forces that are present in other well-established representative democracies. For example, party membership has declined radically over the last half century (Kosiara-Pedersen, 2010; Van Beiten, Mair, & Poguntke, 2012). In the early 1960s, around 25% of the population were party members, whereas that figure is now a mere 4%. Political party members do not play the same active role in policy formation as they once did. As is true elsewhere, the surge of catch-all and cartel parties leaves policy-making in the hands of a few leading politicians who mainly confer with their staff of policy advisors, spin doctors and leading civil servants (Detterbeck, 2005; Loomes, 2012; Mair, 2013). Political parties are less focussed on ensuring ongoing dialogue between elected politicians, the party members, their local constituencies and the public at large (Andersen, 2006; Katz, 1990). Their main focus is on controlling the political agenda and strategically monitoring and influencing public opinion. In multi-party systems, this development has triggered a surge in new parties with an intention of giving members a more active role in policy-making, but their membership basis is often limited. And when leading politicians face the realities of 24/7 mediatised political communication, they tend to adopt a similar leadership style (Bolleyer, 2013).

There has also been a general shift in the political culture in Western liberal democracies. As documented in a large comparative study of the political culture in the United States, United Kingdom and Europe (Dalton & Welzel, 2014, p. 11), there is very little left of the civic culture of allegiant, satisfied and obedient citizens prevalent in the late 1950s (Almond & Verba, 1963). Citizens have become increasingly assertive, self-confident and anti-authoritarian. Although there are marked differences between countries, the general trend is that citizens have strong opinions and want a say on the matters affecting them, seek more influence than mere voting can give and they are critical of political elites who are not responsive to their demands. This shift in political culture challenges the traditional party government models (Schattschneider, 1960), and it undermines the twentieth century folk theory of sovereign political leadership (Bang & Sørensen, 1999; Clarke, Jennings, Moss, & Stoker, 2018).

In the 1990s and early 2000s, the Danish response to the crisis of party government and sovereign political leadership styles was a wave of reforms introducing supplementary forms of political participation. These reforms grant citizens direct influence on the matters affecting their daily lives in a range of venues, including public services and local communities (Bang, Box, Hansen, & Neufeld, 2000; Sørensen, 1997). The hope was that more scope for local participation would both dampen the demands and criticism directed towards government elites and engage citizens in the governance of local matters (Yetano, Royo, & Acerete, 2010). Today, Danes can choose between various public service providers, sit on so-called 'user boards', join citizen panels or village councils, take part in hearings and comment on infrastructure projects (Christiansen & Togeby, 2006). Although the new forms of citizen participation give Danes a more active role in democracy, this has not always strengthened the dialogue or reduced politician–citizen tensions (Andersen, 2006). In fact, in this environment, citizens have a plethora of opportunities to join forces and voice political demands for their particular corner of society, while leaving concerns for the whole of society to the politicians. Moreover, politicians continue to develop policies without (or with very late) citizen input. So although representative democracy assigns politicians the obligation to do what they consider good for each as well as for all, they often do not receive the input required to make informed and legitimate policies, because they are surrounded by assertive citizens organised around special issue interests. In short, the efforts to adapt Danish democracy to the reality of a political culture of assertive citizens has produced an institutional divide between a direct democracy where citizens participate in governing matters that affect their everyday lives and a representative democracy where politicians govern society. The weak link in this model is that there are very few arenas and occasions where citizens and politicians talk together as they once did in the party organisations.

Over the last decade, however, these conditions have started shifting with the introduction of innovative forms of Danish hybrid democracy that engage politicians and citizens in the joint discussion of political goals and strategies. Many new arenas and occasions integrate the direct democracy in user boards and civil society networks with the representative democracy of political assemblies and committees, promoting a more interactive citizenship and political leadership style among citizens and politicians alike (Sørensen, 2020; Sørensen & Torfing, 2019). This chapter describes these recent developments in Danish democracy and considers how they inform the search for ways to adapt representative democracy to the reality of the day. We believe there are lessons to be gleaned from this movement, both for Denmark and other countries around the world.

Here, we first provide a brief outline of changes in the Danish democratic culture in the post-war period, paying specific attention to how it articulates the politician–citizen relationship. We then describe the reforms that contributed to the development of a counter democracy before analysing the recent surge in hybrid forms of democracy and interactive political leadership. We discuss the potential and perils of this development, concluding with discussion of what other representative democracies might learn from the current developments in Denmark.

Danish Democracy: Past and Present

In Denmark, the mainstream narrative about the history of Danish democracy is that it stands on two legs: political institutions, which regulate the battles for power in society, and political culture, which places deliberation and dialogue at centre stage of all social, economic and political interactions and decision-making. These two legs resemble what is known as the procedural and the substantive aspect of democracy. In the years after World War II, these understandings were condensed in the celebrated writings of theologian Hal Koch and law professor Alf Ross, who focussed on building a democracy strong enough to avoid the rise of dictatorship as seen in 1930s Germany. Ross (1949), who was actively involved in writing the 1953 revisions to the Danish Constitution, argued that the staying power of a democracy relies on a number of facts. The most essential is a constitution that both installs and protects a set of political institutions separating power between the judiciary, lawmakers and the executive and which accommodates strong political leadership with the protection of citizens' political rights, liberty and privacy (Ross, 1949).

Somewhat in line with John Stuart Mill (1961), Hal Koch's (1945) contribution was to argue that the backbone of a strong democracy is a deliberative political culture permeating all aspects of political, social and economic life, the family, local communities, voluntary organisations, the education system and the workplace. Deliberative political culture becomes a way of life. People find sensible ways to resolve disputes by exchanging views and ideas, and they seek some sort of mutual understanding and agreement. In their co-authored book *Nordic Democracy* (1949), Koch and Ross conclude that the Nordic democracies were strong because of both the structure of political institutions and the public education system that empowered citizen participation. In Denmark, a well-organised civil society dates back to the late nineteenth century, when Danish farmers formed dairy cooperatives, the labour movement was strong and folk high schools were created (Begtrup, Lund, & Manniche, 1926; Chloupkova, Svendsen, & Svendsen, 2003; Korsgaard, 2000).

In the following decades, this portrait of Danish democracy – a happy marriage of solid institutions of representative democracy and a strong deliberative political culture – served as a hegemonic point of reference for most Danes and still influences how international researchers characterise Danish democracy (See e.g. Rhodes, 1999; Runciman, 2014). This portrait grants a novel role to civil society as the site for building a deliberative political culture, just as it creates a relatively sharp demarcation between political decision-making in and around representative government and interaction between citizens within a self-regulating civil society and a market economy. Like Alex de Tocqueville (1835) and John Stuart Mill (1961), the overarching idea is that although participation in deliberative processes in everyday life is an indispensable training ground for citizens, the political decisions of consequence for the greater society should be left to elected politicians. Responsive political leaders, party organisations and sub-national political institutions are the connecting points between the two legs in Danish democracy.

This understanding of democracy lost its salience in the late 1960s. As citizens became wealthier and better educated, women entered the labour force in great numbers, the youth movement challenged existing authority structures, and the political culture took an anti-authoritarian turn. The battleground was initially the social life in the family, the local community and the workplace. Young people wanted to live a different life than their parents, women demanded that men took their turn washing the dishes, and workers wanted influence on their working conditions. From the late 1970s onwards, however, this attention also turned towards the institutions of representative government, which were increasingly seen as paternalistic and out of tune with popular views, wants and needs. While the criticism specifically targeted the national government and state apparatus, growing criticism focussed on counties and municipalities that had grown larger and become more professionalised, more beholden to party politics, and distant from the people (Blom-Hansen, 2012).

The criticism of representative government came from both the right and left sides of the political spectrum (Dich, 1975; Kristensen, 1980; Meyer, Petersen, & Sørensen, 1978), and supplementary forms of political participation that gave citizens a direct influence on matters affecting their daily lives were introduced (Sørensen, 2020). In the 1980s and 1990s, different public sector reforms provided citizens with new means to influence public governance besides voting in national and sub-national elections. The users of public services could vote with their feet by shopping around between service providers. They were also invited to take part in the governing of local public institutions, such as schools and childcare institutions, by voicing their views and opinions in user boards (Sørensen, 1997). Additionally, municipalities gave village committees and neighbourhood councils the authority to govern certain local affairs (Bang et al., 2000). Finally, a new citizen information law gave civil society organisations direct influence on the distribution of funding for culture and sports activities (The Public Information Act, 1991; Yndigegn, 1994). By the turn of the 21st century, Danes had grown used to participation and making their voices heard between elections; in 2000, a large survey documented how a huge majority of the Danes had begun to expect and demand much more political influence than they could get from merely voting (Andersen, Torpe, & Andersen, 2000, p. 154).

Yet, as citizens became engaged in matters that directly affected them, their involvement in party politics continued to decline (Andersen, 2006; Katz et al, 1992). Although the Danes continued to vote in high numbers (around 85% in national elections, 70% in local elections), very few were political party members; and those who were found that they had little influence on the formulation of party politics, as the party leaders controlled the party line. In 2007, a second amalgamation reform of sub-national governments further deepened the politician–citizen distance (Lassen & Serritzlew, 2011).

As a result of these different developments, there were growing tensions and wavering distrust between politicians and citizens, which was particularly striking in that it counters the rise in social trust (Andersen, 2006; Denters, 2002; Edelman, 2020; Sønderskov & Dinesen, 2014). The institutional divide between a direct democracy, where increasingly assertive citizens vote with their feet or take part in decentred decision-making, and a representative democracy, where elected politicians and political leaders make sovereign authoritative decisions for society, is at the root of such tensions. In the end, there are very few arenas and occasions where citizen and politicians meet, exchange views and perspectives and discuss political matters of mutual concern. Politicians have little opportunity to get a feel for what occupies citizens, and citizens in turn have little opportunity to consider political issues related to the governing of society as a whole.

A Trend towards Hybrid Democracy and Interactive Political Leadership

Interestingly, these conditions have now triggered both a plethora of new institutional innovations in Danish democracy and the surge of a new political leadership style among some politicians. An underlying aspiration of these actions is to improve the politician–citizen relationship and mutual understanding by strengthening the dialogue between them. Establishing some form of hybrid democracy that integrates the decentred citizen engagement process with society-level political decisions is beginning to occur (Sørensen & Torfing, 2019). Hybrid democracy comes in the shape of institutionalised arenas and occasions that engage citizens and politicians in the joint discussion of a pressing political issue. The purpose is to exchange views and ideas both to create a more nuanced understanding of the matter at hand and to develop political strategies or policies that reflect this knowledge. Citizens continue to govern themselves through direct forms of participation, and politicians continue to make authoritative decisions; but the dialogue provides a means for developing a bridge of mutual understanding – if not agreement – on a given matter.

One potent example is the introduction of citizen proposals, an idea that was introduced by a new political party, *Alternativet*, which first gained election to the Folketing, the Danish parliament, in 2015. Their agenda: to engage citizens in policymaking by giving them opportunity to influence the political agenda and discussion in the formal political institutions and force the political parties to address pressing issues, even when doing so is inconvenient (Bischoff & Christiansen, 2017). In 2017, the Folketing passed a temporary law committing the Folketing to debate and vote on all policy proposals supported by 50,000 citizens and seconded by at least one elected official (Danish Ministry of Justice, 2017). Any Dane can initiate the collection of the 50,000 signatures from eligible voters willing to support a given policy proposal. Proposals with enough signatures are then discussed and voted on in the Folketing. There is an increasing number of cases of this process; while most of them die in parliament, this mechanism does give citizens a new role in setting the political agenda (Sejr, 2021). Elected politicians are forced to take a stand on a matter of concern to many. On a number of occasions, this process has begun to influence the parliamentary political process; for example, while a proposal committing the Folketing to pass a climate law every year was first rejected, it became a central issue in the next election campaign, which the Folketing ultimately passed in a new form after the election. Interestingly, numerous municipalities have mirrored this national innovation, and some now allow a smaller number of citizens (e.g. 1,000) to formulate policy proposals that the municipal council must take up (see, e.g. Holbæk Municipality, 2020).

Other recent developments are changes in political procedures and practices that may have significant long-term consequences (Sørensen, 2020). Politicians have begun to seek input from the citizenry early in the political process rather than merely hosting hearings that symbolically get feedback on decisions. At the national level, ministers and parliamentary committees have intensified their efforts to involve stakeholders in thematic discussions and special issue commissions composed of a broad variety of stakeholder organisations and policy experts. Some committees have begun inviting citizens to discuss specific issues, and meetings are sometimes held in relevant localities to engage in face-to-face dialogue regarding those policy concerns.

At the regional and local levels, politicians increasingly engage with citizens in workshops, innovation camps, townhall meetings, seminars and conferences to find inspiration and develop new policies that enjoy broad ownership. For example, when the municipal council in Fredericia set out to formulate a new political vision and strategy, they spent six months collecting input from all of the different groups in the municipality. And when Roskilde started to plan the closing of an industrial area, politicians invited civil society actors and different investors not only to mobilise their resources but also to engage in crafting a vision and strategy to develop the new experimental neighbourhood, Musicon (https://Musicon.dk). And when a fireworks factory exploded in Kolding, destroying almost an entire neighbourhood, the local schoolchildren presented the results of a week's efforts to specify what a good neighbourhood looks like, facilitating discussion between politicians and community residents on how to rebuild the area.

Initiatives aiming to promote dialogue and interaction around the formulation of policies between user board members and politicians are growing in frequency. Many municipalities have formed digital citizen panels to provide a sounding board to develop their understanding of a policy problem more fully or to generate ideas for how to tackle them. 'Citizen salons' are a form of engagement in which politicians ask a specific group of people to discuss a matter of concern and then forward their thoughts to a municipal council. In 2011, the so-called *Folkemøde* (people meeting) came to be a setting where politicians from different levels in the political system meet with different stakeholders and citizens to discuss a wide range of issues. Held annually in June, around 100,000 Danes meet with the politicians over four days on Bornholm, a Danish island in the Baltic Sea south-east of Sweden. In more than 100 small tents, hour-long panel sessions are hosted around the clock, each hosted by people from various walks of life. Each session tends to involve a couple of politicians, some stakeholders and a citizen audience (https://folkemoedet.dk/). Overall, the *Folkemøde* reinforces the notion that effective and legitimate politics is produced in the intersection between politicians and citizens.

In the same vein, it is becoming increasingly common for politicians to solve disputes with citizens by involving them in political problem-solving. In the thinly populated rural Guldborgsund Municipality, citizens protested when the municipal council cancelled a bus route, despite few people actually using it. Instead of insisting on their right to decide and explaining their decision to the critics through the local media, politicians hosted a workshop asking citizens about their transport needs. When it became clear that those who used the bus line were mainly schoolchildren, decision was made to introduce a school bus, which both saved the municipality a lot of money and improved children's transport. In Syddjurs, when the municipal council needed to cut costs, they made several changes to the service structure. At the same time, a number of villagers got together to develop their own competing proposal that saved the same amount of money but looked different. To resolve the matter, the municipal council invited the villagers to a meeting to integrate the two proposals and develop an agreement. These events further illustrate how a turn to hybrid democracy and an interactive political leadership style can reduce politician–citizen tensions by linking representative and direct democracy.

Finally, Danish municipalities have intensified their use of political task committees. Since 1968, it has been possible for regional and municipal politicians to form so-called advisory ad hoc committees to engage people who are not politicians. Danish municipalities rarely used this opportunity before 2010, but a quick Google search documents how almost all of the 98 Danish municipalities have established one or more such committees in the last five years. These committees are generally used when a municipal council wants to focus on a specific policy problem that demands their special attention. The task committees are not permanent, typically developed to convene for 3–10 months. Although the composition of such task committees differs significantly, they often include several citizens. To illustrate, in 2020 the regional council in the Copenhagen Metropolitan Area had four political task committees, each consisting of three regional politicians, two municipal politicians and one citizen to focus on various dimensions of health (Copenhagen Metropolitan Area, 2020).

The most intensive use of task committees is found in Gentofte Municipality. In 2015, the municipal council decided to reduce the time spent in standing political committees and to dedicate more time to developing policies on pressing issues. Over a 5-year period, 50 task committees have proposed policy on a wide range of issues from finding paid employment for refugees, over assistance to kids in need, to traffic planning and the promotion of healthy living. And the process is yielding results. All of the policy proposals produced by the committees were later passed by the municipal council, which was possible in part because politicians from the different parties had participated in the discussions from beginning to end, ensuring that the municipal council's concerns and perspectives were voiced in the process.

There is little indication of having reached a peak in the surge of hybrid forms of democracy in Denmark. In 2019, the Folketing decided to make the temporary law permanent. With the exception of a single sceptical party, the other parties all found that the many citizen proposals had reinvigorated the Folketing debate, and the individual parties have started to view them as an integrated part of the formal political process. The use of task committees with citizen involvement continues to spread and is taking new forms. Other forms of citizen involvement in formal political processes are also spreading and assuming new forms. A sign of this trend is how providing all sorts of courses and advice on how to organise productive citizen–politician dialogue has become a niche industry in itself (see, e.g. Local Government Denmark (KL), 2017; Technology Council, 2019).

Although it is difficult to say where this development will take Danish democracy and how much hybridity it will produce, it is fair to say that the emerging results are consequential. They integrate policymaking into the many diverse arenas for self-governed citizen participation and policymaking in representative assemblies. They also push Danish politicians away from a traditional, sovereign political leadership style. Instead, what is being witnessed here is the establishment of an interactive political leadership style that seeks authorisation to lead not only on Election Day but through continuous negotiations with other political leaders and, of interest here, the affected stakeholders and general public. In recognition of the fact that politicians who make sovereign decisions without consulting anyone tend to be attacked from all sides, it is becoming increasingly common to bring relevant and affected stakeholders and citizens to the table early in the policymaking process to secure their support and ownership of the final decisions (Sørensen, 2020).

Implications for Danish Democracy

While hybrid forms of democracy and interactive political leadership seem to have considerable potential, they also raise new challenges. As the examples shared here suggest, municipalities that have moved towards hybrid democracy and interactive political leadership seem to experience numerous benefits. At a minimum, there are more informed and innovative political decisions, higher levels of trust and mutual understanding between politicians and citizens, and more engagement to support implementation (Bentzen, Sørensen, & Torfing, 2020; Kjær & Opstrup, 2016; Røiseland & Vabo, 2020; Sørensen, 2020; Torfing & Sørensen, 2019; Bentzen, Sørensen, & Torfing, 2020). For example, an evaluation of the Gentofte task committees documents how both the politicians and participating citizens regard this new way of organising the policymaking process as a great achievement. Politicians and citizens grow wiser in the process and develop mutual respect and understanding (Sørensen & Torfing, 2016). Generally, politicians who engage in early dialogue with citizens report that it gives them a much better understanding of the problems calling for political action (Agger, 2015). Citizens also state that they obtain much better understanding of the difficulties and dilemmas involved in developing viable ways of dealing with complex and turbulent problems, as well as the need to balance between different interests and concerns (Agger, 2015; Torfing & Sørensen, 2019).

But these innovations in the democratic process also raise challenges. For one, politicians may struggle to maintain the arms-length distance to citizens required to make the autonomous decisions of political leadership. Political leaders need space to see into the future, to strategize, prioritise, focus and act (Kane & Patapan, 2012). Although close dialogue with all those with something to offer in terms of insights and support provides a solid foundation, elected leaders sometimes need space and autonomy to act decisively, i.e. as in the face of a sudden crisis, e.g. a pandemic or a natural disaster. Hybrid democracy should not marginalise representative democracy.

Secondly, this emerging type of engagement raises new questions related to accountability. Although holding representative assemblies and cabinets to account can be difficult, it seems straightforward in comparison to accountability for decisions made in hybrid democracy (Papadopoulos, 2007). Very often and for good reason, the dialogue between politicians and relevant and affected citizens regarding policy development takes place out of the media spotlight, as it would hamper free and open debate and the testing of new ideas and perspectives. Moreover, the outcome tends to be collaborative; no single political actor can be held to account although the formal decision-making power continues to lie in the hands of the politicians. In a hybrid democracy, it is not sufficient to secure accountability through a formal distribution of responsibilities and authority. It also relies on various forms of social accountability in the form of informal checks and balances that empower politicians when it comes to explaining and defending their stance on a given topic and the decisions they make and enabling citizens to challenge their views and actions (Sørensen & Torfing, 2019).

Finally, there is a risk of hybrid democracy exacerbating the political inequalities between those with strong participatory skills and high social standing and those with weaker political standing and fewer participatory capabilities. International research documents that participatory democracy may create structural inequalities (Hildreth, 2012; Young, 2002). Research suggests the importance of design and facilitation in mitigating inequity (Bryson, Quick, Slotterback, & Crosby, 2013; Sandfort & Quick, 2015). For example, inviting those who would not otherwise attend and get their input in other forms are important parts of the engagement design. Integrating participatory and representative forms of democracy requires a different type of attention to new practices.

What Can Other Countries Learn from Denmark?

While the Danish context and institutional history is rather unique, we believe the Danish case highlights some important themes for other advanced democracies. In the face of growing democratic disenchantment and the criticism of sovereign forms of political leadership, the Danes have found a number of ways to respond. Rather than abolishing representative democracy in favour of direct democracy, they have started to develop new ways to integrate direct and representative forms of participation. When the types of expertise brought by politicians and citizens alike are recognised as legitimate, new insights and pragmatic proposals can be developed. New alliances can be forged to overcome political disagreements.

There are early indications of the Danish developments also appearing in other countries. For example, a parliamentary committee in the United Kingdom interviewed affected citizens to obtain input to the development of a policy on honour killings (Ercan, 2014). In another comparative study, politicians from

Canada, United Kingdom, Australia, New Zealand and the United States report adopting a praxis of talking to a broad variety of relevant and affected actors before developing policy proposals (Lees-Marshment, 2015). In 2017, the Irish parliament commissioned a citizen assembly to propose a new abortion policy that the Irish people later accepted in a referendum (Suiter, Farrell, & O'Malley, 2016). In the United States, a series of research experiments documents how online conversations between governors and members of their constituencies considerably enhanced the level of trust and mutual understanding between them (Neblo, Enderling, & Lazer, 2018). An analysis of 28 case studies of politicians and citizens engaged in collaborative policymaking around the world documents that the legitimacy of the policy process and its outcome is connected by the degree to which the two parties meet face to face (Sørensen, Edelenbos, Hendriks, & Herrting, 2020).

Yet in-depth knowledge of the Danish developments highlights how the engagement format varies. Citizen proposals, innovation camps, townhall meetings, citizen panels and political task committees all require new government capacities. Attention to engagement design, invitation, authentic hosting and intentional harvesting are required if public bureaucracies are to deliver on the potential of these practices (Bryson et al., 2013). And yet the legacies of New Public Management – which reduced citizen needs to consumer tastes, and the purpose of the public sector was seen not as convener but as performance assessor – are now deeply rooted in public organisations (Phinney & Sandfort, 2021). Undoing this legacy and supporting the ability of public organisations to enhance the capacity of citizens and politicians to engage in evolutionary learning (Ansell, 2011) requires intentional investment of time and resources in the public sector. It involves a persistent effort to institutionalise opportunities and arenas in which politicians and citizens can develop nuanced relationships and broad ownership to negotiated collective decisions, even in the face of disagreement.

While Denmark has important institutional assets – being a small, rather homogenous country with a lengthy democratic history and relatively high levels of trust – the innovations developed here can provide insight to others about what it takes to move in this direction.

Summary

In Denmark and internationally, growing distrust in politicians from increasingly assertive citizens challenges representative democracy. While many countries gave citizens more voice and exit opportunities in the final decades of the twentieth century, the surge of more direct forms of democracy has tended to intensify citizen–politician tensions. But Denmark also saw the development of new democratic innovations at the national, regional and – most intensively – the municipal levels. Bringing politicians into society and citizens into politics, these innovations foster citizen–politician dialogue. They pull citizens into political decision-making with societal implications and enrol politicians in dialogue with citizens around the concrete challenges they face. While it remains too early to say where this development will take Danish democracy, we believe it is important to document these trends and to consider the lessons they may hold for other representative democracies facing similar challenges at this stage in their history.

References

Agger, A. (2015). Hvilke potentialer og udfordringer er der ved tidlig inddragelse af borgere i samproduktion af styring. *Politica, 47*(2), 185–201.

Almond & Verba. (1963). The civic culture. *Political Attitudes and Democracy in Five Nations*. Scranton, PA: Princeton University Press.

Andersen, J. G. (2006). Political power and democracy in Denmark: Decline of democracy or change in democracy? *Journal of European Public Policy, 13*(4), 569–586.

Andersen, J. G., Torpe, L., & Andersen, J. L. (2000). *Hvad folket magter: Demokrati, magt og afmagt*. Copenhagen: DJOEF Publishers.

Ansell, C. K. (2011). *Pragmatist democracy: Evolutionary learning as public philosophy*. Oxford: Oxford University Press.

Bang, H. P., Box, R. C., Hansen, A. P., & Neufeld, J. J. (2000). The state and the citizen: Communitarianism in the United States and Denmark. *Administrative Theory & Praxis, 22*(2), 369–390.

Bang, H. P., & Sørensen, E. (1999). The everyday maker: A new challenge to democratic governance. *Administrative Theory & Praxis, 21*(3), 325–341.

Begtrup, H., Lund, H., & Manniche, P. (1926). *Folk high schools of Denmark and the development of a farming community*. Oxford: Oxford University Press.

Bentzen, T. Ø., Sørensen, E., & Torfing, J. (2020). Strengthening public service production, administrative problem solving, and political leadership through co-creation of innovative public value outcomes? *Public Innovation Journal, 25*(1), article 4.

Bischoff, C. S., & Christiansen, F. J. (2017). Political parties and innovation. *Public Management Review, 19*(1), 74–89.

Blom-Hansen, J. (2012). Local government in Denmark and the 2007 municipal reform. In A. Moisio (Ed.), *Rethinking local government: Essays on municipal reform* (pp. 43–70). Helsinki: Government Institute for Economic Research.

Bolleyer, N. (2013). *New parties in old party systems: Persistence and decline in seventeen democracies*. Oxford: Oxford University Press.

Bryson, J. M., Quick, K. S., Slotterback, C. S., & Crosby, B. C. (2013). Designing public participation processes. *Public Administration Review, 73*(1), 23–34.

Chloupkova, J., Svendsen, G. L. H., & Svendsen, G. T. (2003). Building and destroying social capital: The case of cooperative movements in Denmark and Poland. *Agriculture and Human Values, 20*(3), 241–252.

Christiansen, F. J., & Pedersen, H. H. (2014). Minority coalition governance in Denmark. *Party Politics, 20*(6), 940–949.

Christiansen, P. M., & Togeby, L. (2006). Power and democracy in Denmark: Still a viable democracy. *Scandinavian Political Studies, 29*(1), 1–24.

Clarke, N., Jennings, W., Moss, J., & Stoker, G. (2018). *The good politician: Folk theories, political interaction, and the rise of anti-politics*. Cambridge: Cambridge University Press.

Copenhagen Metropolitan Area. (2020). Om regionens opgaveudvalg. Retrieved from https://www.regionh.dk/politik/politiske-udvalg-og-fora/Oevrige-politiske-fora/Opgaveudvalg-Boern-og-unge-som-patienter-i-optageomraade-midt/Sider/Om-regionens-4-opgaveudvalg.aspx. Accessed on November 24, 2020.

Dalton, R. J., & Welzel, C. (Eds.). (2014). *The civic culture transformed: From allegiant to assertive citizens.* Cambridge: Cambridge University Press.

Danish Ministry of Justice. (2017). Lov om etablering a en ordning for borgerborslag med henblik på behandling i folketinget. LOV no. 1672 á 26.12.2017.

De Toqueville, A. (1835). *Democracy in America.* New York, NY: A Mentor Book from New American Library.

Denters, B. (2002). Size and political trust: Evidence from Denmark, the Netherlands, Norway, and the United Kingdom. *Environment and Planning C: Government and Policy, 20*(6), 793–812.

Detterbeck, K. (2005). Cartel parties in Western Europe? *Party Politics, 11*(2), 173–191.

Dich, J. (1975). *Den herskende klasse.* Copenhagen: Gyldendal.

Edelman. (2020). *Edelman trust barometer 2020, global report.* Retrieved from https://cdn2.hubspot.net/hubfs/440941/Trust%20Barometer%202020/2020%20Edelman%20Trust%20Barometer%20Global%20Report.pdf?utm_campaign=Global:%20Trust%20Barometer%202020&utm_source=Website. Accessed on March 20, 2021.

Elklit, J. (2005). Denmark: Simplicity embedded in complexity (or is it the other way round)? In M. Gallager & P. Michell (Eds.), *The politics of electoral systems* (pp. 453–471). Oxford: Oxford University Press.

Ercan, S. A. (2014). Same problem, different solutions: The case of 'honour killing' in Germany and Britain. In A. K. Gill, C. Strange, & K. Roberts (Eds.), *Honour killing and violence* (pp. 199–217). London: Palgrave Macmillan.

Heinze, A. S. (2018). Strategies of mainstream parties towards their right-wing populist challengers: Denmark, Norway, Sweden and Finland in comparison. *West European Politics, 41*(2), 287–309.

Hildreth, R. W. (2012). Word and deed: A Deweyan integration of deliberative and participatory democracy. *New Political Science, 34*(3), 295–320.

Holbæk Municipality. (2020). Borgerforslag. Retrieved from https://holbaek.dk/politik/kommunalbestyrelsen/borgerforslag/. Accessed on November 24, 2020.

IDEA. (2004). *Voter turnout in Western Europe since 1945. Research report.* Stockholm: International Institute for Democracy and Electoral Assistance.

Kane, J., & Patapan, H. (2012). *The democratic leader: How democracy defines, empowers and limits its leaders.* Oxford: Oxford University Press.

Karp, J. A., & Banducci, S. A. (2008). Political efficacy and participation in twenty-seven democracies: How electoral systems shape political behaviour. *British Journal of Political Science, 38*(2), 311–334.

Katz, R. S. (1990). Party as linkage: A vestigial function? *European Journal of Political Research, 18*(1), 143–161.

Katz, R. S., Mair, P., Bardi, L., Bille, L., Deschouwer, K., Farrell, D., ... Poguntke, T. (1992). The membership of political parties in European democracies, 1960–1990. *European Journal of Political Research, 22*(3), 329–345.

Kjær, U., & Opstrup, N. (2016). *Variationer i udvalgsstyret.* Copenhagen: Kommuneforlaget.

Knudsen, T., & Rothstein, B. (1994). State building in Scandinavia. *Comparative Politics, 26*(2), 203–220.

Koch, H. (1945). *Hvad er demokrati?* Copenhagen: Gyldendal.

Koch, H., & Ross, A. (Eds.). (1949). *Nordisk Demokrati.* Copenhagen: Westermann.

Korsgaard, O. (2000). Learning and the changing concept of enlightenment: Danish adult education over five centuries. *International Review of Education, 46*(3–4), 305–325.

Kosiara-Pedersen, C. (2010). *Danish party membership.* CVAP Paper, Center for Voting and Parties. København: Department of Political Science, Copenhagen University.

Kristensen, O. P. (1980). The logic of political-bureaucratic decision-making as a cause of governmental growth. *European Journal of Political Research, 8*(2), 249–264.

Lassen, D. D., & Serritzlew, S. (2011). Jurisdiction size and local democracy: Evidence on internal political efficacy from large-scale municipal reform. *American Political Science Review, 105,* 238–258.

Laursen, F., & Andersen, T. M. (2018). *Denmark report. Sustainable governance indicators.* Gütersloh: Bertelmann Stiftung.

Lees-Marshment, J. (2015). *The Ministry of Public Input: Integrating citizen views into political leadership.* London: Routledge.

Local Government Denmark (KL). (2017). Det kommunale demokrati er i forandring. Hvor skal vi hen? Local Government Denmark. Retrieved from https://www.kl.dk/media/7966/det-kommunale-folkestyre-er-i-forandring.pdf. Accessed on March 20, 2021.

Loomes, G. (2012). *The impact of cartel strategies in France, Greece, Denmark and Ireland.* Working Paper 35. Keele European Parties Research Unit. Retrieved from https://www.keele.ac.uk/media/keeleuniversity/group/kepru/KEPRU%20working%20paper%2035_Loomes.pdf. Accessed on May 20, 2017.

Mair, P. (2013). *Ruling the void: The hollowing of Western democracy.* London: Verso.

Meyer, N. I., Petersen, K. H., & Sørensen, V. (1978). *Oprør fra midten.* Copenhagen: Gyldendal.

Mill, J. S. (1961). *The philosophy of John Stuart Mill: Ethical, political, and religious.* New York, NY: Modern Library.

Neblo, M. A., Esterling, K. M., & Lazer, D. M. (2018). *Politics with the people: Building a direct representative democracy.* Cambridge: Cambridge University Press.

Papadopoulos, Y. (2007). Problems of democratic accountability in network and multilevel governance. *European Law Journal, 13*(4), 469–486.

Phinney, R., & Sandfort, J. (2021). Discover together: Attempting to alter understanding and practices in governments' work with citizens. In E. Loeffler & T. Bovaird (Eds.), *Palgrave handbook on co-production of public services and outcomes* (pp. 211–228). London: Palgrave Macmillan.

Rhodes, R. A. (1999). Traditions and public sector reform: Comparing Britain and Denmark. *Scandinavian Political Studies, 22*(4), 341–370.

Røiseland, A., & Vabo, S. I. (Eds.). (2020). *Folkevalgt og politik leder.* Oslo: Cappelen Damm Akademisk.

Ross, A. (1949). *Hvad er demokrati?* Copenhagen: Nyt Nordisk Forlag.

Runciman, D. (2014). *Politics, ideas in profile.* London: Profile Books.

Sandfort, J. R., & Quick, K. S. (2015). Building deliberative capacity to create public value: The practices and artifacts of the art of hosting. In J. M. Bryson, L. Bloomberg, & B. C. Crosby (Eds.), *Public administration and public value* (pp. 39–52). Washington, DC: Georgetown University Press.

Schattschneider, E. E. (1960). *Party government.* New Brunswick, NJ: Transaction Publishers.

Sejr, K. (2021). *Politikernes kontrol over den politiske dagsordensætning.* Master thesis, Department of Social Sciences and Business, Roskilde University, Roskilde.

Sønderskov, K. M., & Dinesen, P. T. (2014). Danish exceptionalism: Explaining the unique increase in social trust over the past 30 years. *European Sociological Review*, *30*(6), 782–795.

Sørensen, E. (1997). Democracy and empowerment. *Public Administration*, *75*(3), 553–567.

Sørensen, E. (2020). The future of democratic governance lies in interactive political leadership. *PUBLIC, ESADE, E-Bulletin, 39.*

Sørensen, E., Edelenbos, J., Hendriks, C., & Herrting, N. (2020). Political boundary spanning: The role of politicians in collaborative governance. *Policy & Society*, *39*(4), 530–569.

Sørensen, E., & Torfing, J. (2016). Samlet evaluering af den nye politiske arbejdsform i Gentofte kommune: Slutrapport. Gentofte Municipality.

Sørensen, E., & Torfing, J. (2019). Towards robust hybrid democracy in Scandinavian municipalities? *Scandinavian Political Studies*, *42*(1), 25–49.

Suiter, J., Farrell, D. M., & O'Malley, E. (2016). When do deliberative citizens change their opinions? Evidence from the Irish Citizens' Assembly. *International Political Science Review*, *37*(2), 198–212.

Technology Council. (2019). Nye politiske arbejdsformer. Teknologirådet. Retrieved from https://tekno.dk/methods/?lang=en

The Public Information Act (Folkeoplysningsloven). (1991). Danish law on citizen information. Ministry of Culture. Retrieved from https://www.retsinformation.dk/eli/lta/2011/854

Torfing, J., & Sørensen, E. (2019). Interactive political leadership in theory and practice: How elected politicians may benefit from co-creating public value outcomes. *Administrative Sciences*, *9*(3), 51.

Van Biezen, I., Mair, P., & Poguntke, T. (2012). Going, going,… gone? The decline of party membership in contemporary Europe. *European Journal of Political Research*, *51*(1), 24–56.

Yetano, A., Royo, S., & Acerete, B. (2010). What is driving the increasing presence of citizen participation initiatives? *Environment and Planning C: Government and Policy*, *28*(5), 783–802.

Yndigegn, C. (1994). *Ny folkeoplysning? Ny fritidspolitik?: En undersøgelse af folkeoplysningslovens indførelse i kommunerne og folkeoplysningsudvalgenes virkemåde.* AKF-Papers. Copenhagen: AKF Publishing.

Young, I. M. (2002). *Inclusion and democracy.* Oxford: Oxford University Press.

Section III
Public Sector Effectiveness and Efficiency

Chapter 7

The Danish Control–Trust Balance in Public Governance

Jacob Torfing and Tina Øllgaard Bentzen

Abstract

Denmark is characterised by high levels of trust between citizens and public authorities as well as between public leaders and employees, providing a comparative advantage when it comes to expanding public welfare, enhancing economic performance and handling a crisis like COVID-19. Public governance, however, requires a delicate balance between trust and the legitimate need for control to secure accountability This chapter explains how the high levels of trust in the Danish public sector are wedded to a pragmatic combination of various public governance paradigms, which has produced a 'hybrid governance system' balancing the legitimate demand for control with widespread trust in public employees. Traditional Weberian bureaucratic values of regularity, impartiality and expertise are combined with a limited and selective introduction of New Public Management reforms. Simultaneously, a dynamic neo-Weberian state works to satisfy an increasingly demanding citizenry while new platforms for developing collaborative solutions to complex problems are designed and developed at the municipal level. This hybrid governance system produces a virtuous circle of trust sustained by trust-based systems of evaluation, assessment and accountability developed in close dialogue between public managers and employees. The chapter demonstrates how a long-lasting political-administrative culture based on trust and a pragmatic, non-ideological combination of different governance paradigms has generated a positive trust–public governance feedback loop. Striking the right control–trust balance remains a continual challenge, however, to avoid governance failures eroding citizen trust in the public sector and to safeguard public values of transparency, accountability and performance.

Keywords: Trust; control; hybrid governance; public governance; public governance paradigms; trust-based management

Public Governance in Denmark, 111–129
Copyright © 2022 by Emerald Publishing Limited
All rights of reproduction in any form reserved
doi:10.1108/978-1-80043-712-820221007

Introduction

Most countries are currently witnessing mediatised government scandals in which public employees are accused of providing poor service, showing monitoring or regulatory neglect, squandering taxpayer money on failing projects or allowing private interests and money to prevail over the public interest. Together with the ubiquitous neoliberal criticism of public employees as self-serving agents, such scandals have strengthened the demand for control-based performance management that defines performance targets, measures results and punishes malperformance (Dooren, Bouckaert, & Halligan, 2015). While the demand for mechanisms preventing sabotage, shirking and opportunistic behaviour in the public sector has increased, the problem is that governance tools that are perceived to be controlling tend to crowd out the intrinsic task motivation and public service motivation (PSM) of public employees (Jacobsen, Hvitved, & Andersen, 2014). A decline in these vital forms of employee motivation will inevitably reduce the quality of public services and ultimately leave citizens dissatisfied, thus undermining their trust in the public sector. To animate public sector employees to use their professional skills and competences to produce public value for and with public service users and other relevant actors, they must be shown trust, defined as the willingness to absorb the risk ensuing from the expectation that the other part will refrain from acting opportunistically in a situation that allows them to do so (Six, 2013).

It is frequently asserted that trust provides a welcome alternative to control-based governance relying on insistent auditing and the use of sticks and carrots to ensure compliance (Nyhan, 2000; Sønderskov & Dinesen, 2016). However, the paradox seems to be that the more public managers trust public employees to do good, the greater the risk that they merely act in their own best interest and eventually erode citizen trust in the public sector. The question becomes, then, how to balance the legitimate demand for control with widespread trust in the commitment and skills of public employees? The answer might be found in the historical development of the Danish public sector.

Despite decades of strong government oversight, budget control and performance management, Denmark remains the world champion in trust, followed closely by the other Scandinavian countries (Delhey & Newton, 2004; Edelman, 2016; Torpe, 2003). Evidence of the high levels of Danish trust is provided in Table 1.

The recent experience with COVID-19 reveals the positive impact of the high levels of trust. Public leaders, partly out of necessity, trust that their employees will solve new, emerging tasks with little or no supervision and with much less control than usual, the result being that new, creative solutions have been fostered, which helped to avoid a major health crisis (Bentzen & Torfing, forthcoming). Citizen trust in government ensured high compliance with the constantly changing health regulations; consequently, the Danish infection and mortality rates have been relatively low (Olagnier & Mogensen, 2020). This experience is by no means unique to Denmark and has also been observed in the other Scandinavian countries, which bears evidence to the fact that trust is a central

Table 1. High Levels of Danish Trust.

Danes trust one another	86% of all Danes – the highest figure in the world – agree that most people can be trusted (https://www.pewresearch.org/fact-tank/2020)
Danes trust government	In 2018, Denmark was the country with the lowest perceived corruption in the public sector (https://www.transparency.org/en), and 88% and 84% of the population reported being satisfied with the health and education systems, respectively (https://www.oecd.org/gov/gov-at-a-glance-2019-denmark.pdf)
Leaders trust their employees	83% of all Danish employees claim that they are able to choose and make changes to how they do their work. Only Malta and Norway have higher figures (https://www.eurofound.europa.eu/data/european-working-conditions-survey)

component of Nordic governance and provides a comparative advantage, both with respect to expanding public welfare and enhancing economic performance (Delhey & Newton, 2004; Svendsen & Svendsen, 2016).

High levels of trust in and within public institutions constitute a valuable asset for the public sector, as they tend to facilitate rapid, high-quality leader–employee communication, secure efficient and holistic service delivery, enhance citizen participation, spur multi-actor collaboration and stimulate public innovation. It is well-documented that people tend to communicate and work better together with those they trust (Hunt, Burke, Sims, Lazzara, & Salas, 2007; Nyhan, 2000). Service delivery is improved when public professionals are trusted to do their best within the limits set by budgets and legislation and to trust that they will each do their part and coordinate their efforts (Oliver, 1997; Spreitzer & Mishra, 1999). Citizens are willing to participate in public governance when they trust public authorities to listen respectfully and to provide an adequate response (Corbett & Le Dantec, 2018; Fledderus, 2018). Actors trusting other actors to constructively manage differences and to implement joint solutions tend to promote collaborative problem-solving (Costa, Fulmer, & Anderson, 2018; Dirks, 1999; Gray, 1989). Finally, innovative solutions are more easily created and adopted when relevant and affected actors trust that eventual risks will be dealt with collectively (Nooteboom, 2013; Torfing, 2016).

Trust is not only important in times of crisis and turmoil, when public and private actors struggle to find new and better solutions; it is also important in the day-to-day running of the public sector. An illustrative example of the value of trust for public service organisations is the introduction of unmanned opening hours in Danish public libraries, which improves services despite severe fiscal constraints. Citizens are trusted to take good care of the books and library; and in exchange for acting responsibly, they enjoy access to high-quality services in the later hours when libraries are usually closed. At a more general level, trust is a precondition for the Danish welfare state: Citizens trust one another to work and pay their taxes, and they trust the public sector to deliver high-quality services, to be efficient and not to squander their taxes. By the same token, the public welfare systems trust that people do not cheat.

Trust begets trust, leading to positive trust spirals; however, such spirals become vulnerable when trust is abused. Although Denmark is the country with the perceived lowest corruption in the world, spectacular examples of trust abuse still occur (Mungiu-Pippidi, 2013). It was recently revealed that thousands of private firms and financial investors have illegally exploited the trust-based procedures for VAT reimbursement, resulting in massive losses of tax revenue. And in a case that received extensive media attention, an office clerk employed in the National Board of Social Services was convicted of having funnelled almost €16 million into her own private account over a 25-year period, money that had been earmarked for social purposes, which triggered huge public outrage. Finally, lax control with private banking led to the largest ever money laundering scandal in the Baltic branch of Danske Bank. Trust is regularly abused and breaks down, but prompt trust repair work normally succeeds in restoring the high levels of trust that seem deeply embedded in the DNA of Danish society. We saw this in the wake of the 2007–08 financial crisis, which damaged the public trust in government; already in 2019, after a decade of economic recovery policy, trust in government had been completely restored (Pedersen & Pedersen, 2020).

The high levels of generalised trust are the result of early efforts to curb corruption, longstanding traditions for collaborative governance and a homogenous society in which 'other people are just like me' and therefore to be trusted. However, in an attempt to further explain trust relations between public leaders and employees – and, consequently, between citizens and the public sector – this chapter points to the impact of the pragmatic, non-ideological combination of public governance paradigms. The claim here is that the Danish 'hybrid governance system', which pragmatically combines different public governance paradigms, has both benefited from and further promoted trust-building in a sound balance with legitimate forms of control.

The Rise and Fall of Public Governance Paradigms in Denmark

To trace the emergence of the Danish control–trust balance, this section analyses the shifting public governance paradigms in the Danish public sector. Public governance paradigms are defined here as more or less coherent ideas and perceptions about how to organise, govern and manage the public sector and its relations to its social and economic surroundings (Torfing, Andersen, Greve, & Klausen, 2020). Although they change more frequently, public governance paradigms tend to behave in much the same manner as the scientific paradigms described by Kuhn (1962): A new paradigm develops in response to problems with the old one, it gains growing support and acquires 'new normal' status, only to lose traction over time due to the steady accumulation of new problems.

The Rise of Bureaucracy and Professional Rule

The rise of the Absolutist State in the seventeenth century led to the gradual removal of the trade privileges of the Danish aristocracy and increasingly emphasised the role of bureaucratic rules and professional skills. It also created an efficient tax collection system, meaning that the King could hire competent civil servants based on their merits. The bureaucracy was further expanded after the introduction of constitutional monarchy and representative democracy resulting from the so-called 'peaceful revolution' in 1848, which ended Danish absolutism. The gradual expansion of insurance-based public welfare programmes in the early twentieth century was based on the rule of law and bureaucratic administration of welfare programmes within a unitary state.

Public bureaucracy was combined with professional rule that grew strong in the decentralised and increasingly universalistic welfare state founded in the 1930s and which expanded dramatically in the 1960s. An informal 'service contract' gave professional public employees bounded autonomy to govern local welfare institutions in the fields of health, education and welfare in return for the promise that they would use their professional skills, competences and values to produce and deliver high-quality welfare services. This service contract rests on a delicate balance between central rule-governing and local professional discretion. Too much room for local discretion enhances the risk of opportunistic behaviour by self-serving professionals, whereas excessive central control threatens to deprive public professionals of the ability to use their skills and competences in the provision of services tailored to citizens' needs (Torfing et al., 2020).

The combination of bureaucracy and professional rule impacts trust both positively and negatively. The positive effect results from the development of strong professional norms and the competences of the public employees and an equally strong adherence to bureaucratic rules. This development encourages public managers to trust their employees, possibly spurring the development of positive trust spirals. Another positive effect is that bureaucratic values such as legality, predictability, fairness and equity, in tandem with high-quality services delivered by professional public employees, tend to enhance citizen trust in the public sector (du Gay, 2000).

By contrast, the negative effect is that the centralised, hierarchical control inherent to public bureaucracy tends to leave little space for trust in public employees who are expected to follow rules and commands. Fortunately, the combination of bureaucracy with professional rule counteracts this negative effect by trusting public professionals to excel when given the autonomy to do so. However, another negative effect may spring from the paternalistic behaviour of well-intended public sector professionals who think they know what is best for their clients and therefore tend to disempower citizens, who are reduced to passive service recipients (Andersen & Pedersen, 2012). While the latter might work in times with predominantly allegiant citizens, recent anti-authoritarian revolutions in education and culture more generally have fostered a new, assertive citizen who tends to distrust public professionals who disregard their lay knowledge and expertise (see Dalton & Welzel, 2014).

Since the 1970s, there has been growing scepticism towards public bureaucracy, which in the Anglo-Saxon research literature is criticised for being ossified (Downs, 1967), costly (Niskanen, 1971) and rule-fixated (Osborne & Gaebler, 1992). Neoliberal bureaucracy bashing has been accompanied by strong criticism of professional rule as overly paternalistic (Grand, 1997) and for spurring opportunistic behaviour among public professionals who enjoy excessive autonomy, have gained considerable power and are notoriously difficult to control (Lane, 2005). These criticisms also found their way to Denmark. Danish political scientists criticised the role played by public professionals and other 'spenders' in driving up public expenditure (Kristensen, 1980, 1987). In the same vein, the economist Jørgen Dich wrote a bestselling book in 1975 describing public professionals as the new ruling class that exploits the population by expanding welfare services beyond their marginal utility. This book greatly inspired the welfare-professional bashing promoted by the new Progress Party (*Fremskridtspartiet*), which enjoyed landslide electoral success in 1973.

The strong criticism of public bureaucracy and professionals was fuelled by the publication of the Trilateral Commission's report on *The Crisis of Democracy* (Crozier, Huntington, & Watanuki, 1975), which presented a bleak diagnosis of how the public sector faced twin problems of 'government overload' and 'societal ungovernability' and how this critical situation could undermine citizen trust in government and liberal democracy. The report generated considerable debate regarding the future sustainability of the Danish welfare state. This dispute coincided with the first energy crisis in 1973, which triggered a deep economic recession in Denmark. The combined effect was mounting political pressure to rethink the role and organisation of the public sector.

The Introduction of New Public Management – And by Default the Neo-Weberian State

With the Anglo-Saxon countries as the epicentre, the world was hit by a tsunami of New Public Management (NPM) reforms that began in the 1980s (Hood, 1991). NPM offered a moderate version of the neoliberalist attempts made by Reagan and Thatcher to roll back the welfare state and replace it with market-based solutions. The wholesale privatisation of public service organisations was replaced by outsourcing based on the construction of quasi-markets and the introduction of free service choice, allowing the users of services to choose freely between public and private service providers. In order for public managers to handle the competition for contracts and customers, they must act as private business leaders by strengthening their entrepreneurial spirit and strategic leadership and subjecting their organisation to rigorous performance management focussed on achieving results rather than following rules.

The Danish public sector was prompted to implement NPM reforms in 1983, when the Ministry of Finance started publishing a series of annual so-called 'Modernisation Accounts' that set a new reform agenda for the public sector. Deregulation, new technologies, increasing use of internal and external contracting, performance management, wage bonuses and corporate governance were some of the main themes. Since everyone in the public sector depended on Ministry of Finance funding, the pressure to adopt at least some of the new measures was strong. However, the key tenets of NPM, such as marketisation and control-based managerialism, were at odds with Danish traditions for publicly provided welfare, trust-based management based on a low degree of rule-based work structuration, short manager–employee distances and collaboration within an elaborate system of macro- and micro-corporatism (Klausen & Ståhlberg, 1998). Moreover, the underlying economic-man model stressing individual utility maximisation was foreign to the humanistic and bureaucratic conception of motivation, stressing the intrinsic task motivation of professionals enjoying doing what they are trained to do and the PSM of altruistic managers and employees aiming to do good for citizens, society and the public sector (Torfing et al., 2020).

The opposition to NPM was considerable, especially among public administration researchers and the professional associations of which public professionals are members. But while NPM never became an ideological project for the successive right- and left-wing governments, the Ministry of Finance and its new Modernisation Agency were strong supporters of NPM and continued to recommend NPM-inspired reforms. Even the Social Democratic Minister of Finance, Bjarne Corydon (2011–2015), supported NPM out of concern for securing tight budget control and the ability to finance future welfare spending. While the Ministry of Finance held some sway over the other ministries that are part of the central unitary state, it proved more difficult to persuade the local municipalities, which deliver the lion's share of public services in Denmark, to adopt the NPM measures recommended in the annual financial accord between the Ministry of Finance and the municipalities, as represented by Local Government Denmark (KL).[1] Thus, a recent Danish survey – administered to municipal directors for social welfare and technical services and measuring the organisational focus on a randomised series of public governance measures on a 5-point Likert scale – shows that only one of eight NPM items (the use of management by objectives) had a positive opinion balance indicating a high organisational focus (Torfing & Køhler, 2016). As such, it is fair to conclude that NPM was never fully implemented and that the 'layering' of new governance measures on top of old ones dominated over 'displacing' previous governance ideas with new ones (see Mahoney & Thelen, 2010).

Countries that follow the NPM recipe partially and selectively – seeking to maintain classical bureaucratic virtues and merely using NPM to strengthen strategic management, enhance organisational and economic efficiency and increase user satisfaction – have been labelled 'neo-Weberian states' (Pollitt & Bouckaert, 2011). Whether the neo-Weberian state is a paradigm in its own right or merely a default option in countries that did not wholeheartedly embrace NPM is open to debate (Torfing et al., 2020). In the Danish case, however, the selective incorporation of NPM elements (e.g., strategic management, stricter budget rules, enhanced focus on user satisfaction) together with the addition of a novel ingredient in terms of enhanced centralisation through organisational amalgam- ations and the concentration of standardised tasks (e.g., tax assessments, social benefits) provided a relatively coherent set of governance ideas that revamped bureaucracy, making it more efficient and responsive. The goal was to create the 'smiley state': a well-driven, dynamic bureaucracy capable of satisfying the increasingly demanding citizenry and society in general.

The impact of the somewhat limited implementation of NPM and, by default, the emergence of the neo-Weberian state on the trust–control nexus is mixed. NPM builds on a fundamental mistrust in public employees who are assumed to be driven by extrinsic motivation encouraging them to seek rewards and avoid punishment. Opportunistic behaviour is supposed to be counteracted by control- based performance management based on conditional positive and negative sanctions, but that tends to further enhance the extrinsic motivation of public employees and potentially crowd out their intrinsic task motivation and PSM, which creates a workforce of cynics (Jacobsen et al., 2014; Moynihan, 2010); hence, the NPM assumption that public employees are self-interested opportun- ists becomes a self-fulfilling prophecy.

That said, we should bear in mind that the negative effects of NPM on trust relations were mitigated by its less than wholehearted implementation and the maintenance of classical bureaucratic values, including faith in the merits and competences of those hired in the public sector and the belief that compliance is ensured through rules. Still, as explained above, NPM reforms have eroded the trust in public employees. Several empirical incidents support this interpretation. Hence, the state-employed policemen and regional hospital personnel were sub- jected to a very strict performance management regime based on targets for different tasks, and performance-related pay expanded throughout the public sector. The most spectacular incident was a schoolteacher lockout in 2013, where the government sought to find the financing for a massive reform of the public school system by changing the working-hour regulations for schoolteachers, who were seen to be slacking – teaching only a few hours per week and going home far too early. The changes to their working conditions were driven by a deep mistrust in the ability of schoolteachers to regulate themselves as professional employees, which sparked a lengthy conflict that took many years to settle (a compromise was first reached in 2020).

Turning briefly to the assessment of citizen trust in the public sector, the impact of the selective use of NPM – associated with the neo-Weberian state – is more positive. On the one hand, a major corruption scandal in relation to private contracting in a Danish municipality, implicating a well-known mayor, served to undermine trust in the public sector. Citizen trust in government was further undermined by the centralisation of municipal tax collection and the creation of a new national tax agency that sought to realise huge savings by replacing human resources (staff) with new digital technologies. The subsequent crash of these digital solutions was devastating and costly for Danish taxpayers. On the other hand, trust in the public sector was sustained by its increasing efficiency, stricter

budget control that almost eliminated budget transgressions, enhanced trans
parency regarding outputs and outcomes and greater service choices coupled with
the introduction of user boards in kindergartens, schools and eldercare facilities.
The reinforcement of bureaucratic values associated with the neo-Weberian state
also contributed to enhancing trust in the public sector.

In sum, while trust in public employees may have waned, citizen trust in the
public sector has been maintained through a combination of enhanced efficiency
and the revaluation of traditional bureaucratic values.

New Public Governance Sets a New Course

Despite some positive effects on budget discipline, political and administrative
goal-steering and enhanced transparency and responsiveness via-à-vis the citizenry, there has been mounting criticism of performance management for eroding
trust, spurring goal displacement and stimulating sub-optimisation (Torfing et al.,
2020). NPM was also criticised for fragmenting the public sector by creating a
growing number of special-purpose agencies and contracting out services, which
rendered coordinated policy implementation and holistic service provision more
difficult (Dunleavy, Margetts, Bastow, & Tinkler, 2006). The neo-Weberian state
aimed to solve the latter problem through re-centralisation but was criticised for
its romantic celebration of the time before NPM and its failure to mobilise
societal resources and stimulate public innovation in the face of the financial crisis
and rising demands on the public sector.

Hence, since 2010, new ideas about public innovation, co-creation, networked
governance and not least trust-based management – increasingly associated with
New Public Governance (NPG) (Klijn, 2010; Osborne, 2006) – began attracting
increasing attention in the Danish public sector. The pervasiveness of complex
problems in an increasingly turbulent world called for innovative public solutions,
and innovation can be spurred by co-creation, which mobilises the ideas and
competences of a plethora of public and private actors, including citizens (Bason,
2018; Bentzen, Sørensen, & Torfing, 2020; Torfing, 2016). Co-creation requires
the formation of networks and partnerships that could also help counteract the
fragmentation caused by NPM through pluri-centric coordination based on cross-
boundary dialogue and alignment. The focus on distributed problem-solving and
goal attainment requires more outgoing and collaborative public employees
(Agger & Sørensen, 2018), which in turn calls for enhancing the trust in their
skills, intrinsic task motivation and PSM (Bentzen, 2020a, 2020b; Gronn, 2002;
Louis, Mayrowetz, Smiley, & Murphy, 2009). This move required the abandoning
of agency theory and the adoption of stewardship theory, which assumes the
existence of a high degree of goal and value congruence between principals and
agents and renders it reasonable for the former to trust the latter (Schillemans,
2013; Torfing & Bentzen, 2020). Finally, in order to secure the political and
democratic anchorage of cross-boundary collaboration in networks, partnerships
and local forms of co-creation, NPG advocates have recommended that political
and administrative leaders should exercise metagovernance, defined as the effort

to influence processes and outcomes of networked collaboration without reverting too much to old-fashioned command and control (Sørensen & Torfing, 2009).

In 2011, an inter-university group of public administration researchers published a manifesto criticising NPM and recommending public sector reforms drawing on a combination of ideas associated with the neo-Weberian state, digital era governance and not least NPG. The manifest was downloaded more than 26,000 times, and the researchers behind it were invited to present their main ideas to scores of municipalities, the regional authorities and an inter-ministerial forum of permanent secretaries, which stimulated debate about public administration reform. While most central state actors were very negative about the new ideas, claiming that the NPM-associated problems were mainly caused by its incomplete implementation, the local municipalities held a much more positive view of the recommended changes. Mobilising additional resources through networks, partnerships and co-creation with citizens and civil society and removing red tape to boost public employee motivation seemed attractive in the light of the cross-pressure between growing expectations to public services and public problem-solving combined with scarce public resources.

Then-Minister of the Interior Margrethe Vestager supported the local efforts to supplement and supplant bureaucracy and NPM with new ideas about the need to mobilise public employee competences, motivations and energies through a more trust-based management system and to involve citizens in service delivery and service innovation. In 2013, she launched a major 'trust reform' consisting of seven principles for public governance developed in close dialogue with the professional employee organisations. The reform had no direct impact on public administration, because the principles appeared to be fairly banal and the reform failed to assign responsibility for making concrete changes to the relevant actors. Nevertheless, it served to legitimise local experiments aimed at removing bureaucratic rules and performance indicators.

Local experiments with NPG-inspired reforms were further stimulated by the municipal amalgamation reform in 2007, which created larger and gradually more self-confident municipalities with a strategic capacity for setting their own reform agenda and engaging in experimentation. Hence, many municipalities tested new ideas about trust-based management aimed at creating room for public employees to draw on their professional skills and knowledge and to collaborate with each other as well as with citizens and users to spur public innovation (Bentzen, 2019). This trend is evidenced by the survey referred to above, which found a high organisational focus on all of the NPG-related items in both the municipal departments on social affairs and the more technical planning and environment departments (Torfing & Køhler, 2016).

The growing embrace and promotion of NPG-associated reform initiatives is conditioned by the high levels of trust established over the course of Danish history in Danish culture and solidified through the combination of bureaucracy and professional rule. Denmark has longstanding traditions for corporatist collaboration in the labour market and the involvement of the social partners in policymaking (Svendsen & Svendsen, 2016). Corporatist wage negotiations began in the wake of a major industrial conflict in 1898, resulting in the formation of a set of ground rules for labour market negotiations that still exist to this day. In the 1930s, the Folketing passed a large social reform complex after corporatist policy negotiations with the social partners. Until the late 1970s, tripartite negotiations were the norm in Denmark and served to cultivate strong norms among both public and private actors about trusting each other to honour joint agreements and to focus on public value production rather than the narrow pursuit of short-term organisational interests. Corporatism works in tandem with bureaucracy and professional rule in the sense that negotiated solutions are expected to be carefully and effectively implemented and to be supported by professional expertise. Hence, the corporatist actors trust that the administrative apparatus of central and local government will carry out negotiated policy solutions.

The corporatist breeding ground for interorganisational trust has weakened steadily since the 1980s, however, as corporatist representation in the policy-making process has declined and changes in executive–legislative relations have augmented the Folketing's power. Organised interests have generally adapted to these changes, however, partly by lobbying the civil servants in the policy-formulating ministries and partly by lobbying the elected representatives in the Danish parliament and government (Opedal, Rommetvedt, & Vrangbæk, 2012). Hence, corporatism remains in operation, albeit in a different form. There are even signs of a revival of corporatism during the COVID-19 epidemic (Junk, Crepaz, Hanegraaff, Berkhout, & Aizenberg, 2020).

Although some negative effects may also be observed, the overall impact of NPG ideas and practices on trust relations is positive. NPG introduces more trust-based management aimed at combining trust in the commitment and skills of public employees with the legitimate need for control. Trust-based management involves reducing the number of bureaucratic rules and the number of performance indicators about which frontline personnel must collect data and report. This is hard work and requires the ability to challenge and remove rules and performance indicators that are particularly burdensome but may be defendable as seen from the perspective of bureaucratic control and performance management. An emblematic and oft-mentioned example of a successful combination of trust and control is found in the Culture and Leisure Administration in the City of Copenhagen, where then-Director Carsten Haurum decided that employees should be trusted to determine how their daily tasks are carried out provided that they meet three simple performance indicators: they should be within budget, sick leave should be low and user satisfaction should be high. Indeed, control with a few parameters helped to liberate the employees to use their skills and competences to improve services and produce innovative solutions through internal and external collaboration.

Studies have found that there is good experience with enhancing trust-based management in organisations that firmly anchor new initiatives in executive leadership, involve the local workplace council and organise joint and local discussions between managers and employees about how to clarify, change, retain or remove rules and indicators (Bentzen, 2020a). Perhaps most importantly, trust-based management requires the development of a new mindset focussed on the shared goals of managers and employees and the need for continuous dialogue about both the daily operations and more strategic management issues (Bentzen, 2020b). To ensure that trust-based management does not lead to a lack of control and opportunistic behaviour, evidence shows that it is paramount to find new ways of ensuring the evaluation and assessment of results that are meaningful to employees and to facilitate learning-enhancing accountability (Torfing & Bentzen, 2020). When control is decreased, it is vital to absorb risk in alternative ways. Hence, trust-based management entails not only structural changes to control systems but also the development of organisational competences and new forms of joint learning-based evaluation (Bentzen, 2019).

Not only does NPG have a positive impact on the trust relations between public managers and their employees, it also enhances citizen trust in the public sector by using innovation to make the public sector 'work smarter' and to produce better services and by inviting users, citizens and stakeholders to participate in networks and partnerships through which they co-create public solutions together with public administrators and/or elected politicians. The rosy picture of the trust-building effects of collaborative governance and co-creation must be counterbalanced by a sobering view on the negative effects. Hence, citizen trust in the public sector tends to decline when collaborative governance in networks and partnerships fails to produce the expected solutions; when the co-creation of public value outcomes is replaced with the co-destruction of public value due to negligence, incompetence or over-zealous vigilante behaviour and when collaborative governance arrangements lack public transparency and fail to secure accountability (Fledderus, 2018; Steen, Brandsen, & Verschuere, 2018). To curb these risks, trust-based collaboration must be supplemented with legitimate forms of control.

Despite the growing embrace and positive impact of NPG, the Ministry of Finance stubbornly insisted on further NPM reforms when everyone seemed to feel, 'enough already'. This insistence triggered massive conflict around the public wage negotiations in 2018, which resulted in the demonisation of the Ministry of Finance and its NPM-focussed Modernisation Agency. The fear of losing credibility and legitimacy as a public agency finally led to critical self-examination and ultimately to the termination of the agency, which has been completely reorganised and re-named.

On this background, Danish Social Democratic Prime Minister Mette Frederiksen (2019–present) has repeatedly declared NPM to be dead, and she has called for public administration reforms reducing bureaucratic red tape and control-fixated performance management. What will a much awaited 'proximity reform' accomplish? It remains too early to say. Apparently, the reform intends to remove bureaucratic control and give more freedom to local welfare institutions to boost trust, professionalism and job satisfaction. However, it remains unclear how this new political vision will be carried out in practice. So far, the government has only launched one new reform: it has transferred administrative resources from the police at the national level to local police precincts and exempted particular sector departments in seven municipalities from all legislation for the next three years, thus giving them free rein to innovate their schools, employment services and eldercare based on bottom-up initiatives. Experiences from the local experiments will drive future reforms.

Still, no matter the outcome of these new reform efforts, there is no indication that NPG will replace the limited Danish version of NPM and the longstanding integration of bureaucracy and professional rule. NPG may be the current fad and fashion, but all of the abovementioned governance paradigms are pragmatically combined, and therein lies the explanation of the high degree of trust in the Danish public sector.

Public Governance in Denmark – Between Control and Trust

The above analysis shows how public governance in Denmark is blessed with high levels of trust, both between public leaders and employees and between the public sector and citizenry. Public leader–employee trust is important for securing the effective execution of political decisions and for motivating and enabling frontline personnel to pursue quality and excellence in public service production. The citizen trust in the public sector in general and government in particular is equally important, as it not only helps to ensure compliance with public regulation but also makes the population less prone to support populist political leaders who thrive on popular distrust and alienation vis-à-vis the political and administrative system and who often ultimately undermine the core principles and procedures of liberal democracy.

The analysis also reveals how the pragmatic combination of different public governance paradigms positively impacts the high levels of trust:

(1) The net effect of the combination of bureaucracy and professional rule on trust along the vertical axis is positive. First, the trust in public employees is reduced by bureaucratic control and command but enhanced by professional rule that creates space for professional discretion and self-regulation. Second, while professional rule may create conditions for paternalistic behaviour, bureaucracy ensures that citizens can rely on bureaucracy to provide services and public regulation based on legal rules and rights, impartiality, equity and meritocratic professionalism.

(2) NPM builds on an almost axiomatic mistrust in public employees, but its limited and selective implementation and its layering on top of bureaucracy mitigate its negative impact on manager–employee trust. The mistrust in public employees is combined with high trust in the competences of citizens, who are expected to act as rational consumers in newly created welfare markets and invited to participate in user boards. Although the extent to which citizens take up these exit and voice options is quite limited, NPM and the neo-Weberian state default option have changed the public sector discourse in the direction of greater appreciation of input from empowered citizens.

(3) NPG further nurtures the trust relations between the public sector and a broad range of citizens and private stakeholders by inviting the latter to

participate in governance networks, partnerships and more broadly the co-creation of public solutions. Citizens and other private actors are valued for their input, but they are also perceived as the co-producers of services and co-designers of new and better solutions. At the same time, NPG replaces agency theory with stewardship theory, thereby paving the way for more trust-based relationships between public managers and employees, who are assumed to share core goals and values and must therefore coordinate their efforts to deliver high-quality services.

The pragmatic, non-ideological approach to public governance has helped to secure valuable trust relations. Some may speculate that the strong post-war support for the universalistic welfare state model explains the pragmatic approach to public governance, which revolves around the key question of how tax revenues can be spent most efficiently to produce welfare outputs and public value outcomes. The shifting public governance paradigms hold different answers to this pertinent question. Bureaucracy and professional rule aim to provide rule-based and rights-based welfare delivered by professional employees using their skills and norms to govern local service production. NPM and the neo-Weberian state aim to enhance the focus on results and empower citizens by giving them voice and exit options. Finally, NPG aims to expand the space for public professionals to use their knowledge and competences, working together across silos and involving citizens, volunteers and stakeholder organisations in both the co-delivery and co-creation of public solutions, albeit based on political and administrative metagovernance that provides a clear political, discursive and budgetary framing of the local collaboration.

The high degree of devolution within the Danish unitary state coupled with the commitment to the universal provision of high-quality welfare services has supported the integration of bureaucracy and professional rule, and the political support for public welfare and an organisational culture praising informality, professional intuitions and egalitarianism have combined to prevent wholesale conversion to NPM, thereby paving the way for the emergence of the neo-Weberian state. The continued opposition to and accumulation of empirical observations of the unintended negative consequences of NPM paved the way for the adoption of key ideas associated with NPG, which is supported by the longstanding traditions for collaborative governance that connect the strong Danish state with a well-organised civil society. Resting on a conducive set of historical socio-political conditions, the pragmatic combination of the different public governance paradigms has further enhanced the trust between public managers and employees and between the public sector and citizenry.

While trust-based public governance has major advantages, it may foster anti-social and sub-optimising behaviour among public employees with mixed motives and lead to governance failures that erode citizen trust in the public sector. Nevertheless, high levels of trust by no means exclude legitimate forms of control aiming to curb the abuse of trust; rather, trust and control tend to co-exist. While trust reduces complexity by excluding negative possibilities from consideration, thereby absorbing risk and enabling action, control seeks to minimise complexity by regulating and reducing possibilities for action (Edelenbos & Eshuis, 2012; Möllering, 2006). Hence, trust and control are similar in their ambition to reduce complexity, but the mechanisms by which they do so differ significantly. This difference does not necessarily mean that trust and control are opposites; indeed, new research demonstrates that trust and control may support and even reinforce each other (Vallentin & Thygesen, 2017; van Thiel & Yesilkagit, 2011). Control with key parameters may render it easier to trust a group of employees to use their professional skills, and trusting public employees may make it easier to involve them in the development of control systems that support learning and excellence (Bentzen, 2020a).

In short, the Danish public sector has exploited its historical conditions to pragmatically combine a broad range of governance paradigms that together have enabled the public sector to strike a healthy balance between trust and control that both motivates frontline personnel to produce high-quality welfare and secures a high level of citizen trust in government.

Implications for Practice

In Denmark, it is clearly the 'mix that matters' in the sense that the combination of different governance paradigms explains the relatively high levels of trust and how trust is balanced by legitimate control. This finding begs the questions why and how Denmark has managed to constructively combine different visions of how to govern the public sector and what other countries can learn from the Danish way.

Regarding lesson-drawing, there is little reason to refer to the unique historical factors that have helped create a high-trust culture. More interestingly, three replicable factors seem to have supported the measured combination of different governance paradigms. The first is that public governance reforms have not been subject to ideologisation, as we have otherwise seen in a number of Anglo-Saxon countries where political leaders have recently campaigned in the pursuit of NPM reforms. With the exception of those in the Modernisation Agency and some executive managers in the Ministry of Finance, Danish politicians and executive public managers have all taken a pragmatic approach to public governance reform. Even staunch NPM supporters have argued that marketisation and performance management help to consolidate the welfare state by cutting slack. As such, the preservation of the universalistic welfare state is the gold standard when pragmatically combining elements from different public governance paradigms.

The second factor is the close interaction between researchers and practitioners that has helped to preserve a critical distance to new governance fashions and to provide research-based evaluation and discussion of the results of administrative reforms. Leaders in the public sector are generally very well educated in public leadership and management (e.g., through academic studies and mid-career master programmes), which provide them with the latest research in the field of public administration. Public administration researchers are frequently invited to speak at meetings at the local, regional and national levels. One explanation for this is that Danish public administration research engages with relevant real-life problems and has found ways to manoeuvre between unconstructive criticism and descriptive commentary.

The third factor is the involvement of professional organisations representing public leaders and professional employees in the debate about public governance issues. This involvement, which is indebted to lengthy corporatist traditions, means that administrative reforms are evaluated from different perspectives, and new reforms are based on broad agreements and political compromise.

Whether these factors can be replicated in other countries is debatable, but depending on national conditions, policymakers may want to 'depoliticise' and take a more pragmatic approach to public governance reform, base reforms on scientific evidence and advice, and generally seek to create a common sense of ownership to the modus operandi of public administration by involving key stakeholders such as public managers and employees and other downstream actors in administrative reforms. That said, we should bear in mind that the inclusive consensus culture in Denmark also poses a democratic dilemma, since it limits the ability of elected government to reform the public sector based on its political orientation and convictions. It is difficult for a new government to use its democratic mandate to set a new course for the public sector.

Conclusion

As a purposeful intervention in the ongoing debate about trust and control, this chapter has demonstrated the presence of a positive, self-reinforcing feedback loop between a longstanding socio-political and administrative trust culture and a pragmatic combination of different public governance paradigms that tend to produce trust relations with legitimate control. The virtuous trust–governance circle enables the Danish public sector to reap the fruits of a sound trust–control balance and to maintain trusting relations between public sector and citizenry.

The development in the Danish public sector shows how some forms of control might even support trust-building and how trust may facilitate joint efforts to curb the expansion of control mechanisms that straightjacket the public sector. Yet the current control–trust balance in the Danish public sector is unstable in the sense that the pendulum continues to swing back and forth. Still, for historical reasons, the amplitude of this swinging is limited, since a relative balance has been achieved. Herein lies one of the most interesting features of Danish public governance.

Note

1. KL is a private organisation representing the interests of the 98 Danish municipalities.

References

Agger, A., & Sørensen, E. (2018). Managing collaborative innovation in public bureaucracies. *Planning Theory*, *17*(1), 53–73.

Andersen, L. B., & Pedersen, L. H. (2012). Public service motivation and professionalism. *International Journal of Public Administration*, *35*(1), 46–57.

Bason, C. (2018). *Leading public sector innovation*. Bristol: Policy Press.

Bentzen, T. Ø. (2019). The birdcage is open but will the bird fly? *Journal of Trust Research*, *9*(2), 185–202.

Bentzen, T. Ø. (2020a). *Samskabt styring: Nye veje til afbureaukratisering*. Copenhagen: Samfundslitteratur.

Bentzen, T. Ø. (2020b). Continuous co-creation. *Public Management Review*. doi:10.1080/14719037.2020.1786150

Bentzen, T. Ø., Sørensen, E., & Torfing, J. (2020). Strengthening public service production, administrative problem solving, and political leadership through co-creation of innovative public value outcomes? *The Innovation Journal*, *25*(1), 1–28.

Bentzen, T. Ø., & Torfing, J. (forthcoming). COVID-19 induced organizational transformation: How external shock may spur cross-organizational collaboration and trust-based management.

Corbett, E., & Le Dantec, C. A. (2018). Going the distance: *Trust work* for citizen participation. In Proceedings of the 2018 CHI conference on human factors in computing systems (pp. 1–13).

Costa, A. C., Fulmer, C. A., & Anderson, N. R. (2018). Trust in work teams. *Journal of Organizational Behavior*, *39*(2), 169–184.

Crozier, M., Huntington, S. P., & Watanuki, J. (1975). *The crisis of democracy*. New York, NY: New York University Press.

Dalton, R. J., & Welzel, C. (2014). *The civic culture transformed: From allegiant to assertive citizens*. Cambridge: Cambridge University Press.

Delhey, J., & Newton, K. (2004). *Social trust: Global pattern or nordic exceptionalism?* Retrieved from http://www.econstor.eu/handle/10419/44134

Dich, J. (1975). *Den herskende klasse: En kritisk analyse af social udbytning og midlerne imod den*. Copenhagen: Gyldendal.

Dirks, K. T. (1999). The effects of interpersonal trust on work group performance. *Journal of Applied Psychology*, *84*(3), 445.

Dooren, W., Bouckaert, G., & Halligan, J. (2015). *Performance management in the public sector*. Abingdon: Routledge.

Downs, A. (1967). *Inside bureaucracy*. Boston, MA: Little Brown & Co.

Dunleavy, P., Margetts, H., Bastow, S., & Tinkler, J. (2006). New public management is dead. Long live digital-era governance. *Journal of Public Administration Research and Theory*, *16*(3), 467–494.

Edelenbos, J., & Eshuis, J. (2012). The interplay between trust and control in governance processes. *Administration & Society*, *44*(6), 647–674.

Edelman, D. J. (2016). *Edelman trust barometer 2016: Annual global study*. Chicago: Edelman, 70.

Fledderus, J. (2018). The effect of co-production on trust. In T. Brandsen, T. Steen, & B. Verschue (Eds.), *Co-production and co-creation engaging citizens in public services* (pp. 258–265). London: Routledge.

du Gay, P. (2000). *Praise of bureaucracy: Weber, organization, ethics*. London: Sage.

Grand, J. L. (1997). Knights, knaves or pawns? *Journal of Social Policy*, *26*(2), 149–169.

Gray, B. (1989). *Collaborating*. San Francisco, CA: Jossey-Bass.

Gronn, P. (2002). Distributed leadership as a unit of analysis. *The Leadership Quarterly*, *13*(4), 423–451.

Hood, C. (1991). A public management for all seasons? *Public Administration*, *69*(1), 3–19.

Hunt, J. G., Burke, C. S., Sims, D. E., Lazzara, E. H., & Salas, E. (2007). Trust in leadership. *The Leadership Quarterly*, *18*(6), 606–632.

Jacobsen, C., Hvitved, J., & Andersen, L. (2014). Command and motivation: How the perception of external interventions relates to intrinsic motivation and public service motivation. *Public Administration*, *92*(4), 790–806.

Junk, W. M., Crepaz, M., Hanegraaff, M., Berkhout, J., & Aizenberg, E. (2020). Interest representation during the corona virus crisis. Retrieved from https://staticcuris.ku.dk/portal/files/251739870/EU_Report_Interest_Representation_under_the_Corona_Virus_Crisis.pdf

Klausen, K. K., & Ståhlberg, K. (1998). *New public management i Norden*. Odense: University Press of Southern Denmark.

Klijn, E. H. (2010). Trust in governance networks: Looking for conditions for innovative solutions and outcomes. In S. P. Osborne (Ed.), *The new public governance?* (pp. 303–321). Abingdon: Routledge.

Kristensen, O. P. (1980). The logic of political-bureaucratic decision making as a cause for governmental growth. *European Journal of Political Research*, *8*(2), 249–264.

Kristensen, O. P. (1987). *Væksten i den offentlige sektor: Institutioner og politik*. Copenhagen: DJØF Publishers.

Kuhn, T. S. (1962). *The structure of scientific revolutions*. Chicago, IL: University of Chicago Press.

Lane, J.-E. (2005). *Public administration and public management: The principal–agent perspective*. London: Taylor & Francis.

Louis, K., Mayrowetz, D., Smiley, M., & Murphy, J. (2009). The role of sensemaking and trust in developing distributed leadership. In A. Harris (Ed.), *Distributed leadership: Different perspectives* (pp. 157–180). London: Springer.

Mahoney, J., & Thelen, K. (2010). A theory of gradual institutional change. In J. Mahoney & K. Thelen (Eds.), *A theory of gradual institutional change: Ambiguity, agency and power* (pp. 1–37). New York, NY: Cambridge University Press.

Möllering, G. (2006). *Trust: Reason, routine, reflexivity*. Oxford, Amsterdam: Elsevier.

Moynihan, D. P. (2010). A workforce of cynics? The effects of contemporary reforms on public service motivation. *International Public Management Journal*, *13*(1), 24–34.

Mungiu-Pippidi, A. (2013). Becoming Denmark: Historical designs of corruption control. *Social Research: An International Quarterly*, *80*(4), 1259–1286.

Niskanen, W. A. (1971). *Bureaucracy and representative government*. Chicago, IL: Aldine-Atherton.

Nooteboom, B. (2013). Trust and innovation. In R. Bachmann & A. Zaheer (Eds.), *Handbook of advances in trust research* (pp. 106–124). Northampton: Edward Elgar.

Nyhan, R. C. (2000). Changing the paradigm: Trust and its role in public sector organizations. *The American Review of Public Administration*, *30*(1), 87–109.

Olagnier, D., & Mogensen, T. H. (2020). The COVID-19 pandemic in Denmark. *Cytokine & Growth Factor Reviews, 53,* 10–12.

Oliver, A. L. (1997). On the nexus of organizations and professions: Networking through trust. *Sociological Inquiry, 67*(2), 227–245.

Opedal, S., Rommetvedt, H., & Vrangbæk, K. (2012). Organised interests, authority structures and political influence: Danish and Norwegian patient groups compared. *Scandinavian Political Studies, 35*(1), 1–21.

Osborne, S. (2006). The new public governance? *Public Management Review, 8*(3), 377–387.

Osborne, D., & Gaebler, T. (1992). *Reinventing government.* Reading: Addison-Wesley.

Pedersen, R. T., & Pedersen, L. H. (2020). Citizen attitudes on politicians' pay: Trust issues are not solved by delegation. *Political Studies, 68*(2), 389–407.

Pollitt, C., & Bouckaert, G. (2011). *Public management reform.* Oxford: Oxford University Press.

Schillemans, T. (2013). Moving beyond the clash of interests. *Public Management Review, 15*(4), 541–562.

Six, F. (2013). Trust in regulatory relations. *Public Management Review, 15*(2), 163–185.

Sønderskov, K. M., & Dinesen, P. T. (2016). Trusting the state, trusting each other? The effect of institutional trust on social trust. *Political Behavior, 38*(1), 179–202.

Sørensen, E., & Torfing, J. (2009). Making governance networks effective and democratic through metagovernance. *Public Administration, 8*(7), 234–258.

Spreitzer, G., & Mishra, A. (1999). Giving up control without losing control trust and its substitutes' effects on managers' involving employees in decision making. *Group & Organization Management, 24*(2), 155–187.

Steen, T., Brandsen, T., & Verschuere, B. (2018). The dark side of co-creation and co-production seven evils. In T. Brandsen, B. Verschuere, & T. Steen (Eds.), *Co-production and co-creation engaging citizens in public services.* New York, NY: Routledge.

Svendsen, G. T., & Svendsen, G. L. H. (2016). *Trust, social capital and the Scandinavian welfare state.* Cheltenham: Edward Elgar.

van Thiel, S., & Yesilkagit, K. (2011). Good neighbours or distant friends? *Public Management Review, 13*(6), 783–802.

Torfing, J. (2016). *Collaborative innovation.* Washington, DC: Georgetown University Press.

Torfing, J., Andersen, L. B., Greve, C., & Klausen, K. K. (2020). *Public governance paradigms: Competing and co-existing.* Cheltenham: Edward Elgar.

Torfing, J., & Bentzen, T. Ø. (2020). Does stewardship theory provide a viable alternative to control-fixated performance management? *Administrative Sciences, 10*(4), 86.

Torfing, J., & Køhler, T. B. (2016, April). *Styringskløft mellem Finansministeriet og kommuner.* Altinget.

Torpe, L. (2003). Social capital in Denmark: A deviant case? *Scandinavian Political Studies, 26*(1), 27–46. Retrieved from http://onlinelibrary.wiley.com/doi/10.1111/1467-9477.00078/full

Vallentin, S., & Thygesen, N. T. (2017). Trust and control in public sector reform. *Journal of Trust Research, 7*(2), 150–169.

Chapter 8

Digitalising Denmark: Efficiency versus privacy

Peter Aagaard and John Storm Pedersen

Abstract

For many years, one of the central ambitions of shifting Danish governments has been to maintain the position as an e-government frontrunner. The overall dream of administrators has been and remains to produce personalised social services efficiently. Shifting Danish governments have followed a centralised, party-neutral and consensual path to digitalisation. The efforts have been based on a centralised civil registration number system (CPR) established in 1968. However, the quest for efficient, personalised services has also stimulated debate in Denmark as to whether the state is obtaining too much personalised information and risks violating the privacy of its own citizens. Digitalisation efforts, especially the out-of-office efforts, cannot be pushed without public legitimacy attached to the process. Furthermore, Danish legislation must be changed substantially to pave the way for the increased use of advanced digital tools. Algorithmic tools cannot be trusted to solve all tasks. These dilemmas illustrate that the days of high political consensus in the Danish digitalisation efforts may very well be over. Other countries can learn four overall lessons from the Danish experiences: (1) although a high level of digitalisation can be reached using a top-down, nonpartisan approach, digitalisation will always be political, (2) experimentation and the failures attached to digitalisation can come at a very high cost, (3) effort will benefit greatly from citizen trust, especially in out-of-office efforts and (4) the public legitimacy of digitalisation must be based on strong mechanisms of social and political accountability.

Keywords: Privacy; personalised services; legitimacy; digitalisation; digital governance; IT scandals

Public Governance in Denmark, 131–146
Copyright © 2022 by Emerald Publishing Limited
All rights of reproduction in any form reserved
doi:10.1108/978-1-80043-712-820221008

For over a decade, a range of international organisations have ranked Denmark among the most digitalised countries in the world (Department of Economic and Social Affairs, 2020; OECD, 2010). According to Statistics Denmark, 92% of all Danes have home access to the Internet and use it daily. Danes increasingly search for information on public sector websites and homepages (86% in 2019), and Danes increasingly access public services via digital self-service (71% in 2019). For many years, successive Danish governments consisting of parties from both sides of the political spectrum have aspired to maintain the status of the country as an e-government frontrunner. The overall dream of administrators has always been to produce personalised social services efficiently (Jæger, 2020), and the potential efficiency gains have been calculated repeatedly. A business leader panel estimated in 2017 that the government could save DKK 90 billion (ca. €12 million) in 2025 (Digital Vækstpanel, 2017). While this number has never been verified, the quest for efficiency has been steady and ongoing. However, the quest for efficient, personalised services has also triggered a new debate in Denmark as to whether the state is accessing too much personalised information and risks violating the privacy of its own citizens.

Internationally, digital governance proponents have argued for years that computer technology will significantly change the conditions for public service production and delivery (Lupton, 2015; Pedersen & Wilkinson, 2019). The promise is that digital governance holds the potential to support more efficient, equitable, transparent and responsive public services (Margetts & Dorobantu, 2019). Dunleavy and Margetts (2005) famously claimed the advent of digital era governance (DEG), where digitalisation substantially changes public service production and delivery. Digital governance renders it possible for state agencies to gather data on citizens in very narrow segments of the population or specific neighbourhoods. Based on the large-scale gathering of data, digital governance allows state agencies to build a new layer of algorithmic governance (Danaher et al., 2017) based on machine learning/AI and intelligent feedback systems. Algorithmic governance is based on 'datafication', which is the transformation of human activity into data (Mayer-Schönberger & Cukier, 2013); or, to be more specific, it is the transformation of the digital traces left by people and the 'integration, analysis and visualisation of data patterns for purposes of decision-making' (Flyverbom, Deibert, & Matten, 2017, p. 4). And the data has become a valuable resource in public service for the same reason. However, the 'tech backlash' caused by the NSA scandal in 2012 and the Facebook scandal in 2018 have put more focus on surveillance, privacy and data ethics in the international debate. Supported by big tech companies, state agencies engage in surveillance and data tracking, also on behalf of privacy concerns (Zuboff, 2019). Personal and private data can be used to nudge people to follow certain patterns of behaviour of benefit to a range of different policies in health, security, transport, etc. AI tools can also 'black box' authority (Pasquale, 2015), dehumanise citizens, ingrain patterns of discrimination and stigmatisation, increase intrusion into privacy, exclude citizens (Brown, Chouldechova, Putnam-Hornstein, Tobin, & Vaithianathan, 2019; Gillingham, 2016; Metcalf & Crawford, 2016) and compromise the professionalism of welfare workers (Busch & Henriksen, 2018;

Desouza & Jacob, 2017). Citizens must accept nudging from digital infrastructure in their everyday lives, with the risk of violating norms and standards relating to privacy. This development emphasises the need for more public and political attention to digitalisation efforts; it is no longer merely a matter of finding and implementing the right technology, but also a matter of balancing political interests and values (Pors & Ejersbo, 2020).

Analysis

The Danish roadmap to lead the world in digitalisation has increasingly been a centralised, party-neutral and consensual path. The first generation of IT development in Denmark, from 1960 to the 1980s, was characterised by the development of central administrative systems capable of making calculations based on national data sets, like taxes or national budget planning (Jæger & Pors, 2017). Much of the Danish success is linked to a highly centralised civil registration system, CPR, which Denmark founded in 1968. Here, all Danes are registered from birth (and immigrants and refugees upon the issuance of their first residence permit). All public agencies use the CPR system, which makes it possible to collect and match massive amounts of data for every resident of the country across different databases regarding health, occupation, income, education, family relations and more. The CPR system remains the backbone of the Danish digitalisation system, as it sustains digital taxation, control of social benefits, storage of personal medical records and much more.

The next phase, from the 1980s to the 2015s, was characterised by 'front office digitalisation' in the form of personal computers and local intranets. Nevertheless, for many public services, case work was still often handled on paper and stored in hard copy filing systems. Many producers of the digital infrastructure were privatised in this phase, such as TDC (TeleDanmark), Datacentralen (owned by CSC) and KMD (Kommunedata). As the Internet emerged in the late 1990s, the focus of the front office gradually shifted from internal affairs to include communication with citizens. Citizens could communicate with public authorities via the Internet, and public services could be produced and delivered on the Internet. Front offices developed websites and homepages full of interactive formulas and information for the citizenry and moved frontline meetings with citizens to the Internet. Once the smartphone technology had become widespread, it was decided that the Internet should be the primary public sector–citizens meeting ground (aka. digital-first approach). The third and current phase focusses on out-of-office efforts, involving direct participation, surveillance and measurement of citizen behaviour based on digital technologies like IoT and big data sets combined with AI. Here, big tech companies play a major role. The backbone of the health platform is provided by an American company, Epic, while the police platform, Pol-Intel, is provided by American NSA contractor Palantir. The medical industry, including the Novo Nordisk Foundation investment in the Danish National Genome Centre, has also become directly involved in the creation of the digital infrastructure (see Table 1).

Table 1. Digital Efforts and Strategies in Denmark since World War II.

Year	1945–1980	1980–2015	2015–
Focus of strategy	Back office	Front office	Out of office
Type of technology	Backbone, mainframe computing	PC, intranet and Internet, 2g, 3g	Wearables, IoT, 4g, 5g, supercomputers
Digital purpose	Calculation	Documentation, digital services	Big data sets, algorithms, AI
Strategic actors	Local IT officers	National task force, data centres, privatised agencies	National data agencies, private companies, big tech companies
Infrastructure development	Local	National, centralised	Privatised, transnational
Legitimacy and accountability	Professional accountability through IT expertise	Bureaucratic accountability	Increased social and legal accountability
Privacy issues	No controversy	Surveillance by auditing employees and employee–citizen interaction	Growing challenges regarding surveillance and privacy

Each of these phases of digitalisation has been marked by different forms of accountability (Ejersbo & Greve, 2017). The ambition was (and remains) to push digitalisation out into the daily operation of all welfare services. Consequently, as digitisation has moved closer to the front office and citizens, the public interest has increased, and the legitimacy and accountability of the digitalisation efforts have become more politically important. While there was emphasis on professional accountability (proper norms and standards) in the beginning, greater emphasis has since been placed on bureaucratic accountability (internal control through rules and procedures), and more recent efforts are moving towards greater emphasis on social accountability (responsiveness to key stakeholders) and legal accountability (oversight by a legal authority), not least because citizen privacy issues become more important as digitalisation moves 'out of office'.

The National Strategy

Digitalisation in Denmark has followed a nonpartisan, top-down reform strategy for several decades, where central government, represented by the Ministry of

Finance, has collaborated with regions and local governments (Ejersbo & Greve, 2017). This top-down approach has been a key factor in the Danish success. The first national strategy on digitalisation, 'Info-society 2000', was published in 1994. It emphasised the need for public sector experimentation based on values of societal equality, digital rights and local democracy. Since the turn of the Millennium, however, digitalisation efforts have taken a very different direction. A government report, 'The Digital Denmark' (Dybkjær & Lindegaard, 1999), identified a need for overview and a coordinated governance approach, and another government report issued two years later, 'IT for all: Denmark's future' (Ministeriet for Videnskab Teknologi og Udvikling, 2001), viewed digitalisation as a means to become an even more efficient and competitive nation. In 2001, the key player and 'chief whip' behind the digitalisation efforts, The Digital Task-force, emerged (Jæger, 2020). Based on a network approach, five ministries, the national association of municipalities (Local Government Denmark – KL), Danish Regions joined forces with the City of Copenhagen and the Municipality of Frederiksberg. Together, representatives from these actors formulated four-year plans for digitalising the Danish public sector. This centralisation was further accelerated by the founding of the National Digitalization Agency in 2011. Together, these actors have coordinated the digitalisation efforts for two decades with a national, top-down and highly political, consensual strategic approach (Jæger, 2020; Pors & Ejersbo, 2020). This approach built on a sharp politician–administrator distinction, where politicians determine the objectives whereas administrators decide on the technologies and how to achieve the objectives (Jæger, 2020) as well as the means and measures, such as common standards or the formation of data centres. One such data centre was Udbetaling Danmark (founded in 2012), which took over the payment of unemployment assistance from municipalities to their residents. These initiatives were negotiated with the municipalities (KL) and regions. KL and Danish Regions then formulated their own strategies (the first in 2010), in the light of the negotiated results with the state representatives (Jæger & Pors, 2017). The ambition has been to push digital tools out into the individual welfare service fields, such as employment, health, social benefits and schools as well as security, taxation, etc.

This was primarily due to the financial squeeze of the welfare state (Lipsky, 2010, p. 27). This is also the case in Denmark, creating a permanent squeeze between the demand for public welfare services and public finances. The financial squeeze has fuelled the aim for more efficient digitalisation, including more efficient communication with citizens and social service delivery (Hundebøl, Pors, & Sørensen, 2020). Expectations regarding efficiency gains have often been associated with savings resulting from synergy effects, as the IT projects often centralise public services. Increased digitalisation has also made it possible to benchmark municipalities, schools and hospitals and to carry out result-based management on the basis of increasingly narrow KPIs.

The top-down reform strategy has spawned a range of services, including a single travel card for public transport throughout the country, secure email from authorities, secure identification on the Internet (NemID), secure payment (NemKonto), digital post to the public sector, digital power of attorney as well as a handful of Internet portals for citizens (borger.dk), health (sundhed.dk) and private businesses (virk.dk). In particular, the services for unemployed people have become highly digitalised, with huge amounts of information stored for each citizen in the system. All in all, digitalisation investment, efficiency measures and centralisation have been highly interconnected (Jæger & Löfgren, 2010). This development took place with little public debate. Unions raised concern occasional, like when the representatives of case workers critiqued the cutbacks and digitalisation of the taxation services (Borre, 2016), but criticism was largely disregarded.

Efficiency Failures

However, underneath the success of the Danish digital strategy lies a graveyard of digitalisation failures in diverse policy fields, such as defence (Daccis, Demars), police (Polsag), employment services (Proask, Amanda), public health (G-EPJ) and taxation (EFI). These failures demonstrate the challenges of harvesting the promised financial gains to be achieved via improved efficiency. The failures, not least EFI, have also re-politicised the digital agenda somewhat, calling for the digitalisation efforts to be more politically accountable. EFI, launched in 2013 by the Tax Agency, became a huge scandal, undermining not only public trust in the taxation agency but also in the political establishment more generally and its ability to balance efficiency, rationalisation, quality of services and legal rights issues. In 2006, the right-of-centre Venstre government decided to lay off 40% of the Tax Agency employees over six years. Instead, digital technology should take over the jobs. Even though the 2008 Financial Crisis increased the Tax Agency workload, the politicians maintained the plan. EFI was to be ready for operations in 2007, tasked with collecting debt from citizens as well as police fines, custom duties, etc. Despite internal consultancy reports warning about the inaccuracy of the system, the Tax Agency launched it in 2013. The failures were grave, and employees constantly had to clean up EFI messes. There were particular problems with the payment of property taxes, and the Minister for Taxation finally pulled the proverbial plug in 2015. In the space of time in which it operated, the flawed EFI is estimated to have incurred DKK 700 million (almost €100 million) in extra administration costs – and outstanding tax payments amounting to a whopping DKK 90 billion (ca. €12 billion), DKK 14 billion (€2 billion) of which is probably never going to be collected. In 2017, 2000 additional Tax Agency employees were hired to do the job that EFI could not (Aagaard, 2017). Political accountability failed, because political parties across the aisle in the Folketing (Danish Parliament) were indirectly made responsible for the scandal. Denmark had nine different ministers of taxation from four different parties over this 10-year period.

Efforts in the health field have also had efficiency-related problems. Launched in 2016 and 2017 in the Copenhagen Metropolitan Area and Zealand Region, the health platform was delivered by Epic, an American company, at a price of DKK 2.8 billion (ca. €375 million). The portal was supposed to collect information on hospital patients, consultations with GPs and health services throughout the region, and the aim was to create one single medical journal for each patient. The system was also to be used for medicine prescriptions, the prompt delivery of test results, ordering of tests, etc.; however, the technical barriers proved much worse than expected. Communication between the health platform and national systems has been particularly difficult, and medical staff have harshly criticised the system for being slow, illogical and not least for prescribing the wrong medicines for patients. Instead of enhancing efficiency, the system actually made health services less efficient, and cases of maltreatment and unintended events among patients increased, including six deaths that are suspected of being due to the system (Olling, 2018).

All in all, the Danish top-down strategy has created a highly digitalised country in which citizens have digital access to a long range of public sector services. However, the creation of the digital infrastructure has also been marked by severe and costly scandals and sustained inefficiency.

Out-of-Office Efforts

Digitalisation efforts are proceeding at a rapid pace in Denmark. Currently, the ambition is to move public services from the front office to 'out of office', which is being enabled by the third phase of digitalisation IT service tools, which have made it possible for citizens no longer to have to attend meetings in job centres, social agencies, etc. Besides many new apps regarding rehab, the out-of-office monitoring of chronic diseases makes it possible to keep citizens out of public welfare institutions (Breit, Egeland, & Løberg, 2019). In Denmark, it is now possible to receive medical treatment from home using digital patient monitoring tools.

In 2019, the government, regions and municipalities agreed on a Digitalisation Pact, where artificial intelligence (AI) was prioritised in health, social services and employment services. For instance, when citizens call emergency services, AI helps to identify heart attacks. AI is also used when allocating public support for cleaning as part of eldercare, rehabilitation, reducing the time used on case work in construction approval applications, decision-making based on fixed, neutral criteria, such as applications for student grants and property valuation (Rasmussen & Klit, 2020), the automated collection of documents for open access applications and reports for sickness benefits (Høybye-Mortensen, 2020).

The out-of-office strategy is especially profound in healthcare. Here, efforts encompass projects for how to monitor seniors at home or to collect health data from patients at home via wearables. A new strategy for personalised medicine was already decided in 2016 to use data on citizens' DNA to provide better diagnostics and tailored treatment. The Danish National Genome centre was established in 2018 to implement the strategy. In 2019, the Novo Nordisk Foundation supported the effort with DKK 1 billion (ca. €135 million); money that will be used to build the digital infrastructure and for the first initial analysis of the system. The system will be based on written patient consent, and patients will be able to decide for themselves if their data can be used for research. As indicated, private enterprises increasingly play a role in the digitalisation efforts. In a collaboration between Danish Regions and the Confederation of Danish Industry, industry and researchers will gain better access to health data (Mølsted, 2019). The combination of the Civil Registration System (CPR) and the many data points on the health of Danish citizens provides a unique opportunity for the medical industry and government to join forces. However, the collaboration with private businesses also intensifies the focus on privacy matters and personal data ownership.

Privacy and Lack of Security

The public IT services have raised security challenges and privacy concerns. Danish citizens have repeatedly fallen victim to cyberattacks and security breaches. The digital identification app, NemID, was hit by a cyberattack in 2012, the national police in 2013, and in 2018 a social benefits programme was subject to fraud for DKK 117 million (ca. €16 million) by one of their own employees due to inadequate IT security. Hospital health data storage has been the subject of security breaches for years. The Statens Serum Institute (SSI) has also had its share of data-related scandals. In 2016, the data and civil registration numbers of 5 million Danes were mistakenly transferred to a Chinese company, and SSI transferred the health data of 2000 Danish women to an American research facility without consent in 2016 and again in 2018 (Lehmann, 2020).

Rigsrevisionen (the national audit office) has repeatedly criticised the IT security in Danish public agencies, most recently in 2020, when six ministries were criticised for inadequate security. After the implementation of the General Data Protection Regulation (GDPR), Rigsrevisionen also criticised the inadequate security and lack of risk assessment when public agencies outsource citizens' private information to third parties. Denmark implemented the GDPR regulation with a new Data Protection Act in 2018. While this legislation sets new and high standards for privacy and data administration, it has also been criticised for allowing public authorities to cross-reference (public) databases without the consent or even orientation of the involved citizens. The legislation enables state authorities to profile Danes based on data from public records, such as dentists, schools or social welfare case work. The Minister of Justice dismissed this criticism, saying: 'This is not the GDR or the USSR' (Ritzau, 2018).

The Minister's remarks point out how Denmark has historically and generally maintained a high degree of public trust in public authorities when it comes to collecting personal information. Statistics Denmark surveys reveal a decline in citizen trust in the ability of public authorities to handle personal data. In 2017, 83% of all citizens had some or a high degree of trust in public authorities (37% 'high', 46% 'some'). By 2019, however, these numbers had declined: Only 76% of the citizens had some/a high degree of trust, and only 27% a high degree of trust (Tassy, Nielsen, & Jakobsen, 2020). The aforementioned failures might have impacted this result. Furthermore, as digitalisation efforts get closer to out of office, scandals violating privacy emerge.

The so-called 'Telecommunications data' scandal broke in 2019, when it was revealed that the police had made mistakes with localisation data from mobile phones in an extensive number of cases and that possibly up to 10,000 court cases had been settled partly based on such data. Danish National Police employees report being told to lie by the Ministry and to cover up mistakes (Goos, 2019). The Danish Defence Intelligence Service (DDIS) was also hit by a serious scandal in 2020 based on a whistle-blower contact to a government control organ, a scandal that was rather similar to the American NSA scandal in 2013. For years, and with help from the NSA, the DDIS had mass-surveilled communication among Danes via a Danish data centre (Fastrup, Quass, Moltke, Nielsen, & Lindegaard, 2020). The Danish welfare services have also been criticised for surveillance of citizens. The national data and benefits centre, Udbetaling Danmark, has been criticised for carrying out systematic surveillance in their work to root out fraud with social benefits. The data centre has been granted extensive access to collect data on citizens without consent. These are data from citizens who have applied for or already received social benefits, but the sur-veillance also includes their family and household members. Both public and private databases are merged in this search for fraud (Eiriksson, 2019).

The combination of the many public databases in Denmark has become a new strategic effort in the digitalisation of the Danish welfare state. The aim is to be able to use machine learning methods to predict social marginalisation and to deploy early and more individualised intervention in the lives of citizens. Such *Predictive Risk Assessment Tools* (PRATs) are the new frontier for Danish public authorities. PRATs can be used to risk-profile citizens and the needs of entire families for efforts and benefits. One example has been a profiling tool employed by STAR, the national employment agency. The tool is supposed to profile the risk of newly unemployed citizens remaining unemployed for a longer period. The Human Rights Institute has criticised STAR for discriminating against non-Western ethnic groups, because ethnicity is one of the parameters used by the tool to make predictions (Andersen, 2019).

Discussion

Is Danish Digitalisation Really That Efficient?

While Denmark has determinately initiated and implemented new digital infra-structure, from back office to out of office, the process has focussed rather narrowly on efficiency. The efforts have been driven by a perceived need to reduce welfare service costs. Previous governments have even claimed that cost reduction would be so high that would be no problem to finance the entire welfare state (Jæger, 2020, p. 59). Many of the services provided by the Danish welfare system have been digitalised: taxation, medical record archives, communication with public authorities, real-estate transactions, public transport payments and much more, creating a significantly digital-supported welfare state for Danish citizens. However, Rigsrevisionen has recently criticised the efficiency of Danish IT pro-jects (Statsrevisionerne, 2020). From 2011 to 2020, the state launched 115 IT projects with budgets of at least DKK 10 million (ca. €1.3 million). Rigsrevisionen studied 44 of these projects (all completed by late 2018), only half of which realised the planned revenues, and the ministry in question had not even calculated whether planned revenues had been achieved in one-third of them. The same picture is found on the municipal level (Fribo, 2018). According to the Local Government Denmark (KL) Technology Radar, which is a facility mapping the technologies used in the daily municipal operations regarding solutions to challenges regarding social, health, care and other welfare issues, positive business cases have been made regarding administration, logistics and planning. In relation to core services such as eldercare and primary school teaching, however, positive business cases have yet to be made (www.kl.dk/teknologier/kommunernes-teknologiradar).

This questions the overall goal of the decade-long reform strategy as well as the current notion of the Danish success found in the academic literature. Increasing social services costs also raise serious questions regarding the efficiency of the new digital governance. Danish municipalities have used digitalisation to establish a high degree of control and regulation based on the legal demands for documentation and the need to control costs. While legislative demands for documentation have been reached, social service costs continue to rise.

Continued Privacy Challenges: The End of Political Neutrality?

Issues like security, privacy and citizen rights have become key challenges as digitalisation has eased into everyday life, from back office to front office and more recently out of office. The digitalisation effort has been marked by a range of major public scandals in the Danish Tax Agency, the Health Platform, the Danish Defence surveillance scandal and the misuse of mobile phone data in court proceedings. In addition to raising questions regarding the efficiency of digitalisation, these events have also shaken the public trust. Coming from high levels of trust, citizen trust in the ability of public authorities to handle personal information is waning. The privacy discourse has also reached Denmark, partly inspired by the Silicon Valley tech backlash, partly by the introduction of the GDPR in 2018 and partly by homegrown Danish IT scandals. The partners in the digitalisation pact consider trust vital, forcing them to place greater emphasis on privacy issues. While Denmark may aspire to become a future leader on the privacy front, it would be wrong to claim that the country has been proactive on privacy issues. For many years, Danish digitalisation efforts focussed on efficiency but neglected security, privacy and citizen rights issues, and the Danish public authorities continue to walk a thin line between improving personalised services and violating privacy. Data collection and surveillance have been increased, ultimately on the behalf of citizen privacy. As mentioned, the digitalisation efforts suffer from a lack of public trust. Accordingly, the Danish way of doing digitalisation demonstrates how digitalisation can become counterproductive without privacy by design. This development challenges the nonpartisan political approach to digitalisation.

Transformation of the Role of Public Service Semi-professionals: Conflict versus Consensus?

The next frontier in the digitalisation effort involves AI elements, particularly predictive tools, which are currently very limited in the Danish welfare services. This is mostly due to legislation, although the 2018 Data Protection Law lays the groundwork for deploying such tools. The lack of AI tools and predictive tools may also be due to scepticism among professionals and even open resistance to deploying digital tools. Many professionals fear becoming what Bovens and Zouridis (2002) have coined 'production managers' in screen-level bureaucracies; that is, professionals mainly relying on digital tools, including tools that predict which services best solve citizens' challenges, and subsequently deliver the services prescribed by the tools. Obviously, professionals are going to perceive such a development as devaluing their key competences and position in the welfare state. Susskind and Susskind (2017) take this feared vision a step further, predicting that welfare professionals will be marginalised or even eliminated from street-level bureaucracy (Lipsky, 2010) once the digital tools have been fully developed. At the societal level, a new social contract among welfare professionals, administrators, citizens and politicians must therefore be reached.

Additional Points for Future Research

The Danish Society of Engineers (IDA) argues that the Danish CPR data security system is outdated and that it is too easy for public authorities to merge large data sets without proper citizen consent (Andersen, 2019). But what should replace the system? Considering the low level of security and the continued rapid pace and levels of ambition regarding digitalisation efforts, future security breaches are likely. Another overlooked issue in the literature is the changing role of Danish municipalities: The increased centralisation of social service production has changed the municipal remit. Will continued digitalisation efforts render Danish municipalities redundant as local polity, or can they re-invigorate this role? The role played by commercial enterprises also raises privacy concerns. Since the 1980s, private firms have had a high stake in back office, front office and out-of-office infrastructure. Many of the digital tools are developed by big tech firms and sold to the welfare state. The involvement of private companies in solving welfare challenges will probably increase. However, this development can become a challenge for transparency and accountability, raising further privacy concerns: Who owns the data in the partly privatised infrastructure? How can public authorities prevent personal data misuse when the data are stored in databases that may be located abroad?

Lessons Learned and Implications for Practice

Even though Denmark has topped rankings of international indices of digitalisation for years, it is unclear whether the promise of significant efficiency increases has materialised in the daily operations of welfare state institutions. To harvest such efficiency windfalls, several practical challenges and dilemmas must be dealt with:

(1) The Danish development demonstrates how it is counterproductive to sacrifice privacy concerns for efficiency. The inability of public authorities to handle privacy issues will lead to citizen distrust. The legitimacy of the digitalised governance system will suffer. Digitalisation efforts, especially the out-of-office efforts, cannot be pushed without a legitimate process.
(2) Danish legislation must be changed substantially to pave the way for the increased use of advanced digital tools in public welfare institutions. Privacy concerns in particular render this difficult.
(3) Algorithmic tools can be trusted to solve some tasks but not others. A cost-effective, 'moving' balance between 'old' and 'new' ways of producing and delivering public welfare services to citizens must therefore be found.
(4) In Denmark, the municipalities enjoy political and administrative autonomy in the production and delivery of most public welfare services to the citizenry. The combination of the municipal autonomy and responsibility for public welfare services has important consequences for the top-down implementation of digitalisation. This leaves the central government with two options: (1) It can reduce municipal autonomy substantially and continue the long tradition of top-down implementation of digitalisation or (2) the government can leave it to the municipalities to do the implementation bottom-up. The latter would represent a novel breach of decades of top-down strategies. One advantage of such a strategy might be that it could motivate the municipalities to promote the use of digital tools in everyday operations better than a top-down strategy.

These dilemmas illustrate that the days of high political consensus in the Danish digitalisation efforts may well be a thing of the past. They all illustrate how politics and the digitalisation of public services are highly interconnected and are no longer the isolated domain of specialised data experts and consultancy firms.

Other countries can learn four general lessons from the Danish experience: (1) Although a high level of digitalisation can be reached by applying a top-down, nonpartisan approach, digitalisation will always be political, (2) digitalisation experimentation – and failures – can come at a very high cost, (3) digitalisation efforts benefit greatly from citizen trust, especially out-of-office efforts and (4) the public legitimacy of digitalisation must be based on strong social and political accountability mechanisms.

Conclusion

Decades of digitalisation have changed the production, provision and distribution of welfare in the Danish public sector. The current ambition is to take public service from front office to 'out of office' by involving citizens directly in the collection of information, while digital tools are used to adjust citizen behaviour. These efforts have put Denmark at the top of world digitalisation rankings. The approach has increasingly been a centralised, party-neutral and consensual path that builds on a sharp distinction between politics and administration: Politicians decide on goals, administrators decide on technologies and how to accomplish goals. More recently, however, the overall goal of the digitalisation efforts – enhancing efficiency – has been questioned by Rigsrevisionen, the national auditing authority. And underneath the success of the Danish digital strategy lies a graveyard of digitalisation failures. These failures, not least in the Danish Tax Agency, have re-politicised the digital agenda to some degree, calling for a more politically accountable digitalisation effort. As digitalisation moves closer to the front office and the citizenry, the public interest also increases, and the legitimacy and accountability of digitalisation efforts have also become more politically important. Digitalisation now challenges ethical norms and individual privacy. Moreover, surveys reveal a decline in citizen trust in the ability of public authorities to handle personal data. This decline could very well be the result of failures and scandals as well as a more general neglect of security, privacy and citizen rights issues in the hunt for efficiency gains and personalised welfare production. Privacy is pivotal for maintaining the continued high levels of trust (despite recent setbacks) among Danish citizens. This culture of trust has been essential for the public acceptance of digitalisation efforts. Digitalisation also challenges the role of professions in the welfare production, especially professional autonomy. Technology must be legitimate in the eyes of both citizens and professionals to have a positive impact, which makes a new societal contract in Denmark necessary. Legislators must re-negotiate the structure of the digitalised welfare state so that welfare professionals, administrators and data analysts can collaborate on how to use digitalisation to solve challenges regarding welfare issues.

References

Aagaard, P. (2017). Den perfekte skandale – et casestudie af SKAT. In P. Aagaard & A. Agger (Eds.), *Ledelse i politisk styrede organisationer* (pp. 199–209). Copenhagen: Hans Reitzels.

Andersen, T. (2019). Jurist: Dataprofilering af langtidsledige med etnicitet er ulovlig. Ekspert: Det er diskrimination. Version2.

Borre, M. (2016). Historien om skandalen Skat: 9 ministere, 5000 færre ansatte og danskernes tabte milliarder. *Berlingske*.

Bovens, M., & Zouridis, S. (2002). From street-level to system-level bureaucracies: How information and communication technology is transforming administrative discretion and constitutional control. *Public Administration Review*, *62*(2), 174–184.

Breit, E., Egeland, C., & Løberg, I. B. (2019). Cyborg bureaucracy: Frontline work in digitalized labor and welfare services. In J. S. Pedersen & A. Wilkinson (Eds.), *Big data: Promise, application and pitfalls*. Cheltenham: Edward Elgar. doi:10.4337/9781788112352.00012

Brown, A., Chouldechova, A., Putnam-Hornstein, E., Tobin, A., & Vaithianathan, R. (2019). Toward algorithmic accountability in public services. In *CHI paper* (pp. 1–12). doi:10.1145/3290605.3300271

Busch, P. A., & Henriksen, H. Z. (2018). Digital discretion: A systematic literature review of ICT and street-level discretion. *Information Polity*. doi:10.3233/IP-170050

Danaher, J., Hogan, M. J., Noone, C., Kennedy, R., Behan, A., De Paor, A., … Shankar, K. (2017). Algorithmic governance: Developing a research agenda through the power of collective intelligence. *Big Data & Society*, *4*(2), 1–21. doi:10. 1177/2053951717726554

Department of Economic and Social Affairs. (2020). *E-government survey 2020*. New York, NY: UN. Retrieved from https://publicadministration.un.org/egovkb/Portals/egovkb/Documents/un/2020-Survey/2020%20UN%20e-government%20survey%20(Full%20Report).pdf

Desouza, K. C., & Jacob, B. (2017). Big data in the public sector: Lessons for practitioners and scholars. *Administration & Society*. doi:10.1177/0095399714555751

Digital Vækstpanel. (2017). Danmark som digital frontløber. Copenhagen.

Dunleavy, P., & Margetts, H. (2005). New Public Management is dead: Long live digital-era governance. *Journal of Public Administration Research and Theory*, *16*, 467–494. doi:10.1093/jopart/mui057

Dybkjær, L., & Lindegaard, J. (1999). *Det digitale Danmark: Omstilling til netværkssamfundet*. Copenhagen.

Eiriksson, B. A. (2019). *Udbetaling Danmarks systematiske overvågning*. Copenhagen: Justitia.

Ejersbo, N., & Greve, C. (2017). Digital era governance reform and accountability: The case of Denmark. In T. Christensen & P. Lægreid (Eds.), *The Routledge handbook to accountability and welfare state reforms in Europe* (pp. 267–279). London: Routledge.

Fastrup, N., Quass, L., Moltke, H., Nielsen, M. K., & Lindegaard, L. (2020). Ny afsløring: FE masseindsamler oplysninger om danskere gennem avanceret spionsystem. Retrieved from https://www.dr.dk/nyheder/indland/ny-afsloering-fe-masseindsamler-oplysninger-om-danskere-gennem-avanceret-spionsystem. Accessed on November 13, 2020.

Flyverbom, M., Deibert, R., & Matten, D. (2017). The governance of digital technology, big data, and the internet: New roles and responsibilities for business. *Business & Society*, 1–17. doi:10.1177/0007650317727540

Fribo, A. (2018). IT-projekter i København forsømmer business case og gevinstrealisering. Retrieved from https://www.version2.dk/artikel/it-projekter-koebenhavn-forsoemmer-business-case-gevinstrealisering-1085999. Accessed on November 13, 2020.

Gillingham, P. (2016). Predictive risk modelling to prevent child maltreatment and other adverse outcomes for service users: Inside the 'black box' of machine learning. *British Journal of Social Work*. doi:10.1093/bjsw/bcv031

Goos, S. (2019). Forstå skandalen om brugen af teledata. Retrieved from https://nyheder.tv2.dk/krimi/2019-10-04-forstaa-skandalen-om-brugen-af-teledata. Accessed on November 13, 2020.

Høybye-Mortensen, M. (2020). Sagsbehandlerens roller i den digitale forvaltning. In J. Hundebøl, A. S. Pors, & L. H. Sørensen (Eds.), *Digitalisering i offentlig forvaltning* (pp. 165–186). Frederiksberg: Samfundslitteratur.

Hundebøl, J., Pors, A. S., & Sørensen, L. H. (2020). *Digitalisering i offentlig forvaltning*. Frederiksberg: Samfundslitteratur.

Jæger, B. (2020). Digitalisering af den offentlige sektor i et historisk perspektiv. In J. Hundebøl, A. S. Pors, & L. H. Sørensen (Eds.), *Digitalisering i offentlig forvaltning* (pp. 31–50). Frederiksberg: Samfundslitteratur.

Jæger, B., & Löfgren, K. (2010). The history of the future: Changes in Danish e-government strategies 1994–2010. *Information Polity*, *15*(4), 253–269.

Jæger, B., & Pors, A. S. (2017). Ledelse af digitalisering: Fra projekt til præmis. In P. Aagaard & A. Agger (Eds.), *Ledelse i politisk styrede organisationer*. Copenhagen: Hans Reitzels.

Lehmann, C. (2020). Ulovlige dataoverførsler fortsatte i næsten et år trods henvendelse fra Datatilsynet. Retrieved from https://www.altinget.dk/forskning/artikel/ulovlige-dataoverfoersler-fortsatte-i-naesten-et-aar-trods-henvendelse-fra-datatilsynet. Accessed on November 13, 2020.

Lipsky, M. (2010). *Street-level bureaucracy: Dilemmas of the individual in public services*. New York, NY: Russell Sage.

Lupton, D. (2015). *Digital sociology*. London: Routledge.

Margetts, H., & Dorobantu, C. (2019). Rethink government with AI. *Nature*, *568*(7751), 163–165. doi:10.1038/d41586-019-01099-5

Mayer-Schönberger, V., & Cukier, K. (2013). *Big data: A revolution that will transform how we live, work, and think*. Boston, MA: Houghton Mifflin Harcourt.

Metcalf, J., & Crawford, K. (2016). Where are human subjects in big data research? The emerging ethics divide. *Big Data & Society*. doi:10.1177/2053951716650211

Ministeriet for Videnskab Teknologi og Udvikling. (2001). *IT for alle: Danmarks fremtid*. Copenhagen.

Mølsted, H. (2019). DI og regioner vil skabe en førende sundheds-it-nation: Nu skal alskens sundhedsregistre kobles sammen. Version2.

OECD. (2010). *Efficient e-government for smarter public service delivery Denmark 2010*. Paris. Retrieved from https://www.oecd.org/gov/digital-government/45382562.pdf

Olling, J. (2018). De første år med Sundhedsplatformen: Her var udfordringerne med systemet. Retrieved from https://www.tv2east.dk/region-sjaelland/det-forste-ar-med-sundhedsplatformen-her-var-udfordringerne-med-systemet. Accessed on November 13, 2020.

Pasquale, F. (2015). *The black box society*. Cambridge MA: Harvard University Press. doi:10.4159/harvard.9780674736061

Pedersen, J. S., & Wilkinson, A. (2019). *Big data: Promise, application and pitfalls*. Cheltenham: Edward Elgar.

Pors, A. S., & Ejersbo, N. (2020). Offentlig styring i den digitaliserede forvaltning. In J. Hundebøl, A. S. Pors, & L. H. Sørensen (Eds.), *Digitalisering i offentlig forvaltning* (pp. 31–54). Frederiksberg: Samfundslitteratur.

Rasmussen, N., & Klit, M. L. (2020). Brug af big data og kunstig intelligens i den offentlige forvaltning. In J. Hundebøl, A. S. Pors, & L. H. Sørensen (Eds.), *Digitalisering i offentlig forvaltning* (pp. 223–243). Frederiksberg: Samfundslitteratur.

Ritzau (2018). Pape efter LA-kritik af dataforslag: Vi er jo ikke DDR. *Berlingske*. Retrieved from https://www.berlingske.dk/politik/pape-efter-la-kritik-af-data-forslag-vi-er-jo-ikke-ddr

Statsrevisionerne. (2020). Rigsrevisionens beretning om IT gevinstrealisering. Copenhagen.

Susskind, R., & Susskind, R. (2017). *The future of the professions: How technology will transform the work of human experts.* Oxford: Oxford Univerisity Press.

Tassy, A., Nielsen, M. B., & Jakobsen, D. T. (2020). *IT-anvendelse i befolkningen 2019.* Copenhagen: Statistics Denmark. Retrieved from http://www.dst.dk/Publ/ItBefolkning

Zuboff, S. (2019). *Surveillance capitalism: The fight for the future at the new frontier of power.* London: Profile Books.

Section IV
Climate Change and Biodiversity

Chapter 9

Climate Politics and Renewable Energy in Denmark 1975–2020

Karsten Bruun Hansen and Peter Enevoldsen

Abstract

Sustainable energy has been on the political agenda in Denmark for decades. This chapter will highlight how wind turbine production quite unforeseen became a great success in Denmark before the turn of the Millennium. An integrative public leadership approach using a mix of supportive institutional designs and instruments, combined with an unexpected bottom-up pressure for alternatives to nuclear power, promoted ways for wind turbine innovation and production in the 1970s. After the turn of the Millennium, being a huge financial success creating many new jobs and export has it developed into a cluster based on huge investments and professionalised developers. The comprehensive transition of wind turbine production in Denmark, from small scale to large scale, has however provided a counterproductive decrease in community commitment for local renewable energy production.

Denmark is known internationally as a climate frontrunner and not only due to wind turbine production and planning. The status is obtained by polycentric governance applied in cooperative-owned energy systems. The Danish response to climate change is a concerted effort of a plethora of public and private actors, providing a crucial momentum and robustness in climate politics not at least generated from a genuine civic society involvement. 'The Danish Energy Model'; a withhold strategic effort to combine ambitious renewable energy goals, energy efficiency targets and political support of technical and industrial development has for four decades, succeeded in providing high levels of cheap energy supply, while partly reducing fossil fuel dependency at the same time.

Keywords: Climate politics in Denmark; the Danish energy model; renewable energy from below; wind turbine innovation and production; cooperative-owned energy companies; community commitment

Public Governance in Denmark, 149–167
Copyright © 2022 by Emerald Publishing Limited
All rights of reproduction in any form reserved
doi:10.1108/978-1-80043-712-820221009

Introduction

According to the Paris Agreement (2015), global warming is a massive, manmade crisis.[1] Despite the COVID-19 pandemic, global greenhouse gas (GHG) emissions continue to increase (IEA, 2021), jeopardising future generations if global temperatures rise over 1.5–2.0 degrees Celsius. In 2020, the COVID-19 crisis triggered the largest annual drop in global energy–related CO_2 emissions since World War II. The overall estimated decline of about 6% during 2020 is in line with the COP21 recommendations for GHG cuts *every* year, but global emissions rebounded in December 2020, an estimated 2% higher (60 million tonnes) than in December 2019.

For decades, the UN has urgently recommended substituting fossil fuels with renewable energy sources, but hitherto with limited success. All countries must promote fossil-free energy production and consumption if global warming is to be kept below recommended UN limits.

Sustainable energy has been on the political agenda in Denmark for decades, which renders the lessons learned in Denmark interesting for other countries. This chapter will provide insights into these lessons and bring new perspectives to the table. It will highlight how wind turbine production unexpectedly became a rather great success in Danish climate and energy politics before the turn of the millennium. In Denmark, an integrative public leadership approach (Crosby & Bryson, 2010) using a mix of supportive institutional designs and instruments combined with unexpected bottom-up, polycentric pressure for alternatives to nuclear power promoted wind turbine innovation and production in the 1970s. Since the turn of the Millennium, the wind sector has become a huge financial success and created many new jobs and exports, and it has developed into a cluster or sub-sector based on massive investments and professionalised developers.

However, the comprehensive transition of wind turbine production in Denmark from small scale to large scale, not least regarding investments and financing, has resulted in a counterproductive decrease in community commitment regarding renewable energy production.

The early interest in and success of wind power were not seen in the other Scandinavian countries, such as Sweden, where wind resources are otherwise comparable to Denmark (Enevoldsen, 2016). In some countries, such as Germany and the United States, large companies made massive investments in the 1970s–80s in wind turbine development, but none of them with success similar to the trial-and-error, low-cost innovation and implementation in Denmark. Some research has been dedicated to understanding how Denmark succeeded in forming an apparently 'unplanned' wind turbine cluster (Karnøe & Garud, 2012) and became a global wind turbine pioneer. Scholars such as Meyer (2007) have suggested explanations to this paradox primarily in terms of differences in leadership and technological approaches, facilitated by national energy policies supporting and stabilising the development of more sustainable energy systems in Denmark. By applying historical and bottom-up perspectives, we reveal this not to be the whole story. We argue that public commitment (e.g. from laypeople) is crucial to understanding the Danish success.

Denmark currently enjoys international renown as a climate front runner; also for more than wind turbine production. This status has been achieved via the polycentric, multi-level development and government approach (Vedeld, Hofstad, Solli, & Sandkjær, 2021) that initiated the development of 'the Danish Energy Model' in the 1980s. The Danish model consists of a strategic effort to combine ambitious renewable energy goals, energy efficiency targets and political support for technical and industrial development. Over the course of four decades, Denmark has developed a model that produces cheap energy supply while partly reducing fossil fuel dependency. Since 1990, Denmark has reduced adjusted GHG emissions by approximately 40% (Danish Energy Board, 2020), albeit relying on a rather problematic degree of wood-based biomass conversion of combined power and heating plants. Biomass has been questioned worldwide by environmental NGOs in the late 2010s, as this conversion presumably emits more GHGs than do fossil fuels such as coal and oil (e.g. Beddington et al., 2018).

The three-legged foundation of the Danish Energy Model – renewable energy, energy efficiency and system integration (electrification), and cleantech innovation – is key to understanding the Danish success. The facilitation of public–private cooperation, coupled with stable political and regulatory integrative frameworks, has for decades fostered important innovations and breakthroughs in new Danish energy solutions. These solutions include widespread efficient, decentralised district heating systems operating in most Danish municipalities. The extensive use of decentralised combined heat and power (CHP) production in consumer- or public-owned district heating systems and organisations has allowed Denmark to integrate large amounts of wind into the energy grid together with large amounts of cheap biomass. Conversion to biomass in Danish CHP stations has tripled in the last 20 years (DEB, 2018).

Although the Danish government decided in 2020 to end all of its oil and gas exploration in the North Sea by 2050, putting pressure on other large oil producers such as Norway and Great Britain, questions continue to be raised in the popular debate if Denmark should be termed a climate frontrunner nation regarding renewable energy production and climate-friendly consumption. Environmental NGOs are critical of why 64% (2018) of all renewable energy consumed in Denmark is from imported, wood-based biomass (Information, 2021).

This chapter describes how, 30–40 years ago, polycentric, bottom-up commitment dramatically changed the Danish heating and electricity sector. In the early 1980s, the Danish energy system was based on coal and Danish-produced natural gas. We will unfold how a rather surprising bottom-up engagement in wind energy emerged in opposition to the prevailing interest of the Folketing, the Confederation of Danish Industry and the trade union movement, which were otherwise working with plans for the rapid implementation of nuclear power plants after the first OPEC-induced energy crisis in the winter of 1973/74 (Meyer, 2007).

The analysis below posits that there are more perspectives to bring forth to understand the successes and failures of the Danish Energy model, especially regarding renewable energy.[2] We will focus on important implications for maintaining the extraordinary results regarding wind turbine innovation. We believe that many countries can learn applicable lessons from the last years of the past millennium regarding wind energy production in Denmark. We also claim that current climate and energy policy in Denmark could learn from the previous period to promote important implications for cleantech innovation and renewable energy production.

After interviewing some 30 central actors, we have analysed how one of the most hotly debated topics in Denmark – nuclear power planning in the 1970s – made wind turbines a power source supported broadly by local actors and laypeople for several decades throughout most of Denmark.

Danish Climate Politics

To understand the context and important aspects of climate policy in Denmark in the early 2020s, we begin by analysing what happened after the 2019 Folketing election, which has since come to be referred to as 'the Climate Election'. In agreement with almost all of the parties in the Folketing, the new Social Democratic government adopted binding climate legislation in the summer of 2020 aimed at cutting 70% of CO_2 emissions before 2030 (ca. 21 million tonnes CO_2 annually). 'Climate' was evaluated as one of the most important topics in this election. In the spring of 2021, however, the Government was criticised for only deploying roughly one-third of the 70/30 goal (Energywatch, 2020). The (internal) public government advisor, 'the Danish Council on Climate Change' (Klimarådet), issued a status report declaring that the official GHG reduction target for 2030 will not be met unless the government prioritises climate mitigation higher.[3] Besides high COVID-19 expenditures, the government claims that climate-related costs in the early 2020s will result in lost jobs and that green taxes may exacerbate social inequalities (Ritzau, 2020). To fulfil the 70/30 goal, the Danish government therefore placed its trust in the development of innovative technologies in the late 2020s, including immature technologies such as 'Power to X' and 'Carbon Capture Utilisation'. Independent energy experts question if this allows sufficient time to develop these expensive and rather questionable technologies (Information, 2020). Laypeople, NGOs and researchers are criticising the government for not increasing investments in more mature technologies, such as photovoltaic cells, large heating pumps, geo-thermal power and further electrification. At the same time, large (international) energy companies, such as Better Energy and European Energy, started organising large-scale solar cell farms in many municipalities in Denmark in 2018. Local communities have nevertheless criticised these large-scale energy investment projects for insufficient citizen ownership and involvement (Nielsen, 2020).

We draw on two strands of theory in our exploration of the Danish wind energy success: climate governance theory and polycentric theory. Climate governance theory is used to analyse the integrative dimensions regarding hori zontal and vertical mainstreaming in multi-level governance approaches (van der Heijden et al., 2019). Elinor Ostrom's polycentric 'theory' (2010a, p. 552) is used to analyse the climate governance landscape and modes of operation as "interconnected, evolving polycentric systems from below". Ostrom (2010b) state that many actors, NGOs, universities, private companies, charities etc., for many years, below, to the side and besides national and international bodies, are directly involved in governing climate change. Ostrom (2009) describes this as 'polycentric', as based on bottom-up self-organisation involving a greater variety of actors and institutions operating on multiple levels in opposition to (or in balance with) monocentric, top-down governance approaches (van der Heijden, 2018). The polycentric–monocentric axis is not either–or; rather, it is always a balance, in one direction or the other, possibly mirroring the pre-dominant governance paradigm, embedded context and specific leaders. Climate change is addressed in various fragmented ways, with overlapping multiple centres working across many geographical levels, which renders it polycentric in nature (Abbott, 2018). In an anthology edited by Jordan, Huitema, Schoenefeld, van Asselt, and Forster (2018), polycentric climate governance is conceptualised as consisting of a set of five intertwined theoretical propositions able to describe and explain the climate governance landscape and as prescribing how to make it function more effectively in terms of reduced GHG emissions. The propositions are: (1) self-organised 'local action', (2) 'mutual adjustment', (3) 'experimentation', (4) 'trust' and (5) 'overarching rules/targets'. In this chapter, polycentric theory is applied as a framework for understanding in greater detail how and why Danish wind turbine innovation and implementation, against all odds, became a rather impressive success, not least for Danish exports.

In 2019, more than 47% of the electricity consumed in Denmark was produced by wind turbines (see Fig. 1), and days where 100% of the electricity consumed in the country is produced by wind are no longer unusual. There are days where Denmark actually exports wind-produced electricity e.g. to Germany and Norway (Winddenmark, 2020). That same year, Denmark exported wind turbine technology for €14.3 billion.[4] Wind turbine technology exports have increased by about 60% since 2010 and have become one of the most important Danish exports. As of 2021, Denmark has more than 4,000 large onshore wind turbines and 558 offshore wind turbines (see Fig. 2). The total number is expected to decrease in the years to come due to a repowering strategy favouring larger, more efficient wind turbines.

To unfold how Denmark became a wind turbine pioneer in greater detail, our historical analysis focuses on the two important aspects unfolded below.

The Emergence of Wind Energy in Denmark

The status of Denmark as a wind power pioneer can be traced back to the work of Poul la Cour at Askov Folk High School in the 1890s. La Cour was a Danish meteorologist, inventor and folk high school teacher. His local experiments

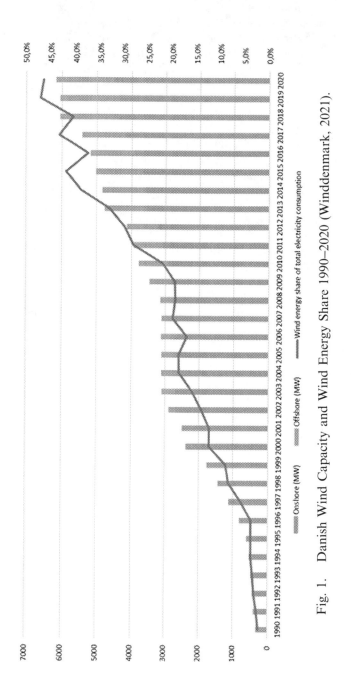

Fig. 1.   Danish Wind Capacity and Wind Energy Share 1990–2020 (Winddenmark, 2021).

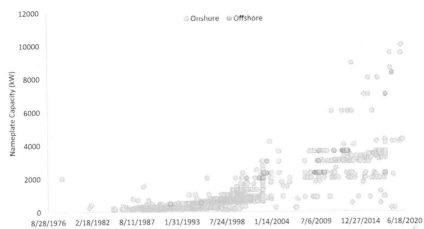

Fig. 2.   An Overview of Development in Installed Nameplate
Capacity (kW) of Danish Wind Turbines in the Period 1978–2020. *Source:*
Data collected from the Danish Energy Agency (2020).

included the conversion of classical windmills to produce DC electricity. La Cour
even used electrolysis to store energy in the form of hydrogen to light the school
where he was working. He was highly determined to find sources capable of
providing rural, 'self-organised', small-scale electricity plants based on cooperative principles (Petersen, 2018). As described below, there are several polycentric
propositions at stake here, including the self-organisation, local action and
experimentation criteria.

At the folk high school, la Cour educated young men to become what he called
'countryside electricians' or 'wind electricians', skilled at establishing small-scale
cooperative power plants. Although the combustion engine and cheap diesel
outcompeted wind power in the 1910s, many such wind electricians were mobilised and became skilled at planning local cooperative power plants, including
wind turbine construction. Some of these men improved on la Cour's inventions
in the following decades.

In 1903, la Cour established the Danish 'Wind Turbine Organization', the
mission of which was to disseminate knowledge about how to erect wind turbines.
Based on la Cour's expertise, a company on the island of Fuen started producing
the 30 kW 'Lykkegaard wind turbine', which was erected on many sites
throughout the country during World War II due to oil shortages.

After World War II, cheaper fossil fuel prices undermined the Danish interest
in wind energy. In the early 1950s, however, a chief engineer for a large power
company who was reaching retirement age, Johannes Juul, returned to his old
interest in wind energy, which he had originally picked up in one of la Cour's
courses in 1903. Juul constructed a number of experimental machines and became

the first to connect a wind turbine with an AC generator to the electricity grid. In 1956, Juul built the first Gedser wind turbine, erected with Marshall Fund support, which became a pioneering design for modern wind turbines. For many years, the 200 kW Gedser turbine remained the largest in the world. It operated without any major maintenance issues for 11 years but abandoned in the late 1960s. Nonetheless, the turbine was refurbished in the mid-1970s at the request of the US Energy Research Development Agency (ERDA), which needed performance and measurement results for a new US programme for the construction of large turbines. The Gedser machine subsequently operated for another three years, giving Denmark and ERDA important knowledge about 'The Danish Concept' regarding wind turbine production and maintenance. The Gedser Mill concept boiled down to three blades on a horizontal axis in an up-wind position. An asynchronous generator and stall regulation were further developed step by step by *local* industrial entrepreneurs in the mid-1970s, experimenting from the outset with rather small turbines (ca. 22 kW) (Petersen, 2018). In other countries, such as the US, Sweden and Germany, researchers developed large-scale wind turbines, whereas the Danish craftsmen and small companies were developing these rather small-scale machines and applying learning-by-doing and trial-and-error principles.

But few of these small industrial entrepreneurs and craftsmen in the 1970s survived in the longer term – they were financially vulnerable despite the introduction of public economic support schemes in the late 1970s, which were partly the result of the popular resistance to nuclear power. We now turn to the second historical aspect.

The Energy Crisis in the 1970s Accelerates Wind Turbine Experimentation

The energy crises in 1973 and 1979 were wake-up calls for new strategic political decisions regarding energy production and consumption, as Denmark relied almost entirely on (OPEC) oil imports at the time. In the winter of 1973–1974, oil shortages resulted in 11 car-free Sundays. The Folketing reached agreement on a systemic transition to nuclear power supplemented by natural gas and oil, the latter two from the Danish part of the North Sea, which was urgently required to secure an energy supply and low prices to maintain the national wealth and welfare (Meyer, 2004).

Nuclear Power versus Renewable Energy

Simultaneously, only 20 km from the Danish capital, on the Swedish side of the Øresund strait, the Swedish authorities constructed Barsebäck, a large nuclear power plant that was visible from Copenhagen on clear days. Two newly established Danish NGOs – the Organisation against Nuclear Power (OOA) and the Organization for Renewable Energy (OVE) – criticised the location of a nuclear plant so close to Copenhagen. They succeeded in mobilising broad engagement in the early 1970s against nuclear power and for renewable energy, notably sun and wind power. Although the Folketing, the Confederation of Danish Industry and the trade union movement had all agreed on plans for the development of nuclear power, the majority of Danes soon came to share the NGOs' anxiety. By 1976, the resistance to Danish – and Swedish – nuclear power plants was manifest in demonstrations and protest marches. This unexpected popular reaction forced the authorities to find alternatives to nuclear power, such as natural gas, oil and coal, and renewable energy sources (albeit reluctantly) became part of the national political agenda. Just as politicians after the 2019 elections were forced to implement an ambitious climate law, the politicians of the late 1970s suddenly found renewable energy to have become a high priority on their agenda due to bottom-up pressures.

OOA and OVE diligently worked the public media, framing renewable energy as David versus Goliath, the huge, evil 'expensive and unsecure energy solutions', which lacked transparency and democratic legitimacy. In this context, Goliath was the Folketing, the Confederation of Danish Industry, Danish Energy (the largest energy companies) and the trade union movement. OOA and OVE engaged in dialogue with farmers, a culture valuing cooperative and private ownership still existing in the Danish countryside, seeing itself in opposition to large energy companies.

What made OOA and OVE so influential was also that craftsmen and workers supported their statements in the media regarding more environmentally benign energy production and locally owned, small-scale energy solutions. OVE was able to establish local 'collaborative energy offices' in almost all regions of Denmark, in many places at folk high schools, providing technical knowledge about how to realise local renewable projects, primarily based on cooperative principles. A new organisation, Danish Wind turbine owners (DV), was born in 1978, in some respects a child of OVE, providing knowledge about the construction and operation of small wind turbines.

The large energy companies were (and still are) primarily consumer- or public-owned. Many were the offspring of the early cooperative movement but had been thoroughly institutionalised and professionalised. In late 1970s, around 100 energy companies operated in Denmark. Following the energy crisis and the EU's liberation of the sector, the companies started merging in the early 1990s and coordinated their activities in two national organisations, Elsam (West Denmark) and Elkraft (East Denmark), which aimed at securing stable supply and low prices. Hence, in the decades to come, after operating the largest power plants in Denmark in rather *monocentric* and professionalised ways, Elsam and Elkraft often questioned if wind power was the best and cheapest solution. They were generally sceptical of the prospects for Danish wind power, as they also suspected politicians and other actors of deviating from plans or solutions, 'interfering' in their rather monocentric and monopolistic energy planning in Denmark. Nonetheless, being publicly owned, the energy companies had to accept guidelines from their boards with e.g. municipal mayors, demanding leeway for renewable energy experimentation (Petersen, 2018).

The Danish Academy of Technical Sciences (ATV) also played an important role in the gradually shifting energy strategies. They provided prompt support to the financially vulnerable, small-scale wind turbine entrepreneurs of the mid-1970s. ATV was able to impact national energy and environmental policies. One person in particular, ATV President Professor Niels I. Meyer, has been crucial to Danish wind turbine progress in the early, vulnerable phase. Having read Meadows' *Limits to Growth* (1972), Meyer abandoned a promising career as vice-chancellor at the Technical University of Denmark, to become a researcher – and an environmental activist on the side – focusing on alternative renewable energy sources. The large Danish energy companies demanded that Meyer be removed as DATS president (Meyer, 2020). Before being dismissed, however, Meyer established DATS working groups and committees focusing on the potential for wind power in the Danish energy system. He successfully used his position and personal network to make renewable energy 'acceptable' and 'interesting' for some parties in the Folketing, not least two centrist parties (the Social Democrats and Social Liberals) and the left-of-centre parties. In the 1980s, Meyer was appointed chairman of a government committee established to promote renewable energy in the Danish energy grid. In the late 1980s, the committee also promoted new offshore windfarm programmes to overcome foreseen obstacles, such as complaints from neighbours regarding onshore turbines. As wind power economics improved during the 1980s, the subsidies were gradually reduced and finally eliminated in 1989.

The prevailing integrative governance and public leadership approach (Crosby & Bryson, 2010) in Denmark, based on a strong institutional design and multiple instruments and incitements, was reinforced in 1993, when a powerful, unified Environmental and Energy Ministry was headed by Svend Auken, a charismatic and highly climate engaged Social Democrat. Although New Public Management–inspired professionalism and market liberalisation were evident, universities, NGOs, folk high schools, the cooperative movement and small Danish industrial entrepreneurs/companies had crucial shares in what may be denoted a polycentric/co-creational approach. This comprises of the promotion of several of the core principles of polycentric actions, including self-organised local action, experimentation, mutual adjustment, trust and overarching rules. By combining an integrative governance approach with a polycentric – some say co-creational (Sørensen & Torfing, 2020) – governance and leadership approach, Denmark paved the path to success for small, locally or regionally owned innovative wind turbine producers (Petersen, 2018). 'Local action', in terms of local, self-organised industrial entrepreneurs who were experimenting with step-by-step learning-by-doing were observable until the late 1990s, as opposed to the large-scale strategic planning seen in the US, Sweden and Germany.

Due to the lack of a national strategic master plan and roadmap for implementation, some scholars have attributed the Danish wind turbine success to 'good luck'. On the contrary, we interpret it as an example of a successful, combined top-down integrative and polycentric bottom-up practice, where mutual adjustment, action and trust are supported by financial incentives and public quality testing programmes. It has been crucial in Denmark to secure stable frames for an ongoing evolution of larger and larger machines developed throughout the 1980s–90s. Quality proof standards, or 'overarching rules' in Ostrom's (2010a) terminology, in this case means that all wind turbines should be certificated at the national test laboratory, launched at the Risø National Laboratory, previously a nuclear test facility. This was important to secure market credibility, preventing sub-standard technologies from being marketed at home and abroad (van Est, 1999). According to a law passed in 1979, private wind turbine investors were reimbursed 30% of the turbine's price *if* the machine was certified by the Risø Laboratory (Meyer, 2004).

There were many disagreements in this period between utilities/energy companies and local wind turbine owners/producers regarding prices for grid connection and tariffs. This was solved in 1992 by a national regulation giving turbine owners attractive prices and a tax refund, which triggered dramatic growth in land-based wind capacity throughout the 1990s (Beuse et al., 2000). The predominance of consumer/public ownership of the energy companies meant that the authorities could require companies to accept attractive grid connection prices and tariffs to wind turbine owners. Consequently, the energy companies had to pay for part of the grid connection for added local wind turbines, and the energy companies and private investors took over the erection of wind turbines, as the necessary investment increased together with the increasing size of the wind turbines.

In sum, despite almost all of the influential players in Danish society in the 1970s preferring nuclear power, it was rejected by a broad popular majority, primarily 'orchestrated' by two newly established NGOs: OOA and OVE. They succeeded in organising, informing and educating laypeople in a rather complicated (energy) topic, and mobilised many citizens committed to propel more environmentally benign energy sources (Nielsen, 2020). The planning for nuclear power in the 1970s led to a significant, widespread debate about more benign renewable energy alternatives. Ultimately, the Folketing abandoned nuclear power in 1985 (Petersen, 2018) and, rather surprisingly, wind turbines became a sunrise industry in Denmark with broad public engagement for the next two decades.

Accompanied by supportive public structures and funding, an integrative and polycentric public governance and leadership approach made a significant difference for small Danish wind turbine entrepreneurs and producers in the first phase (1975–1995). As we interpret it in this in generally accepted narrative, however, there is one pivotal aspect that is partly neglected but nevertheless important to understand the Danish success more profoundly.

Local Engagement, Local Ownership

Almost 80% of the Danish population supported wind power in the early 1990s (Damborg, 1999). This is often attributed to the fact that most Danish wind turbines at the time were partly owned by private households, often organised in neighbourhood cooperatives. Noise, flicker effects and the visual pollution of a turbine are presumably easier to accept if you benefit directly from the electricity it generates.

As Fig. 3 visualises, the number of onshore turbines increased rapidly in the late 1990s. Despite efforts to separate dwellings and turbines through municipal planning, more groups vocally opposed wind energy, and some media, primarily right-of-centre newspapers, were eager to disseminate these 'scandals'. Wind power became a political and ideological issue, where mainly right-of-centre opponents declared sustainable energy to be too expensive compared to fossil fuels (Petersen, 2018). In parallel, wind turbines were growing in size, making them more efficient. The signs of the future wind turbines were already established more than four decades earlier when the first multi-megawatt turbine was commercialised in Denmark in 1978 (see Fig. 2) with a nameplate capacity of 2 MW and a 54 m hub height (Nissen & Christensen, 2009). Nevertheless, this turbine was ahead of its time, and turbines with 600–1,000 kWh capacities first became the new normal in the mid-1990s.

Large wind turbines were much more costly to develop and produce, which demanded professional (international) investor groups. But as the investor-owned turbines grew, so did the numbers of complaints regarding onshore machines. This also partly explains why large wind turbine farms were placed offshore. Vindeby, the first such offshore windfarm, was erected in Danish waters in 1991.

Figs. 2 and 3 illustrate the increasing physical size and nameplate capacity of all of the Danish wind turbines. Every Danish wind turbine commercialised with a nameplate capacity of >99 kW has been included, resulting in data points from 5,919 onshore and 558 offshore wind turbines in the period 1978–2020.

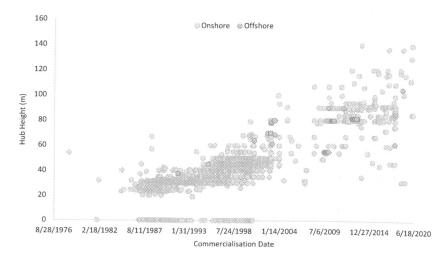

Fig. 3.   An Overview of Development in Hub Heights (m) of Danish Wind Turbines in the Period 1978–2020. *Source:* Data collected from the Danish Energy Agency (2020).

The figures confirm existing research on the clear global trend of increasing wind turbine sizes. Closer examination of the figures also reveals a pattern of fewer but larger wind turbines being installed in Denmark, which is also seen in other countries (Enevoldsen, Valentine, & Sovacool, 2018).

Not only did larger wind turbines require larger investments, these large-scale building projects also required professional developers and large-scale entrepreneurs. This resulted in more critical public attitudes towards wind turbines, at least in some regions of Denmark. Especially after 2009, when 150m-tall multi-megawatt turbines were erected, more local communities became critical, perhaps also because they were not a part of the projects (Enevoldsen & Xydis, 2019).

Local ownership had been a key topic when securing community acceptance in the 1980–1990s (Baark, 1997). The ownership structures changed dramatically after the turn of the century, when politicians removed the requirement that turbine owners should live close to the machine. The numbers of community cooperatives decreased considerably. Erecting a wind turbine had become a large-scale investment and technical, complicated project, now primarily carried out by professional developers. Nonetheless, some large-scale onshore and offshore windfarm projects were still partly locally owned due to legal regulations until 2020.[5] Although it is possible to find partly community-owned projects until June 2020, wealthy (international) investors, developers and/or energy companies had and have the economic and organisational muscles to conduct multi-megawatt building project. Since June 2020, it is no longer mandatory to offer local citizens the opportunity to buy at least 20% of the project.

Sovacool and Blyth (2015) found that more than one-third of the Danish population believed that local energy and climate plans 'had not gone far enough'. It is important to foster commitment when seeking wind power acceptance and the successful implementation and integration of renewables from a theoretical standpoint (Sovacool & Ratan, 2012). This commitment can be divided into three levels of acceptance: socio-political, market and community acceptance (Wüstenhagen, Wolsink, & Bürer, 2007).

A 2020 dispute on the Danish island of Bornholm offers an illustrative example. Citizens and local actors planned a 100% community-owned 100 MW offshore wind project. However, it was rejected due to interference with a Danish government–backed, large-scale 2 GW offshore wind project, adopted to reach the new Danish Climate Act goal (2020). While the 2 GW 'Energy Island' and large offshore windfarms are seen as important solutions, providing 100% renewable, cheap energy, it is also worth noting how the 'Danish Model' is now partly moving offshore and large scale, relying on huge investments and professional developers. This seems to collide with the third level of acceptance: community commitment to renewable energy production.

Another interesting example was an onshore wind project in Hirtshals harbour in Jutland in 2019, where local community members were invited to buy shares in a wind turbine. More than 218% of the originally allocated shares were bought up by locals, and the project became the first to be commercialised without financial support from the Danish state (TV2Nord, 2019). This demonstrates how local engagement is possible and wanted in large-scale energy projects, and that deliberative political (economic) regulations on ownership possibly foster increased commitment on the crucial community level.

Discussion and Lessons Learned

The Danish integrative and polycentric governance and leadership approach in environmental and climate politics in the 1970s–1990s was comprised of dialogue mechanisms involving many relevant actors, which, according to polycentric theory, enhance local action, experimentation, innovation and trust. And that was exactly what happened. The distributive and integrative governance approaches included not only the industry, energy companies and the trade union movement, but also environmental groups, other citizen groups and independent experts (Wallace, 1995) – *because of* the bottom-up mobilisation.

As NGOs, OOA and OVE seem to be good examples of what polycentric theory denote bottom-up self-organisation. At the same time, OOA and OVE also *facilitated* more self-organised local action and education. These two NGOs became central actors in energy planning in the 1970–1980s. They are great examples of what Ostrom (2010a) termed self-organised 'experimenters'. They applied skillful *dialogical*, face-to-face communication and were able to bridge socio-cultural changes between scholars, farmers and workers, for example. In the popular debate, OOA and OVE often succeeded in taking the role as 'David', giving the impression that their counterpart, 'Goliath' – the government and large energy companies – was trying to neglect small-scale, locally owned energy solutions.

Polycentric self-organised governance and planning approaches are not always the best solution to wicked societal issues; there are many factors in play, including context, time and topic. Nevertheless, in the 1980s, the large energy companies had to accept guidelines from their public board members and politicians demanding space for *long*-term experiments regarding the promotion of renewable energy sources. The energy companies were public- or consumer-owned and had started many years earlier as small cooperatives. On the liberalised energy market in the 1990s, they were merged and demanded a strong focus on price and supply security, but not exclusively. They were – and are still today – guided mainly by publicly designated (political) board members. Although the energy companies have grown large and are highly professionalised, they are often consumer-owned, and the companies are generally acknowledged as being loyal public service providers (Petersen, 2018). Hence, the governance approaches applied in Denmark may be seen as a balance between two poles: the polycentric–monocentric axis. Applied governance approaches are always a balance; in this case, a balance mainly leaning towards the former pole before the turn of the Millennium and primarily against the monocentric pole after the turn.

From the mid to late 1990s, the Danish state and energy companies again took a more predominant role in national energy and climate planning, being professionalised actors on a liberalised energy market. The Danish state also assumed a key role on the international stage to promote renewable energy. The national authorities guaranteed the financing of new, large-scale wind turbine projects carried out by private Danish companies worldwide. However, the decrease in NGO and public engagement in renewable energy implementation in the late 1990s could partly be interpreted as a result of a more professional, more monocentric approach in large, merged energy companies and ministries. Local action, experimentation and local engagement came to play a less significant role after the mid-1990s, when wind turbine projects became large-scale technical investments on a liberalised energy market.

The introduction of wind power on a commercial scale in Denmark in the 1980s received acceptance on all three levels (Wüstenhagen et al., 2007). Wind power (1) received adequate political and economic support and attention, (2) developed into an attractive energy solution on the market, as one of the main growth sectors in the Danish economy, and, finally, (3) was perceived as a greater community good and subjected to comprehensive community support.

It is therefore interesting to acknowledge how, despite the successful upscaling of wind turbine production in the 1990s, wind power in Denmark lost social acceptance after the turn of the Millennium, presumably due to missing community acceptance. Kirkegaard, Cronin, Nyborg and Karnoe (2020) explain that social opposition to wind power in Denmark not only has to do with the usual nimbyism, but also with the liberalisation of the energy markets and increasing commercialisation in the industry, resulting in communities being marginalised in the decision-making processes and ownership. Considering results from Sovacool and Blyth (2015), the truth is probably hidden in the relationship between nimbyism and the maturing and upscaling of the wind industry. Expanding market demands for cheap energy have resulted in larger turbines with greater visual impact, which has made it more difficult for local investors to take part in wind turbine development and construction (Enevoldsen & Sovacool, 2016), although law regulation made it possible until mid-2020. A predominantly professionalised, monocentric governance and leadership approach focusing on low prices and supply security on a free, commercialised energy market seems to neglect the importance of the broader social acceptance of renewable energy production in Denmark.

An important lesson for decision-makers is that the Danish model consists of a hybrid integrative and polycentric governance approach, a balancing between bottom-up and top-down governance approaches. The success criteria for the transition towards renewables in the 1980s was mainly based on experimentation, local self-organisation and action, trust and interconnectivity between manufacturers, suppliers, policymakers and, not least, energy consumers and ordinary people, mobilised by two NGOs. If nothing else, the Danish cooperative and polycentric tradition has proved vital for establishing a vibrant wind turbine sector, which is estimated to be a main contributor in the battle against climate change. However, if the world is to reach the Paris Agreement (COP21) deep decarbonisation target, it seems crucial that decision-makers must orchestrate broad community mobilisation and motivation in balanced governance and leadership approaches applied to facilitate benign energy innovation, – production and – consumption.

Conclusion

Despite resistance from a reluctant political system, wind turbine innovation and production paradoxically became a great success in Denmark, very much due to a broad, bottom-up, polycentric commitment combined with a mainly top-down–oriented integrative governance approach.

Ingenuity, innovation and experimentation were driving factors behind the pioneering work of Poul la Cour in the 1890s. The same trial-and-error approach drove small industrial entrepreneurs to develop 22 kW wind turbines in the late 1970s. The first commercial multi-megawatt wind turbine was erected at a folk high school in 1978, and the first offshore windfarm in the world opened in Danish waters in 1991. The outcome of such ingenuity is exemplified by a Danish company 'Vestas', which has become the largest wind turbine manufacturer in the world, and the 'Ørsted' energy company, which is now the largest offshore wind project developer. Moreover, almost all global wind turbine manufacturers now have a Danish R&D setup, which is mainly due to the world-leading Danish wind component suppliers and universities producing state-of-the-art wind research and students, respectively. Nevertheless, ingenuity and technologies, innovation competencies and capabilities cannot stand alone. It is also the syntheses of political and socio-cultural actors, the mobilisation of citizens that may foster robust innovation and benign cultural transformation processes.

The question that remains is whether the Danish wind power future mainly belongs to large investors and energy companies or if the Danish bottom-up, polycentric planning approach applied until the late 1990s can re-innovate itself. In other words: Do political leaders today acknowledge the importance of synthesising a polycentric approach with the widespread top-down integrative governance approach widespread in e.g. Denmark at the turn of the Millennium? Local ownership seems to be the primary motivation behind the record-breaking, first subsidy-free wind turbines in Hirtshals in 2019 and the forces behind a community-owned offshore windfarm on Bornholm. However, community-owned windfarms – and mushrooming photovoltaic cell farms – seem to compete with large, professional developers and investors looking for attractive large-scale energy projects.

Leading politicians should keep all three – integrated – levels in mind: the political, the economic and civic society are key to successful cleantech innovation and environment-friendly transformation processes; or that which has been termed 'Ecological Modernisation' in a green growth perspective (Dryzek, 1997; Huber, 2007), endeavoured by many national and sub-national decision-makers throughout the world (e.g. in the C40 city network). It seems crucial that citizens and other local stakeholders are mobilized and engaged in huge, self-organised, locally meaningful and robust transformation processes, if we are ever to reach the Paris target.

Notes

1. https://unfccc.int/process-and-meetings/the-paris-agreement/the-paris-agreement.
2. https://ens.dk/en/our-responsibilities/global-cooperation/danish-energy-model (the Danish Energy Agency, November 11, 2021).
3. https://klimaraadet.dk/da/rapporter/statusrapport-2021.
4. https://energiwatch.dk/Energinyt/Cleantech/article12118550.ece.
5. https://ens.dk/ansvarsomraader/stoette-til-vedvarende-energi/fremme-af-udbygning-med-vindmoeller/koeberetsordningen.

References

Abbott, K. (2018). Orchestration. In A. Jordan, D. Huitema, H. Van Asselt, & J. Forster (Eds.), *Governing climate change: Polycentricity in action?* Cambridge: Cambridge University Press.

Baark, E. (1997). Environmental technology policy in a consensus mode: The case of Denmark. In A. Jamison & P. Østby (Eds.), *Public participation and sustainable development*. Aalborg: Aalborg University Press.

Beddington, J., Berry, S., Caldeira, K., Cramer, W., Creutzig, F., Duffy, P., . . . Arber, W. (2018). Letter from scientists to the EU parliament regarding forest biomass. Retrieved from https://www.euractiv.com/wp-content/uploads/sites/2/2018/01/Letter-of-Scientists-on-Use-of-Forest-Biomass-for-Bioenergy-January-12-2018.pdf

Beuse, E., Boldt, J., Maegaard, P., Meyer, N. I., Windleff, J., & Østergaard, I. (2000). *Renewable energy in Denmark: History of 25 years of growth 1975 to 2000* (in Danish). Aarhus: OVE Publishers.

Crosby & Bryson. (2010). Integrative leadership and the creation and maintenance of cross-sector collaborations. *The Leadership Quarterly, 21*(2). Retrieved from https://www.sciencedirect.com/science/article/pii/S1048984310000226

Damborg, S. (1999). *Public attitudes towards wind power*. Danish Wind Industry Association. Retrieved from http://windpower.org/media(485.1033)/Public_Attitudes_Towards_wind_power.pdf. Accessed on September 10, 2007.

Danish Energy Board. (2018). Retrieved from https://ens.dk/ansvarsomraader/bioenergi/fast-biomasse

Danish Energy Board. (2020). Retrieved from https://ens.dk/en/our-responsibilities/global-cooperation/danish-energy-model

Dryzek, J. (1997). *The politics of the earth*. Oxford: Oxford University Press.

Energywatch (2020). Interview with Peter Birch Sørensen, former chairman of the Danish Council on climate change. Retrieved from https://energiwatch.dk/Energinyt/Renewables/article12346024.ece. Accessed on September 17, 2020.

Enevoldsen, P. (2016). Onshore wind energy in Northern European forests: Reviewing the risks. *Renewable & Sustainable Energy Reviews, 60*, 1251–1262.

Enevoldsen, P., & Sovacool, B. K. (2016). Examining the social acceptance of wind energy: Practical guidelines for onshore wind project development in France. *Renewable & Sustainable Energy Reviews, 53*, 178–184.

Enevoldsen, P., Valentine, S. V., & Sovacool, B. K. (2018). Insights into wind sites: Critically assessing the innovation, cost, and performance dynamics of global wind energy development. *Energy Policy, 120*, 1–7.

Enevoldsen, P., & Xydis, G. (2019). Examining the trends of 35 years growth of key wind turbine components. *Energy for Sustainable Development, 50*, 18–26.

van Est, Q. C. (1999). *Winds of change: A comparative study of the politics of wind energy innovation in California and Denmark*. Amsterdam: International Books, University of Amsterdam.

van der Heijden, J. (2018). City and subnational governance. In A. Jordan, D. Huitema, H. Van Asselt, & J. Forster (Eds.), *Governing climate change: Polycentricity in action?* (pp. 81–96). Cambridge: Cambridge University Press.

van der Heijden, J. (2019). Studying urban climate governance: Where to begin, what to look for, and how to make a meaningful contribution to scholarship and practice. *Earth System Governance, 1*, 100005.

Huber, J. (2007). Pioneer countries and the global diffusion of environmental innovations: Thesis from the viewpoint of ecological modernization theory. *Global Environmental Change, 18*, 360–367.

IEA. (2021). Retrieved from https://www.iea.org/news/after-steep-drop-in-early-2020-global-carbon-dioxide-emissions-have-rebounded-strongly. Accessed on March 23, 2021.

Information. (2020). Interview with Minister for Finance Nikolai Wammen. Retrieved from https://www.information.dk/telegram/2020/09/wammen-advarer-unoedigt-dyr-vej-klimamaal

Information. (2021). Retrieved from https://www.information.dk/indland/2021/02/forskere-opraab-biden-von-leyen-stop-afbraending-biomasse

Jordan, A., Huitema, D., Schoenefeld, J., van Asselt, H., & Forster, J. (2018). Governing climate change polycentrically: Setting the scene. In A. Jordan, D. Huitema, H. Van Asselt, & J. Forster (Eds.), *Governing climate change: Polycentricity in action?* Cambridge: Cambridge University Press.

Karnøe, P., & Garud, R. (2012). Path creation: Co-creation of heterogeneous resources in the emergence of the Danish wind turbine cluster. *European Planning Studies, 20*(5), 733–752.

Kirkegaard, J. K., Cronin, T., Nyborg, S., & Karnoe, P. (2020). Paradigm shift in Danish wind power: The (un)sustainable transformation of a sector. *Journal of Environmental Policy & Planning, 23*(1), 1–17.

Meyer, N. I. (2004). *Fra højre mod venstre [From the right to the left]*. Copenhagen: Tiderne Skifter.

Meyer, N. I. (2007). Learning from wind energy policy in the EU: Lessons from Denmark, Sweden and Spain. *European Environment, 17*, 347–362.

Meyer, N. I. (2020). Interview conducted by the authors (September 10, 2020).

Nielsen, J. S. (2020). Retrieved from https://www.information.dk/indland/2020/10/indtager-solcelleparkerne-danske-marker-naboer-foeler-belejret. Accessed on October 27, 2020.

Nissen, P.-O., & Christensen, B. (2009). *Wind power – the Danish way: From Poul la Cour to modern wind turbines*. Vejen: Poul la Cour Foundation.

Ostrom, E. (2009). *A polycentric approach for coping with climate change*. World Bank Policy Research Working Paper Series, 5095.

Ostrom, E. (2010a). Polycentric systems for coping with collective action and global environmental change. *Global Environmental Change, 20*(4), 550–557.

Ostrom, E. (2010b). A long polycentric journey. *Annual Review of Political Science, 13*, 1–23.

Petersen, F. (2018). *Da Danmark fik vinger* [*When Denmark got wings*]. Copenhagen: Wind Denmark.

Ritzau. (2020). Interview with Minister of Finance Nicolai Wammen. Retrieved from https://policywatch.dk/article12436074.ece

Sørensen, E., & Torfing, J. (2020). Co-creating ambitious climate change mitigation goals: The Copenhagen experience. *Regulation & Governance*. doi:10.1111/rego. 12374

Sovacool, B. K., & Blyth, P. L. (2015). Energy and environmental attitudes in the green state of Denmark: Implications for energy democracy, low carbon transitions, and energy literacy. *Environmental Science & Policy, 54*, 304–315.

Sovacool, B. K., & Ratan, P. L. (2012). Conceptualizing the acceptance of wind and solar electricity. *Renewable and Sustainable Energy Reviews, 16*(7), 5268–5279.

TV2Nord. (2019). Retrieved from https://www.tv2nord.dk/hjorring/vild-med-vind-moller-350-borgere-fra-hirtshals-har-kobt-anparter-i-vindmoller. Accessed on November 12, 2020.

Vedeld, T., Hofstad, H., Solli, H., & Sandkjær, G. (2021). Polycentric urban climate governance: Creating synergies between integrative and interactive governance in Oslo. *Environmental Policy and Governance*. doi:10.1002/eet.1935

Wallace, D. (1995). *Environmental policy and industrial innovation: Strategies in Europe, the USA and Japan* The Royal Institute of International Affairs, the Energy and Environmental Programme. London: Earthscan Publications.

Winddenmark. (2020). Retrieved from https://en.winddenmark.dk/wind-in-denmark/ statistics. Accessed on November 23, 2020.

Winddenmark. (2021). Figure 1 is provided by Jacob Møldrup. Winddenmark. Accessed on April 28, 2021.

Wüstenhagen, R., Wolsink, M., & Bürer, M. J. (2007). Social acceptance of renewable energy innovation: An introduction to the concept. *Energy Policy, 35*, 2683–2691.

Chapter 10

Resilience and Adaptability Capacity in the Danish Agriculture and Food System: Continuity and Change

Sevasti Chatzopoulou and Kostas Karantininis

Abstract

Being constantly exposed to emerging economic and environmental challenges and other external shocks, such as the recent pandemic, agrifood systems must be resilient and adaptive. The Danish AgriFood System (DAFS) adopted a number of organisational changes in response to environmental demands and external shocks, both in the sector and the management by public authorities, leading to the development of new strategies and instruments. The DAFS has demonstrated an ability to anticipate, to be proactive and to recover quickly from difficulties, exhibiting remarkable resilience and the capacity to adapt and to position itself as a frontrunner in sustainable agrifood. In this process, the organisational institutional settings play a prominent role, where public and private actors interact and coordinate their activities, develop synergies and resolve conflicts within collaborative governance structures. The DAFS provides four interlinked and equally important success stories worth emulating: governance, cooperation, professionalism and social capital. Governance structures incorporating the state-administration-agrifood sector in close collaboration provide the necessary institutional conditions for adaptation and the accommodation of new solutions to emerging problems. Integrated cooperative organisation ensures the fair distribution of the added value and enables the resolution of conflicts and consensus-driven decisions. High levels of expertise and professionalism support the sector to identify new strategies and viable innovative solutions in the long term, responding to new demands while remaining competitive by promoting and externalising sector interests. Strong social capital binds everything together and ensures sustainability and resilience.

Public Governance in Denmark, 169–188
doi:10.1108/978-1-80043-712-820221010

Keywords: Danish agrifood system; governance; resilience; adaptability; organisation; agricultural policy

Introduction

Agrifood systems (AFSs) around the world are expected to produce food for all, contribute to rural economies and provide income and revenue to farmers, other stakeholders and businesses. They are also expected to maintain rural landscapes, improve the environment and biodiversity and reverse climate change. Being constantly exposed to emerging economic and environmental challenges and other external shocks, such as the recent COVID-19 pandemic, AFSs must be resilient and adaptive. Like all other AFSs, the Danish agrifood system (DAFS) includes all actors from production to processing and distribution, to the final consumption of food, such as farmers, the HORECA sector (hotels, restaurants, catering), the institutions, processes, infrastructures and resources, the environment and activities including socio-economic and environmental outcomes (Food & Agriculture Organisation, 2014). This chapter investigates *what and how has enabled the resilience and adaptability capacity to emerging challenges of the DAFS over time?*

Responding to environmental demands and external shocks, the DAFS has displayed remarkable resilience: able both to increase production and exports while reducing its environmental footprint by reducing GHG emissions, ammonia emissions and phosphorus surplus and using new energy sources, positioning itself as a sustainable agrifood frontrunner. Throughout its history, the DAFS managed not only to adapt to changes but also to anticipate and be proactive, recovering quickly from difficulties. These achievements are attributed to organisational capacity and collaborative governance, the application and development of new technologies, supported by professionalism and expertise. Collaborative governance interconnects the various actors, public and private, in the DAFS, combined with strong, farmer-owned cooperatives dating back to nineteenth-century land reforms, which have integrated the entire agrifood sector vertically and bottom-up. The DAFS faces important challenges, since intensive industrialised agriculture burdens the environment considerably and depends on continuous investments in technology and land that are mostly financed by expensive loans that lead to debt. This chapter presents the DAFS as a useful and crucial case to investigate its strengths and weaknesses, drawing useful lessons on how to build sustainable and resilient AFSs.

Analysis

This section analyses the governance initiatives and sector-specific organisational changes that the DAFS adopted to address the emerging challenges. First, the overall situation of the DAFS is characterised using descriptive statistics. Based on public documents and secondary literature, the governance initiatives and measures and the organisational changes in the DAFS are then discussed. We argue that, throughout its history, the DAFS has demonstrated resilience and an adaptability capacity to internal and external challenges, such as changes to the Common Agricultural Policy (CAP), the financial crisis, climate change and the recent COVID-19 pandemic, which enable it to develop new strategies and means to achieve its goals under the new circumstances. The resilience of AFSs in crises is a multifaceted concept that includes three dimensions: anticipation (to predict and prepare), adaptability (to withstand and survive) and robustness (to 'bounce back') (Meuwissen & Feindt, 2020). More specifically, 'adaptability capacity refers to the ability of an organisation to adjust, reorganise and restructure in response to changing circumstances' (Chatzopoulou, 2020a, p. 37).

In Denmark, more than half of the land (51% or 42,916 km^2) is rural, 66% of which is agricultural land. Agrifood production is characterised by rather large farms (67.5 hectares compared to the EU-28 average of 16.1 hectares), but 20.3% of all holdings have more than 100 hectares (compared to 3.1% in EU-28).[1] The sector is mostly specialised in livestock production (28% is swine). Danish farmers are highly skilled and generally younger than the EU-28: 2.5% of farmers are under 35 years old (5.9% in EU-28) and 24% are older than 64 (30.6% in EU-28). Although the primary sector accounts for only 1.6% of the country's economy (total GVA) (1.6% in EU-28) and 2.5% of total employment (4.7% in EU-28), the Danish agrifood sector contributes significantly to the national economy through innovation, job creation and the export of high added-value processed food products (5.6% of GDP in 2015).[2] The Danish food-manufacturing sector is internationally renowned for its advanced knowledge transfer and innovation capacities, combining natural resources with science (https://investindk.com). For instance, two significant companies, Chr. Hansen and DuPont, account for an 80% share of the global market for (ingredients) cultures (Chatzopoulou, 2020a), and two of the farmer-owned cooperatives are the largest in the world (Arla Foods Amba, Trifolium DLF).[3,4]

Similar to all European Union (EU) member states, Danish agriculture is subsidised and regulated by the CAP, the single most integrated EU policy since 1959. In 2019, Denmark's 35,000 farmers received a total €934 million (€833 million in direct payments, €101 million in rural development). This constitutes 1.7% of the annual CAP budget, which is roughly similar to Denmark's share of gross value added (GVA) of agriculture (1.9% of the EU). The CAP subsidies constitute 26% of the Danish agriculture GVA (the EU27 average is 33%). Meanwhile, Danish agriculture emits 16.8 million tonnes of GHG (3.7% of the total agricultural emissions in the EU). Danish agriculture accounts for 30.9% of the country's total GHG emissions (the EU27 average is 12.7%). For every €1 GVA, Danish agriculture emits 4.8 kg of GHG (the EU27 average is 2.5 kg/€) (OECD, 2020a). But, the EU is not alone worldwide in financing agricultural production, and EU agriculture is not the most heavily subsidised.[5] Agricultural subsidies are not the sole culprit of climate change. For example, agriculture accounts for 8.9% of the total GHG emissions in the EU, whereas the same figure for New Zealand is 48.1%, despite their having abolished agricultural subsidies in the 1980s (OECD, 2020b).

Denmark initially supported a market intervention approach for the CAP due to the benefits enjoyed by the agrifood sector from the higher prices for agricultural products, access to the EU market (e.g. the United Kingdom and Germany were the two major importers of Danish agricultural products at the time) and the agricultural export subsidies that boosted trade (Chatzopoulou, 2020b). Over time, however, Denmark became a net contributor to the EU budget due to various EU enlargements and CAP reforms. In addition, WTO agreements eliminated trade-distorting export subsidies, which affected the Danish export benefits. Responding to new circumstances, the agrifood sector shifted its position from a supporter of the protective CAP towards a liberal market-oriented approach and limited market intervention, focussing on efficiency, competitiveness and exports of both primary and processed agrifood products (Daugbjerg, Andersen, Hansen, & Jacobsen, 2020; Jensen & Nedergaard, 2020). The DAFS adopted a number of organisational changes (e.g. mergers) and developed new strategies that enabled it to address the emerging circumstances.

During the Eurozone crisis (2008–2018) and the 2020 COVID-19 pandemic, the DAFS demonstrated resilience, similar to most AFSs around the world.[6] Fig. 1 illustrates the developments in Danish agrifood imports and exports (food, beverages and tobacco – FBT) in the period 2002–2019, organic exports in particular. Following the financial crisis, With the exception of 2009, the year following the financial crisis, when both FBT exports and imports decreased significantly (exports decreased from €13.5 billion to €12.7 billion, and imports from €8.6 billion to 7.9 billion, or −6% and −9%, respectively), both exports and imports increased by an annual average of +3.8% and +4.4%, respectively. Consequently, the balance of trade of FBT remained positive and relatively constant during the entire crisis period, fluctuating roughly around €5 billion (€5.324 billion in 2019). The export of organic products also grew steadily, increasing more than tenfold in the period 2005–2018 (from €250 million to €2.9 billion). FBT exports to non-EU countries increased (€4.7 billion in 2002, €7.3 billion in 2019) more than to EU-27 countries (65.4% and 45.3%, respectively). Organics now constitute more than 17% of total Danish FBT exports.

Governance of the DAFS: Since Denmark's accession to the EU in *1973*, the governance of the Danish agrifood policy has followed the CAP rules and regulations and the changes introduced by successive CAP reforms, which significantly changed the policy orientation and instruments over time. For example, since the 1992 MacSharry reform of the CAP, responding to criticism of overproduction due to CAP subsidies ('butter mountains', 'milk lakes'), financial support was linked to farm size (versus production and export amounts), the multifunctionality of agriculture and now to environmental initiatives. The DAFS actors, both public and private, were particularly prepared to shape and adapt the CAP reforms, lobbying for a market-oriented approach to the CAP. Additionally, since *2004*, Denmark has applied the EU General Food Law (GFL) with respect to safety and food and feed labelling, which is particularly relevant for livestock production, that constitutes the major agricultural activity in Denmark. The EU CAP and food policies follow the ordinary legislative procedure, while the implementation of the decisions are the responsibility of the member states.

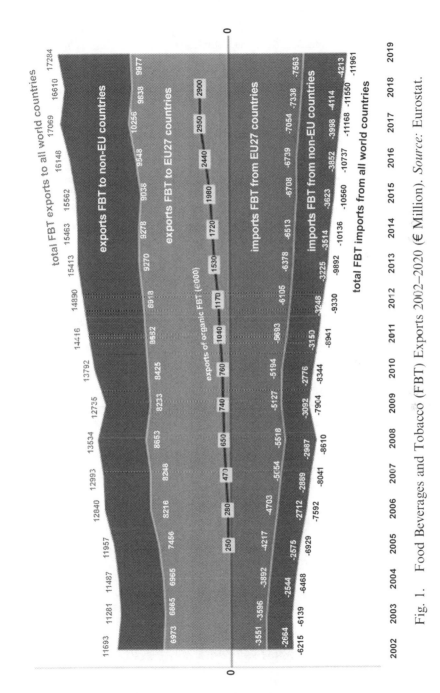

Fig. 1.   Food Beverages and Tobacco (FBT) Exports 2002–2020 (€ Million). *Source:* Eurostat.

National policy instruments and legislation complement the EU legislation, such as legislation on land ownership or the protection of the environment, but always in accordance with the EU regulatory framework. For instance, numerous action plans in Denmark complemented the EU Habitat, the Seveso and the Nitrate Directives.[7–9]

A broad range of formal and informal Danish actors influence the agrifood policy process and policy implementation (Chatzopoulou, 2020b; Martinsen, 2013), including politicians, members of the agriculture committee and the EU committee in the Danish Parliament, administrators (Minister of Food, Agriculture and Fisheries, Food Agency and local authorities), interest organisations (e.g. Danish Agriculture & Food Council) and businesses, many of which are farmer-owned cooperatives (e.g. Arla, Danish Crown) or investor-owned firms (Chr. Hansen, DuPont, Novo-Nordisk, etc). Some of the actors have decisive competences, while others influence decisions through frequent interactions, consultation and lobbying. Supported by high levels of professional expertise, these actors facilitate the collaboration between the state, administration and the sector, which enables the adaptation of new strategies for Danish agriculture (Chatzopoulou, 2015).

In 2009, the Danish government introduced the *Green Growth Agreement (GGA)* in response to EU developments on *climate change*, emphasising the need for a transition towards a sustainable food system and promoting the increase of organic agricultural production, which marked a 'paradigm shift' in Danish agrifood policy (Altinget, 2015).[10] The Danish farmers and slaughterhouses contested the GGA due to concerns over both domestic and EU regulations for their high administrative demands, resulting in over-implementation practices, which increase production costs and hurt competitiveness, especially compared to neighbouring countries (e.g. Sweden, Germany) (Danish Agriculture & Food Council, 2013). The extent to which the implementation of the EU directives led to over-implementation has not been settled because the way the civil servants have interpreted and transposed these directives into national law has often delayed compliance with EU demands (Martinsen, 2013). In response, the agrifood transferred agricultural activities abroad (e.g. Poland), resulting in the loss of around 2,000 jobs in the primary sector (Nørby, 2013). Hence, one of the challenges for Danish agrifood governance is about balancing high standards and timely compliance with EU rules against limited administrative burdens for the sector.

In *2010*, the Danish government issued a report, '**Towards a New Common Agricultural Policy**', aiming to contribute to the 'Europe 2020' strategy and to foster green growth (Ministry of Agriculture and Food, 2010). The report acknowledged the need for a common policy for agriculture due to fears that a renationalisation of the CAP could deteriorate the functioning of the Internal Market, the competitiveness of the agrifood sector globally and potentially harm EU consumers (Ministry of Agriculture and Food, 2010).[11] The government also underlined the significance of common rules for food safety, environmental standards, animal welfare norms, trading standards and labelling rules, and it proposed new objectives and principles for the CAP concerning green growth.

The proposals emphasised the need to focus on research, innovation and professional development instead of subsidies and financial support mechanisms, which represented a shift in Danish agrifood towards new ways to address environmental challenges (Ministry of Agriculture and Food, 2010).

As Danish agriculture faced high debts due to increased investments and high land prices that burdened the sector in recent decades, the government loosened some land ownership restrictions (Daugbjerg, Andersen, Hansen, & Jacobsen 2020). In the early 2000s, Danish agrifood experienced growth, and primary producers took out loans to increase investments (Altinget, 2013a). Meanwhile, Danish agriculture experienced a financial crisis, and land prices increased by more than 80% from 2003 to 2008, creating a 'land bubble' (Pedersen, Buchholst, & Drejer, 2014), when poorly serviced loans exceeded 25% of total loans. The government had to enact a bailout package in 2005, *Dansk Landbrugskapital*, to rescue farmers from bankruptcy.[12] The Landbrugskapital loans were expensive (10%) in contrast to the going interest rates (0–2%).

In *2011, measures to reduce nitrogen-related water pollution stemming from agriculture* were introduced by a Social Democrat-led coalition government. To ensure clean drinking water, the government adopted new legislation requiring a 10-metre buffer zone (*randzoner*) around cultivated areas.[13] This legislation was justified by the high cost of purifying the water polluted by agricultural activities, which would otherwise burden taxpayers. The agricultural organisations strongly contested the legislation, as it added to production costs, which triggered hard negotiations and challenged the state–agrifood sector relations in this period (Chatzopoulou, 2020b). Despite being financially compensated when they implemented the law, the farmers refused to comply with the buffer zone legislation and instead accepted the relevant legal sanctions (Altinget, 2013b).

In December *2013*, the appointment of Minister for Agriculture and Food Dan Jørgensen (Altinget, 2013b) prompted new DAFS dissatisfaction due to his strong environmental and animal welfare views, strong commitment to green agriculture and criticism of pesticide and chemical use in intensive agriculture. Two years later (28 June *2015*), a minority right-of-centre, Venstre-led government supported by the Liberal Alliance and the Danish People's Party merged the Ministry of Agriculture and Food with the Ministry of Environment, renaming it the Ministry of Food and Environment. This merger increased concentration at the political level but also signalled the internal conflicting dynamics and the potential undermining of environmental concerns due to the strong relations between the Ministry of Food and Agriculture and the agrifood sector. In response to the dissatisfied farmers, in December 2015, the right-of-centre government introduced the Food and Agricultural package, which included 30 policy and finance-specific initiatives (Altinget, 2016). This package would abolish the buffer zones (*randzoner*), allowing farmers to cultivate that part of their land again. New environmental regulations complemented the package (the Fertilizer Act and Animal Husbandry Act), which would target nutrient pollution mitigation, strengthen collaboration in the sector, improve the agrifood business, increase commodity exports and create growth and new jobs in Denmark in relation to nature and the environment.[14] In reaction, environmental organisations and the media criticised the government as being captured by the agricultural interests at Axelborg, which have traditionally been associated with the Liberal Party (Christiansen, 2020).[15] These critics claimed that the package mainly supported the already highly industrialised, intensive agricultural production in Denmark – and not the environment. The European Commission also declared its concerns to the then Minister of Environment and Food that the package did not comply fully with the EU's Water Framework Directive, Nitrates Directive and the Habitats Directive (Euroactiv, 2016). Increased pressure from the Conservative Party resulted in the resignation of then-Minister of Food and Agriculture Eva Kjær, who was replaced by Esben Lunde Larsen in February 2016.[16] The frequent ministerial rotations in this period are uncommon in the Danish context (Chatzopoulou, 2020b). This merger ended on 19 November 2020, resulting in two Ministries: the Ministry of Environment and the Ministry of Food, Agriculture and Fisheries.

Organisational changes in the sector: The sector carried out a series of organisational changes, not least including mergers between major cooperatives. These changes first began in the 1970s in response to the forthcoming 1973 EU accession and the 1990s food crises (e.g. mad cow disease). The Danish agricultural sector had been organised cooperatively since the 1800s, when the first cooperatives emerged in response to increasingly competitive international markets in the late 1880s, with the support of the bourgeois and agricultural elites of the day (Bogason, 1992). These actors aimed to introduce a liberal and progressive view on agriculture, emphasising the role of skills and knowledge, which remains important to this day and constitutes a benchmark for the state–agrifood sector relations. The cooperatives played a significant consultative role at the domestic level and contributed to the founding and institutionalisation of agricultural education and training that supported the development of expertise and professionalism in the sector.

The cooperative structures, which constitute a key component of the DAFS, are linked through board 'interlocks'; that is, a number of directors holding (a large number of) positions in various different organisations (Karantininis, 2007). Interlocking board members transfer information and monitor the actions and performance of the linked firms in the chain. These board members represent the knowledge and values of the entire industry, and they guarantee the continuity, legitimacy and homogeneity of values and ideas. Being the 'bridges' connecting individual members and organisations, the interlocking directors contribute to the creation and deepening of social capital in the DAFS. This social capital and capabilities are valuable, non-tangible, non-copyable resources, and they constitute much of the competitive advantage, adaptability and resilience of the DAFS.

In *2009, reorganisation* of the Danish agrifood sector was underway. The merger of five organisations (*Danish Agriculture*, the *Danish Bacon and Meat Council*, the *Danish Agricultural Council*, the *Danish Dairy Board* and *Danish Pig Production*) was intended to strengthen competition and resulted in the renaming of the *Danish Agricultural Council* to *Danish Agriculture and Food Council* (DA&FC). This reorganisation demonstrated the adaptability of the sector and its prompt responsiveness to economic shocks, such as the Eurozone crisis in 2007–2008, climate change and environment as well as the 2009–2010 food crisis, the latter characterised by increased food prices.[17] In 2019, the DA&FC includes 30,000 primary producers, associations and private companies together with 300 cooperative and private enterprises from primary agriculture and the secondary food processing industry sectors.[18] This expanded DA&FC membership signalled the prominent role of the agrifood sector as well as the strong collaboration between primary agriculture and the processing food sector (Chatzopoulou, 2020b). The reorganisation also further concentrated the representation of diverse sectoral interests while strengthening the sector's bargaining capacity with the state (Chatzopoulou, 2020b). Economically, vertical integration, both downstream into processing–distribution (e.g. Arla, Danish Crown) and upstream into the provision of inputs (e.g. DLG), empowered the agrifood sector, which expanded its activities on international markets (Chatzopoulou, 2020b). Nevertheless, this reorganisation emphasised the promotion of the food processing industry's interests rather than those of the primary producers, which marked a new type of politicisation of the state–agrifood sector relations in Denmark (Chatzopoulou, 2020c). During the Eurozone crisis, falling agricultural product prices and lower primary sector earnings, accompanied by depreciating asset values led to insolvency, liquidity problems and more expensive loans (Schou & Bramsen, 2020). Moreover, farmers felt they were losing with the DA&FC after the 2009 merger and criticised it for concentrating on the food processing industry and large producers who focused more on exports than production-related problems (Altinget, 2010). A small number of producers responded in 2010 by founding the Sustainable Agriculture (SA) group (*Bæredygtig Landbrug*) (Altinget, 2010). These internal disagreements intensified internal DA&FC conflicts. The SA group demanded the eradication of the costly aspects, such as taxes and increased costs due to the GGA. Moreover, the eurozone crisis and the most recent EU CAP reform discussions provided a new window of opportunity for change in Danish agrifood politics and policy. Facing reduced production subsidies (e.g. dairy sector) and their conditioning to environment-friendly production, primary producers started reconsidering their production types. Similar changes are also observed in the processing sector, which started to invest in the production of environment-friendly methods and products.

Initiatives targeting environmental concerns: The highly industrialised and intensive Danish livestock production, which requires extensive natural resources and energy, was already contested in the 1980s (Daugbjerg, 1998). Since then, the agrifood sector has been criticised extensively in the media and society more generally for its impact on animal welfare and the environment, specifically regarding soil degradation and water pollution (lakes, coastal marine areas). According to a recent Eurobarometer survey (2016), it is widely held in Denmark that farmers should ensure the welfare of farmed animals (50% compared to 35% EU-28); protect the environment (44% vs. 30% EU-28) and demand that the EU should ensure a 'sustainable way to produce food' (61% vs 43% EU-28). Societal perceptions have challenged the image of the agrifood sector, exerted pressure on policymakers and demanded new, more environment-friendly strategies. Such criticism became even more prominent due to their connection to the EU green growth and sustainability strategy and the 2015 UN Sustainable Development

Goals (SDGs). Denmark played a leading role in the Agenda 2030, as reflected in its Action Plan for the Implementation of the 2030 Agenda and SDGs (March 2017), which introduced 37 targets and national indicators.[19] In response, the agrifood sector tried to maintain high productivity and economic resilience combined with reduced GHG emissions; that is, to increase production while reducing the environmental impact. As Fig. 2 shows, while production increased over time (1990–2015) GHG emissions, ammonia emissions and phosphorus surplus decreased.[20]

The DA&FC also established a specific department promoting and encouraging organic agricultural interests and production. Although this trend became especially salient in 2009–2010, organic farming in Denmark had already started in the 1980s, and the first act concerning organic agricultural production was introduced in 1987, followed by the introduction of the Danish organic label (the red *Ø-label*) shortly thereafter, which marked Denmark as one of the first countries worldwide to introduce relevant legislation.[21] Organic standards inspections are carried in Denmark out by the Food Agency. The fact that the *Ø-label* represents a state-controlled labelling scheme, often supported financially, increased its legitimacy and consumer confidence (Hjelmar, 2011). Food labelling contributes to informed consumer choices by providing comprehensive information about food product ingredients and composition. At roughly the same time, the EU also introduced rules in *1991* regarding organic vegetable production, followed by rules for organic livestock in 2000. During this process, Denmark worked actively to 'export' its rules to the EU.

In *2013*, the government introduced the Growth Plan for the Food Industry, focussing on five areas emphasising efficiency, exports and research:

(1) Sustainable, resource-efficient food production
(2) Solution-oriented regulations and control
(3) Talent, dynamism and food industry exports
(4) Growth-oriented food R&D
(5) Strengthened access to finance (Ministry for Industry, Business and Financial Affairs, 2013).

In *2015*, the Ministry of Food, Agriculture and Fisheries developed a plan for more organic production (Ministry of Food, Agriculture and Fisheries, 2015). In *2018*, the government, supported by the Danish Peoples' Party, financed the promotion of organic production beyond the Food and Agriculture package as part of the growth plan for food (Ministry of Environment and Food, 2018). The areas pertaining to organic crops and milk both increased, while organic meat was hit hard in 2018 (mainly due to swine fever). This organic production increase has also been promoted by regulating mineral fertiliser and synthetic pesticide use, which demonstrates the state intervention that provided the conditions for expanding organic farming. Farmers also received financial support from the EU and Danish programmes. The introduction of the unique eco-labelling certification (*økologisk*) by the government clearly differentiated the organic production

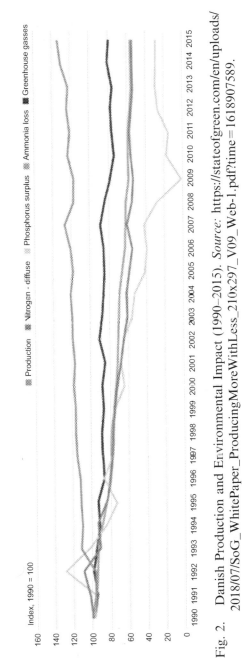

Fig. 2.   Danish Production and Environmental Impact (1990–2015). *Source:* https://stateofgreen.com/en/uploads/2018/07/SoG_WhitePaper_ProducingMoreWithLess_210x297_V09_Web-1.pdf?time=1618907589.

and strengthened the organic food consumption (Sønderskov & Daugbjerg, 2010). Consequently, the market share of organic consumption increased from 3.5% in 2005 to 12.1% of total retail food sales in 2019, which represents, proportionally, the largest organic market share in the world ahead of Switzerland and Sweden.[22] These changes also resulted in increased organic agrifood exports (Fig. 1), especially after the mid-2010s.

The adoption of strategic initiatives by the government in collaboration with the Danish agrifood sector aimed to promote organic agricultural production, both internally and externally. In so doing, the DAFS is adapting to the EU Green growth initiatives, the recent EU Green Deal and the farm to fork strategy.[23,24]

In *2019*, the DA&FC launched a *strategy for climate-neutral agrifood production by 2050*, aiming for: better natural resource management, encouraging climate-friendly farming practices and a doubling of organic farming areas; investments to improve the environmental performance of farms, restructuring farms in the pig and cattle sector; and boosting innovation and creating rural jobs.[25] Achieving these targets requires partnerships and collaborations among the different actors, companies, authorities and research institutes in the entire AFS, R&D investment, job creation and wiser resource consumption for environmental care. The DA&FC therefore invites policymakers, researchers, advocacy groups, businesses and consumers to collaborate in developing solutions, transferring information across the system, achieving cohesion and creating social capital. These solutions include circular economy methods by optimising everything and reducing waste, reflecting the adaptability capacity of the sector; for example, using animal blood for medicine, processing offal into mink food, animal's rumen for biogas production, etc.

In March *2020*, the *COVID-19 pandemic* closed national borders, raising concerns regarding Danish agrifood exports. On 9 March 2020, the DA&FC met with the government to discuss the challenges and necessary measures for the sector, such as transportation across the EU and potential financial support in the form of bailouts or the connection of agrifood to the spreading of COVID. Between 2019 and 2020, Danish dairy exports dropped by DKK 1.2 billion (€161 million), which has been primarily attributed to the COVID-19 pandemic.[26] Dairy sales fell significantly, especially cheese and other value-added products that were supplied to restaurants and hotels. However, both prices and demand largely recovered in 2021. In collaboration with its member states, the EU introduced so-called 'green lane' border crossings aimed at alleviating supply chain disruptions. The green lanes facilitated the quick checks and health screenings of product, permitted the mobility of all freight vehicles carrying goods and enabled the import and export of goods throughout the EU.[27] This has been crucial for Danish agrifood exports. In response to the EU strategy and requirements, the Danish government, in collaboration with SEGES (the Danish agricultural extension agency), has launched a pilot scheme for *multifunctional land consolidation* to consider multiple tasks on each plot simultaneously (e.g. nature, environment, climate, rural development).[28]

Discussion

Our analysis demonstrates the resilience of the DAFS and its adaptability capacity to emerging challenges, such as the Eurozone crisis, climate change, the COVID-19 pandemic and CAP reforms (Altinget, 2015; Chatzopoulou, 2020b). These characteristics are attributed to the cooperative organisational structures that enabled proactive, collaborative, consensus-driven responses to challenges. The consensus-driven Danish cooperative AFS is more adaptive to external challenges, as actors are willing to take risks, share adaptation costs and accommodate changes (Börzel & Panke, 2019; Chatzopoulou, 2020b).

Despite the broadly liberal, market-oriented stance in the DAFS, successive Danish governments, working in close collaboration with the agrifood sector, introduced national legislation and guidelines that complement the EU rules (e.g. the 2015 Agriculture and Food package). These initiatives follow the EU-level strategies, such as the EU *Green Deal* and *Farm to Fork*.

In the meantime, the administrative and organisational capacity characterising both the state and the sector supports the policymaking process to ensure continuity and high compliance with the EU rules over time (Martinsen, 2013). Even if disagreements and diverse views in the development of policies exist, as discussed above, such disagreements do not affect the Danish compliance with the EU rules. Instead, any obligation regarding compliance prevails over disagreements and opposing national preferences (Martinsen, 2013). In this way, the DAFS has displayed resilience to external change.

At the same time, in coordination with the agrifood sector, the government is continuously and proactively developing new, long-term strategies (e.g. Green Growth), taking into account the EU and international developments. By expanding into external markets, Danish agriculture contributes to the economic growth of the agrifood sector, the country and society more broadly. As Brexit and the recent COVID-19 crisis have shown, however, high exports also increase dependence on external demand and competition.[29] Additionally, the transport of agricultural exports burdens the environment and requires energy. Industrialised agriculture resulted in high exports, while intensive animal production requires expansive feed imports. For instance, Denmark imports approximately 1.5 million tonnes of Latin American soya for animal feed, which is unsustainable, as it externalises Denmark's shortages.[30] Finally, AFS industrialisation disconnects rural and urban areas, and while food is produced in the rural areas, young generations have no contact with how it is produced. This rural–urban disconnect alienates us from nature and food production activities and increases potential health and safety risks, emphasising the need for local production and shorter supply chains. Recent efforts, campaigns, gastronomic events and fairs involving the Ministry and the agrifood sector, from primary producers to restaurants, have been carried out to address this disconnect; although useful, these events are often characterised by an urban understanding of food and do not provide an inclusive, pragmatic approach to addressing sustainability challenges sufficiently and effectively.

While the DAFS demonstrates resilience and adaptability, it is not necessarily adequately sustainable. For instance, the percentage of reduced GHG emissions due to agrifood is not the lowest in the EU (Jacobs et al., 2019), and the turn to organic agriculture can ensure a sustainable AFS. Industrialised, intensive organic agriculture also contributes to soil degradation and CO_2 emissions.

> Greenhouse gas emissions per kilogram of organic and conventional products are more or less the same, and a number of technological measures are likely to be unacceptable in organic farming.
>
> (Hutchings & Dalgaard, 2021 own translation)

New agrifood models are therefore required that reconsider the food system and could replace the Danish industrialised AFS by focussing on the development and use of technological innovations combined with social innovations. This transition cannot occur without consumer involvement. New, less meat-intensive diets, together with more plant and legume-based nutrition, can contribute to sustainable agrifood. Furthermore, the development of innovative technologies that can use organic waste to produce protein-rich, organic fertilisers or animal feed could replace soya imports. Such solutions, which are also under DAFS consideration, contribute to innovation, create jobs and ensure sustainable resource consumption. Hence, the relation between organic agriculture, food and sustainability requires further research.

Lessons Learned and Implications for Practice

What lessons can we draw from the development and characteristics of the DAFS? How can we understand the impact of the diachronic transformations in the DAFS, its resilience and adaptability to emerging challenges? To what extent and under what conditions are these transformations able to address environmental and climate change challenges and to respond to societal concerns about sustainable agriculture?

Our analysis shows that the creation and institutionalisation of the unique cooperative organisational structures enable the establishment of collaborations and synergies among the public and private actors at all levels in the DAFS and contribute to long-term solutions and strategies. Moreover, themselves part of these structures, actors are willing to take new risks, as they do not have to bear the potential failure costs alone. Consequently, they are unafraid of trying new approaches and adapting to new circumstances, providing the basis for innovation. Innovation empowers the AFS, creating or providing access to new niche markets. But society does not necessarily accept all innovative solutions, which are therefore not necessarily legitimate due to uncertainties, unless their creation involves the affected actors more broadly. As the analysis in this chapter shows, one significant challenge concerns the costs–benefits balance between the DAFS transformations, namely the extent to which economically viable agrifood businesses can simultaneously take care of the environment and contribute to social cohesion. Both the government and the sector's governance and policy measures aim to achieve such a balance. Such transformations require time, resources and social capital.

Furthermore, policy and organisational learning among differentiated systems is not a straight-forward process. The adoption of the Danish organisational and technological innovations by the AFSs in other countries also includes challenges. First, every country has its own institutional and organisational structures, both on the political and sectoral levels, which may differ significantly from the Danish structures and can impede change. Different territorial and geographical characteristics represent different resources, climate conditions, gastronomical traditions and cultures. Countries also differ in terms of the level and structure of their social capital; in other words: 'one size fits all' cannot be applied.

Nevertheless, there are three important lessons to be learned from the DAFS: (1) Collaborative governance structures (2) Cooperative organisation in the sector, (3) Professionalism and social capital. *Collaborative governance structures* that incorporate the state–administration–agrifood sector, provide the necessary institutional conditions for adaptation and the accommodation of new solutions to emerging problems. *Cooperative organisation of the sector* under a single umbrella organisation ensures the fair distribution of the added value and enables conflict resolution and consensus-driven decisions. *High levels of professionalism* and expertise generates valuable social capital that supports the sector in identifying new strategies and viable, innovative solutions in the long term, responding to new demands while remaining competitive by promoting and externalising sector interests.

The characteristics above, which enabled and enforced innovation, resilience and adaptability during crises in the DAFS can, to some extent, provide useful lessons, be adapted by others and adjusted to their own needs and challenges. While collaboration and coordination are crucial to the success of future endeavours, they might not be always successful, legitimate and/or approved by all actors. Nevertheless, through deliberation and dialogue within institutionalised organisations, compromises can be reached and disagreements resolved. While collaborative governance is no panacea, it conditions resilience and adaptation by facilitating democratic access to resources in the system and laying the framework for long-lasting solutions to emerging challenges. Instead, top-down hierarchical and conflictual structures, without the involvement of relevant stakeholders, could lead to one-sided, top-down, non-feasible, non-resilient solutions. The successful legacy of the DAFS demonstrates how public–private collaboration, together with highly organised and professional structures, enables the development of new ideas and enhances innovation, and it can ensure feasibility and implementation. This is reflected in the most recent strategies and policy instruments with respect to climate and environmental change and the adaptive efforts throughout the agrifood value chain.

Conclusions

Agrifood enjoys an important position in Danish politics, which has remained strongly corporatist over time, dating back to the early days of the Danish welfare state. This positioning has been enabled by the unique cooperative model, collaborative governance and high levels of professionalism in both the public and private sectors. Consequently, the DAFS adequately and proactively addresses internal and external challenges, crises and competition, regulatory burdens and public perceptions. This renders the DAFS highly resilient, adapting to changes, while building on pre-existing policies and structures. Despite these characteristics, important aspects must still be addressed since the existing changes did not lead to a fully sustainable AFS, especially in lieu of SDG commitments. Thus, there is a need to reconsider and seek new ways for how the industrialised DAFS can ensure care for the environment, biodiversity, clean water, animal welfare and avoid dependence on unsustainable imports. Only then can the DAFS be truly sustainable, connecting the urban with the rural and providing safe and healthy food.

Notes

1. EUROSTAT. We use 28 members, as Brexit is a recent phenomenon (since 31.12.2020) and data are not yet available.
2. https://www.agriworker.eu/en/danmark/country-information-menu/agriculture-in-denmark#:~:text=The%20contribution%20of%20agriculture&text=The%20food%20sector's%20direct%20and,which%20is%205.6%20%25%20of%20GDP
3. DuPont, a US chemical giant, took over the Danish food ingredient and enzyme giant Danisco in 2011.
4. Danish Agriculture and Food Council https://agricultureandfood.dk/
5. CAP subsidies as percentage of gross farm receipts in the EU is 19%, higher than the United States (10.6%) and China (13.2%), but lower than Japan (41.4%), Korea (47.9%) and Norway (59%) (OECD, 2020a).
6. During the writing of this chapter the pandemic was still unfolding.
7. Council Directive 92/43/EEC of 21 May 1992 on the conservation of natural habitats and of wild fauna and flora https://eur-lex.europa.eu/legal-conte https://ec.europa.eu/environment/water/water-nitrates/index_en.html nt/EN/TXT/?uri=celex%3A31992L0043
8. The Seveso-III-Directive (2012/18/EU) aims at the prevention of major accidents involving dangerous substances. However, as accidents may nevertheless occur, it also aims at limiting the consequences of such accidents not only for human health but also for the environment. https://eur-lex.europa.eu/legal-content/EN/TXT/PDF/?uri=CELEX:31982L0501&from=EN, https://eur-lex.europa.eu/legal-content/EN/TXT/?uri=CELEX:01996L0082-20120813
9. 19/10/2020 – NAPINFO: publication of the final report on the identification of approaches and measures in action programmes under the Nitrates Directive and the database of measures from Member States' action programmes

16/09/2020 – JRC report on Technical proposals for the safe use of processed manure above the threshold established for Nitrate Vulnerable Zones by the Nitrates Directive

17/07/2020 – Commission Implementing Decision (EU) 2020/1074 granting a derogation requested by Denmark

13/07/2020 – Commission Implementing Decision (EU) 2020/1073 granting a derogation requested by the Netherlands

02/07/2020 – Water: The Commission is calling on Spain to protect its waters from nitrate pollution

02/07/2020 – The Commission is urging Belgium to comply with the EU's Nitrates Directive

03/10/2019 – Court of Justice confirms standing of individuals to challenge Nitrate Action Programmes

25/07/2019 – Water pollution: Commission urges Germany to implement judgment on breach of EU rules on nitrates

04/05/2018 – Publication of the latest Commission Report on the implementation of the Nitrates Directive, https://ec.europa.eu/environment/water/water-nitrates/index_en.html

10. https://mfvm.dk/fileadmin/user_upload/FVM.dk/Dokumenter/Servicemenu/Publikationer/Groen_vaekst.pdf
https://eng.mst.dk/media/mst/69152/Danish%20Agreement%20on%20Green%20Growth_300909.pdf
https://www.ft.dk/samling/20111/almdel/miu/bilag/21/1030569.pdf

11. A renationalisation of the CAP would allow each member state to provide financial support to agriculture (which the CAP now restricts) and increase competition among nations, as some states (e.g. Denmark) have more capacity to do so.

12. https://landbrugskapital.dk/investor/investeringsstrategi

13. LOV nr.591 af 14/06/2011 Gældende (Randzoneloven), Offentliggørelsesdato: 15-06-2011, amended by LOV nr 563 af 18/06/2012 Gældende, Offentliggørelsesdato: 19-06-2012, Fødevareministeriet.

14. http://mfvm.dk/fileadmin/user_upload/FVM.dk/Dokumenter/Landbrug/Indsatser/Foedevare-_og_landbrugspakke/Aftale_om_foedevare-_og_landbrugspakken.pdf

15. Axelborg is the name of the Copenhagen building in which the Danish Food and Agriculture interest organisation is located.

16. https://www.b.dk/nationalt/bred-enighed-om-at-kigge-paa-landbrugspakken-igen, http://cphpost.dk/news/danish-minister-on-the-verge-of-being-sacked.html

17. https://www.nationalgeographic.com/magazine/2009/06/cheap-food/
https://www.un.org/esa/socdev/rwss/docs/2011/chapter4.pdf

18. https://agricultureandfood.dk/

19. https://www.oecd-ilibrary.org/sites/1eeec492-en/1/2/2/3/index.html?itemId=/content/publication/1eeec492-en&_csp_=1a16badfe958d9223522404bb31624d9&itemIGO=oecd&itemContentType=book#section-d1e12030

20. https://stateofgreen.com/en/uploads/2018/07/SoG_WhitePaper_ProducingMoreWithLess_210x297_V09_Web-1.pdf?time=1618907589

21. https://www.foedevarestyrelsen.dk/english/Food/Organic_food/Pages/default.aspx

22. https://www.organicdenmark.com/facts-figures-about-danish-organics?fbclid=Iw AR3cn7SHVopc_5VXf3HZUN0LL6_mPMNVks81XIpIrzyTyXQ2SlnvHV15 L74
23. https://ec.europa.eu/info/strategy/priorities-2019-2024/european-green-deal_en
24. https://ec.europa.eu/food/horizontal-topics/farm-fork-strategy_en
25. https://agricultureandfood.dk/climate-neutral-2050/climate-neutral-2050#
26. https://maelkeritidende.dk/dairynordic/news/covid-19-costly-experience-dairy-exports
27. https://ec.europa.eu/commission/presscorner/detail/en/IP_20_510
28. https://water-drive.eu/multifunctional-land-consolidation-in-denmark-2020-2021/
29. https://www.oecd.org/officialdocuments/publicdisplaydocumentpdf/?cote=ECO/ WKP(2019)13&docLanguage=En
30. https://agricultureandfood.dk/danish-agriculture-and-food/responsible-soy-production

References

Altinget. (2010). Vrede landmænd vil stævne staten, by Emilie Iess Halberg, 31 August 2010. Retrieved from https://www.altinget.dk/miljoe/artikel/vrede-landmaend-vil-staevne-staten

Altinget. (2013a). Landbruget tegner fremtiden sort trods milliardoverskud, by Kjeld Hansen, 27 February 2013. Retrieved from https://www.altinget.dk/foedevarer/artikel/landbruget-tegnerfremtiden-sort-trods-milliardoverskud

Altinget. (2013b). Ny tvivl om randzoner, by Anders Jerking, 22 November 2013. Retrieved from https://www.altinget.dk/miljoe/artikel/130809-ny-tvivl-om-randzoner

Altinget. (2015). Paradigmeskifte i dansk fødevareproduktion, by Britta Riis, 27 May 2015. Retrieved from https://www.altinget.dk/foedevarer/artikel/paradigmeskifte-i-dansk-foedevareproduktion

Altinget. (2016). Overblik: Forstå dramaet om landbrugspakken, by Anders Jerking, 23 February 2016. Retrieved from https://www.altinget.dk/artikel/overblik-forstaa-dramaet-om-landbrugspakken

Bogason, P. (1992). Strong or weak state? The case of Danish agricultural export policy, 1849–1906. *Comparative Politics*, *24*(2), 219–227.

Börzel, A. T., & Panke, D. (2019). Europeanisation. In M. Cini & B. Pérez-Solórzano (Eds.), *European union politics* (pp. 115–126). Oxford: Oxford University Press.

Chatzopoulou, S. (2015). When do national administrations adapt to EU policies? Variation in Denmark and Greece. *International Journal of Public Administration*. doi:10.1080/01900692.2014.930752

Chatzopoulou, S. (2020a). Europeanization and domestic administrative adaptation. In *The Europeanization of national administrations* (pp. 23–54). Cham: Springer.

Chatzopoulou, S. (2020b). The Danish case. In *The Europeanization of national administrations* (pp. 55–97). Cham: Springer.

Chatzopoulou, S. (2020c). Administrative adaptation during the Eurozone crisis in the Europeanization of national administrations. In *The Europeanization of national administrations* (pp. 157–177). Cham: Springer.

Christiansen, F. J. (2020). The Liberal Party. From agrarian and liberal to center right catch all. In P. M. Christiansen, J. Elklit, & P. Nedergaard (Eds.), *The Oxford handbook of Danish politics* (pp. 296–312). Oxford: Oxford University Press.

Danish Agriculture & Food Council. (2013, November). Overimplementering af EU regler. Retrieved from https://lf.dk/om-os/vores-holdning/erhvervspolitik/over-implementeringer-af-eu-regler

Daugbjerg, C. (1998). Linking policy networks and environmental policies: Nitrate policy making in Denmark and Sweden 1970–1995. *Public Administration*. doi:10.1111/1467-9299.00101

Daugbjerg, C., Andersen, P., Hansen, H. O., & Jacobsen, B. H. (2020). Agricultural and fisheries policy: Towards market liberalism. In P. M. Christiansen, J. Elklit, & P. Nedergaard (Eds.), *The Oxford handbook of Danish politics* (pp. 627–643). Oxford: Oxford University Press.

Euroactiv. (2016). Commission warns Denmark over its new agriculture package. Retrieved from https://www.euractiv.com/section/climate-environment/news/commission-warns-denmark-over-its-new-agriculture-package/

Food & Agriculture Organisation. (2014). *Food losses and waste in the context of sustainable food systems. A report by the High Level Panel of Experts on food security and nutrition of the Committee on World Food Security*. Rome: FAO.

Hjelmar, U. (2011). Consumers' purchase of organic food products: A matter of convenience and reflexive practices. *Appetite*, *56*(2), 336–344.

Hutchings, N., & Dalgaard, T. (2021). Udledninger fra landbruget er en stor barriere for at blive klimaneutrale i 2050. Retrieved from https://www.altinget.dk/foedevarer/artikel/forskere-landbrugets-stigende-drivhusgasemissioner-er-en-stor-barriere-for-at-naa-2050-maal-om-kulstofneutralitet?fbclid=IwAR0KP02eaiRGsI MkWQBXzdOn8w8T16WX6pQgZiMoR7u4AGVldrOmFx6exGo. Accessed on May 7, 2021.

Jacobs, C., Berglund, M., Kurnik, B., Dworak, T., Marras, S., Mercu, V., & Michetti, M. (2019). *Climate change adaptation in the agriculture sector in Europe*. Report, European Environmental Agency (EEA). Luxembourg: Publications Office of the European Union.

Jensen, D. M., & Nedergaard, P. (2020). Danish European Union policies sailing between economic benefits and political sovereignty. In P. M. Christiansen, J. Elklit, & P. Nedergaard (Eds.), *The Oxford handbook of Danish politics* (pp. 487–501). Oxford: Oxford University Press.

Karantininis, K. (2007). The network form of the cooperative organization: An illustration with the Danish pork industry. In K. Karantininis & J. Nilsson (Eds.), *Vertical markets and cooperative hierarchies: The role of cooperatives in the agri-food industry*. Dordrecht: Springer.

Martinsen, D. S. (2013). Danmarks implementering af EU-politik. *Politica*, *45*(4), 437–456.

Meuwissen, M. P. M., & Feindt, P. H. (2020). Multiple suggestions to enhance resilience. *EuroChoices*, *19*(2), 3–3.

Ministry of Agriculture and Food. (2010). Towards a new common agricultural policy comments from the Danish government to the Commission's public debate. Ministry of Foreign Affairs in Denmark, The Danish Food Sector. Retrieved from https://investindk.com/publications/danish-food-industry

Ministry of Environment and Food. (2018). Vaekstplan for_dansk_oekologi. Retrieved from https://mfvm.dk/fileadmin/user_upload/MFVM/Vaekstplan_for_dansk_oekologi.pdf

Ministry of Food, Agriculture and Fisheries. (2015). Økologi plan sammen om mere økologi. Retrieved from https://mfvm.dk/fileadmin/user_upload/FVM.dk/Dokumenter/Landbrug/Indsatser/Oekologi/OekologiplanDanmark.pdf

Ministry for Industry, Business and Financial Affairs. (2013). *Danmark i arbejde-Vækstplan*. Retrieved from https://em.dk/media/9170/vaekstplan-for-foedevarer.pdf

Nørby, T. E. (2013, November 7). Randzoner spænder ben for danske arbejdspladser. *Debat*. Retrieved from https://dbrs.dk/artikel/randzoner-sp%C3%A6nder-ben-for-danske-arbejdspladser

OECD. (2020a). *Agricultural policy monitoring and evaluation 2020*. Paris: OECD Publishing. doi:10.1787/928181a8-en

OECD. (2020b). *Environment at a glance 2020*. Paris: OECD Publishing. doi:10.1787/4ea7d35f-en

Pedersen, E. H., Buchholst, B. V., & Drejer, P. A. (2014). Danish agriculture. *Danmarks Nationalbank Monetary Review, 2nd Quarter*. Retrieved from https://www.nationalbanken.dk/en/publications/Documents/2014/06/Monetary%20Review%202nd%20quarter%202014.pdf. Accessed on April 4, 2021.

Schou, J. S. r. & Bramsen, J. M. R. (2020). Hvis der er styr på indtjeningen, er gæld ikke et problem. *Altinget*, 29 January 2020. Retrieved from https://www.altinget.dk/foedevarer/artikel/ifro-hvis-der-er-styr-paa-indtjeningen-er-gaeld-ikke-et-problem

Sønderskov, K. M., & Daugbjerg, C. (2010). The state and consumer confidence in eco-labeling: Organic labeling in Denmark, Sweden, The United Kingdom and The United States. *Agriculture and Human Values*, 28(4), 507–517.

Section V
Demographic Changes and Immigration

Chapter 11

One of the Best Pension Systems in the World?

Fritz von Nordheim and Jon Kvist

Abstract

The transition from large to small working age cohorts and perpetually increasing longevity presents major challenges to pension systems around the world. In this context, the Danish system has been highlighted as particularly adequate and sustainable, although often developed more as element in macro-economic and fiscal policies than pension visions and certainly enabled and bolstered through other policies, such as fixed exchange rates, debt reduction, wage restraint, employment maximation and tax reform. The combined effect of six distinctive pension policy features places Danish pensions in the super-league of national systems: (1) a generous minimum pension providing all residents with basic old age security; (2) progressive redistribution resulting from the integration of public and private pension benefits; (3) high occupational pension coverage, with sizable contributions offering immediate membership, vesting and full portability of rights; (4) the tax regime, where investment return taxation substantially reduces the fiscal pressure from tax-exempting gross income in the build-up period and deferral of income tax until benefits are paid out, secures a revenue windfall at the height of ageing; (5) the linking of pensionable ages to life expectancy, which aims to lower pension costs, increases labour supply, growth and tax revenue and (6) the regime for third pillar schemes preventing their use in tax planning. Although the Danish pension experience has its obvious peculiarities, lessons for other governments can be found in the public–private benefit integration, the tax regime, the life expectancy indexing of pensionable ages and the use of pensions in economic policies.

Keywords: Pensions; ageing population; longevity risk; retirement age; older workers; pension reforms

Public Governance in Denmark, 191–208
Copyright © 2022 by Emerald Publishing Limited
All rights of reproduction in any form reserved
doi:10.1108/978-1-80043-712-820221011

Introduction

Population ageing represents a serious challenge to viable pension systems (e.g., World Bank, 1994). Since the 1990s, politicians have struggled to devise a pension system that can be both adequate and economically viable in ageing societies (e.g., Holzmann & Hinz, 2005).

In the renowned Melbourne Mercer Global Index of pension system performance (Mercer, 2012–2020), the combined score of the Danish pension system has consistently been highlighted as one of the best in the world: 'A first class and robust retirement income system that delivers good benefits is sustainable and has a high level of integrity' (Mercer, 2020, p. 6). Danish and international experts largely concur (e.g., European Commission, 2015, 2018a, 2018b; Pensionskommissionen, 2015).

The Mercer scoring is based on a weighted index of adequacy (40%), sustainability (35%) and integrity (25%). It also focusses on how schemes are supported by economic performance indicators, such as public debt, national and household savings, employment rates and economic growth. Indeed, without the policies adopted ahead of or parallel to changes to the retirement system, the Danish pension system would be much less impressive. Long-term commitment to fixed exchange rates, debt reduction, wage restraint, activation, employment maximation and tax reform has helped prepare for and bolster pension reforms.

Remarkably, Mercer scores Denmark well ahead of Sweden and Norway. Sweden twice excelled as the global leader in grand pension design (1960 and 1998), and Norway followed suit (Von Nordheim, 2012). In contrast, Denmark was long the Nordic pension laggard, and when the current three-pillar structure emerged, developments followed more from macro-economic concerns and ad hoc decisions than from any clear pension vision (Larsen & Andersen, 2004, pp. 52–121).

By 2012, however, when Mercer first assessed Danish pensions, a remarkable system of pension provision had been formed. Key was pioneering legislation, which raised the pensionable age and linked it to developments in life expectancy while restricting access to early retirement.

We present the Danish pension system below, highlighting its distinctive qualities and tracing how it came about, before discussing its pros and cons, lifting out some lessons of general relevance and concluding.

Analysis

The Present Danish Pension System

For old-age provision, Denmark has a three-pillar pension system with statutory, occupational and personal schemes, respectively, covering the classic functions of poverty prevention, income maintenance and additional savings, while sharing the insurance function and representing robust risk diversification (see Fig. 1). Retirement practices are also affected by schemes for early withdrawal and disability (European Commission, 2018a, 2018b; Finansministeriet, 2017a).

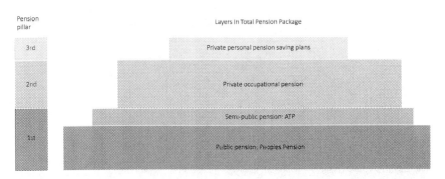

Fig. 1.   Structure of the Danish Pension System.

The three-pillar structure in itself says little about the merits of the Danish system. Some of its qualities emerge from how the various details add up. But it is primarily six distinctive features, which elevate Danish pensions into the super-league of national pension systems. We highlight these qualities after presenting the main current elements of the system (2020).

The first pillar consists of three statutory schemes: the national old-age pension covering all residents, known as the Folkepension (literally: People's Pension); the ATP (Arbejdsmarkedets Tillægspension), covering all employed people; and the OP (Obligatorisk Pension), covering those on social security.

The *Folkepension*, which still accounts for almost two-thirds of all pensioner income, is a universal, non-contributory scheme financed from general taxation on a pay-as-you-go basis. To qualify for the full pension, people must reside at least 40 years in Denmark between age 15 and the pensionable age. Benefits are taxed as personal income and consist of a flat-rate basic amount and an income-tested supplement. Further supplementary benefits include a generous housing benefit, some heating and health allowances and a reduced owner-occupier housing tax. Pensioners with little to no savings or income in addition to the old-age pension receive a complementary benefit (ATP, 2013a). Pensions can be combined with moderate earned income without affecting the income-tested supplement and be deferred up to 10 years with an actuarial bonus.

The *ATP* is a fully funded, defined-contribution scheme financed by moderate flat-rate contributions from all employed persons and all working-age claimants of cash benefits. The mandatory ATP covers about 85% of the working-age population. Self-employed individuals can join on a voluntary basis. The ATP, which offers a moderate, supplementary annuity, is organised in a separate fund under tripartite management.

The *OP* is a new, fully funded, defined-contribution scheme financed by small, income-related contributions from cash benefit recipients.

The second pillar consists of occupational schemes based on collective tariff agreements providing compulsory coverage for all workers employed on such terms. These primarily sector-wide schemes administered in pension funds under social partner control cover 94% of all full-time employees and about 65% of the working-age population (ATP, 2013b). While the coverage rate in the public sector is almost 100%, it is about 75% in the private sector. The bulk of occupational schemes are fully funded, defined-contribution, pension insurances with obligatory, in-house annuitisations. Schemes are devoid of any inter- or intragenerational transfers other than those attributed to the insurance coverage. Income-tax-exempt contributions vary. Skilled and unskilled workers contribute 12%, while people with mid-level professional training (e.g., schoolteachers) pay 15% and academics 18%. Benefit packages typically include a 10–15-year annuity, an annuity for life and a lump sum upon retirement. Schemes also offer disability and survivor pensions. The share of occupational schemes in overall pension income is steadily rising as the payouts from the major sectoral schemes established around 1990 expand and earlier schemes begin to mature.

The third pillar consists of a wide range of voluntary, personal life insurance and pension savings plans with uneven coverage and differing scope. Most savings schemes allow lump-sum payments with no annuitisation obligation. Schemes are used for a top-up to secure a higher level of pension income or to compensate for a lack of savings in second pillar schemes. Earlier lucrative possibilities to use schemes for tax speculation have largely been eliminated, but top-up savings schemes remain quite widespread. While compensatory savings are particularly relevant for the self-employed and employees not covered by collective agreements offering occupational pensions, they are on average unevenly covered and their savings rates insufficient (ATP, 2013c, 2015).

The public and private pensions interact (see Fig. 2); the higher the private pension, the lower the public pension, although the basic amount of the Folkepension is always paid out.

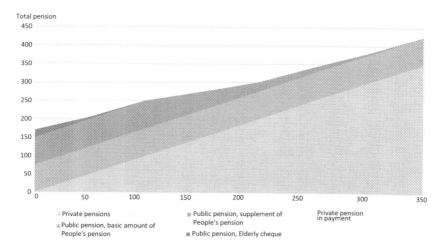

Fig. 2.   The Interaction between Public and Private. Pensions, 1,000 DKK. *Source:* Pensionskommissionen (2015).

Early retirement is not possible with the Folkepension. Instead, needs for premature labour market exit are served by four separate schemes. The Voluntary Early Retirement Pay Scheme, 'VERPS', is a voluntary, contributory scheme tied to the unemployment insurance scheme. Entitlement 3 years before the pensionable age is predicated on a 30-year contribution record and eligibility for unemployment benefits. A so-called *Seniorpension* can be claimed 6 years before reaching the pensionable age by people incapable of working more than 18 hours per week. Those who have a work record of 42, 43 or 44 years by age 61 obtain the right to an 'Early Pension' 1, 2 or 3 years before the pensionable age, respectively (Beskæftigelsesministeriet, 2020). The disability pension is for those with a permanent loss of a major part of their capacity to work.

The Danish Pension System – Six Distinctive Characteristics
The distinctive features of the Danish three-pillar system are (1) a relatively generous minimum pension reducing the poverty risk and providing basic old-age security for all residents (ATP, 2013a; Beier Sørensen & Keldorff, 2015); (2) the progressive redistribution resulting from the integration between the public and private tiers in the pension package, where the private pension income testing of the pension supplement curbs the inequality effect from earnings-related occupational pensions and reduces public pension expenditure (Beier Sørensen, 2015); (3) the high occupational pension scheme coverage with sizable contributions offering immediate membership and vesting without health criteria as well as full portability of rights in case of job changes, under bi-partite, quality pension fund administration (Von Nordheim, 2004); (4) the positive fiscal implications of the special ETT tax regime (tax exemption of contributions, taxation of investment returns and pension in payment), where the 15.3% so-called 'PAL' (*Pensionsafkastbeskatningsloven*) tax on returns substantially reduces the fiscal pressure from tax-exempting 12–14% of gross income in the build-up period, and the deferral of income tax until benefits are paid out imply a windfall of extra revenue at the height of ageing, which can help cover the extra cost of providing care for the increasing share of very old persons (Nielsen, 2012); (5) the linking of all pensionable ages to developments in life expectancy for 60-year-olds is aimed at limiting average public pension duration to 14.5 years. This is an important instrument in government efforts to expand the labour supply by raising exit ages, thereby counteracting the demographic shrinkage in the share of people of traditional working age (20–64); (6) the tax and regulatory regime for third pillar schemes largely pre-empts their use in tax planning and secures that members are well informed about their pension prospects.

How the Danish Pension System Evolved

When Gøsta Esping-Andersen (1990) developed his seminal typology of welfare capitalisms and categorised the Danish welfare model as social democratic and universalist, this included reference to the characteristics of the Folkepension at that time. Later developments have turned the pension system into a hybrid, mixing social democratic and liberal features, albeit in a distinctively Nordic manner.

To understand why Denmark did not follow the public pension route of Sweden and Norway, instead ending up with a pension system like the one the World Bank began promoting in the mid-1990s, we must examine the developments since the early 1960s (Green-Petersen, 2007).

The foundation of the present Danish pension system came with the so-called 'full Folkepension' for all residents, irrespective of gender, labour market record, income and wealth, which took effect in 1970 (Petersen & Petersen, 2012). At the time it was widely perceived to be a major achievement, it is indeed the part of the pension system that has since guaranteed all Danish residents basic security in old age (Petersen & Petersen, 2013, 2014). Internationally, it was also rather unique for its universality (i.e., equal pension rights for women), benefits levels and full financing through general taxation. Even today, none of the parties in the Folketing object to the Folkepension, and there is no part of the welfare state that enjoys greater or wider support in the electorate. Currently, it still provides about two-thirds of all pension income, and even when occupational pensions are mature in 2080, it is expected to constitute almost 40% of pension income (Finansministeriet, 2017a).

The Folkepension has also been the pivotal point in the evolution of the Danish pension system, both because the Folkepension has remained the foundation of the entire system and because key developments have revolved around its inherent limitations: The pensionable age and flat-rate benefit applies to everyone, irrespective of considerable differences in retirement and income maintenance needs. These inadequacies became recurring themes in subsequent reforms.

The VERPS, the Seniorpension, Early Pension and the possibility to defer one's pension represent attempts at meeting the need for a differentiated pension age. The late 1970s saw the introduction of the VERPS, which afforded insured workers the right to retire up to 7 years before the pensionable age of 67. Initially motivated by the fact that almost two-thirds of all unskilled workers were either dead, sick or unemployed before they could claim a pension, it also made sense with large numbers of youth entering the labour market to open jobs by allowing worn-out, ageing workers to retire early (Petersen 2011, 2014). Originally targeting blue-collar workers, who were insured through the union-affiliated voluntary unemployment schemes, the VERPS developed into an exceedingly popular early exit route as white-collar employees unionised and massively joined redundancy insurance schemes when unemployment was high in the 1980s (Larsen & Andersen, 2004, pp. 241–259).

When, in the search for better income maintenance, all attempts to agree on a public pillar of earnings-related pensions failed for 20 years, the foundation for the spread of occupational schemes grew. The proliferation of such schemes was greatly boosted by two factors: (1) The exemption of pension savings from taxation in a country with a high marginal tax rate provided strong economic incentives. (2) When the public sector underwent rapid expansion beginning in the late 1960s, governments sought to contain civil servant employment by hiring contract employees and readily agreeing to offer them occupational pension coverage as part of their terms of employment. Although schemes for white-collar elements in the private sector also became more commonplace, the bulk of the new occupational coverage was in the public sector.

Shortly after a centre-right government succeeded a Social Democratic administration in 1982, the latter having struggled with excessive budget and trade balance deficits, three policy changes of fundamental importance for the success of the later pension system occurred. Firstly, the new government decided to commit to a fixed exchange rate and forego devaluations once and for all, thus establishing a core precondition for a pension system involving massive, long-term savings. Secondly, to find instruments for inoffensive extra taxes to help close deficits, the government reluctantly agreed to legislate a tax on pension fund returns. The tax soon generated revenue of such a magnitude that it became impossible to remove. Thirdly, the cost-of-living adjustment mechanism, which had been driving run-away national inflation, was abolished. Again, this removed an important macro-economic barrier to large-scale pension savings. While none of these decisions was motivated by concerns for pension provision, they happened to open avenues for a particular version of this.

Danish politicians never made a grand decision about an earnings-related pension pillar taking the form of collectively agreed occupational schemes. But this is actually what happened, as they were unable or unwilling for decades to agree to and establish a public scheme (Larsen & Andersen, 2004, pp. 52–121).

By the early 1980s, about one-third of all wage earners had obtained some form of occupational pension rights. But manual workers had no part in this and did not strive for it before 1984, when the Danish Union of Metalworkers pondered whether they should prioritise an occupational pension in the upcoming national tariff negotiations. In the first instance, the national peak organisation asked the metalworkers to wait while it developed a proposal for a single common scheme, where the pension fund would be controlled by the union movement. Unsurprisingly, both the employers and the centre-right government fiercely opposed this proposal. As routes to legislation closed, however, industrial relations dynamics took over from the politicians and assisted in the birth of a comprehensive pillar of sector-wide, occupational pensions (Due & Madsen, 2003). A decentralised breakthrough for occupational pension agreements in the 1989 public sector negotiations opened the way for similar developments in the 1991 private sector tariff talks. The employers and unions initially clashed over the design and legal form of schemes, but practical compromises were soon found.

Once major conflict over pensions and scheme design had been avoided, union–employer collaboration secured a prompt build-up of occupational pension institutions under two-partite management. From 1990 to 1992, occupational pension coverage was raised from approximately 1/3 to about 90% of full-time employees through free collective tariff agreements. Moreover, from 1992 to 2003, contribution rates for workers were raised from 0.3% to 9% and then again to 12% in 2009. This would not have been possible if the Danish industrial relation system had not been as comprehensive, capacious and consensus oriented as is the case (see Chapter 3). In fact, industrial relations experts convincingly argue that occupational pensions have helped resurrect and solidify the consensual character of the Danish labour market model after the strife and conflict of the late 1970s and early 1980s (Due & Madsen, 2005).

A disharmonious pension system consisting of diverging parts was avoided as key legislation to ensure the integration of public and private benefits soon followed. As part of the 1994 tax reform, engineered by a new Social Democrat-led coalition government, all cash benefits (including the Folkepension) were raised ('grossified') to allow them to be subject to normal income tax. Since it was the income-tested supplement of the Folkepension that was raised, the total amount of the Folkepension would be tapered by other income, such as benefits from private pension schemes (Petersen & Petersen, 2014). The increasing income inequality emanating from earnings-related occupational schemes would be curbed and would free up expenditure, which could be used for allowances and services for more needy pensioners.

Another adaptation of the public pillars in view of the expanded role of the occupational pillar came in the form of two changes to the ATP pillar. Contribution levels were raised and indexed to wage developments. At the same time, the government sought to compensate for the lack of legislation addressing the needs of non-covered groups by extending ATP coverage to working-age persons outside the labour force, such as the disabled. Similarly, it eased the effects of the interruption of occupational pension contributions during periods of absence due to unemployment, maternity and longer-term sickness by paying double-ATP contributions (Petersen & Petersen, 2014).

With the build-up of occupational schemes well under way and a sensible integration of public and private benefits in place, concern shifted to the impact of early retirement on labour supply and public expenditure. Employment and social policy reforms in the 1990s meant a shift from passive to active policy approaches to unemployment – including among older workers (Andersen & Jørgensen, 2020). This led rather directly to the first major restrictions in access to early retirement through the VERP and the disability pension system. The 1998/99 VERP reform led to a sudden drop in entry followed by a long decline in membership (Jensen & von Nordheim, 2020). This was followed in 2001 by a disability pension reform that shifted focus from 'faculties lost' to 'remaining work ability', which subsequently ended the privileged access of older workers to disability pensions.

Meanwhile, new political circumstances after 2001 led to improvements in the minimum public pension package. In exchange for their support for the budget proposals of the centre-right minority governments (2001–2011), the Danish People's Party secured annual improvements in a new supplement for pensioners subsisting solely on their Folkepension income (Petersen & Petersen, 2014). Consequently, the minimum social pension came to offer steadily better protection against old-age poverty.

The concern of policymakers shifted in the early 2000s towards the impacts of the impending demographic transition. One main reason was that longevity growth, which thus far had appeared to be a very manageable part of population ageing (Finansministeriet, 1995; Regeringen, 2000), began to accelerate. Life expectancy at age 60 had increased by as much as 2 years from 1995 to 2005, which truly worried politicians (Sundhedsudvalget, 2006). If this trend continued, pension duration could expand by an extra 7 years by 2040. Since average pension duration in 1995 had amounted to 14.5 years, one was looking at a 50% expansion in pension expenditure merely from longevity growth, which would add to costs of the adjacent doubling of the number of pensioners.

As this prospect sunk in, expert commissions were asked to determine which changes in welfare and employment policies would be needed to counter the negative impacts of ageing on labour supply and pension costs. The so-called 'Welfare Commission' suggested immediate reforms aimed at ensuring that longer lives would also result in longer working lives (Smith & Petersen, 2006). The centre-right Prime Minister initially flatly refused suggestions to start raising eligibility ages for VERPS and the Folkepension already from 2009 and 2013, respectively. Aside from the Conservatives, all of the political parties reacted in similarly negative ways. It was therefore rather surprising when, a mere six months later, the Minister of Finance was able to get most of the opposition parties to agree to a major retirement reform (Regeringen, 2006). The Social Democrats needed to demonstrate their willingness to take responsibility for prudent fiscal policies while also ensuring the continuation of the VERP. The Danish People's Party was motivated partly by their need to gain acceptance as a reliable partner and partly by some further restrictions on immigration and integration, which were hitched to the deal. Nevertheless, although aided by the Danish political culture of broad compromises, what really paved the way for the agreement was that the timing had become fundamentally different from the one suggested by the experts (Petersen & Petersen, 2014).

The pension age would be raised from 65 to 67 in the period 2024–2027. The pensionable age would thereafter be linked to developments in life expectancy for 60-year-olds, meaning that the average duration of pension receipt would approach the 14.5 years to which it had amounted in 1995. Since 2015, the pensionable age would be raised in line with longevity growth every fifth year, with a maximum of 1 year and a 15-year warning; that is, people could prepare for the increase to take effect in 15 years. Hence, the first increase would occur in 2030 (Finansministeriet, 2006).

While the VERPS and its 5-year duration would be maintained, the earliest age for receiving VERPS would likewise increase from 60 to 62 years. Thereafter, it would also be linked to life expectancy. Importantly, the restricted access to early retirement for older workers was balanced with regained rights in the labour market. For decades, the right to claim unemployment benefits and to draw on the services of the employment office had ceased when people reached VERPS eligibility age. But by 2006, workers aged 60–64 years had regained full access to job centre services, and follow-up legislation outlawed mandatory retirement and firings on grounds of age.

In 2011, with reference to the economic crisis, a centre-right government argued for the necessity of boosting late-career employment and lowering early exit costs by phasing out the VERPS. Over opposition from the Social Democrats, the government found a majority for its proposal to move the 2006 reform

5 years forward while gradually downsizing and phasing out the VERPS (Finansministeriet, 2011; Regeringen, 2011). To meet the needs of people with severe attrition, the government at the same time proposed a fast track in the disability scheme for older workers. The VERPS reform took effect from 2014, and the Folketing adopted the first life-expectancy-growth-induced increase in the pensionable age in 2015 (Finansministeriet, 2015). It will increase from 67 to 68 years in 2030.

In 2016, the government failed to find a majority for its proposal to raise the pensionable age by another six months by 2030 (Regeringen, 2016). It had more success with its 2017 proposals to allow pension receipt to be combined with a higher amount of earned income and to lower the period that private pensions can be taken out ahead of the pensionable age from 5 to 3 years (Finansministeriet, 2017b).

Claiming that the phasing out of VERP had unhinged the pension system and left people with long, strenuous working lives at high risk of prematurely wearing down without a dignified route to retirement, the Social Democrats campaigned in the 2019 election for a new right to an earlier Folkepension (Socialdemokratiet, 2019). Sixteen months later, this resulted in parliamentary agreements on two new early retirement schemes: the Seniorpension and the Early Pension (Regeringen, 2020). The current government sees these schemes as paving the way for broader public acceptance of the longevity linking of the pensionable age. Accordingly, the new early retirement options were adopted on the same day that the Folketing decided to raise the pensionable age to 69 in 2035. The absence of serious protests from major trade unions, which formerly had mobilised against further increases, reflects how opposition subsided with the introduction of these new schemes.

Discussion

Longevity Linking of the Pensionable Age

The life-expectancy indexing of pensionable ages is a core strength of the Danish pension system, but its implementation and likely long-term social and economic consequences are less impressive.

Intergenerational and Gender Inequities

Raising the pensionable age in line with longevity growth can be an immensely powerful way of limiting the negative impacts of population ageing. But the way Danish politicians have chosen to execute it weakens the beneficial effects and creates intergenerational inequities.

While 'life-expectancy linking' was legislated in 2006, the first increases in pensionable ages were only planned to take effect from 2019 and 2024. Even if the reform exercise was moved 5 years forward in 2011, implementation still represented a grandfatherly approach. Age cohorts born 1940–1953 escaped the reforms altogether. For them, the pensionable age was even lowered to 65 years. Persons born in 1954 are the first to experience a rise in the pensionable age.

Other aspects result in further intergenerational inequities. Younger age cohorts will have to work increasingly longer and receive pension for ever shorter periods than the pensioners of today, both in absolute and relative terms. While a 65-year-old male is on average currently receiving 16 pension years after 40.5 years of work, a 25-year-old will receive a mere 14 pension years after 48.5 years of work. Since women live longer, all female age groups will have more pension years, but the intergenerational inequities are similar (Kvist, 2019).

The universal and unisex features of the Folkepension protect women particularly well given their somewhat lower labour market activity and longer life expectancy. By contrast, the occupational pension pillar as a mirror image of labour market performance tends to benefit men more than women. Still, in terms of occupational pension coverage, women are in a far more equal position vis-à-vis men than in many countries thanks to the gender equality rules in the individual schemes.

Longer-term Risks of Social Inequities and Dwindling Economic Gains
Successive governments have been fascinated by how restrictions in access to early retirement seem to have underpinned structural trends towards higher employment and rising exit ages (Finansministeriet, 2007, 2017a). In long-term national budgeting, the longevity linking of the pension age has come to be portrayed as the *sine qua non* of fiscal sustainability, with a surplus at the height of population ageing (Finansministeriet, 2019a, 2019b).

What started as successful efforts to reverse a longstanding fall in effective exit ages and to limit the cost of early retirement has evolved into a major effort to counter the negative impacts of ageing by expanding the labour supply of older workers (Finansministeriet, 2014, 2017c, 2017d).

However, as the increasing life expectancy, which is primarily caused by better medical treatments for people in their 80s and 90s (Lunenfeld & Stratton, 2013), cannot be equated with a proportionally increasing work ability for those in their 60s and 70s, the strategy of ever later pensionable ages is likely to meet its limits in both social and economic terms.

With rising pensionable ages, ever-increasing segments of workers will come to find their work ability seriously ebbing before becoming eligible for a public pension. Unless they qualify for the new early-exit schemes, they will be compelled to use some of their occupational pension savings (ATP, 2013b). In both instances, the income inequalities between those who can continue working until the pensionable age and those who cannot will take off. As a growing number of Danish wage earners will have to revert to part-time work or retire before reaching the pensionable age, the expected economic benefits will also wane. The hoped-for contributions to GDP and tax revenue will dwindle and, as people flow onto whichever scheme will help them survive until they can claim a pension, the cost of early retirement, unemployment and sickness benefits will increase. In the longer run, life-expectancy indexing may thus threaten the social and economic merits of the current pension model (Jensen & von Nordheim, 2020). Thus far, politicians are at a loss to overcome this challenge, as their mid- to long-term fiscal planning is based on the rather optimistic expectation of a continual rise in effective exit ages (Finansministeriet, 2018, 2019a). Further research is needed to help quantify the challenge and clarify its timing.

Use of Pension Savings as an Economic Policy Instrument

From the beginning, considerations about an earnings-related pension pillar have been overlayered with macro-economic, fiscal and wage policy concerns (Larsen & Andersen, 2004). As Denmark suffered from insufficient national savings and deficits in the balance of payment in the 1960s and 1970s, earnings-related pensions were perceived from the outset as possible vehicles for massive long-term savings. This view also defined government interest in the establishment and build-up of occupational pension schemes (Andersen, 2011). Moreover, governments have tended to see and use funded pensions as a significant instrument both for stop-go policies and for long-term fiscal planning.

Sensitivity to Economic Downturns

The integration of public and private pension benefits has been highlighted as a strength when viewed from the angles of redistribution and public expenditure (Beier Sørensen, 2015). Likewise, we have pointed to the advantages of the tax regime from a revenue perspective. However, both advantages entail vulnerabilities with fluctuations in the economic cycle. While the risk diversification across the pillars will help insulate pensioners from the worst consequences of longer term, low or negative returns on pension savings to some extent (ATP, 2019), such a scenario will seriously reduce the intake from the PAL tax and the income taxing of private pension payouts. Should this occur, the public sector will have to replace income foregone through other taxes or find equivalent savings.

Implications for the National Economy and Its Political Economy

Where the Folkepension is a straightforward old-age provision, the full funding of the earnings-related pension pillar takes Danish pensions into terrain far beyond provisions for retirees: those of macro-economics and a political economy with a steadily growing role for institutional investors (Von Nordheim, 1996).

At the macro-economic level, pension savings have helped transform Denmark from a country with recurrent, sizeable deficits in its balance of payments to one with considerable, stable surpluses. In 2018, the pension fund aggregate of about DKK 4,400 billion (ca. €600 billion) ranked Denmark as the country with the largest GDP share of pension savings (210%) and the second-largest share per capita (OECD, 2018).

Obviously, this represents a formidable economic resource for stability and the financing of challenges such as the green transition (Forsikring & Pension, 2020). But it also compels governments to fend for the peculiar interests of a nation of long-term savers. Quantitative easing and low-interest periods represent major worries, and devaluations are no longer possible.

In the early 2000s, political attempts to have pension savings legally equated with individual life-time investment projects – instead of rightly as collective pension insurances – were averted, but other investment-related, non-pension perspectives keep flaring up (e.g., Økonomi-og Erhvervsministeriet, 2003).

The new pension institutions have excelled thus far. They have been so well-managed and invested so successfully that they have drawn international recognition and received awards (IPE, 2018, 2019, 2020). But large-scale money management brings with it the risk of mismanagement and misappropriation.

There are also the dangers of political raiding: With lots of money steadily accumulating in pension funds, there will often be ideas for how it could be used to achieve other objectives before it is needed for its primary purpose.

Lessons Learned and Implications for Practice

Major Danish politicians, government officials, pension experts and pension industry professionals are largely united in their appreciation of the Danish pension system and its performance. Apart from the possible need for early retirement rights for workers with particularly long working lives, they concur that further reforms may only be called for at the margins (Pensionskommissionen, 2015). Still, they also often busy themselves with various tinkering to maintain and slightly improve the public pillars and the regulation of personal pension savings.

For politicians from the main Danish parties, the lessons learned include that (1) the ETT tax regime functions well, (2) the double-payment challenge when funded systems are introduced can be handled, (3) it is important to maintain the integration of public and private benefits, (4) the occupational pillar can be safely left in the hands of the social partners and the pension institutions that they have established, while (5) it is important to build sound collaboration between government and the pension industry, (6) life-expectancy linking appears to be able to markedly ease the budgetary implications of population ageing (Finansministeriet, 2017a).

From the convoluted, incremental and somewhat messy story of the development of the Danish pension system set out in previous sections, one might easily get the impression that none of its qualities can be emulated in the systems of other countries.

But that is not the case. There are important possible lessons for other countries in the (1) principles of public–private benefit integration, (2) the ETT taxation – particularly the PAL tax, (3) the life-expectancy indexing of the pensionable age, (4) the central involvement of the social partners and (5) the handling of the double-payment challenge. The underpinning of the savings emphasis in the pension system through economic policies preventing inflation also calls for attention, as does the use of funded pensions in fiscal policies.

The important thing is to be aware of some of the dilemmas and trade-offs in the distinctive qualities of the Danish pension system.

The integration of benefits from public and private pillars as well as the taxation of returns obviously also compel the public purse to bear the economic consequences if pension fund returns drop to low levels and remain there for extended periods.

If the pensionable age keeps rising as foreseen, major new income inequalities in old age are likely to emerge. They will result not just from the wage hierarchy and labour-market-career-induced differences in savings, but from a growing gap between effective exit ages and the statutory pension age.

The key role for the social partners in the provision of earnings-related pension obviously also implies that governments have far less control and are dependent on the continued ability of the industrial relations system and the autonomous pension institutions to deliver.

Countries often shy away from funding parts of the pension system because they fear the double-payment challenge (i.e., sizeable private contributions to future pensions on top of taxes for current pensions). Even if the Danish case demonstrates that it can be handled while Danish governments simultaneously managed to reduce the public debt from 53% in 1994 to 11% of BNP in 2008, one should be aware of how this required favourable economic conditions in addition to a rare kind of long-term commitment.

Irrespective of the qualities inherent in the Danish pension system, its relative success continues to rely on flanking policies, such as fixed exchange rates, balanced public budgets, wage moderation, activation of the unemployed and employment maximation.

Noteworthy also is how it is the combined score of the Danish system in a weighted index that ranks it as a top performer. On traditional performance scores, such as poverty prevention, income maintenance and pension benefit duration, other national pension systems perform better than the Danish system on the one dimension or the other.

Conclusion

We have highlighted a number of distinctive qualities, which we believe will continue to place the current Danish pension system among the best in the world. Still, observers should also be aware of some of its dilemmas and longer-term weaknesses.

Currently, life-expectancy indexing as a key feature of the Danish pension system seems set to meet major challenges in two areas:

(1) Politically, it is currently being tested for the first time, which follows from the fact that it is first now that the agreed increase in the pensionable age is taking effect.
(2) Its long-term ability to curb inequality is likely to be waning. If it evolves as planned, an increasing gap between the effective retirement age and pensionable age will develop.

In the longer run, life-expectancy indexing may become a major challenge to the fairness and social sustainability of the current Danish pension model. Under social and political pressure, the Ministry of Finance is beginning to nuance and correct its basic assumptions about the economic gains that are likely to result from a linear continuation of longevity linking (Altinget, 2020a). The union movement is demanding that the Ministry also examines alternative and supplementary ways of handling upcoming ageing challenges (Altinget, 2020b). The extent to which this will lead to changes in how pensionable ages are indexed to life expectancy remains to be seen.

References

Altinget. (2020a). Pres på regeringen vokser: HK kræver opgør med stigende pensionsalder. 9 October 2020.

Altinget. (2020b). Regeringen ændrer regnemetode og gør det billigere at stoppe stigende pensionsalder. 27 October 2020.

Andersen, J. G. (2011). Denmark: The silent revolution toward a multipillar pension system. In B. Ebbinghaus (Ed.), *The varieties of pension governance: Pension privatization in Europe* (pp. 183–209). Oxford: Oxford University Press.

Andersen, N. A., & Jørgensen, H. (2020). Udviklingslinjer og sporskifte i dansk arbejdsmarkeds- og beskæftigelsespolitik. In M. P. Klint, S. Rasmussen, & H. Jørgensen (Eds.), *Aktiv Arbejdsmarkedspolitik: Etablering, udvikling og fremtid* (pp. 89–118). Copenhagen: DJØF Publishers.

ATP. (2013a). Næsten alle folkepensionister modtager indkomstafhængige tillæg. Faktum no. 119, August.

ATP. (2013b). Hver fjerde indbetaler ikke til en arbejdsmarkedspension. Faktum no. 123, December.

ATP. (2013c). Tidlig tilbagetrækning uden efterløn kan koste tre fjerdedele af pensionsformuen. Faktum no. 122, November.

ATP. (2015). *Pensionssystemets restgruppe.* Hillerød: ATP.

ATP. (2019). Lavere fremtidige afkast på private pensioner bliver kompenseret af højere offentlig pension. Faktum no. 182, January.

Beier Sørensen, O. (2015). *The interaction of public and private pensions – the Danish Case.* Hillerød: ATP.

Beier Sørensen, O., & Keldorff, S. T. (2015). *Boligydelse til folkepensionister, dens betydning og dens incitamentsmæssige virkninger.* Hillerød: ATP.

Beskæftigelsesministeriet. (2020). *Aftale om en ny ret til tidlig pension – 10 October 2020.* Copenhagen: Ministry of Employment.

Due, J., & Madsen, J. S. (2003). *Fra magtkamp til konsensus: Arbejdsmarkedspensionerne og den danske model.* Copenhagen: Djøf.

Due, J., & Madsen, J. S. (2005). Et tilfældigt sammenfald af særlige omstændigheder: Arbejdsmarkeds-pensionernes indførelse i 1980'erne. In J. H. Petersen & K. Petersen (Eds.), *13 Reformer af den danske velfærdsstat* (pp. 189–202). Odense: University Press of Southern Denmark.

Esping-Andersen, G. (1990). *The three worlds of welfare capitalism.* Cambridge: Polity Press.

European Commission. (2015). *The 2015 pension adequacy report. Vol I and Vol II.*

European Commission. (2018a). *The 2018 ageing report*. Institutional Paper 065.

European Commission. (2018b). *The 2018 pension adequacy report. Vol I and Vol II*.

Finansministeriet. (1995). *Pensionssystemet og fremtidens forsørgerbyrde*. Copenhagen: Ministry of Finance.

Finansministeriet. (2006). *Aftale om fremtidens velstand og velfærd*. Copenhagen: Ministry of Finance.

Finansministeriet. (2007). *Fakta om udviklingen i arbejdsstyrken frem mod 2040 i lyset af allerede vedtagne reform*. Copenhagen: Ministry of Finance.

Finansministeriet. (2011). *Aftale om senere tilbagetrækning*. Copenhagen: Ministry of Finance.

Finansministeriet. (2014). *Finansredegørelse 2014*. Albertslund: Schultz.

Finansministeriet. (2015). *Pressemeddelelse vedr. lovforslag om levetidsindeksering af folkepensionsalderen af 15. september*. Copenhagen: Ministry of Finance.

Finansministeriet. (2017a). *Det danske pensionssystem nu og i fremtiden*. Copenhagen: Ministry of Finance.

Finansministeriet. (2017b). *2025-forløb og reformudspil*. Copenhagen: Ministry of Finance.

Finansministeriet. (2017c). *De ældre bliver længere på arbejdsmarkedet*. Finansministeriet. brief, 3 February 2017.

Finansministeriet. (2017d). *Stigende beskæftigelse og arbejdstid for seniorer – både blandt lavt- og højtuddannede*. Finansministeriet. brief, 17 May 2017.

Finansministeriet. (2018). Finansministerens svar til Folketingets Finansudvalg af 2. juli 2018 på Finansudvalgets spørgsmål nr. 386 af 6. juni 2018.

Finansministeriet. (2019a). Opmærksomhedspunkter i forhold til differentieret folkepensionsalder. Brief, 22 January 2019.

Finansministeriet. (2019b). *Teknisk briefing om pensionsalder*. Copenhagen: Ministry of Finance.

Forsikring & Pension. (2020). Pensionsbranchen offentliggør rekordstort tal på 50 mia. kr. for grønne investeringer. Nyheder 3 November 20220. Copenhagen. Retrieved from https://www.forsikringogpension.dk/nyheder/pensionsbranchen-offentliggoer-rekordstort-tal-paa-50-mia-kr-for-groenne-investeringer/. Accessed on September 9, 2020.

Green-Petersen, C. (2007). Denmark: A 'World Bank' pension system. In E. M. Immergut, K. M. Anderson, & I. Schulze (Eds.), *The handbook of West European pension politics* (pp. 454–498). Oxford: Oxford University Press.

Holzman, R., & Hinz, R. (2005). *Old-age income support in the 21ˢᵗ Century: An international perspective on pension systems and reforms*. Washington, DC: World Bank.

IPE. (2018). IPE conference: PensionDanmark is Europe's best pension fund. IPE News 5 December 2018. Retrieved from https://www.ipe.com/ipe-conference-pensiondanmark-is-europes-best-pension-fund/10028468.article. Accessed on November 03, 2020.

IPE. (2019) UN climate summit: Danish pensions to lead green transition with €47bn pledge. IPE News 24 SEPTEMBER 2019. Retrieved from https://www.ipe.com/un-climate-summit-danish-pensions-to-lead-green-transition-with-47bn-pledge/10033458.article. Accessed on November 03, 2020.

IPE. (2020). Danish pension funds on track to hit green goal three years early. IPE News 4 November 2020. Retrieved from https://www.ipe.com/news/danish-pension-funds-on-track-to-hit-green-goal-three-years-early/10048799.article. Accessed on November 03, 2020.

Jensen, P. H., & von Nordheim, F. (2020). Tilbagetrækning mellem flexicurity og økonomisk råderum. *Nordisk Välfärdsforskning, 5*(2), 109–121.

Kvist, J. (2019). Det egentlige pensionsproblem: meget længere arbejdstid og kortere otium for unge. *Politiken*, May 18.

Larsen, C. A., & Andersen, J. G. (2004). *Magten på Borgen*. Aarhus: Aarhus University Press.

Lunenfeld, B., & Stratton, P. (2013). The clinical consequences of an ageing world and preventive strategies. *Best Practice & Research Clinical Obstetrics & Gynaecology, 27*(5), 643–659.

Mercer. (2012–2019). *Mercer Melbourne global pension index*. Melbourne: Mercer.

Mercer. (2020). *Mercer CFA institute global pension index*. Melbourne: Mercer.

Nielsen, A. Ø. (2012). Pensionisterne betaler for sig selv. Forsikring & Pension, Brief.

OECD. (2018). *Pension outlook*. Paris: OECD.

Økonomi- og Erhvervsministeriet. (2003). *Storre valgfrihed i pensionsopsparingen*. Copenhagen: Ministry of Economic Affairs.

Pensionskommissionen. (2015). *Det danske pensionssystem: International anerkendt, men ikke problemfrit*. Copenhagen: Ministry of Taxation.

Petersen, K. (2011). *Bastarden: Historien on efterløn*. Odense: University Press of Southern Denmark.

Petersen, K. (2014). Efterløn. In J. H. Petersen, K. Petersen, & N. F. Christiansen (Eds.), *Hvor glider vi hen? Dansk velfærdshistorie, 1993–2014* (*Bind VI andet halvbind*, pp. 997–1100). Odense: University Press of Southern Denmark.

Petersen, J. H., & Petersen, K. (2012). Alderdomsforsørgelse og ældrepolitik. In J. H. Petersen, K. Petersen, & N. F. Christiansen (Eds.), *Velfærdsstatens storhedstid: Dansk velfærdshistorie, 1955–1973* (*Bind IV*, pp. 239–346). Odense: University Press of Southern Denmark.

Petersen, J. H., & Petersen, K. (2013). Alderdomsforsørgelse og ældrepolitik. In J. H. Petersen, K. Petersen, & N. F. Christiansen (Eds.). *Velfærdsstatens storhedstid. Dansk velfærdshistorie, 1973–1993* (*Bind V*, pp. 243–360). Odense: University Press of Southern Denmark.

Petersen, J. H., & Petersen, K. (2014). Alderdomsforsørgelse og ældrepolitik. In J. H. Petersen, K. Petersen, & N. F. Christiansen (Eds.). *Hvor glider vi hen? Dansk velfærdshistorie, 1993–2014* (*Bind VI forste halvbind*, pp. 337–468). Odense: University Press of Southern Denmark.

Regeringen. (2000). *Et bæredygtigt pensionssystem*. Copenhagen.

Regeringen. (2006). *Aftale om fremtidens velstand og velfærd og investeringer i fremtiden*. Albertslund: Schultz.

Regeringen. (2011). *… vi kan jo ikke låne os til velfærd!* Copenhagen.

Regeringen. (2016). DK 2025: Et stærkere Danmark. Copenhagen.

Regeringen. (2020). *Ny ret til tidlig pension: Værdig tilbagetrækning for alle* Copenhagen.

Smith, N., & Petersen, J. H. (2006). Tilbagetrækning og pension. In J. H. Petersen & K. Petersen (Eds.), *13 løsninger for den danske velfærdsstat* (pp. 151–166). Odense: University Press of Southern Denmark.

Socialdemokratiet. (2019). De mest nedslidte fortjener også en værdig pension. Hentet fra. Retrieved from https://www.socialdemokratiet.dk/media/7959/en-ny-ret-til-tidlig-folkepension-til-de-mest-nedslidte.pdf

Sundhedsudvalget og det Politisk-Økonomiske Udvalg. (2006). Kraftig stigning i befolkningens levealder. Brief, 18 October. Copenhagen: Parliament.

Von Nordheim, F. (1996). Danish occupational pensions in the 1980s: From social security to political economy. In M. Shalev (Ed.), *The privatization of social policy? Occupational welfare and the welfare state in America, Scandinavia and Japan* (pp. 241–260). New York, NY: St. Martin's Press.

Von Nordheim, F. (2004). Danske pensionskasser i EU perspektiv. In *PFA: Pensioner på arbejde 1954–2004* (pp. 54–61). Copenhagen: PFA.

Von Nordheim, F. (2012). On the first wave of NDC schemes. In R. Holzmann, E. Palmer, & D. Robalino (Eds.), *NDC pension schemes in a changing pension world: Progress, lessons and implementation* (pp. 122–126). Washington, DC: The World Bank.

World Bank. (1994). *Averting the old age crisis. Policies to protect the old and promote growth.* Washington, DC: World Bank.

Chapter 12

Ensuring Public Health Care and Tackling Growing Expenditures

Erik Bækkeskov and Peter Triantafillou

Abstract

Healthcare provision in Denmark reflects some of the key principles of the welfare state. By securing relatively easy and equal access for all Danish residents regardless of income via general tax financing, the Danish healthcare system has strong ethical merits. All residents are entitled to comprehensive healthcare services. The Danish healthcare system is also relatively efficient. Total healthcare expenditures – including public and private – amount to 10% of GDP, above the OECD 8.8% average but well below the costs in the other Nordic countries, Germany, Switzerland and the United Stated. Notwithstanding its merits, healthcare in Denmark shares key predicaments with other OECD countries, primarily how to improve health outcomes while containing care expenditures. All of the OECD countries aim to improve population life expectancy and health quality. Yet their ageing and increasingly obese populations are exacerbating the demands on their respective healthcare systems. This chapter examines changes in how Denmark has managed these challenges. The main argument is that the healthcare system performance on managing health outcomes and costs improved remarkably from the 1990s to the early 2020s, although outcome inequalities remain. Notable changes in the system were targeted innovations in treatment procedures and expansion of municipal rehabilitation and preventive efforts, along with strict budget controls.

Keywords: Public health; equity; efficiency; effectiveness; health status; life quality

Introduction

Healthcare provision in Denmark reflects some of the key principles of the welfare state. By securing relatively easy and equal access for all residents of the country

Public Governance in Denmark, 209–226
doi:10.1108/978-1-80043-712-820221012

regardless of income and with its general tax financing, the Danish healthcare system has strong ethical merits. The 'equal' treatment principle was adopted in the early nineteenth century and then gradually institutionalised. All residents are entitled to comprehensive healthcare services, a principle that enjoys broad support among residents and political parties (Larsen, 2020, p. 603).

Fast and effective healthcare has the macro-economic benefit of people returning to work and other activities sooner than otherwise might be the case (Saha, Gerdtham, & Johansson, 2010). The Danish healthcare system is also relatively efficient. Total healthcare expenditures – including public and private – amount to 10% of GDP, which is above the 8.8% OECD average but well below the costs in other Nordic countries, Germany, Switzerland and the United States (OECD, 2020a).

Compared to other countries, Danish public health has been less severely affected by issues such as HIV/AIDS (WHO Regional Office for Europe, 2019, p. 38), obesity (OECD, 2017a), antimicrobial resistance and novel communicable diseases like the 2009 H1N1 flu and COVID-19. Such outcomes suggest that the Danish healthcare system has coped relatively well with significant challenges in the past few decades.

Notwithstanding its merits, healthcare in Denmark shares key predicaments with other OECD countries, primarily how to improve health outcomes while containing care expenditures. The OECD countries all aim to improve population life expectancy and health quality. Yet their ageing and increasingly obese populations are imposing steadily greater demands on their healthcare systems. This chapter examines changes in how Denmark has managed these challenges. Its main argument is that the healthcare system performance on managing health outcomes and costs improved remarkably from the 1990s to the early 2020s, even though outcome inequalities remain (Statens Institut for Folkesundhed, 2019).[1] Notable changes in the system were targeted innovations in treatment procedures and the expansion of municipal rehabilitation and preventive efforts, along with strict budget controls.

The chapter is organised as follows. After describing the structure of healthcare system, evidence on Danish public health, healthcare service costs and survival rates are summarised. The chapter then discusses public policy initiatives that have addressed the challenges facing the system. Finally, it pinpoints the economic and political trade-offs implied by the ongoing Danish attempts to ensure high-quality healthcare for all, to contain growing expenditures and to respond adequately to emerging threats like COVID-19.

Analysis

Organisation of Danish Healthcare

Around 85% of all Danish healthcare services are funded via general taxation (Larsen, 2020, p. 596). A 1971 reform introduced public healthcare for all residents and disbanded private – albeit publicly subsidised – health insurance pools that had existed since the late nineteenth century. These pools had covered less than 10% of the population, so the popular impact of the reform was low. Nevertheless, it gave government greater control over general and specialist medical practices, which remain privately owned but depend on government pricing and permits. Private co-payments were retained outside of medical practices. Dental care, physiotherapy, psychological counselling and certain other healthcare services involve large co-payments. Moreover, direct access to private clinics and hospitals (as opposed to practices) is not tax-financed, in principle (notably, however, a public treatment guarantee within one month of diagnosis has pushed publicly funded demand towards private hospitals since the early 2000s). The use of such privately funded services further increased as companies increasingly began offering employees private health insurance packages (Holstein, 2017).

The Danish healthcare system mixes central and local governance (Knudsen & Nielsen, 2000). Under the Ministry of Health, the Danish Health Authority (*Sundhedsstyrelsen*) is the key advisor to the government and regions on all health-related matters, and it certifies medical staff (rather than the medical community itself; Starr, 1982). The Danish Medicines Agency, also under the Ministry of Health, is solely responsible for regulating the availability and quality of pharmaceuticals. In turn, public hospitals are organised under and managed by five regional authorities, which also regulate the number of general practitioners (GPs) and specialists and their fees for services. The regions collect no taxes, depending on Ministry of Finance transfers and payments from municipalities.

Healthcare services are provided by hospitals and clinics, independent GPs and specialists, and municipal healthcare services.

Denmark has 43 public and 20 private hospitals. Public hospitals are managed regionally and funded by central and municipal authorities, and they contain a broad range of medical specialities. Following a consolidation from 14 counties to 5 'regions' in 2007, several smaller public hospitals were closed and larger, more centrally located hospitals expanded. These consolidations aimed to improve specialist quality and to achieve economies of scale. While relatively numerous, private hospitals are small, with a combined financial turnover of less than 1% of the total hospital revenue (Sundhed Danmark, 2018). They focus primarily on lucrative medical specialities that public hospitals are short on, such as cosmetic surgery.

Almost all Danish residents have a designated GP, who functions as the gatekeeper to most other healthcare services, granting access through referrals to specialists and hospitals. GP gatekeeping helps to contain public health expenditures, as referrals determine whether treatments are free of charge to patients (patients can pay out of pocket for specialised examinations or treatment in practices or private hospitals, but not in public hospitals). While GP-based healthcare is quite common outside of Denmark (e.g., in the United Kingdom, Australia, New Zealand), many other OECD countries rely more on citizens' own discretion and do not require GP referrals (Austria, Greece, Sweden, Switzerland), allowing citizens to skip the referral and pay for treatment at public hospitals (Belgium, France, Germany), or by a wide variety of private and public healthcare delivery mechanisms (the United States) (Reibling & Wendt, 2012).

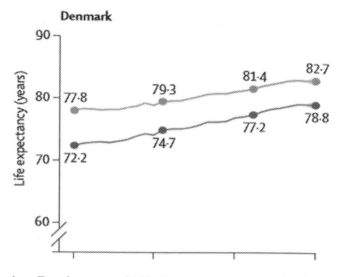

Fig. 1.   Development of Life Expectancy for Females (Red) and
Males (Blue) in Denmark from 1990 to 2017. *Source:* (Knudsen et al.,
2019, e661).

Finally, Danish municipalities provide health promotion and sickness prevention services, as well as rehabilitation and training programmes that follow up
on hospital treatment (Pedersen & Petersen, 2014). This includes programmes and
courses to help local citizens adopt healthier lifestyles and, in the case of rehabilitation, assist citizens to regain their ability to return to work. The municipalities also administer and finance services for the physically disabled, and they
provide eldercare, including retirement housing and homecare. These activities
are primarily financed by municipal tax collection and supplemented by central
government funding.

Three Key Public Health Challenges and Their Development

This section focusses on how three public health policy challenges, which are
widely shared by high-income countries, have developed in Denmark since the
late 1990s: securing public health outcomes such as life expectancy and quality of
health; overcoming capacity limitations and containing healthcare expenditures.

Contemporary states all work to secure long and healthy lives for their populations; indeed, life expectancy is a metric for successful governance. In Denmark,
however, improving life expectancy has proven surprisingly difficult. The challenge
became evident in the early 1990s, when multiple epidemiological studies revealed
that Danish citizens had lower average life expectancies and higher incidences of

several cardiovascular diseases and cancers than other Nordic (i.e., otherwise very similar) countries (Dansk Institut for Klinisk Epidemiologi, 1993).

Average life expectancy has improved significantly since the 1990s (Fig. 1) yet remains below the levels achieved in the other Nordic countries (Knudsen et al., 2019) and several other OECD countries, including Australia, Belgium, France, Italy, the Netherlands and Spain (OECD, 2020b).

Another measure of population health status is health-adjusted life years (HALE), which indicates how many years a person on average lives without disabling diseases.

Table 1 shows how the quality of health measured in 2017 for Denmark using HALE is somewhat below that of the other Nordic countries and France, while at roughly the same level as Germany and the United Kingdom. Japan and the United States constitute two extreme cases among high-income countries, the former with persistently high HALEs and the latter with very low HALEs. The table also suggests that the Danish HALE improvement from 1990 to 2017 is quite impressive for males (7.7 years), but less so for women (only 4 years). These improvements differ little from the other high-income countries (except the United States, which is an outlier in this selection); that is, the Danish public health outcomes have generally improved at-pace with neighbouring countries, even if their relative positions have not been altered.

In Denmark as elsewhere, disability and death are strongly associated with growing disease burdens from cancers, cardiovascular diseases and diabetes. Danish healthcare services have generally maintained relatively high standards. During the 1990s, however, policymakers became aware that survival rates from some forms of cancer and heart disease in Denmark were dramatically lower than in the other Nordics (Engeland et al., 1998). In the intervening decades, a combination of changes has led to improvements in these outcomes (described in the next section). Thus, by 2011, the mortality rates for patients with cardiovascular

Table 1. Development of Health-adjusted Life Years (HALE) and Healthcare Costs.

Country	1990 HALE (Female/ Male)	2017 HALE (Female/ Male)	Change 1990–2017 (% Points)
Denmark	66.9/63.7	70.6/68.6	4.0/7.7
Norway	68.1/64.0	71.1/69.3	4.4/8.3
Sweden	68.8/66.0	71.4/70.4	3.8/6.7
France	69.8/64.7	73.4/70.0	5.2/8.2
Germany	67.4/63.5	70.8/68.3	5.0/7.6
Japan	71.2/68.0	74.6/71.4	3.4/3.4
UK	67.3/64.1	70.0/68.5	4.0/6.9
US	66.8/62.6	67.9/65.3	1.6/4.3

Source: (GBD 2017 DALYs and HALE Collaborators, 2018, 1864–1865).

Table 2. Development of Healthcare Expenditures (Public and Private).

Country	1990 Healthcare Costs (Percentage of GDP) (%)	2018 Healthcare Costs (Percentage of GDP) (%)	Change 1990–2018 (% Points)
Denmark	8.0	10.1	2.1
Norway	7.1	10.0	2.9
Sweden	7.2	10.9	3.7
France	8.0	11.3	3.3
Germany	8.0	11.5	3.5
Japan	5.8	11.0	5.2
UK	5.1	10.0	4.9
US	11.3	16.9	5.6

Source: OECD Health Data.

diseases were significantly lower in Denmark than in most other OECD countries, including Norway and Sweden (OECD, 2015, p. 41). Moreover, this high performance was achieved with relatively low healthcare costs (OECD, 2015, p. 151). Survival rates for most forms of cancer have also seen significant improvements in the last two decades, even though Denmark continues to lag behind the other Nordic countries (Arnold, Rutherford, & Bardot, 2019).

Danes also tend to make more lifestyle choices that harm their health and life expectancy than is the case in the neighbouring countries. Danish alcohol consumption has dropped over the last two decades but remains significantly higher than in the other Nordic countries and OECD countries such as Greece, Italy, the Netherlands and the United States (OECD, 2019). Alcohol consumption contributes to liver diseases and certain forms of intestinal cancer that shorten health and life. In addition, Denmark's smoking rates remain higher than those in the surrounding countries despite decades of anti-smoking campaigns and recent regulations (Lykkegaard & Kristensen, 2016). Smoking contributes to lung cancer and chronic obstructive pulmonary diseases, which remain relatively common in Denmark. Finally, diabetes case numbers in Denmark doubled from 2000 to 2016, 4.5% of the population being afflicted as of 2020 (Diabetesforeningen, 2020), almost 90% being the lifestyle-related type 2 diabetes. This incidence rate is higher than in other Nordic countries as well as in Australia, France, Greece, Italy and Japan (OECD, 2017b, p. 67).

The second challenge facing the Danish healthcare sector relates to capacity problems. Several medical specialities, including psychiatry, cardiology and anaesthesiology, suffer from insufficient numbers of doctors (Eienstrand, 2019), and there is also a shortage of GPs. This problem is most acute in rural areas, where individual GPs in extreme cases have been asked to serve more than 1,800 citizens (Praktiserende Lægers Organisation, 2018). There is also a lack of nurses, particularly in the hospital sector, which has delayed surgeries and other treatments (Danmarks Radio, 2019). Many nurses work part time, and nursing capacity could be boosted by around 10% if all nurses worked full time (Dansk Sygeplejeråd, 2019). Part of this capacity problem has to do with the 2002 decision in the Folketing to impose a maximum of two months between diagnosis and treatment for a wide range of diseases, and public hospitals have often been unable to fulfil this requirement. This was further reduced to one month in 2007. While this has led to improvements in critical treatments, hospitals complain that they lack the sufficient financial and personnel resources to fulfil this patient right. In turn, untreated patients are entitled to treatment in private clinics and hospitals at no out-of-pocket cost.

Thirdly and finally, as in most other OECD countries, healthcare expenditures constitute a large share of the Danish economy. Since the late 2000s, the costs have been around 10% of GDP (OECD, 2020c). As of 2019, this makes Danish costs relatively modest among rich OECD countries (see Table 2), but higher than the overall OECD average of 8.8%.

Table 2 shows that healthcare expenditures have grown in all of the illustrated high-income countries over the last three decades. It is worth noting that the expenditures have grown much faster in Japan and the United States. Japan's growth is most likely due to its ageing ageing population. The growth in the United States, which has by far the highest healthcare expenditures in the world, may at least partly be ascribed to a dual system of public and private deliverers and a private insurance system creating very high transaction costs and overtreatment (Garber & Skinner, 2008). In Denmark, the growth in healthcare expenditures has been quite moderate and only slightly exceeded growth in GDP. Nonetheless, expenditures grew in absolute terms by 43% from 2000 to 2017, which was faster than other Danish public sector expenditures in the same period (Finansministeriet, 2018).

Analyses of these growing absolute expenditures reveal several contributing factors. The most important ones seem to be the political imposition of waiting time caps on the treatment of a wide range of diseases in 2001, treatment of diseases that previously received little or no medical attention, the construction of new, centralised 'super-hospitals', rapidly growing prices on medicine and medical treatments and an ageing population (although the demographic impact is disputed) (Draborg, 2017; Iversen & Kjellberg, 2018; Rasmussen & Kristensen, 2019).

So how effective is Danish healthcare when compared to other OECD countries? There is admittedly no perfect indicator of this, because lifestyles and social and environmental conditions confound the effects of healthcare itself. Using HALE as the indicator, public health outcomes suggest that Denmark roughly resembles Germany and the United Kingdom as of 2018 and has been catching up to Norway and Sweden since 1990, but remains worse than France and Japan (Table 1). Using cost share of GDP as the indicator, Denmark is remarkable for its ability to contain healthcare costs relative to other rich OECD members. Between 1990 and 2018, its healthcare costs as a percentage of GDP increased just 2.1 percentage points, which is lower growth than in other Scandinavian and large

OECD countries (Table 2); that is, Denmark maintained public health outcomes at the level of the United Kingdom and Germany between 1990 and 2018, but at lower cost. Clearly, initiatives such as lifestyle-oriented public health campaigns (e.g., smoking, drinking, diet) could also play parts here (described in the next section). But these indicators suggest that Denmark has been able to move healthcare costs from levels at the midrange of spending amid rich OECD countries in the early 1990s to the lower end in 2018 without commensurately losing ground on public health outcomes.

Handling the Three Public Health Challenges

Denmark has launched initiatives to address the key challenges facing its public health and healthcare system, some of which it has been able to handle quite successfully.

As described, some of the most important drivers of public health outcomes in Denmark relate to smoking, alcohol consumption and obesity. In turn, several policy interventions have targeted these phenomena together with physical exercise habits. All have been intensely debated, with liberal principles (e.g., limiting state actions affecting citizens' private lives) juxtaposed against public health principles (e.g., maximising population health). Overall, Denmark has adopted more liberal approaches than have the other Nordic countries. Right- and left-leaning governments alike have consistently been reluctant to increase tobacco taxes, which were introduced for fiscal reasons, and to prohibit smoking in certain areas (Pedersen, 2018, pp. 132–133, 149–152). Attempts at increasing tobacco taxes for public health reasons were unsuccessful until 2019. Similarly, attempts to prohibit smoking in public places and spaces in the early 1980s were widely resisted on the grounds that they infringed on individual autonomy. It took another two decades, following campaigns on the dangers of second-hand smoking, before smoking was banned on public transport and in selected public spaces. Then in 2007, a law was passed banning smoking in all indoor spaces with public access, such as hospitals, schools, workplaces, restaurants and bars. The following year, a new regulation meant that only people aged 18 and older can buy tobacco products. These regulatory changes seem to have further contributed to the dropping smoking rates since the late 1970s (Pedersen, 2018, p. 148). At least, the proportion of daily smokers fell from 31% to 17% between 2000 and 2014 (The European Commission, 2018, p. 4). While Danish smoking statistics remain substantially higher than in the other Nordic countries, they have crept below those in France, Italy and Spain (OECD, 2020d).

Campaigns and bans aimed at reducing alcohol consumption have also been introduced over many decades. Like tobacco, Danish alcohol consumption is also substantially higher than in the other Nordic countries, but lower than in countries such as France, Germany and Spain (OECD, 2019). While the other Nordics strictly regulate the sale of alcohol and have at least partial, state-owned retail monopolies, most Danish convenience stores and supermarkets can sell alcohol of any kind to anyone 18 or older and 'light alcohol' (beer, wine) from age 16.

A prevailing, key argument against stricter regulations is that excessive alcohol consumption only hurts the drinker (i.e., no 'second-hand drinking'). Questions remain about whether the commercial interests of Danish breweries have contributed to obstructing regulations (Vallgårda, 2017). While high levels of taxation on alcohol played an important role in reducing consumption between the late 1910s and the 1960s, taxation levels did not follow real income growth between the 1960s and early 1980s, where alcohol consumption more than tripled (Eriksen, 2011). Following systematic public information campaigns, introduction of citizen courses for controlling alcohol abuse and the voluntary adoption of alcohol policies in most public and private workplaces (e.g., prohibiting alcohol during working hours), alcohol consumption has dropped: Where 11% of the population's alcohol consumption exceeded the official safety levels in 2010, this figure was 7% in 2019 (Sundhedsstyrelsen, 2019).

A set of direct healthcare system changes have addressed diseases associated with contemporary lifestyle and social conditions. As described in the previous section, the system achieved relatively poor outcomes in the 1990s from treatments for some cancers and cardiovascular diseases but has markedly improved since (Arnold et al., 2019; OECD, 2015, pp. 41, 151). Significant changes in healthcare governance and organisation contributed to these improvements. Earlier diagnosis and treatment were identified as critical to better cancer and heart disease outcomes. This helped governments justify 'treatment guarantees' within limited times from diagnoses, introduced in 2002 and shortened in 2007 (as described above). Although many hospital physicians have complained that these guarantees offer no medical benefits for many diseases, shorter wait times have been associated with substantially improved cancer survival rates (Allemani et al., 2018). The treatment of cancer, heart diseases and certain other diseases was also centralised. As part of regional consolidations after 2007, the number of public hospitals was reduced from 40 in 2007 to 21 in 2016 (Christiansen & Vrangbæk, 2018, p. 323), which allowed many specialised treatments to be consolidated in hospitals with more qualified medical personnel (Albinus, 2010, 2012).

Healthcare policy instruments were also augmented through municipal-level organisational and governance reforms. Municipalities were merged in 2007 into larger units and made responsible for new sickness prevention and rehabilitation services. With restructuring, the new, larger municipalities also gained professional capacity to deal with health issues. Through coordination with the Danish Health Authority and the national association of GPs (Praktiserende Lægers Organisation), the municipalities have launched concerted initiatives aimed at stepping up the rehabilitation of patients coming out of hospital treatment together with preventive efforts seeking to motivate citizens to adopt healthier diets and to exercise more (Triantafillou & Vucina, 2018). These rehab and prevention programmes have yielded many successes among individual cases, and all have been significantly expanded (Jakobsen, Sølvhøj, & Holmberg, 2020; Sundhedsstyrelsen, 2020; VIVE, 2019). However, their population-level effects on lifestyle have been limited thus far. Obesity has increased: Where 13.6% of the population had a BMI over 30 in 2010, the figure was 16.8% in 2017 (Sundhedsstyrelsen, 2018, p. 97). While this is lower than in many other OECD countries, it contributes directly to increases in diseases such as diabetes (as previously described, diabetes cases doubled in Denmark from 2000 to 2016).

The second healthcare challenge described in the previous section, insufficient sector capacity, is exacerbated by persistent and increasing staff shortages. Several initiatives have been launched in recent years to alleviate this problem, and successive governments allocated more funding to medical education in the 2010s (Sundheds-og Ældreministeriet, 2018). However, expanded training has yet to affect the shortage. It takes many years to educate a medical doctor, and the students themselves (not their employers) decide their areas of specialisation. The system has bridged the gap mainly by paying existing specialists to work more and by recruiting specialists from other countries. The GP shortage is further complicated by newly trained doctors being reluctant to work in rural areas and some urban areas with large ethnic-minority populations (Drejer, Holm, & Petersen, 2016). In order to attract more doctors to rural areas, regional governments have encouraged the establishment of clinics where two or more GPs share facilities and can exchange expertise (Sundheds-og Ældreministeriet, 2018). This has proven attractive to some younger doctors, who would otherwise have remained where there is greater potential for professional and collegial interactions. Nevertheless, the long-term, aggregate effects of this programme remain unclear. Finally, nurses are in short supply, particularly for hospitals. Many nurses prefer part-time work, in part due to the pressure of hospital work (Christensen, 2018). As with doctors, a key instrument is allocating more resources to educating nurses (Toft, 2020), but education funding is unlikely to overcome the staffing shortage. As long as hospital work is more stressful for nurses than working in private practice or municipal healthcare services, hospitals are likely to remain the less-preferred employer.

As regards the third challenge, healthcare expenditures, Danish spending has increased, but less so than in many similar countries. Until 2000, healthcare costs amounted to around 8% of GDP, which ranks in the middle among affluent OECD countries (see Table 2). Following a series of reforms to improve treatment, such as the 'treatment guarantee' and caps on surgery waiting times, healthcare spending grew to 10% in 2009 (and remained remarkably constant since then; OECD, 2020c). Numerous measures were initiated to contain cost growth. The GP referral system has functioned throughout the period as an important instrument for avoiding unnecessary and costly specialised treatments. Following the creation of five regions in 2007, which eliminated county taxes, the Ministry of Finance has capped increases in the transfers to the regions at a rate roughly similar to GDP growth. This is important, because the regions administer the public healthcare system. Moreover, since 2000, parts of public hospital budgets have been tied to the number of patients treated at the hospitals. Together with an overall budget framework and systematic productivity benchmarking, this resulted in shorter patient hospitalisation periods and more treatments per unit of expenditure (Danske Regioner et al., 2016) (note that this 'payment-per-treatment' regime has recently been partially replaced by specific outcome targets, such as reduced acute readmissions) (Danske Regioner, 2020).

Finally, to curb growing expenditures for medical products and therapies, a council was established in 2016 to guide expensive pharmaceutical purchases. While following the council guidelines is voluntary, they have nudged the regions away from some very expensive medical products. Critics have questioned the council's transparency and methods, however, urging the better use of standards, such as quality-adjusted life years (QALY) (Oxford Research, 2019). While questions remain about the impact of the guidelines on overall costs, the multiple cost-control measures introduced in recent years appear to have been sufficient to contain their growth to about that of national GDP.

Discussion

The Danish Healthcare System – Strengths and Weaknesses

The analysis above reveals important strengths in the Danish healthcare system. Through policy, it has achieved progress on managing some of its important challenges. Against the challenge of poor treatment outcomes that first came to light in the 1990s, particularly for cancer and cardiovascular diseases, the consolidation of public hospitals and shorter waiting times have enabled more qualified and timely treatments resulting in better outcomes. Worth noting also is how municipal prevention and rehabilitation programmes – at least for some people – would appear to have improved outcomes on the conditions and diseases that these address. Against rising healthcare costs, new policies at the national, local and practice levels have consistently helped to avoid cost increases outpacing GDP growth.

Despite such improvements, the Danish health outcomes remain mediocre compared to other northern European countries, albeit much better than the United States. Policymakers have attempted to address insufficient healthcare system capacities by investing in medical and nursing education programmes, but shortages remain. In addition, the legislated treatment guarantee that aids some treatment outcomes exacerbates these shortages, particularly in hospitals. But public health outcomes depend on more than healthcare system governance; for instance, alcohol and smoking habits contribute to many chronic diseases that reduce aggregate public health. To address the country's relatively low life expectancy and other health outcomes, regulations and campaigns have addressed alcohol consumption, smoking and sedentary lifestyles with information and taxes. These interventions have been incremental over many decades rather than drastic reforms. How and the extent to which the state ought to try to 'make' citizens adopt lifestyle changes is politically sensitive, as exemplified by widespread popular resistance against (and slow acceptance of) restrictions on tobacco in the 2000s.

Two additional challenges are emerging for the Danish healthcare system. Firstly, as a result of expenditure controls, governments have recently restricted the availability of certain costly medical treatments, such as a particular medicine for muscular dystrophy (Jacobsen & Schelde, 2019). While this may make fiscal sense, it may also tempt wealthier residents to seek alternatives to the public system (e.g., private health insurance and services in Denmark or abroad), jeopardising longer-term political support for universal healthcare and healthcare equality (Esping-Andersen, 1990). Secondly, strong budget constraints imposed to control healthcare spending crowd out some services, creating trade-offs that breach the general commitment of the system to high-quality and comprehensive healthcare. For instance, recent austerity measures combined with the substantial resources allocated to improve treatments for cancer and other somatic diseases have meant that psychiatric services have been significantly underfunded and are consequently suffering (Lægeforeningen, 2018).

Two Issues Requiring Further Scholarly Research

Despite the extensive literature on the Danish healthcare system, several issues of economic, political and social relevance remain poorly understood. Firstly, health economists continue to struggle with how Danes can achieve healthier and longer lifespans without incurring further increases in healthcare expenditures. Some Danish hospitals have turned to value-based management focussed on health outcomes to seek such efficiencies (Triantafillou, 2020). But effects on health outcomes, rather than simply outputs, remain poorly understood. In particular, studies should examine if and how the principles of value-based management may be translated into a high-performance system that allocates health expenditures in a more cost-effective manner than as currently achieved by the Danish system.

Secondly and relatedly, more research is needed on how to motivate citizens to adopt healthier lifestyles. Chronic diseases driven by lifestyle choices remain too costly. Together with work-related factors, unhealthy lifestyles continue to contribute to diseases such as chronic obstructive pulmonary diseases, lung cancer, several cardiac diseases and type 2 diabetes. Although schizophrenia and arthrosis are the costliest diseases, lifestyle-related diseases, such as chronic obstructive pulmonary diseases, ischaemic (heart) diseases and diabetes, are among the 10 most costly diseases in Denmark (Sundhedsstyrelsen, 2015, p. 26). They also result in reduced capacity to work and, hence, lost income (Kjellberg, Tange Larsen, Ibsen, & Højgaard, 2017). Research should further examine behavioural interventions (e.g., nudging) along with more conventional policy instruments, such as information, incentives and restrictions. Crucially, this should include the scrutinisation of the political and ethical implications of interfering in people's private decisions. Finally, given that past efforts to improve lifestyle choices have had limited effect on low-income groups and those with little education, additional research should consider why interventions work unevenly along socio-economic dimensions.

Lessons and Implications for Practice

Denmark's largely tax-based healthcare system rests on a principle of equal access to high-quality services for all residents and has important ethical and economic merits. It may therefore serve as a source of inspiration for other countries. Most would probably agree that access to healthcare for any person who needs it is ethically sound. There are also important macro-economic rationales for ensuring healthcare for all. Prompt, effective healthcare helps people to return to work and other activities faster than otherwise. By returning to work, citizens are able to pay more taxes and undertake essential care duties for themselves and their families.

As summarised previously, Denmark's principle of equality emerged two centuries ago and was translated into a mostly tax-based, universal system in the early 1970s. As many have observed, such historically derived institutions make policy emulation difficult (Jacobs & Skocpol, 2010; Steinmo & Watts, 1995). Regardless, questions remain as to whether the Danish health system includes unique and useful policy instruments worth imitating. The Danish healthcare system has developed since the 1990s: from poorly performing and more expensive than some similar systems towards relatively well performing and with costs at the low end among similar systems. Its key achievement has been to contain healthcare cost growth while improving treatment outcomes in disease categories that affect many patients.

Attributing this key achievement to any one change is beyond the scope of this chapter given the many different initiatives occurring within the period. It is worth highlighting several shifts that are plausible contributors and, hence, potential grounds for policy and practical lessons.

Although long-standing, the gatekeeper function of Danish GPs could be useful in other systems. As described, all Danish residents are assigned to a GP, and GP consultations are free of charge. One advantage of this arrangement is that citizens can easily consult GPs as soon as they experience health irregularities, which can prevent illnesses from developing into more serious conditions. Another advantage is that GPs determine referrals to specialised treatment, which reduces risks and costs of superfluous medical examinations and treatments. These outcomes are clearly desirable where lifestyle-related conditions and healthcare budgets are increasing burdens.

One potentially instructive change in the system was the 'treatment guarantee' introduced by the Danish government in 2002, ensuring treatment within two months of receiving a diagnosis (reduced to one month in 2007). This has pushed the system to exploit private alternatives that can compensate for public hospital capacity shortages. It has also pressured public hospitals to improve their timeliness, with notable success in cancer and heart disease treatments.

A second change was associated with shorter waiting times pushed by the 'treatment guarantee' and the greater specialisation facilitated by consolidating public hospitals (described above). The combined impact of more timely treatment and more qualified specialists was better outcomes in several areas where the system had been underperforming, most notably cancer and cardiovascular disease survival rates. Unfortunately, other areas have not seen similar improvements, such as mental health.

A third instructive change has been a series of targeted budget and cost controls beyond the long-standing GP referral mechanism. These include the Ministry of Finance's cap on growth in the transfers to the regions of about the rate of

GDP growth, starting in 2007. They also include various hospital-level initiatives, such as 'payments-per-treatment' and, more recently, outcome-based payments. Since the late 2000s, these have effectively helped to contain healthcare costs to about 10% of GDP despite higher demands on services from an ageing and more obese population and the continual introduction of new technologies.

A fourth change has been an organised effort by municipalities to offer services that prevent illness and rehabilitate patients following hospital treatment. While some of these 'extra-medical' services were offered by the counties (until 2007), the larger municipalities have boosted the professional expertise and significantly expanded rehab and prevention programmes. While rehabilitation has undoubtedly improved, preventive efforts have produced less impressive results thus far.

Conclusion

This chapter has described how the Danish healthcare system has moved to a relatively less costly and in some respects more effective model over the past two or three decades. It continues to reflect a key principle of the welfare state: universal accessibility. It remains largely successful in securing easy and equal access for all Danish residents regardless of income via general tax financing. Even the most right-leaning political parties and their voters tend to support publicly funded and managed healthcare (Larsen, 2020, p. 603).

Like most other OECD countries, Denmark is struggling to handle the predicament of increasing pressures on delivering more and better health services to an ageing population with growing expectations while at the same time containing healthcare expenditures. Denmark is not a world leader in handling this predicament, but its improved performance in the area since the 1990s is rather remarkable. Several initiatives have contributed to this development, ranging from national administrative reforms and public health regulations to budget control measures and targeted organisational and treatment programmes in hospitals.

Notwithstanding the improved effectiveness of the Danish healthcare system, it is struggling with shortages in qualified staff and emerging issues related to rationing novel treatments. Like many healthcare systems around the world, it faces rising burdens from chronic diseases related to smoking, excessive alcohol consumption and unhealthy diets. As noted in the Introduction, these problems affect citizens with low-income groups much harder than high-income groups, a fact that challenges Denmark's image as a welfare state. Moreover, while Denmark has contained its healthcare costs relatively well, domestic politics includes calls for more savings, in part because these costs remain the fastest-growing public sector expenditure.

Note

1. Unfortunately, this chapter is unable to address the issue of health outcome inequalities due to a lack of space, which is otherwise an important problem in Denmark.

References

Albinus, N.-B. (2010). Regioner og minister enige: Kræftbehandling skal centraliseres yderligere. *Dagens Medicin*, 19 November.

Albinus, N.-B. (2012). Det kendetegner de bedste kræftafdelinger. *Dagens Medicin*, 7 December.

Allemani, C., Matsuda, T., et al. (2018). Global surveillance of trends in cancer survival 2000–14 (CONCORD-3): Analysis of individual records for 37 513 025 patients diagnosed with one of 18 cancers from 322 population-based registries in 71 countries. *The Lancet, 391*(10125), 1023–1075.

Arnold, M., Rutherford, A., & Bardot, M. (2019). Progress in cancer control: Survival, mortality and incidence in seven high-income countries 1995–2014 (ICBP SURVMARK-2): A population based study. *The Lancet Oncology*. doi:10.1016/S1470-2045(19)30456-5

Christensen, G. (2018). Leder: Nok er nok: Arbejdsmiljøet lider! *Sygeplejersken, 8*, 3.

Christiansen, T., & Vrangbæk, K. (2018). Hospital centralization and performance in Denmark: Ten years on. *Health Policy, 122*, 321–328.

Danmarks Radio. (2019). Massiv mangel på sygeplejersker: 1030 ubesatte job på halvt år. 26 April. Retrieved from https://www.dr.dk/nyheder/indland/massiv-mangel-paa-sygeplejersker-1030-ubesatte-job-paa-halvt-aar

Dansk Institut for Klinisk Epidemiologi. (1993). *Middellevetid og dødelighed: En analyse af dødeligheden i Danmark og nogle Europæiske lande, 1950–1990*. Copenhagen: Middellevetidsudvalget.

Dansk Sygeplejeråd. (2019). DSR notat. Sygeplejernes aftalte og faktiske arbejdstid 2007–2019, Copenhagen.

Danske Regioner. (2020). Finansiering. Copenhagen. Retrieved from https://www.regioner.dk/aftaler-og-oekonomi/oekonomisk-styring/finansiering%0A

Danske Regioner, Finansministeriet and Ældreministeriet, S. (2016). Løbende offentliggørelse af produktivitet i sygehussektoren (XII delrapport). Udviklingen fra 2014 til 2015. Copenhagen.

Diabetesforeningen. (2020). Facts about diabetes in Denmark. Retrieved from https://diabetes.dk/diabetesforeningen/in-english/facts-about-diabetes-in-denmark.aspx

Draborg, E. (2017). Sundhedsøkonom: Flere ældre er ikke skyld i stigende udgifter. *Altinget.Dk*, 1 February.

Drejer, I., Holm, J. R., & Petersen, K. D. (2016). Nuancer af lægemangel i Danmark: Betydningen af den skæve geografiske fordeling af alder og køn. *Samfundsøkonomen, 2*, 41–48.

Eienstrand, K. L. (2019). Pressede lægespecialer fylder mest blandt de højeste lægelønninger. *Dagens Medicin*, 21 June.

Engeland, A., Haldorsen, T., et al. (1998). Relative survival of cancer patients: A comparison between Denmark and the other Nordic countries. *Acta Oncologica, 37*(1), 49–59.

Eriksen, S. (2011). Alkohol (alkoholforbruget i Danmark). In *Den store Danske.* Retrieved from https://denstoredanske.lex.dk/alkohol_(alkoholforbruget_i_ Danmark)

Esping-Andersen, G. (1990). *The three worlds of welfare capitalism.* Cambridge: Polity.

Finansministeriet. (2018). Økonomisk analyse: Udviklingen i de offentlige udgifter 2000 til 2017. Copenhagen.

Garber, A. M., & Skinner, J. (2008). Is American health care uniquely inefficient? *The Journal of Economic Perspectives, 22*(4), 27–50.

GBD 2017 DALYs and HALE Collaborators. (2018). Global, regional, and national disability-adjusted life-years (DALYs) for 359 diseases and injuries and healthy life expectancy (HALE) for 195 countries and territories, 1990–2017: A systematic analysis for the Global Burden of Disease Study 2017. *Lancet, 392*, 1859–1892.

Holstein, M. A. (2017). CEPOS notat: Stor vækst i private sundhedsforsikringer siden ophævelsen af skattefritagelsen. Copenhagen. Retrieved from https://cepos.dk/ media/1580/notat_2017_02_20_sundhedsforsikringer.pdf

Iversen, A. K., & Kjellberg, J. (2018). *Flere ældre og nye behandlinger: Hvad kommer det til at koste? Udviklingen i sundhedsvæsenets økonomi, ressourcer og opgaver.* Copenhagen: PUBLISHER.

Jacobsen, G. D., & Schelde, J. (2019). Medicinrådet afviser atter livsvigtig medicin. Retrieved from https://muskelsvindfonden.dk/nyheder/medicinraadet-afviser-atter-livsvigtig-medicin/

Jacobs, L. R., & Skocpol, T. (2010). *Health care reform and American politics: What everyone needs to know.* Oxford: Oxford University Press.

Jakobsen, G. S., Sølvhøj, I. N., & Holmberg, T. (2020). *Monitorering af kommunernes forebyggelsesindsats 2019.* Odense: PUBLISHER.

Kjellberg, J., Tange Larsen, A., Ibsen, R., & Højgaard, B. (2017). The socioeconomic burden of obesity. *Obesity Facts, 10*(5), 493–502.

Knudsen, A. K., Allebeck, P., Tollånes, M. C., Skogen, J. C., Iburg, K. M., McGrath, J. J., ... Øverland, S. (2019). Life expectancy and disease burden in the Nordic countries: Results from the Global Burden of Diseases, Injuries, and Risk Factors Study 2017. *The Lancet, Public Health, 4*(12), e658–e669.

Knudsen, T., & Nielsen, L. D. (2000). Sundhedsforvaltning 1814–1848. In D. Tamm (Ed.). *Dansk forvaltningshistorie* (Vol. I, pp. 455–464). Copenhagen: DJØF Publishing.

Lægeforeningen. (2018). Styrk psykiatrien nu: Det vedrører os alle. Copenhagen. Retrieved from https://www.laeger.dk/sites/default/files/laegeforeningens_psykia-triudspil_2018.pdf

Larsen, L. T. (2020). Health policy: The submerged politics of free and equal access. In P. M. Christiansen, J. Elklit, & P. Nedergaard (Eds.), *The Oxford handbook of Danish politics* (pp. 592–608). Oxford: Oxford University Press.

Lykkegaard, J., & Kristensen, G. N. (2016). Chronic obstructive pulmonary disease in Denmark: Age-period-cohort analysis offirst-time hospitalisations and deaths 1994–2012. *Respiratory Medicine, 114*, 78–83.

OECD. (2015). *Cardiovascular disease and diabetes: Policies for better health and quality of care.* Paris: OECD Health Policy Studies. Retrieved from https://doi.org/ http://dx.doi.org/10.1787/9789264233010-en

OECD. (2017a). *Obesity update 2017*. Paris. Retrieved from https://www.oecd.org/health/health-systems/Obesity-Update-2017.pdf

OECD. (2017b). *Health at a glance, 2017*. Paris. Retrieved from https://www.oecd-ilibrary.org/docserver/health_glance-2017-15-en.pdf?expires=1597063679&id=id&accname=ocid195399&checksum=BD734241FC32ED18E2DE9371F65D5432

OECD. (2019). Alcohol consumption. *OECD Data*. Paris. Retrieved from https://data.oecd.org/healthrisk/alcohol-consumption.htm

OECD. (2020a). Health expenditure and financing. *OECD.Stat*. Retrieved from https://stats.oecd.org/Index.aspx?DataSetCode=SHA

OECD. (2020b). Life expectancy. *OECD.Stat*. Retrieved from https://stats.oecd.org/Index.aspx?DataSetCode=SHA

OECD. (2020c). Health expenditure indicators. *OECD Health Statistics*. doi:10.1787/health-data-en

OECD. (2020d). Daily smokers. *OECD.Stat*. Retrieved from https://data.oecd.org/healthrisk/daily-smokers.htm

Oxford Research. (2019). *Evaluering af medicinrådet*. Frederiksberg: PUBLISHER.

Pedersen, K. M. (2018). *Dansk sundhedspolitik*. Copenhagen: Munksgaard.

Pedersen, B. M., & Petersen, S. R. (Eds.), (2014). *Det kommunale sundhedsvæsen*. Copenhagen: Hans Reitzels.

Praktiserende Lægers Organisation. (2018). PLO analyse: Antallet af patienter hos de praktiserende læger stiger fortsat. Copenhagen. Retrieved from https://www.laeger.dk/sites/default/files/stigende_antal_patienter_pr_laege_0.pdf

Rasmussen, M., & Kristensen, L. (2019). *DST analyse: De offentlige sundhedsudgifter er steget markant mere endde øvrige offentlige udgifter siden 2000*. Copenhagen: PUBLISHER.

Reibling, N., & Wendt, C. (2012). Gatekeeping and provider choice in OECD healthcare systems. *Current Sociology*, 60(4), 489–505.

Saha, S., Gerdtham, U.-G., & Johansson, P. (2010). Economic evaluation of lifestyle interventions for preventing diabetes and cardiovascular diseases. *International Journal of Environmental Research and Public Health*, 7(8), 3150–3195.

Starr, P. (1982). *The social transformation of American medicine*. New York, NY: Basic Books.

Statens Institut for Folkesundhed. (2019). Social ulighed i sundhed og sygdom: Udviklingen i Danmark i perioden 2010–2017. Copenhagen.

Steinmo, S., & Watts, J. (1995). It's the institutions, stupid! Why comprehensive national health insurance always fails in America. *Journal of Health Politics, Policy & Law*, 20(2), 329–372.

Sundhed Danmark. (2018). Kort om privathospitaler. Copenhagen. Retrieved from https://www.sundheddanmark.nu/media/1195/sundheddanmark-kort-om-privathospitaler-2018.pdf

Sundheds- og Ældreministeriet. (2018). *En læge tæt på dig: En plan for fremtidens almen praksis*. Copenhagen.

Sundhedsstyrelsen. (2015). Sygdomsbyrden i Danmark: Sygdomme. Copenhagen.

Sundhedsstyrelsen. (2018). Danskernes sundhed: Sundhedsprofilen 2017. Copenhagen.

Sundhedsstyrelsen (2019). Nøgletal om alkohol. Retrieved from https://www.sst.dk/da/Viden/Alkohol/Fakta-om-alkohol/Noegletal-om-alkohol

Sundhedsstyrelsen. (2020). Evaluering af puljen til styrket rehabiliteringsindsats for de svageste ældre, Copenhagen.

The European Commission. (2018). *State of health in the EU: Denmark country health profile 2017*. Brussels. Retrieved from https://www.euro.who.int/__data/assets/pdf_file/0009/355977/Health-Profile-Denmark-Eng.pdf

Toft, N. (2020). 1.000 flere sygeplejersker er ikke nok. *Sygeplejersken, 8*, 48–50.

Triantafillou, P. (2020). Accounting for value-based management of hospital services: Challenging neoliberal government from within? *Public Money & Management*. doi:10.1080/09540962.2020.1748878

Triantafillou, P., & Vucina, N. (2018). *The politics of health promotion: Case studies from Denmark and England*. Manchester: Manchester University Press.

Vallgårda, S. (2017). Professor: Gør noget ved alkoholens særstatus i dansk sundhedspolitik. *Altinget.dk*, 21 June.

VIVE. (2019). Evaluering af projektet: Tværsektorielt samarbejde om rehabilitering af borgere med apopleksi. Copenhagen.

WHO Regional Office for Europe. (2019). HIV/AIDS surveillance in Europe 2019–2018 data. Copenhagen. Retrieved from https://www.ecdc.europa.eu/sites/default/files/documents/hiv-surveillance-report-2019.pdf.

Chapter 13

From Homogeneity to Diversity: Societal and Political Responses to Immigration

Carina Saxlund Bischoff and Anders Ejrnæs

Abstract

International migration is a global challenge affecting peoples and nations all over the world. In the advanced economies and welfare states of Western Europe, integrating migrants presents political, social as well as economic challenges. Over the past 50 years, Denmark has made a remarkable U-turn on the immigration question. Once the author of one of the most liberal immigration policies in Western Europe, Denmark presently has one of the strictest. This chapter addresses the causes behind the Danish policy U-turn, and how it has affected the social, economic and political integration of immigrants in Denmark. The chapter shows how Danish immigration politics have turned from low to high salience and have undergone radical changes resulting in a tightening of both internal and external immigration policies. It has become far more difficult to obtain residence and citizenship in Denmark. These measures have limited influx although international refugee crises are difficult to control at the borders. Moreover, Danish integration policies have focused increasingly on obligations and incentives, primarily by cutting benefits. The Danish case however shows that reduction of social benefits only has a marginal positive short-term effect on employment but with some negative side effects. When it comes to education, the Danish welfare state has been relatively successful in integrating immigrants and descendants in the educational system.

Keywords: Immigration; politicization; integration; participation; citizenship; attitudes; ethnic minority

Introduction

International migration is a global challenge affecting nations around the world. Armed conflicts, political persecution and human rights violations, natural

Public Governance in Denmark, 227–245
doi:10.1108/978-1-80043-712-820221013

disasters, poverty and famine afflict peoples in different world regions, creating unprecedented migrant flows. In 2020, the UNHCR estimates that over 80 million people worldwide were displaced by such events. Over four million are asylum-seekers (UNHCR, 2021). That same year, fewer than 500,000 sought asylum in an EU member state. The national responses to the crisis in the EU vary greatly, both in terms of the number of refugees that countries are willing to accept and how they respond to the challenges of integrating them economically, socially and politically. This chapter outlines key features of immigration to Denmark and the Danish response. As an advanced economy with a universal welfare state that has evolved in concert with a highly homogeneous population, the influx of peoples with diverse cultural backgrounds and skillsets has challenged the social and political system, labour market and welfare institutions.

Over the past 50 years, Denmark has made a remarkable U-turn on immigration. In the early decades of this period, the UN highlighted Denmark as an example for other countries to follow (Skaksen & Jensen, 2016, p. 34). The Danish Refugee Council heralded the first comprehensive law on immigration, passed in 1983, as the most 'people-friendly law in the world' (Simonsen, 2020, p. 611), and the Danish commitment to welfare and solidarity did not stop at its borders. Decades later, this rosy image has been shredded by some of the strictest immigration policies in Western Europe. National and international organisations, observers and media have commented on the harshness of the political discourse and Danish policies.[1] Only recently, the UN censured the Danish so-called 'Ghetto Package' for discrimination on the basis of national background (UN Economic and Social Council, 2019).

In this chapter, after presenting a brief overview of immigration to Denmark, the political and policy responses, and the current state of immigrant participation in society, we will address the causes behind the Danish policy U-turn and how it has affected the social, economic and political integration of immigrants in Denmark. The first section describes the development and composition of immigration from the 1980s until today, the second section analyses when, how and why immigration policy became a key issue in Danish elections and party politics, and what laws were passed over the years to address immigration issues, and the third section describes the integration of immigrants in the labour market together with their social and political participation. The chapter is completed with discussion of the pros and cons of Danish integration policy, and we consider a number of implications for practice.

Danish Society, Policies and Politics in Flux

From Homogeneity to Diversity: the Growing Share of Immigrants, Refugees and Their Descendants

Rather than one continuous stream, immigration to Denmark has occurred in successive and overlapping waves with distinct motives behind them. The *leitmotif* of the first wave, in the 1960s, was triggered by an acute labour shortage, attracting immigrants looking for opportunity to work ('labour force immigrants'). From the 1970s onwards, the escape from war, conflict and different forms of oppression became a dominant motivation for those who arrived in Denmark ('refugees'). Adding to their numbers are those who came later because they sought unification with partners or other family members ('immigrants reunited with families'). In the Danish debate on immigration issues, a final group – the so-called 'descendants' – are also included. It includes persons who are born in Denmark to parents neither of whom are born in the country or have citizenship. More than 200 different countries are represented among these people, who are making Denmark more diverse. They represent a wide array of socio-economic and political contexts, climates, cultural and religious traditions. Unless clearly specified in the text, we use the term 'immigrant' broadly to both immigrants – including family reunifications – and refugees. We clearly specify when we refer to 'descendants'.

Fig. 1 shows an increase in the number of immigrants, refugees and their descendants from Western and non-Western countries over the past 30 years. In 2019, the total share of these groups was 13.7% of the population (Statistics Denmark, 2020). Eastern European immigration increased dramatically after the EU enlargement in 2004, and while this influx sparked debate regarding its impact on the labour market ('race to the bottom') and potential 'welfare tourism' (see e.g. Greve, 2019), the challenges related to the integration of non-Western immigrants have been greater and consistently attracted more political attention. We therefore focus on the latter.

The Politics of Immigration: The Danish U-turn

There have been three main phases of Danish immigration politics: Until the 1990s, immigration was a consensus issue in Denmark, whereas it became a left–right issue marked by conflict in the second phase, as in the rest of Europe (e.g. Harmon,

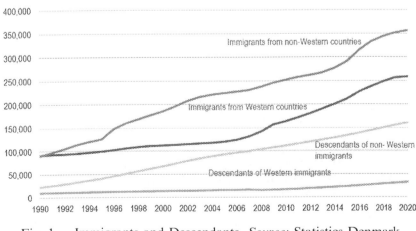

Fig. 1.   Immigrants and Descendants. *Source:* Statistics Denmark (2020).

2018; Koning, 2017), and also highly salient. In the third, current phase, consensus has emerged anew in the party system, where immigration continues to be highly salient.

In the first phase, the political parties collaborated broadly on immigration policies. Dissenting voices were occasionally heard, but the issue had low electoral salience. The first moratorium on immigration, in 1973, was initiated by the left-wing parties to protect Danish workers from competition from low-skilled foreign workers. The aforementioned 'most people-friendly' law of 1983 was originally proposed by the minority right-wing government, although the centre-left did leave a clear mark on the bill, before all of the parties (with the exception of a single party on the extreme right) voted for it (Green-Pedersen & Odmalm, 2008).[2]

In the second phase, immigration becomes a highly salient issue and plays a decisive role in election outcomes from 2001 onwards. Two events play a key role in explaining why the political right began mobilising around the issue in the 1990s. First, the Social Liberals, who had supported right-wing governments in the past, joined the centre-left governing coalition under Social Democratic leadership in 1993. The loss of an ally was a setback for Liberal–Conservative ambitions to reclaim government, but at the same time unmoored them from the Social Liberals' extremely immigration-friendly policy positions. The second event was when the Danish People's Party splintered from the unruly, extreme-right Progress Party in 1995. The new party had a strong anti-immigration platform but was flexible on a wide range of other issues and a viable coalition partner. The right-wing parties could pursue a strategy of politicising the immigration issue without jeopardising ambitions to form government. Stories regularly carried by the media of immigrants exploiting the welfare system made it easy to find an angle (Jønsson, 2013, p. 210). Finally, new Liberal Party leadership in 1998 paved the way for a new stance. From emphasising the rights of immigrants to maintain their own culture, the party moved towards demanding economic and cultural participation (Holm, 2005, pp. 93–113).[3] The Social Democrats failed to formulate a programme to compete with the restrictions proposed on the right and suffered internal dissension on the matter – most visibly between a national elite oriented towards a humanist ideology and solidarity versus the local level, which was experiencing integration problems first-hand. The right-of-centre strategy worked, resulting in 2001 in a Liberal–Conservative government with the Danish People's Party as its stable parliamentary support (Harmon, 2018, p. 1046). Polls indicated that over half of the electorate had immigration as their top priority, and it has generally remained a top priority with voters since. Green-Pedersen and Odmalm (2008) argue that the very different development in Sweden presents a convincing case; that it was indeed the coalition prospects of the political right that played a decisive role in Denmark. In Sweden, the parties on the political right were still beholden to the moderate Centre party, with no other viable majority in sight.

The third phase is characterised by a new consensus and continued high political salience. In the campaign up to the 2019 elections, the Social Democrats pledged a strict, unwavering course on immigration issues. They had already started shifting towards a more restrictive position in the late 1990s (Holm, 2005), but the forces within the party arguing for stricter policies first gained momentum in earnest after the 2001 election defeat. The Social Democrats began shadowing the initiatives of the right and voted for many of its bills, but its governing prospects were tied to the Social Liberals, who made a point of competing on their liberal positions (Green-Pedersen & Krogstrup, 2008). While the Social Democrat–led coalition government of 2011 enacted legislation liberalising immigration in several respects, the current Social Democratic government has made good on promises regarding stricter immigration policies. Policy proposals and public statements made by ministers and party spokespersons signal continuity with the previous right-wing government on immigration issues.[4] There is no viable alternative majority on the issue at present.

The political developments have found support in public opinion where there is broad support behind strict immigration policies. Young people are much more tolerant towards immigrants than older people, but the generations tend to agree on a strict line on new immigration (Reiermann & Andersen, 2019). Danish attitudes do not appear much more anti-immigrant than in countries with less strict policies, however. In the European context, Denmark falls in the middle on anti-immigrant attitudes albeit towards the higher end on some questions, and the polity is more polarised (Simonsen, 2016; Sniderman, Petersen, Slothus, & Stubager, 2014). Generally, the Danes are more sceptical on questions related to immigrant crime and use of welfare, but less concerned about losing jobs to immigrants than in other countries. A large study of Danish values from 2011 concluded that tolerance towards immigrants has increased since the early 1980s (Gundelach, 2011). Much appears to depend on specific questions asked, however. Attitudes on having an immigrant as your neighbour have become much more tolerant. However, asked directly about 'Muslims', a survey from 2019 revealed very low tolerance. Slightly more than 25% agreed with the proposition that Muslim immigrants should be sent out of the country – and less than half disagreed. (Reiermann & Andersen, 2019). Moreover, on the question of living in an area where more than half the residents are non-Western immigrants, 67 pct. of Danish respondents were opposed or strongly opposed, compared to just 47 pct in Sweden (Larsen, 2011). It is likely that the negative public focus on 'ghettos' and 'Muslims' play a role. Studies have shown how the political debate and media discourse impact public opinion (e.g. Hellwig & Kweon, 2016; Klingeren, van Boomgaarden, Vliegenthart, & de Vreese, 2015; Slothuus, Petersen, & Rathlev, 2012). Coupled with high politicisation, the media coverage in Denmark – compared to the other Nordic countries has been found to have a strong negative focus on immigrants (Hovden & Mjelde, 2019; Jørndrup, 2017). This may explain the strength of the anti-immigrant sentiment found in Denmark compared to its Nordic neighbours.

Danish Immigration and Integration Policies

In the following, we will present an overview of the Danish immigration policies of the past two decades. External policies regulate questions of entry, while internal policies concern their social, political and civil rights.

External Policies: An Ever-narrowing Door
In the late 1990s, the centre-left government sought to stem the influx of immigrants by curtailing family reunification, which accounted for the majority of new immigrants. It annulled the right to reunification with parents and introduced 'attachment requirements' for partners who, from that date forward, had to prove stronger ties to Denmark than to other countries.[5] In early 2002, the new right-wing coalition government further restricted reunification by barring couples from applying if either part was younger than 24. The resident partner was also required to place a sum of money as a bank guarantee; they had to demonstrate access to appropriate housing and to have been financially self-sufficient for one year (i.e. having held employment and not been dependent on social benefits). With the sole exception of a few policy reversals introduced by the centre-left government in 2011–2015, which were quickly reinstated again after they lost power, rules have become even stricter. At the time of writing, applicants must be free of public debt (over a certain amount), they must not have been convicted of a range of crimes, and they must have been self-sufficient for four years.

In 2002, the government also tried to stem the influx of refugees by changing the de facto definition of 'refugee' so that only persons under *personal* threat of persecution in their homeland are eligible to apply for asylum. The two most recent governments have followed a similar path. The so-called 'paradigm shift' in 2019 instituted a practice of issuing temporary residence permits to refugees and those reuniting with family. In the spring of 2021, Denmark became the first and only EU country to strip selected Syrian refugees of residence permits, arguing that Damascus is now safe despite reports to the contrary.

Less importantly in terms of sheer volume but with powerful symbolic value, the government reneged in 2016 on a longstanding agreement with the UNHCR to accept so-called 'quota refugees', who are particularly vulnerable. Beginning in 1983, Denmark received 500 such persons annually under the arrangement. The reason given for rescinding the agreement was that Denmark was struggling with the integration of Syrian refugees. In 2017, parliament passed legislation leaving it to the Minister of Integration to decide whether Denmark should accept the quota refugees.[6]

The only exceptions to the increasing restrictions have been for those with specialised skills that are in demand on the labour market. However, as the increasing numbers with non-Western background entering show (see Fig. 1), war and conflict elsewhere are creating flows of refugees that are difficult to control.

Internal Policies: From Equal to Differentiated Treatment
The internal policies cover a broader spectrum of social, political and civil rights of residents without citizenship. While the specifics vary from policy area to policy area, we have seen a general shift from a high degree of uniformity to differentiated rights and duties, depending on status. Until the late 1990s, Danish law made no citizen/non-citizen distinction; all residents enjoyed the same social rights. In 1999, the first policy introducing such a distinction cut welfare payments to create work incentives for immigrants and refugees. The so-called 'introduction

allowance' was struck down just a year later for being in violation of international law prohibiting discrimination. In 2001, the new right-wing government successfully introduced substantial cuts to welfare for immigrants and refugees from outside the EU and the Nordic countries. Until recently, social benefits were the only policy area specifically targeting immigrants; however, the Ghetto Package of 2018 introduced policies aimed at social housing estates with high percentages of non-Western immigrants. An estate where more than half of the residents have a non-Western background qualifies as a 'ghetto'. The package obliges the residents in such areas to enrol their children in childcare already from age 1, and confers powers on the police to introduce zones in areas with a high level of crime where the sentences for such acts are doubled. In theory, the police can introduce such zones everywhere, but so far they have only been enacted in so-called 'ghetto' areas. If an estate is on the ghetto list for several years in a row, it is obliged to moderate the composition of residents by eviction, demolition and/or sale. Rather than eluding the question of discrimination, Prime Minister Lars Løkke Rasmussen bluntly stated that 'Danishness is under threat, and therefore it is necessary to do away with the notion that in Denmark all are treated equally' (*Information*, 27 February 2018).[7] The law has drawn criticism from the UN (UN, 2019).

While refugees basically enjoy the same rights as Danes in the public pension system, entitlement is proportionate to one's length of residence if it is less than 40 years. Labour market pensions work differently, however, and the lower employment rates and employment in professions with lower coverage and incomes place non-citizens at a disadvantage compared to Danish citizens. As regards disability pensions, refugees have the same rights as Danish citizens, but there is a 'duration of residence' requirement for immigrants. In terms of actual allocations, immigrants do not appear disadvantaged in terms of the percentage of immigrants awarded disability pensions. Eldercare is tax-based, free of charge and also provided to immigrants. The same applies to the healthcare system, which also grants equal access for all residents (different rules apply for undocumented immigrants and asylum-seekers, however). Conversely, the government introduced fees for interpreters for immigrants who have been in Denmark more than 3 years. As some 25–35% in this group report problems communicating in Danish (MBU, 2018), this may create a barrier in the health system.

Danish family policies are universal and aimed at creating incentives for both parents to work (Grødem, 2016). Childcare is strongly subsidised and free of charge for low-income families. Immigrants increased use of the childcare system in the 1990s and matched the Danish rates relatively quickly. The only differences are in day care (below age 3), where non-Western immigrants typically sending their children slightly later than ethnic Danes (Glavind, Pade, & Bust Nielsen, 2019).

Labour market policy is generally an area where we find the strongest attempts at differentiating between immigrants/refugees and Danish citizens. The 'start help' programme introduced in 2002 bars those who have not resided in the country for at least seven of the past eight years from receiving social assistance (*kontanthjælp*). Start help was set at about 65% of the amount paid for basic employment assistance and regarded as the least generous scheme in northwestern Europe (Andersen, 2007, p. 263). The primary argument for the deep cuts was to create incentives to find employment – particularly low-wage jobs.

Similarly, while not explicitly targeting immigrants, a ceiling on social assistance introduced in 2004 mainly affected them. In 2015, the unemployment benefit for 'new arrivals' to the country was again cut substantially. The 'integration allowance' was set some 45% lower than social assistance (Jakobsen, Korpi, & Lorentzen, 2019, p. 326).

The final aspect of the internal policies concerns the political rights of immigrants and refugees in Denmark. While citizenship is required to vote at Danish parliamentary elections and national referenda, non-citizens – or denizens – with four years (three years from 1981 until 2019) of uninterrupted residence in Denmark can vote in municipal and regional elections. Only a handful of other European countries grant this right to non-citizens (Simonsen, 2016). The right to run for office follows the right to vote. The road to citizenship for refugees and immigrants is not an easy one, however. The rules on access to citizenship are among the most restrictive in Europe, and they reflect a conception of citizenship as 'a means to make immigrants internalize citizenship norms and competences and to achieve cultural adaptation' (Bech, Borevi, & Mouritsen, 2017).[8] Hence, citizenship is regarded as a reward for integration rather than the starting point of it, as is the case in Sweden (Jensen & Nielsen, 2020). To obtain citizenship, applicants must have eight or nine years of uninterrupted residence (depending on status), they must have been financially self-sufficient for 4.5 of the last five years, and they must not owe money to the state. Moreover, they must demonstrate proficiency in Danish corresponding to the level required to pass the grade 9 final exams in Danish (the final year of primary school). In 2005, the government introduced a test on knowledge of Danish society, history and culture. Conviction of a serious crime bars a person from ever becoming a citizen, while less serious violations of the law result in waiting periods of variable duration. Finally, children born and/or raised in Denmark do not automatically obtain citizenship unless their parents obtain it. They can only apply after turning 18.

In terms of the practical effects of the new citizenship requirements, a study revealed that slightly less than one-third of all immigrants and refugees are able meet all of them. Interestingly, the same study demonstrated that 10% of all citizens with a Danish background would similarly fall short of the requirements (and as many as 20% in the 23–28-year-old group) (Bech et al., 2017, p. 242). The language requirement is the most prohibiting factor (Bech et al., 2017, p. 244). The share of immigrants and refugees with citizenship has dropped dramatically: from around 40% in the early 1980s to 25% in 2017 (Ersbøll, 2018). In Sweden, the figure is 60%. Moreover, only 65% of all descendants in Denmark have citizenship. The consequence is that, in 2019, 9.4% of the adult population residing in Denmark did not have citizenship (55% for those with origins outside the EU) (Danmarks Statistik, 2019).

Table 1 sums up the shift in internal immigration policies in Denmark. Before the turn of the century, integration policy was characterised by efforts to integrate immigrants through the extension of their civil, social and political rights. Since 2001 in particular, there have been successive policy changes aimed at restricting immigrants' political (citizenship) and social rights. Instead of universal social rights for all residents, policies have focused on 'negative selectivism' (Thompson

Table 1. Policy Changes.

	Before 2000	**After 2000**
Social rights	Extension of immigrants' rights	Restricting immigrants' social, civil and political rights
Social policy	*Universalism*	*Negative selectivism*
Ideal of integration	*Mutual integration*	*Assimilation*
Labour market policy	*Investment in human capital*	*Work-first strategy*

& Hoggett, 1996). The aforementioned Ghetto Package is the clearest break with the principle of universalism (Seemann, 2020).

In broader terms, the dominant political ideal for the integration of immigrants in Danish society has changed rapidly and dramatically. Prior to 2000, the ideal was mutual integration; that is, that immigrants and the majority population had to adapt to each other (Betænkning, 1997). In the latter two decades, assimilation has become the dominant ideal, where access to citizenship requires adaptation to Danish values and norms. We also find significant changes in employment policy: where employment policy focused on investing in an individual's skills prior to 2000, since that time, Denmark has adopted a 'work-first strategy' focusing on rapid labour market integration and incentivising immigrants to find employment (Hernes, Arendt, Andersson Joona, & Tronstad, 2020).

The Participation of Immigrants, Refugees and Descendants in Key Areas in Danish Society

We now turn to the question of the social, economic and political integration of immigrants in the Danish society.

Labour Market Participation

Integrating immigrants and refugees in the labour market has been a persistent challenge in all Western countries, where several studies find a persistent employment gap between native citizens and immigrants, refugees and their descendants (OECD, 2020).

As illustrated in Fig. 2, the employment gap has fluctuated greatly over the past 40 years. Non-Western immigrants display labour market participation rates at levels 20–40% lower than those with Danish origins, while descendants perform better. The employment rates of these two groups are subject to more dramatic fluctuations; as employees in industries and companies with changing labour needs, immigrants were more affected by the recession than were ethnic Danes

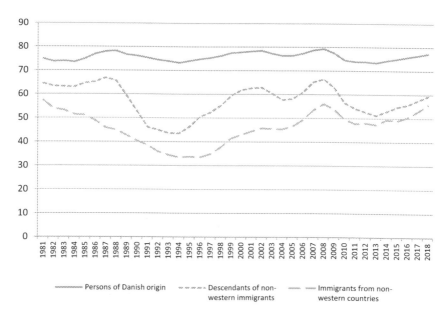

Fig. 2.   Employment by Ancestry and Time. *Source:* Statistics
Denmark, www.statistikbanken.dk/RAS200

(Constant & Schultz-Nielsen, 2004, 135f.). Structural changes in the labour
market, such as the tendency to outsource industry to low-wage countries as well
as organisational changes, may explain some of the massive marginalisation of
immigrants in the 1980s and 1990s (Rosholm, Scott, & Husted, 2006). In addition
to the language barrier – as many as 20% with more than 3 years of residence
report language as an obstacle to work (MBU, 2018) – many immigrants simply
arrive with skillsets ill-equipped to the demands of the Danish labour market.
Moreover, high minimum wages crowd out the types of jobs typically available to
immigrants elsewhere. The composition of the immigrant group also matters. As
mentioned, the first waves of immigrants came to work, where later waves con-
sisted more of refugees who often suffer from debilitating problems, such as war
trauma, which affects their labour market performance. An extended period of
economic growth (1995–2008) drove an increase in the employment of immigrants, who found new employment niches in the post-industrial economy, such
as low-skilled service professions (Ejrnæs, 2008). In particular, the increased
employment in low-skilled service professions, such as cleaning, hotels and restaurants, was a contributing factor to an increase in immigrant employment.
After the economic recession, immigrant employment again declines.

While it is difficult to gauge the magnitude of the effect on employment rates,
studies have revealed considerable discrimination in the Danish labour market.
Particularly, ethnic minority men suffer negative discrimination (e.g. Dahl &

Krog, 2018), and as many as 20% report rejections due to discrimination (MBU, 2018). Ethnic minorities report that they experience lower recognition for their efforts in society – less than half feel adequately recognised in the sense that they do not find employment matching their qualifications (see MBU, 2011, 2016). They place the same or slightly higher premium on being self-sufficient as ethnic Danes (MBU, 2011, p. 36), although there are differences with respect to the role of women. Traditional gender roles may explain some differences in the older generation of immigrants, where elderly women generally have low participation in society, but in the younger group – and particularly the descendants – women have higher labour market participation rates than men.

Education is a key element in solving problems related to qualification mismatch and labour market demands. Compared to employment rates, immigrants and descendants from non-Western countries, especially female descendants, perform better when it comes to education attainment. Fig. 3 shows that an increasing share of immigrants complete an education. As seen in the graph, however, there is currently a considerable gap in education between male and female immigrants and descendants. Among the 16–24-year-olds, the share of descendants enrolled in education programmes is actually higher than the share of Danes, while immigrants still lag behind in this regard.

Immigrants in Danish Society: Values, Social and Political Integration

The question of diversity of beliefs, values and norms prevailing in immigrant communities and Danish society in general has been a source of conflict in shared institutions, and the political debate on how to handle these conflicts has been intense. The so-called 'Citizen Survey' (*Medborgerskabsundersøgelsen*) – first carried out in 2011 to investigate differences between Danish and non-Western immigrants, refugees and their descendants – reveal commonalities and differences in values, practices and experiences between non-Western immigrants and the native population (MBU, 2011–2020).

The 'Citizen Survey' concluded that with respect to civic attitudes related to democracy and rule of law, differences are negligible (MBU, 2011). A later survey revealed stronger support for representative democracy among native Danes, but also that religion does not explain the differences (MBU, 2016). With respect to actual participation, however, immigrants display much lower rates of electoral participation. Immigrant (non-Western as well as Western) electoral turnout is typically estimated at 20–40% lower than those with an ethnic Danish background. There is some indication that descendants participate more in municipal elections but still less than ethnic Danes (see Bhatti & Hansen, 2017). Turnout for both groups increased significantly in the 2019 parliamentary election (Møller-Hansen, 2019), and the harsh anti-immigrant rhetoric, with two new extreme right-wing parties running in the 2019 elections, possibly boosted turnout (Bischoff, 2020). However, Simonsen (2021) finds that anti-immigrant rhetoric generally tends to affect political trust and faith in democracy adversely. Lower electoral participation corresponds to low representation. Only 3% of the candidates – and even fewer of those elected – in the 2013 municipal elections

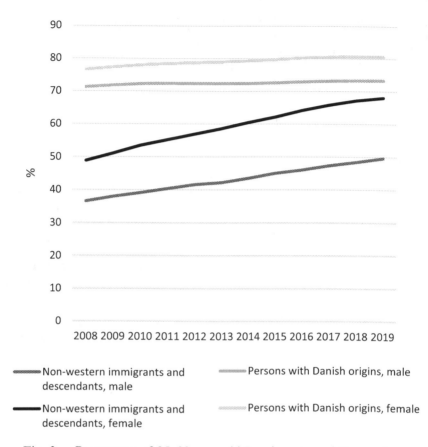

Fig. 3.   Percentage of 25–39-year-old Immigrants and Descendants from Non-Western Countries and Persons with Danish Origins Who Have Completed a Danish Short, Medium or Long Higher Education in 2008–2019. *Source:* The Ministry of Immigration and Integration Affairs' database of foreigners in Statistics Denmark, IMUDD042.

had a non-Western background, while 6.1% of the voting population did. It is worth noting, however, that immigrants of Turkish descent were over-represented, and those of Pakistani descent fairly represented. These nationalities arrived in the first waves of immigration into Denmark, which might indicate that organising political representation simply takes time (Bhatti et al., 2017). In parliament, the representation of non-Western immigrants/descendants is currently at 2.2% (4 members).

Immigrants are less active in civil society associations than the ethnic majority. Corrected for background factors, a recent study estimates that 60% of immigrants and roughly 70% of their descendants are members of at least one such association, compared to 78% for ethnic Danes. Most of this difference is explained by membership in sports associations (MBU, 2018). Association participation is an important integrating factor and typically associated with high levels of trust. In 2019, while Denmark had the second-highest level of generalised trust (trust in other members of society) in the world, it also had the largest differences in the trust levels between the native and immigrant populations. Corrected for background factors, this figure is 16 percentage points lower for immigrants and 24 percentage points lower for descendants. Descendants thus differ more strongly from Danes than do immigrants, despite stronger participation and networks (MBU, 2018). Descendants, however, also consistently report more discrimination than do immigrants; e.g. 23% vs 13% being denied access to places, 34% vs 24% poor service, 52% vs 28% subject of derogatory remarks or offensive comments. Finally, 8% vs 7% report experiences with ethnically motivated physical abuse (MBU, 2018). The high numbers of people experiencing discrimination and having low trust presents a clear challenge for the social integration in the 'Danish model', which builds on high levels of trust and solidarity. Where descendants in most respects (education, labour market participation, social networks, attitudes) are more like the ethnic Danes than are immigrants, this is an opposing trend.

Some of difficulties experienced in 'shared' institutions (e.g. schools, public pools) concern differences in how religious convictions are practised; particularly norms regarding gender and sexuality. Immigrants are generally more religious than Danes and more likely to believe it is important in the education of children. Only 5% of Danes believe it is very important or important, whereas some 60% of immigrants and 40% of descendants do (MBU, 2017). On gender equality, using an indicator from 1–100 measuring attitudes on a number of dimensions, Danes and descendants score the same, while immigrants score lower (85% vs 77%) (MBU, 2020). In terms of lived experience, however, there are strong differences; for instance, female immigrants and descendants report having less freedom to do the same things that the members of the opposite sex do (just under 50%) compared to Danes (just under 30%). On questions of sexual freedom and social control, only 50% of immigrants and 70% descendants, for instance, report being permitted to have a partner before marriage – a freedom that Danes take for granted (MBU, 2018). Such differences create tangible problems. In schools, for instance, it is not uncommon for ethnic minority parents to not permit their children to participate in school trips, sports or social events, which are otherwise viewed as important for the education and socialisation of Danish schoolchildren. But the use of public swimming pools has also caused problems among adults, as some Muslim women will only swim in a pool if it is reserved for women in particular hours. Local institutions and authorities differ in the choices they make, some arguing for the necessity to accommodate diverse practices, others that Danish norms should prevail. Where local practices differ, parliament has passed legislation to send a clear signal that Danish norms rule supreme. The so-called 'burka' and 'handshake' laws from 2018 were more about sending normative messages than addressing pressing issues; the former prohibits masks in public – thereby barring a tiny number from wearing a burka – while the latter requires applicants for citizenship to shake hands as part of the ceremony, which is intended to create difficulties for Muslims who do not wish to shake hands with a member of the opposite sex. The latter has created conflicts within parties between the mayors responsible for enforcing it (who oppose it), and the parties in parliament.

Discussion

Pro and Cons of the Danish Response to Immigration

When comparing different integration policies, we can distinguish between two rationales – equal rights vs obligations and incentives – to promote integration (Borevi, 2014). As described above, Danish policy has focused on the latter, particularly by slashing benefits to create incentives to work. A Danish study found a minor positive effect of reducing benefits on employment (12 percentage points) (Andersen, Hansen, Schultz-Nielsen, Tranæs, & Forskningsenhed, 2012). Comparing the Danish approach to Norway and Sweden, where the focus is on improving immigrants' qualifications, Jakobsen et al. (2019) conclude that the Danish reforms have not had 'any clear-cut effects on either employment or earnings among non-Western immigrants' (p. 325). Specifically for refugees, the effects appear short-lived and vanish in the longer term (Drud-Jensen, 2019). A comparative Scandinavian study reveals that male refugees – but not female – in Denmark are employed faster, whereas refugees in Sweden match Danish employment rates after more years of residence, and refugees in Norway surpass the Danish employment rates (Hernes et al., 2020). The study concludes that the Danish work-first approach may lead to faster labour market integration while weakening long-term labour market activity (Hernes et al., 2020).

Moreover, there are the unintended consequences; 'Start assistance' has put some groups in a situation of absolute – not 'just' relative – poverty (Andersen et al., 2012), and the 'integration assistance' allowance was found to fall short of the sum necessary to subsist in Denmark, causing social and material deprivation (Andersen, Jorsal, & Jørgensen, 2018; Drud-Jensen, 2019). Furthermore, lower benefits are related to higher crime and health issues for refugees (Andersen, Dustmann, & Landersø, 2019).

In contrast to the persistent challenge of integrating immigrants into the labour market, Denmark has been rather successful when it comes to integrating immigrants in the welfare institutions and the formal education system. For instance, immigrants in Denmark make use of voluntary childcare just as much as Danes do. One of the strengths of institutions such as public schools and universal childcare is the ability to foster social bonds between different ethnic and social groups, increasing the level of social cohesion. This critically depends on mixing Danes and immigrants, which is a challenge in the increasingly segmented housing market. Immigrants lag on education attainment, even though more young descendants than Danes are currently enrolled in education programmes.

Creating solidarity and social cohesion between immigrants and natives represents a persistent challenge. Problems such as higher welfare costs for immigrants, higher crime statistics, culture clashes in shared institutions combined with a persistent, strong political and negative media focus that tends to distort public perceptions may well exacerbate tensions. While relatively tolerant on other questions, the percentage of Danes viewing Muslims very negatively is very high. Conversely, large shares of immigrants and descendants have experienced discrimination and have considerably lower levels of interpersonal trust than do those with Danish origins. At the same time, however, an overwhelming majority of immigrants and descendants from non-Western countries feel that they belong in Denmark (MBU, 2020). The question is whether the present political climate and policies will eventually result in more or less inter-group solidarity.

Some Lessons Learnt and Implications for Practice

We have seen a substantial shift in the political rhetoric as well as in the actual immigration and integration policy implemented in Denmark. We can draw four main lessons from this analysis.

(1) The shift from a liberal immigration policy to a more restrictive immigration policy has significantly reduced the number of asylum-seekers. Denmark receives fewer refugees per capita today than do the other Nordic countries and fewer than the EU average.

(2) Despite persistent political efforts to integrate immigrants into the labour market, Denmark experiences the same challenges regarding immigrant labour market participation as found in other European countries. Like other Western European countries, Denmark has a relatively high employment gap between native citizens versus immigrants and refugees from non-Western countries.

(3) The Danish case also demonstrates that reducing social benefits only has a marginal, positive, short-term effect on employment, and that it comes with a cost in terms of poverty and more crime. The dilemma is that the political effort to integrate immigrants into the labour market rapidly by reducing benefits also contributes to further social and economic marginalisation and precarisation.

(4) The Danish welfare state has been relatively successful in integrating immigrants and descendants in the education system. A combination of a publicly financed education system and pro-education values among immigrants may explain the high numbers of immigrants and descendants enrolled in education programmes.

(5) The most significant integration policy in recent years is the aforementioned Ghetto Package of 2018. It aims to combat the 'parallel society' of residential areas characterised by high shares of immigrants together with low employment rates, high crime statistics etc. The strategy has been criticised for embodying discriminatory practices (UN, 2020) and for stigmatising neighbourhoods (Larsen, 2019).

Conclusion

International migration is a global challenge affecting peoples and nations around the world. In the advanced economies and welfare states of Western Europe, integrating migrants presents political, social as well as economic challenges. This chapter shows how Danish immigration politics has turn from low to high salience and policy has undergone radical change, resulting in a tightening of both internal and external immigration policies. Obtaining residence and citizenship in Denmark has become far more difficult, which has had an effect on the influx despite international refugee crises being difficult to control at national borders. Moreover, Danish integration policies have increasingly focused on obligations and incentives, primarily by cutting benefits. The effects on employment are negligible; the approach has negative side effects. A key challenge for the Danish welfare model is how to sustain solidarity between groups, which is key to preserving the welfare state.

Notes

1. In the wake of the Syrian refugee crisis, *The New York Times* editorial board published its opinion on Danish policies under the suggestive headline: 'Denmark's cruelty towards refugees' (NYT, 1 February 2016). The Danish revocation of residence permits for some Syrian refugees in the spring of 2021 – the only EU country to do so – has likewise drawn international attention (e.g. Guardian, 14 April 2021; CNN, 18 April 2021).
2. Minister of Justice Erik Ninn-Hansen (Conservatives) warned that the law would undermine Denmark as a nation-state and cause social unrest (Farbøl et al., 2019).
3. In the Social Democratic Party, prominent mayors experiencing problems with immigration and integration had also started voicing dissent in the late 1980s (see Green-Pedersen & Odmalm, 2008; Holm, 2005).
4. PM Fredriksen's statement in Parliament in January 2021, about how the government aims for zero asylum seekers to Denmark, illustrates its commitment to a strict policy (TV2, 21 January 2021).
5. Refugees – whose rights in this regard are protected by international conventions – are exempted.
6. Only 30 such refugees were allowed entry in 2019, and Denmark accepted 200 quota refugees from Rwanda in 2020 (although their entry was delayed due to COVID-19).
7. A leading tabloid, *Ekstrabladet*, ran a highly critical editorial headlined 'Inequality before the law' as a direct comment on the double punishment clause in the ghetto package (27 February 2017).
8. Author's translation.

References

Andersen, J. G. (2007). Restricting access to social protection for immigrants in the Danish welfare state. *The Policy Press, 15*(3), 257–269.

Andersen, L. H., Dustmann, C., & Landersø, R. (2019). *Lowering welfare benefits: Intended and unintended consequences for migrants and their families.* Study paper 138. The ROCKWOOL Foundation Research Unit, Copenhagen.

Andersen, L. H., Hansen, H., Schultz-Nielsen, M. L., Tranæs, T., & Forskningsenhed, R. F. (2012). *Starthjælpens betydning for flygtninges levevilkår og beskæftigelse.* Rockwool Fondens Forskningsenhed. København: Arbejdspapir 25.

Bech, E. C., Borevi, K., & Mouritsen, P. (2017). A 'civic turn' in Scandinavian family migration policies? Comparing Denmark, Norway and Sweden. *Comparative Migration Studies*, 5(7).

Betænkning. (1997). *Integration. Integration - betænkning afgivet af det af indenrigsministeren nedsatte Integrationsudvalg.* Betænkning nr. 1337. København 1997.

Bhatti, Y. og Møller Hansen, K. (2017). Valgdeltagelsen Blandt Ikke-Vestlige Indvandrere Og Efterkommere. *Politica*, 49(3), 249–272

Bhatti, Y. Møller Hansen, K. og Kjær, U. (2017). Ligner kommunalpolitikerne deres vælgere? I Elklit, Jørgen, Ulrik Kjær, and Christian Elmelund-Præstekær (red.). *KV13 : analyser af kommunalvalget 2013.* Odense: Syddansk Universitetsforlag.

Bhatti, Y. Møller Hansen, K. og Kjær, U. (2017). Forskere: Nydanskere er underrepræsenterede i kommunalbestyrelserne. Fagbladsartikel. København: VIVE.

Bischoff, C. S. (2020). New parties: Game changers or 'much ado about nothing'? *Scandinavian Political Studies*, 43(2).

Borevi, K. (2014). Multiculturalism and welfare state integration: Swedish model path dependency. *Identities: Global Studies in Power and Culture*, 21(6), 708–723.

CNN (2021). In its latest lurch to the far right, Denmark plans to send some refugees back to Syria. By John T. CNN 18 April.

Constant, A., & Schultz-Nielsen, M. L. (2004). Labour force participation and unemployment: Incentives and preferences. In T. Tranaes & K. F. Zimmermann (Eds.), *Migrants, work, and the welfare state* (pp. 147–186). Odense: University Press of Southern Denmark.

Dahl, M., & Krog, N. (2018). Experimental evidence of discrimination in the labour market: Intersections between ethnicity, gender, and socio-economic status. *European Sociological Review*, 34(4), 402–417.

Danmarks Statistik. (2019). Næsten hver tiende voksne i Danmark kan ikke stemme. Retrieved from https://www.dst.dk/da/Statistik/bagtal/2019/2019-03-06-udenstemmeret

Drud Jensen, M. (2019). *Begrænset beskæftigelsesmæssig effekt og negative sociale konsekvenser – en sammenfatning af forskningsbaseret viden om effekter af lave ydelser til flygtninge.* Copenhagen: Dansk Flygtningehjælp.

Ejrnæs, A. (2008). *Integration eller isolation? Etniske minoriteter på arbejdsmarkedet.* Frederiksberg: Nyt fra Samfundsvidenskaberne.

Ersbøll, E. (2018). *Statsborgerskab – Status 2018.* Copenhagen: Danish Institute for Human Rights.

Glavind, N., Pade, S. og Bust Nielsen, L. (2019). Daginstitutioner og børn med etnisk minoritetsbaggrund. - Hvorfor indskrives børnene ofte senere? Bureau 2000 – analyse og forskning. FOA.

Green-Pedersen, C., & Krogstrup, J. (2008). Immigration as a political issue in Denmark and Sweden. *European Journal of Political Research*, 47, 610–634.

Green-Pedersen, C., & Odmalm, P. (2008). 'Going different ways?' Right wing parties and the immigrant issue in Denmark and Sweden. *Journal of European Public Policy, 15*(3), 367–381.

Greve, B. (2019). *Welfare, populism and welfare chauvinism.* Bristol: Policy Press.

Grødem, A. S. (2016). Family-oriented policies in Scandinavia and the challenge of immigration. *Journal of European Social Policy, 27.*

Gundelach, P. (2011). *Små og store forandringer. Danskernes værdier siden 1981.* København: Hans Reitzels Forlag.

Harmon, N. A. (2018). Immigration, ethnic diversity, and political outcomes: Evidence from Denmark. *The Scandinavian Journal of Economics, 120*(4), 1043–1074.

Hellwig, T., & Kweon, Y. (2016). Taking cues on multidimensionalissues: The case of attitudes toward immigration. *West European Politics, 39*(4), 710–730.

Hernes, V., Arendt, J., Andersson Joona, P., & Tronstad, K. (2020). Rapid or long-term employment? A Scandinavian comparative study of refugee integration policies and employment outcomes. *Journal of European Public Policy*, 1–21.

Holm, L. (2005). Folketinget og Udlændingepolitikken. Ålborg: Akademiet for Migrationsstudier i Danmark.

Hovden, J. F., & Mjelde, H. (2019). Increasingly controversial, cultural, and political: The immigration debate in Scandinavian Newspapers 1970–2016. *Javnost - The Public, 26*(2), 138–157.

Information. (2018). Leder. 27 February. Dagbladet Information.

Jakobsen, V., Korpi, T., & Lorentzen, T. (2019). Immigration and integration policy and labour market attainment among immigrants to Scandinavia. *European Journal of Population, 35*, 305–328.

Jensen, K., & Nielsen, L. (2020). Fairness og statsborgerskab. *Politik, 23*(1), 104–118.

Jønsson, H. V. (2013). Ret og pligt til integration: Socialdemokratiet og integrationsloven 1998. *Historisk Tidsskrift, 113*(1), 184–227.

Jørndrup, H. (2017). *'Dem vi taler om': Etniske minoriteter i danske nyhedsmedier.* Foreningen Ansvarlig Presse.

Klingeren, M., van, Boomgaarden, H. G., Vliegenthart, R., & de Vreese, C. H. (2015). Real world is not enough: The media as an additional source of negative attitudes toward immigration, comparing Denmark and The Netherlands. *European Sociological Review, 31*(3), 268–283.

Koning, E. A. (2017). Selecting, disentitling, or investing? Exploring party and voter responses to immigrant welfare dependence in 15 West European welfare states. *Comparative European Politics, 15*, 628–660.

Larsen, C. A. (2011). Ethnic heterogeneity and public support for welfare: Is the American experience replicated in Britain, Sweden and Denmark? *Scandinavian Political Studies, 34*(4), 332–353.

Larsen, T. S. (2019). Fra hårde ghettoer til forsømte områder: Om anvendelsen af socialvidenskabelig refleksivitet i praksis. In B. Greve (Ed.), *Socialvidenskab* (pp. 375–400). Frederiksberg: Nyt fra Samfundsvidenskaberne.

MBU. (2011–2020). Medborgerskabsundersøgelsen. En række selvstændige undersøgelser ved Ministeriet for udlændinge og integration. Retrieved from https://integrationsbarometer.dk/tal-og-analyser/medborgerskab-ligebehandling-og-selvbestemmelse

Møller Hansen, K. (2019). *Valgdeltagelsen ved Folketingsvalget 2019. CVAP WP 2/2020.* CVAP Working Paper Series. University of Copenhagen.

OECD. (2020). *International migration outlook 2020*. Paris: OECD Publishing. doi:10. 1787/ec98f531-en

Reiermann, J., & Andersen, T. K. (2019). Hver fjerde dansker: muslimer skal ud af Danmark. 21 October. Mandag Morgen.

Rosholm, M., Scott, K., & Husted, L. (2006). The times they are a-changin': Declining immigrant employment opportunities in Scandinavia. *International Migration Review, 40*(2), 318–347.

Seemann, A. (2020). The Danish 'ghetto initiatives' and the changing nature of social citizenship, 2004–2018. *Critical Social Policy, 41*(4), 586–560.

Simonsen, K. B. (2016). How the host nation's boundary drawing affects immigrants' belonging. *Journal of Ethnic and Migration Studies, 42*(7), 1153–1176.

Simonsen, K. B. (2020). Immigration and immigrant integration policy: Public opinion or party politics? In P. Munk Christiansen, J. Elklit, & P. Nedergaard (Eds.), *Oxford handbook of Danish politics*. Oxford: Oxford University Press.

Simonsen, K. B. (2021). The democratic consequences of anti-immigrant political rhetoric: A mixed methods study of immigrants' political belonging. *Political Behavior, 43*(1), 143–174.

Skaksen, J. R., & Jensen, B. (2016). *Hvad ved vi om indvandring og integration? Indvandringen til Danmark og forløbet af integrationen fra 1960'erne til i dag*. København: Gyldendal.

Slothuus, R., Petersen, M. B., & Rathlev, J. (2012). Politiske partier som opinionsledere: Resultater fra en panelundersøgelse. *Politica, 44*(4), 544–562.

Sniderman, P. M., Petersen, M. B., Slothuus, R., & Stubager, R. (2014). *Paradoxes of liberal democracy: Islam, Western Europe and the Danish cartoon crises*. Princeton: Princeton University Press.

Statistics Denmark. (2020). Indvandrere i Danmark 2020. Retrieved from https:// www.dst.dk/Site/Dst/Udgivelser/GetPubFile.aspx?id=29447&sid=indv2020

Thompson, S., & Hoggett, P. (1996). Universalism, selectivism and particularism: Towards a postmodern social policy. *Critical Social Policy, 16*(46), 21–42.

UN Economic and Social Council. (2019). Concluding observations on sixth periodic report of Denmark by Committee on Economic. Social and Cultural Rights. 12 November 2019.

UNHCR. (2021). Retrieved from https://www.unhcr.org/refugee-statistics/. Accessed June 18, 2021.

Chapter 14

Public Governance in Denmark – Current Developments and Ways Ahead

Andreas Hagedorn Krogh, Annika Agger and Peter Triantafillou

Abstract

In this concluding chapter, the editors provide an overall assessment of contemporary Danish public governance based on the main findings in the preceding chapters of the edited volume. Surveying the Danish governance responses to contemporary mega-challenges, the chapter reflects on policy implications and contemplate the future of both research and practice related to public administration, politics and governance in Denmark. The chapter argues that recent public governance reforms have turned the Danish welfare state into a mix of a *neo-Weberian state* and an *enabling state*, which deploys its considerable resources to create economic growth for the benefit of the large majority of Danes, to satisfy the needs of citizens and businesses and to develop collaborative solutions to complex problems. While the chapter concludes that this modified version of the well-known universal welfare state is largely apt for meeting the mega-challenges of the twenty-first century, recent reforms seeking to enhance job-seeking incentives for the unemployed and to integrate immigrants have resulted in new forms of marginalisation of weaker societal groups. Moreover, evolving problems such as climate change, an ageing population and digital citizen privacy will require further public governance reforms in the years to come.

Keywords: Public governance; public policy; public administration; neo-Weberian state; enabling state; Denmark

Across the globe, governments and public administrations face major political, economic, social and environmental challenges requiring innovative, adaptive and robust public governance responses (IPCC report, 2018; OECD, 2020; United Nations, 2015). Against a backdrop of lively international debate over the merits and perils of the Danish welfare state model and its ability to deal with the

Public Governance in Denmark, 247–261

Copyright © 2022 by Emerald Publishing Limited

All rights of reproduction in any form reserved

doi:10.1108/978-1-80043-712-820221014

pressing societal problems of the twenty-first century, this edited volume has scrutinised the political system, governance structures and state–society relations underpinning the Danish welfare state. Individually and collectively, the chapters have critically examined the current Danish governance capacity to provide adequate solutions to some of the most daunting mega-challenges facing contemporary societies.

In this concluding chapter, we recapitulate the main findings of the 12 chapters and provide an overall assessment of contemporary Danish governance that can serve to inform the scholarly, political and popular debates regarding the Danish welfare state. First, we survey the Danish responses to the five mega-challenges: creating economic and social equality, strengthening democracy and participation, enhancing public sector effectiveness and efficiency, promoting environmental sustainability and adapting to recent demographic changes and migration patterns. We then reflect on the implications for practice and present our recommendations for policy professionals engaged in formulating and adopting policy reforms and administrative reforms inspired by 'the Danish model'. Finally, we provide some concluding remarks and contemplate on the future of both research and practice, directly or indirectly related to public administration, politics and governance in Denmark.

The Danish Governance Responses

Through nuanced analyses of various aspects of public governance in Denmark, the 12 chapters in this anthology show how the Danish welfare state has changed and developed significantly over the past 40–50 years. In some respects, these developments have geared the Danish welfare state model to meet the mounting challenges of the twenty-first century. In other respects, they have weakened its capacity to solve pressing problems. In the following, we recap the key insights from the five sections on economic and social equality, democracy and participation, public sector effectiveness and efficiency, environmental sustainability, and demographic changes and immigration.

The chapters presented in Section I illustrate three ways in which the Danish governance model achieves relatively high levels of economic and social equality in the form of equal access to public services, social security and affordable housing. In Chapter 2, Bent Greve and Daniel Béland demonstrate how the rather generous Danish welfare benefits, such as free education, health services and social security, funded through relatively high levels of progressive taxation, result in the considerable redistribution of welfare services between rich and poor. While the universality principle remains a central feature in the service sector, recent changes to the income taxation system have influenced the income transfers and resulted in greater levels of inequality. The authors thus find that the levels of equality in contemporary Denmark are less distinct compared to other Nordic countries than was the case in the past.

The Danish labour market model has also changed in recent years. In Chapter 3, Magnus Paulsen Hansen and Janine Leschke describe how the internationally acclaimed 'flexicurity model' combines flexibility and security with an increasing focus on activation and financial incentives to work. Based on collective agreements between employers and employees, the model grants economic compensation to employees when between jobs, while also making it relatively easy for employers to hire and fire people, depending on their needs. The authors argue that the model is successful in the sense that the employment rates are high, wages are comparatively equal and labour conflicts and strikes are few. In recent years, however, it has become increasingly difficult for less educated groups to enter the labour market, and stigmatisation of the unemployed is on the rise. While the flexicurity model still contributes to the relatively high levels of economic and social equality in Denmark, recent reforms and labour market developments have altered the conditions and functioning of the model.

Finally, the social housing sector is another major piece in the puzzle of understanding economic and social equality in Denmark. In Chapter 4, Elizabeth Toft Kristjansen and Jesper Ole Jensen show how the Danish social housing model rests on collective resident ownership of the estates, granting residents a say in the operation of the buildings and development of the housing areas through resident boards. The model generally provides affordable entry to the housing market and contributes to the low levels of homelessness in Denmark. Sustaining a considerable level of democratic innovation in the steering and operation of social housing, the social housing sector has also spurred local engagement and participatory forms of ownership. In recent decades, however, the middle class has increasingly opted for private home ownership, and the percentage of 'weaker' residents, measured in terms of their socio-economic resources, has increased. The demographic development in recent decades has increased the divide between the social housing sector and the rest of the Danish housing market. This development is calling social housing managers to re-think participation in local housing estates.

The chapters in Section II explain how and why Denmark has maintained remarkably high levels of trust in government, political cooperation and political stability despite the recent surge in populism, political turmoil and polarisation seen in many other Western democracies. In Chapter 5, Flemming Juul Christiansen, Peter Heyn Nielsen and Bonnie Field argue that Danish minority governments are unusually durable and consider how they effectively manage to pass major public policy reforms while largely avoiding policy deadlocks. The authors show how formal and informal institutions promote stability in a number of ways. First, the proportional electoral system channels the different views and interests in the population into the formal political decision-making process, whereby most Danes feel represented in the Folketing – the Danish parliament. Second, the low threshold for achieving representation in the Folketing renders it practically impossible for a single party to win an outright majority, prompting political cooperation and negotiation. Third, broad-based legislative agreements grant each party in these settlements a quasi-governmental status, which provides them with informal veto powers with respect to any changes in the agreed-upon policy. Due to its strong institutionalisation, newer parties are quickly absorbed and socialised into the informal system of multi-party agreements, which makes

Danish minority government rule surprisingly stable. However, the authors argue that the multi-party agreements system also comes with a significant risk: since bargaining takes places in closed forums, the stable system risks decoupling public debate, public interests and even parliament to some extent. This, in turn, may hamper the quality of law-making and have negative implications for more participatory forms of democracy.

Other parts of the political system in Denmark work to sustain more interactive forms of political leadership. In Chapter 6, Eva Sørensen and Jody Sandfort examine features of the Danish governance model that facilitate dialogue between politicians and citizens and enable elected officials to make informed political decisions and rally support for policy implementation. First, the highly decentralised political system in Denmark creates a short distance between politicians and citizens, which supports a responsive style of political leadership. Second, a number of innovative initiatives integrate representative and direct forms of democracy and push elected politicians towards a more interactive political leadership style, such as a formal system of citizen proposals, national commissions that invite citizens to discuss specific issues and political task committees where local politicians and citizens meet to develop policy. These 'hybrid forms of democracy' reduce politician–citizen tensions and contribute to the stable, democratic and innovative governance of society. Despite these apparent merits, the authors warn that hybrid forms of democracy also pose several challenges to democratic governance: they may compromise the autonomy of politicians; obfuscate formal forms of accountability and enhance structural inequalities between citizens with different participatory capabilities. Well-functioning hybrid democracy therefore requires new forms of social accountability, checks and balances and appropriate engagement designs.

The chapters in Section III show how the Danish governance model works to sustain public efficiency, effectiveness and innovation despite an array of bureaucratic problems and several instances of poor public service, regulatory neglect and failing public projects. In Chapter 7, Jacob Torfing and Tina Øllgaard Bentzen explain how the high levels of trust in the Danish public sector are wedded to a pragmatic combination of various public governance paradigms, which has produced a 'hybrid governance system' that balances the legitimate demand for control against widespread trust in public employees. The system builds on a continued prevalence of traditional Weberian bureaucratic values of regularity, impartiality and expertise, a limited and selective introduction of New Public Management reforms, and long-standing Danish traditions for short manager–employee distances, a low degree of rule-based work structuration, and an elaborate system of macro- and micro-corporatism. At the state level, a dynamic neo-Weberian state works to satisfy an increasingly demanding citizenry. At the local level, many Danish municipalities design and experiment with new platforms for developing collaborative solutions to complex problems. The hybrid governance system produces virtuous circles of trust, which are continually sustained by trust-based systems of evaluation, assessment and accountability developed in close public manager–employee dialogue. However, there is a continuous need to develop ways of striking the right control–trust balance to avoid governance failures that erode citizen trust in the public sector and to safeguard public values of transparency, accountability and performance.

High levels of trust also provide Denmark with a comparative advantage regarding public service digitalisation. In Chapter 8, Peter Aagaard and John Storm Pedersen demonstrate how the Danish public sector is one of the most digitalised public sectors in the world. Despite several public ICT failures and scandals in recent years, Denmark has maintained high levels of public trust in the ability of public authorities to collect and store personal information safely and securely. Public services have become highly digitalised, including secure electronic mailboxes for all citizens and public Internet portals for citizen services, health services, employment services and private business. Public managers increasingly rely on digital platforms and management systems to manage hospitals, universities, schools and other public institutions. The extensive digitalisation is predicated on the systematic and centralised storing of information on each individual Danish citizen. Aagaard and Pedersen argue that this is the result of an ongoing national, non-partisan reform strategy, where shifting Danish governments have collaborated with regional and local governments over several decades. The high levels of generalised trust in government and a consensual understanding of digitalisation as a crucial means for public sector efficiency have sustained the progressive digitalisation strategy. However, the authors also point to two significant digitalisation risks. First, the government risks violating citizen privacy and eroding public trust if it does not further improve the security of personalised information. Second, the failure of several large public IT projects demonstrates how the digitalisation of public services may incur large and unexpected financial expenses. There is therefore good reason to keep an eye out for data security and to question the widespread belief that digital era governance will always reduce the cost of welfare services.

Internationally, the energy and agriculture sectors contribute significantly to greenhouse gas emissions, soil degradation, air and water pollution and the loss of biodiversity, all of which are high on the list of twenty-first century mega-challenges. International society is increasingly recognising the need for reforms at different levels to halt and reverse the rise in global temperature and the growing pressures on eco-systems worldwide. On this dire background, the chapters in Section IV examine the Danish governance responses to the pressing problems of climate change and sustainable food production. In Chapter 9, Karsten Bruun Hansen and Peter Enevoldsen show how the integrated Danish energy model has secured efficient, affordable and stable supplies of renewable energy. Through a combination of supportive institutional designs, policy instruments and polycentric self-governance, the dependence on coal, natural gas and oil in the 1970s and 1980s has slowly but steadily given way to renewable energy production, especially wind power. The development of renewable energies in Denmark relies on a mix of top-down and bottom-up strategies pertaining to infrastructure change. For example, national authorities have provided political support and opportunities for citizens to buy shares in the wind turbine industry, which has played a crucial role to win broad public acceptance for the comprehensive energy transformation project. However, recent developments towards huge wind turbine projects with international investors would appear to be undermining the public support and causing conflicts around the location of new wind turbines in local communities. These tendencies indicate the need for the constant negotiation of the balance between launching ambitious policies for sustainable energy provision and ensuring public support for large infrastructure projects.

In Chapter 10, Sevasti Chatzopoulou and Kostas Karantininis demonstrate how the Danish agri-food system is generally efficient, resilient and capable of adapting to external and internal pressures over time due to the significant cooperative organisation of the sector and strong ties between stakeholders. The sector plays a significant role for the national economy in terms of GDP, exports, employment and innovation. However, the economic efficiency of the system comes at a price for the environment. The large-scale conventional farming affects the environment negatively in the form of lost biodiversity, nutrient pollution of water and soil degradation. The Danish governance response was an emphasis on organic production, which is now a rapidly growing niche in the Danish agri-food system. Denmark has become one of the countries in the world with the highest consumption of organic products per capita. Already in the 1980s, Denmark introduced an organic agricultural production act followed by a state-issued certification of organic farmers that raised consumer confidence in organic commodities. More recently, the Danish government has collaborated with the agricultural organisations and key market actors in enacting a set of strategic initiatives to promote organic agricultural production, both domestically and internationally. Large-scale industrialised organic agriculture also has environmental implications, however, and the capacity of these efforts to transform the agro-system more fundamentally has yet to be seen.

Last but not least, demographic developments and migration present daunting problems for Western societies today and in the years to come. Ageing populations and mass migration due to climate change, war and poverty pose political, social and economic challenges to the welfare state, not least to the relatively culturally homogenous Scandinavian welfare states. The chapters in Section V consider the Danish governance responses to the challenges in the policy areas of pensions and retirement, healthcare and integration. In Chapter 11, Jon Kvist and Fritz von Nordheim examine the Danish pension system, which is widely recognised as one of the most robust and economically sustainable retirement income systems, offering good benefits with a high level of integrity. Based on public–private benefit integration, the pension system provides statutory, occupational and personal schemes, covering the classic functions of poverty prevention, income maintenance and additional savings. At the same time, it provides robust risk diversification and insurance function. Despite high international appraisal, the model also involves a number of dilemmas and weaknesses, particularly with respect to its ability to curb inequality. In the long run, the indexing of pensionable ages vis-à-vis increasing life expectancy may become a major challenge to the fairness and social sustainability of the current Danish pension system.

The ageing population also raises questions about the capacity and economic viability of the tax-financed public healthcare system. In Chapter 12, Erik Bækkeskov and Peter Triantafillou scrutinise the healthcare system, which propagates equal access to high-quality services for all residents in Denmark. The system provides effective healthcare and fast rehabilitation that enables people to return to work, earn money and pay taxes and to undertake essential care duties for themselves and their family. In order to balance aspirations to improve health outcomes and contain care expenditures, the Danish healthcare model relies on a multi-level governance model that mixes central and local governance strategies. The Ministry of Health certifies all medical staff and advises the government and regions on all health-related matters; the regional authorities operate and manage the public hospitals, regulate the number of general practitioners (GPs) and specialists and price their services, while the local authorities provide rehabilitation and work to promote healthier lifestyles. The authors find that the use of GPs as gatekeepers for most other healthcare services together with efficiency measures in hospitals has proven to be a crucial governance cost-control instrument. Still, the system struggles with rising burdens from chronic lifestyle diseases, a shortage in qualified staff and emerging issues related to the rationing of new treatments. The benefits from a recent turn towards value-based management in hospitals attuned to spur patient outcomes have yet to be seen.

As in many other Western countries, immigration has been another highly politicised topic in Denmark in recent years. In Chapter 13, Carina Saxlund Bischoff and Anders Ejrnæs survey the recent developments in the integration of immigrants into Danish society. An immigration policy U-turn in the 2000s effectively reversed the Danish position: from vocal supporter of human rights to a front runner on restrictions on asylum immigration. Today, Denmark has some of the toughest internal and external immigration policies in Western Europe, resulting in a major drop in applications for asylum and significantly limiting access to social benefits. The increased incentives for rapid labour market integration have resulted in small, positive, short-term effects on employment, but also increasing poverty and precarisation of significant parts of the immigrant population. The authors warn that the most recent and significant addition to the integration policy, the so-called 'ghetto package' of 2018, is stigmatising residential areas with large proportions of immigrants and their descendants and may exacerbate the problem of 'parallel societies' that it aims to combat.

Policy Recommendations and Implications for Practice

While highlighting aspects of current Danish governance responses that are not unequivocally positive and desirable for one-to-one adoption by other states, the 12 chapters justify the general tendency among several policymakers and international institutions to view the Danish welfare state and its capacity to tackle urgent societal challenges in a positive light. At the same time, the chapters have demonstrated how a number of historical, political, economic and social factors condition the workings of public governance in Denmark today, which necessitates substantive translation if policy professionals want to transfer Danish experiences to other contexts. In the following, we consider some of the policy tools – or 'modes of thinking' – that can spark inspiration for politicians and professionals in dealing with some of the core global challenges of today.

In Section I, the three chapters show how the Danish case exhibits a range of policy tools that (more or less effectively) contribute to economic and social equality. In Chapter 2, Bent Greve and Daniel Béland point to the potentials of not only using a 'tax-and-duty system' to finance the welfare state but also using it as a progressive instrument to reduce economic inequality. In order to garner widespread popular support for such a system, however, the middle class must also receive some social benefits in areas such as education, long-term care, pensions and eldercare. Politicians and other policymakers who are looking to reduce inequality through the introduction or radicalisation of progressive taxation with reference to the Danish model must therefore remember the importance of universal social benefits for mobilising support and preserving the legitimacy of such interventions. In Chapter 3, Magnus Paulsen Hansen and Janine Leschke show how 'collective agreements' among employers and employees can promote decent working conditions for workers while providing a stable workforce for employers. Before adopting elements of the popular 'flexicurity model', however, policymakers should be aware of two crucial enabling conditions. First, high levels of trade union membership and informal institutions that ensure high levels of trust between government and the social partners and a shared, pragmatic and compromise-seeking approach to policymaking. Second, a widespread 'public-spiritedness', which makes individuals less prone to cheat on government benefits and exploit the unemployment insurance system. The adoptability of the system thus hinges on the prevalence of such conditions in the adopting country in question. Finally, in Chapter 4, Elizabeth Toft Kristjansen and Jesper Ole Jensen draw attention to yet another possible governance solution to rising social and economic inequalities. The collective ownership of residents, rather than public authorities, in social housing in Denmark is crucial not only for ensuring affordable housing for all but also for the legitimacy of political solutions. In order to successfully develop and realise democratic innovations in social housing projects, policymakers must then consider the issue of ownership structures, be ready to award the necessary resources and actively contribute to building trust between residents, housing organisations and local authorities. The project-based approach has shown potential for enhanced participation, but there is a need for giving the approach strategic direction. Moreover, there is a need to consider how to combine the project-based approach with the formal resident democracy.

Section II demonstrates how Danish public governance relies on a number of instruments for strengthening democracy and participation, more specifically to counteract the growing mistrust in politicians and government along with the concurrent rise in populism, political turmoil and polarisation. In Chapter 5, Flemming Juul Christiansen, Peter Heyn Nielsen and Bonnie Field argue that coalition agreements and legislative agreements, in particular those passed by a broad majority of parties, create predictability and political stability, which is desirable for citizens, commerce and professional organisations. The low entry threshold for political parties (2%) is a crucial precondition for the emergence of these agreements, as the Folketing hosts several political parties, none of which can form governments without the parliamentary support of others. The trust between the political parties and the fear of informal sanctions in case of violation contribute to the durability of the inter-party agreements. However, the agreements involve a risk of closed-door negotiations, which suffer from a lack of input from relevant and affected actors in society and result in agreements that come as a surprise for key stakeholders. In addition, centralised decision-making in cabinets also risks neglecting purview-specific knowledge and expertise. To counteract these risks, politicians should remain in close dialogue with their constituencies and relevant societal actors; parliament should strengthen its capacity to formulate legislative proposals and governments should show greater appreciation for line ministries vis-à-vis the ministry of finance as well as for ministers with knowledge relevant to their portfolios. In Chapter 6, Eva Sørensen and Jody Sandfort suggest that policymakers who wish to reduce tensions between citizens and politicians should not simply expand the citizens' voice and exit opportunities, as through the right to choose between various public service providers or the opportunity to sit on user boards, citizen panels and village councils (as many countries did in the late twentieth century). In fact, the authors argue that such supplementary forms of political participation can be counterproductive to the extent that they widen the institutional divide between direct and representative democracy. Instead, policymakers and politicians should design and engage in arenas and occasions where citizens and politicians can meet and debate pressing political matters in order to strengthen the dialogue and reduce the politician–citizen tensions. It requires the intentional investment of time and resources to undo the legacy of New Public Management as well as careful engagement design in order to promote a more interactive citizenship and political leadership style. If done right, the hybrid forms of democracy found in Denmark hold considerable democratic potential; also for countries with a shorter democratic history, lower levels of trust and a more heterogeneous citizenry.

Section III points to a number of possible avenues for increasing public sector effectiveness and efficiency. In Chapter 7, Jacob Torfing and Tina Øllgaard Bentzen provide recommendations for reformers aiming to prevent bureaucratic problems, poor public service, regulatory neglect, failing projects and inefficient service delivery in the public sector. Instead of introducing extensive control-based performance management, politicians and executive public managers should take a pragmatic approach to public governance reforms that also consider the value of bureaucratic ideals, professional expertise and trust-based collaboration. In order to do so, they should involve professional organisations representing both public managers and employees when formulating new administrative reforms; co-initiate and support research-based evaluations of these reforms and engage both researchers and practitioners in continuous discussions of their results. The Danish experiences suggest that such broad stakeholder involvement in multiple phases of public sector reform processes supports the development of desirable trust–control balance in public governance. In

Chapter 8, Peter Aagaard and John Storm Andersen show how the prospect of enhancing public sector efficiency through digitalisation is not simply a matter of finding and implementing the right technology but also a matter of balancing political interests and values. In the pursuit of more efficient and personalised welfare production, public authorities may easily compromise ethical norms and the privacy of individual citizens. The authors recommend that governments invest in data security to build, guard and maintain public trust and the legitimacy of digitalisation efforts and processes; that they continue to develop and reform legislation to pave the way for the increased use of advanced digital tools within public welfare institutions and that they strike a balance between traditional and digitalised ways of producing and delivering public welfare services.

Section IV considers several policy tools and government strategies for mitigating climate change and environmental deterioration. In Chapter 9, Karsten Bruun Hansen and Peter Enevoldsen show how a combination of hybrid, integrative and polycentric governance approaches is crucial for catalysing emerging green industries, such as the wind turbine industry and district heating industry. To facilitate the transition from the use of oil and coal to renewable forms of energy, policymakers should allow for and actively stimulate experimentation, self-organisation, local action, trust and interconnectivity between manufacturers, suppliers, policy professionals and energy consumers. The Danish experiences suggest that a combination of bold, top-down environmental policies and bottom-up mobilisation though facilitative and interactive forms of leadership is essential for setting direction while creating a market for public investors and mobilising stakeholder engagement, community acceptance and local commitment to cleantech innovation and sustainable energy consumption. In Chapter 10, Sevasti Chatzopoulou and Kostas Karantininis draw out three overall lessons for developing a flexible and sustainable agricultural food system. First, sustainable agri-policies must rely on strong organisational structures, on the public side as well as on the side of the private producers. Second, collaboration between these two sides is crucial to develop durable and effective policy solutions. Third, public policymakers should mobilise agricultural and economic expertise to identify and implement viable solutions and to adapt to new conditions and consumer demands in the market. However, close collaboration between the government and the professional agricultural organisations may also limit the capacity of government to formulate and implement environmental regulations that reduce greenhouse gas emissions and protect biodiversity. Public policymakers must thus involve a broader set of stakeholders and find ways to bridge the gap between the agricultural producers and the environmental movement in order to induce the requisite changes to make agriculture more environmentally sustainable.

Finally, Section V provides a number of suggestions for how to handle vast demographic changes and immigration flows in contemporary Western societies. In Chapter 11, Jon Kvist and Fritz von Nordheim consider how to finance pensions in societies with ageing populations. With the possible exception of climate change policies, no other area is as dependent on durable solutions as the pensions system. The Danish pension system consists of statutory, occupational and personal schemes that supplement each other quite well to secure income for pensioners and prevent poverty. Moreover, the life-expectancy indexing of the pensionable age contributes to the economic sustainability of the pensions system. The prevalence of economic expertise and collaboration between the labour market partners has been key in developing the Danish pensions system. The employer associations and the labour unions fostered the idea of the labour market pension component, and the high level of unionisation made it possible to expand the model to the entire labour market with only a minimum of support from lawmakers. Since few other countries have the same degree of institution- alised labour market collaboration, it may prove difficult for policymakers seeking inspiration in the Danish pensions system to transfer the experiences to other settings. In Chapter 12, Erik Bækkeskov and Peter Triantafillou point to two significant governance solutions for ensuring public healthcare and tackling growing expenditures. First, they stress the great economic and health-related potentials of using GPs as gatekeepers to specialised services. Providing easy access to free-of-charge consultations, the gatekeeper model prevents illness from developing into more severe and resource-demanding sickness and reduces risks and costs of superfluous medical examination. Second, they highlight the positive effects of providing 'treatment guarantees' within two months of diagnosis for certain diseases. Doing so pushes the system to exploit private alternatives in order to compensate for shortages in public hospital capacities and puts pressure on public hospitals to improve their timeliness, which has led to notable improvements in cancer and heart disease treatment outcomes. Finally, in Chapter 13, Carina Saxlund Bischoff and Anders Ejrnæs consider some of the most pivotal policy tools and governance strategies in Danish immigration con- trol. First, a liberal-to-restrictive shift in immigration policies has triggered a significant drop in asylum seekers. Second, the reduction of social benefits has resulted in small, positive short-term effects on employment, but also increasing poverty and precarisation of immigrants. Third, the so-called Ghetto Package of 2018 has effectively stigmatised residential areas with large numbers of immigrants.

Conclusions

In economic terms, the Danish welfare state is comprehensive compared to most other liberal democracies. The public sector makes up about one-fourth of the national economy and employs about one-third of the work force in Denmark. Progressive taxation funds the public hospitals, kindergartens, schools, univer- sities, nursery homes, libraries, roads and water and heating utilities.

Contrary to the worries and warnings of both liberal and conservative observers, however, there is no substantive evidence suggesting that the relatively comprehensive Danish welfare state has stifled the market and crowded out civil society. In fact, the Danish model relies on the co-existence and co-development of a vibrant and self-governing civil society, a robust market economy and a strong welfare state, which is capable of embracing and supporting for-profit and non-profit movements in the private sector. The workers movement and the large cooperative movements in major sectors, such as the food production and distribution sector, the energy sector and the housing sector, have played a historic role in developing the Danish welfare state. In turn, the welfare state continues to provide the education, healthcare, childcare and eldercare needed to maintain high levels of social engagement and private initiative.

The Danish political and public governance system can be characterised in several ways. Apart from the notion of the *welfare state*, which points to the comprehensive public coverage of social needs, it may also be regarded as a *neo-Weberian state*, which focusses on satisfying the demands of citizens, businesses and associations by way of an effective and efficient public sector (Pollitt & Bouckaert, 2011). The high-performing, user-oriented Danish public sector seems to fit this image. In addition, it could also be regarded as an *enabling state*, where the government partners with private actors to create economic growth, catalyse innovation and solve the complex problems that no single actor – public or private – can handle alone (Bevir, 2009; Gilbert & Gilbert, 1989). Almost all of the chapters in this book point to the importance of institutionalised dialogue and collaboration between public authorities and private organisations or citizens to provide governance solutions to societal problems (Ansell & Gash, 2008; Emerson & Nabatchi, 2015). Contrary to popular perceptions, the Danish capacity to tackle rising social, economic and political inequalities and other global problems does not simply hinge on the relative size and functioning of welfare benefits and public services alone. Danish public governance is clearly also a matter of close and sustained collaboration between state, market and civil society. We therefore think that all three terms capture important, albeit different, dimensions of the Danish public governance system in the first quarter of the twenty-first century.

The chapters in this edited volume go to show how the collaborative governance model in Denmark is relatively stable and largely based on socio-political cooperation, equality, trust, pragmatism and an inclusive compromise culture. Despite shifting minority governments and emerging political parties on both wings, the political middle, which embraces gradual reforms of the welfare state, is wide and strong. A generally content and happy citizenry along with both formal and informal institutions of cooperation and pragmatic compromise dampen the radicalism of new governments and ensure a steady reform path.

Yet the Danish welfare state has changed significantly in the past three decades, where the two major governing parties – the Social Democrats and Venstre, the Liberal Party of Denmark – have taken the lead in the slow but steady reform of the Danish welfare state. In the 1990s, Social Democrats directed governments accepted globalisation as a given and introduced market-oriented reforms. From 2001–2019, shifting right-of-centre, liberal–conservative governments and two left-of-centre governments (from 2011–2015) continued to trim the welfare state. These more market-oriented and efficiency-oriented reforms have left their mark on the public sector: an increasing use of performance management has pushed public institutions to perform better for less money, and the reforms have lowered income compensations and reduced social security, especially for immigrants living in social housing areas classified as 'ghettos'.

Some see the developments of the past decades as the beginning of the end for the Nordic welfare state model in Denmark, pointing to the gradual 'hollowing out' of the state and its public institutions and the increasing marginalisation of weaker groups, especially those outside or on the margins of the job market. Others argue that the reforms have been a necessary adaptation to the demands of intensified economic globalisation and a way of maintaining the welfare state in a new and modernised form. As a case in point, they tend to highlight the well-performing national economy, the low public debt and the continuation of a comparatively high level of public welfare vis-à-vis other Western welfare states. To us, both interpretations are true to the extent that they point to two sides of the same coin. The chapters of this edited volume shed light on both the strengths and weaknesses of the delineated developments in various policy fields.

At the general level, the most important takeaway for scholars and practitioners is not to mistake the images of the Danish welfare state and its old public administration in the 1970s and 1980s with the contemporary welfare state and its newer forms of public management and public governance in the 2020s. The modified version of the well-known universal welfare state and the new forms of governance are largely apt for meeting the mega-challenges of the twenty-first century. However, the vast challenges will still require continual adaptation, development and innovation in Danish governance.

One expedient example is the Danish governance response to climate change. In recent years, the international community has praised Denmark as a green pioneer country, and the current Danish government now tours the world with its 'long-term strategy for global climate action' (Danish Government, 2020). The legacy of the state-supported development of the wind turbine industry has given Denmark a head start on intellectual property rights, expertise and infrastructure in the energy supply sector, which provides fertile ground for new green energy adventures that may fund significant parts of the welfare state in the remainder of the twenty-first century. In terms of a green transition in agriculture and transportations systems, however, the Danish strategy relies more on yet-to-come technology fixes than already implemented reforms and solutions. The Danish response to climate change is yet to prove its worth and will require the concerted effort of a plethora of public and private actors to deliver on its praiseworthy promises.

A second example is the recent labour market reforms, pension reforms and healthcare reforms geared to meet the challenges posed by an ageing population. They appear to do the job but rest upon a number of assumptions about increasing average life expectancy and the ability of people to remain longer on the labour market. While the current Social Democratic government has promised to find special solutions for physically worn-out workers who are unable to carry on working within their profession, the political support for early retirement is staggering. The increasing privatisation of income insurance is likely to increase inequality between those who only rely on public solutions and those who can afford to add a private insurance. Time will tell if past and future reforms will catch all and provide adequate levels of compensation.

A third example is the capacity to meet the new challenges arising from the increasing digitalisation and technological developments not only in the public sector but also in the private sector and in the lives of citizens more broadly. Former Danish Minister for Economic Affairs and the Interior and now Executive Vice-President in the European Commission Margrethe Vestager is charged with the responsibility for setting the strategic direction of the political priority, 'A Europe Fit for the Digital Age' (European Commission, 2019). While the European Union is an important player in regulating big tech throughout Europe, not all responsibility for governing the digital lives of the next generations can be allocated to the supranational level. With its high levels of education, a well-functioning digital infrastructure and a state with considerable regulatory capabilities, Denmark appears to be in good shape to handle the digital challenges of tomorrow. Yet Danish governance will have to develop, perhaps at a rapid pace, to keep up with the technological leaps in the years and decades to come.

Scholarly analysis and the practical development of the Danish governance capacity to meet the major societal challenges of our time are thus ongoing projects. Future research in Danish public governance, politics and administration should continue to keep abreast of the small and large transformations of the Danish model in the face of new and demanding developments. More specifically, we would like to see more research on the influence of small policy adjustments and larger public sector reforms on the integrative governance capacity of the Danish governance system as a whole, including the complex interplay between the state, market and third sector. We encourage scholars to continue scrutinising and testing the agility, resilience and robustness of the evolving Danish public governance model as well as the possible adaptations of Danish governance responses in other political, economic, social and cultural contexts.

References

Ansell, C., & Gash, A. (2008). Collaborative governance in theory and practice. *Journal of Public Administration Research and Theory*, *18*, 543–571.

Bevir, M. (2009). Enabling state. In *Key concepts in governance* (pp. 74–78). London: Sage.

Danish Government. (2020). *A green and sustainable world: The Danish government's long-term strategy for global climate action.* Copenhagen: The Ministry of Foreign Affairs of Denmark and the Danish Ministry of Climate, Energy and Utilities.

Emerson, K., & Nabatchi, T. (2015). *Collaborative governance regimes.* Washington, DC: Georgetown University Press.

European Commission. (2019). President von der Leyen's mission letter to Margrethe Vestager. Brussels, 1 December 2019.

Gilbert, N., & Gilbert, B. (1989). *The enabling state: Modern welfare capitalism in America.* Oxford: Oxford University Press.

IPCC. (2018). Summary for policymakers. In V. Masson-Delmotte, P. Zhai, H.-O. Pörtner, D. Roberts, J. Skea, P. R. Shukla, & A. Pirani (Eds.), *Global warming of 1.5°C.* Geneva: World Meteorological Organization.

OECD. (2020). *Life satisfaction.* OECD Better Life Index.

Pollitt, C., & Bouckaert, G. (2011). *Public management reform: A comparative analysis – New Public Management, governance, and the neo-Weberian state*. Oxford: Oxford University Press.

United Nations. (2015). *Transforming our world: The 2030 Agenda for sustainable development*. United Nations Department of Economic and Social Affairs. Retrieved from http://www.un.org/en/development/desa/news/sustainable/un-adopts-new-global-goals.html

Index

Printed in the United States
by Baker & Taylor Publisher Services